ADMINISTERING NDS

Administering NDS

NDS

CORPORATE EDITION

Nancy Cadjan
Jeffrey Harris

McGraw-Hill
New York   San Francisco   Washington, D.C.
Auckland   Bogotá   Caracas   Lisbon   London
Madrid   Mexico City   Milan   Montreal   New Delhi
San Juan   Singapore   Sydney   Tokyo   Toronto

McGraw-Hill

A Division of The McGraw-Hill Companies

Copyright © 2000 by The McGraw-Hill Companies, Inc. All rights reserved.
Printed in the United States of America. Except as permitted under the United
States Copyright Act of 1976, no part of this publication may be reproduced or
distributed in any form or by any means, or stored in a data base or retrieval
system, without the prior written permission of the publisher.

1 2 3 4 5 6 7 8 9 0   AGM/AGM   9 0 4 3 2 1 0 9

ISBN 0-07-212208-0

The sponsoring editor for this book was Michael Sprague and the production
supervisor was Clare Stanley. It was set in Century Schoolbook by D&G Limited,
LLC.

Printed and bound by Quebecor / Martinsburg.

Throughout this book, trademarked names are used. Rather than put a trademark
symbol after every occurrence of a trademarked name, we use names in an editorial
fashion only, and to the benefit of the trademark owner, with no intention of infringe-
ment of the trademark. Where such designations appear in this book, they have been
printed with initial caps.

 This book is printed on recycled, acid-free paper containing a minimum of 50
percent recycled de-inked fiber.

This book is dedicated to our families, who believed in us and supported us through thick and thin. Their support is what makes our dreams attainable.

Nancy's support team includes Arthur (husband), Karen (mom), and George and Mary (grandparents). Also thanks to my in-laws, Gevork and Seda, and my brother-in-law, Meruzhan, who keeps me smiling.

Jeff's support team includes Susan, Tyler, Rylee, Austin, and Joshua. A special thanks to my parents, Lowell and Jan, and my in-laws, Gary and Diane, whose examples of integrity and hard work will serve me throughout my life.

CONTENTS

Contents

PREFACE

The world of networking and Information Technology is becoming a focal point in business, industry, education, and communications. In the age of information, those who can control the flow and manage the chaos around the information are greatly sought after. Managing information about individuals in a company and managing the access they have to information and resources from inside and outside the company has become a huge task. Gone are the days when networking meant a small number of computers sharing disk space. Now networking means a high level of interconnectedness between people, resources, and information. This higher level has created an environment where people can collaborate across great distances and achieve better results. In some instances, networking even means creating new profit centers through the use of such things as e-commerce.

In the fast-paced world of the Information Age, networking professionals need ways to securely and successfully manage the network. Many times these networks are a huge and complex culmination of years of disconnected decisions and missteps in management that must be brought together like a symphony, with the network administrator as the conductor. In order to do their job, network administrators need the correct tools to get all the participants to harmonize.

A directory is generally seen as the best and only way to get people, resources, and information within an organization structured into a harmonious balance. The directory is a database that contains information about people, resources, and the location of information. It provides the ability to grant or limit access and it provides a way for people to look for what they need. It is like the notes on a page of music. Members of the organization read the notes and are able to harmonize their actions and create something better than the sum of its parts. This is the magic of the network.

In the future, the network will continue to grow in complexity as technology progresses. Soon, there will be computers everywhere available for our use—on planes, in cars, and at computing stations. We will no longer use one computer to access the network. Many people will—or do now—regularly use three or more computers. As people travel throughout company offices and throughout the world, they will expect to have the same access and abilities on all these computers whether they are workstations in their main offices, computers in satellite offices, laptops in hotel rooms, or computers in their home offices. This means that somehow the network will need to know the users instead of just knowing the various workstations.

Managing the Future of the Network

As we head into the twenty-first century, the world will become even more interconnected, and network users will constantly become more and more mobile. IP addresses will always be changing, and a person's use of workstations will become ubiquitous. This means that the network will be replaced as the central focus of the IT industry. In the age of information, the individual will become the only meaningful common denominator across devices, services, and applications. Today, there is one directory that understands this vision of the future—*Novell Directory Services* (NDS). It is far advanced in comparison to all other directories and provides more services and means to focus the network on the individual than any other directory available today. It allows the network administrator to orchestrate heterogeneous networks of people, resources, and information, while still keeping the individual user at the center of focus.

NDS has the capability to manage all aspects of an individual's *digital identity* and to break the physical dependencies of location and device. According to Michael Simpson, Novell's Director of Strategic Market Planning, "The aim of NDS is to map the digital identity of people with that of printers, routers, switches, PCs, mobile phones, and palm tops. Doing so creates a world that is not made up of just a bunch of personal computers with different owners—but rather a truly integrated *personal net*. This is the next natural evolution of computing."

Novell did not just come up with the ability to create a world centered around the individual overnight. It has been releasing versions of its NDS database for over 6 years. The latest version—NDS 8 (also known by the code name *Scaleable Kick-Ass Directory* or SKADS)—is now available. It has been tested with as many as a billion users, which is about five times the number of users on the Internet today, and many times more objects than any other directory has even thought about.

NDS also unifies the complex world of multiple-platform networks that are so prevalent in business today. Novell provides not only versions of NDS that run on its own NetWare OS but also provides versions that run on NT and Solaris. IBM has ported NDS to other UNIX versions and even the IBM S/390 mainframe. This integration lets customers use the best platform for the task at hand, while at the same time providing them with a unified directory service from which to manage users and their access to mission-critical applications.

NDS goes beyond just unifying platforms. It also unifies databases and applications within a company. In many companies today, hiring a new employee is a nightmare of paperwork and process to give that new employee access to the correct network resources, a telephone number, and add that employee to any one of a number of databases. NDS simplifies this process. Adding a new employee to an NDS-enabled PeopleSoft HR database starts a process that creates a new user within NDS and provides the employee with immediate access to the correct network resources. There is no longer a need to enter the employee information in multiple databases because changes are automatically recorded in NDS and the PeopleSoft database simultaneously. This means it is no longer necessary to manually synchronize employee data across the many databases.

This is only one example of how NDS allows you to orchestrate the network and create harmony across disparate resources, databases, and platforms. In short, NDS reduces the total cost of ownership and increases the security of your network while still providing network users with access to information and resources, no matter where they are.

Who Should Read This Book?

The goal of this book is to help network administrators become excellent NDS administrators who can bring order and design to the chaotic world of their networks. If you have never used NDS or are contemplating using NDS in your network, this book is an excellent resource that will provide you with the information you need to get started. You will learn how NDS works in a heterogeneous environment, and how you can manage users, applications, security, and network resources using one database. You will learn about the advanced features of NDS that give it greater flexibility than any other directory available. You will learn about how NDS can become the central point of an advanced e-commerce strategy, and how ISPs and others can use NDS to manage user information.

For those who are already using NDS, this book provides you with an understanding of how to use NDS as more than just a means of authenticating to the network. NDS provides advanced functionality and superior security that can be used to expand the scope and capabilities of the network. With the release of native versions of NDS for NT and NDS for Solaris and with the release of NDS 8, the capabilities of NDS continue to expand. You will also learn about the new features such as the ConsoleOne administrative utility and ZENworks, a snap-in to NDS that allows you to manage desktops, applications, and users without having to visit the workstation. You will also learn about integrating disparate networks and application servers that will enable you to manage your entire network from a simple administrative tool—either ConsoleOne or NetWare Administrator. You will learn how to maximize your networking investment and minimize the cost. If you are not currently using NetWare 5, this book provides you information on how upgrading to NetWare 5 adds value to your network.

What This Book Covers

This book covers the concepts and administrative tasks you need to design and implement an NDS directory. Through careful planning and execution, you will be able to prove a high level of network security, while providing the access users need to the network resources and the flexibility you need to manage the network. This book contains 14 chapters that provide step-by-step instructions, checklists, tips and tricks to administering your NDS database.

Chapter 1, "Understanding NDS," provides you with a general description of NDS 8 and how it changes the world of the directory. This chapter also provides information on how NDS works with network operating systems such as NetWare, Windows NT Server, and Solaris. It discusses how NDS differs from other directories such as NT (this includes a discussion of Active Directory). It also explains how NDS for NT and NDS for Solaris can unify your directory and lower the total cost of owning and operating your network.

Chapter 2, "NDS Design Issues" explains the basic concepts of NDS architecture and how NDS administration can be set up in either a centralized or distributed administration structure. It explains how to establish roles and responsibilities for various administrators and others within the company, such as administrative assistants or network print managers, who need access to the database. It gives you several principles for planning your company's NDS design and helps you decide issues based on your company's current and future networking needs, including the importance of establishing standards for naming and access rights.

Chapter 2 also walks you through the processes of creating an NDS tree design, determining replica and partition strategies, and determining time sync strategies. It also outlines the basics of NDS security and the technologies underlying Novell's security features.

Chapter 3, "Installing and Upgrading NDS," explains the NDS server requirements on NetWare, NT, and Solaris. It explains the integration of NDS and NetWare. It provides detailed instructions for upgrading existing NetWare servers to NDS 8. Then, the chapter walks you through the installation process for NDS 8 for NT and NDS 8 for Solaris, including checklists you can use while installing. Finally, it includes instructions for upgrading to NDS 8 on existing NT and Solaris servers.

Chapter 4, "Installing Novell Client," explains different methods to install the Novell Client on your network's Windows 95/98 and Windows NT workstations. By using these methods, you can roll out the client without having to visit each workstation or have users run the software themselves. This chapter also discusses configuring the Novell Client for your network.

Chapter 5, "Administering NDS Objects," chapter explains the various NDS object types shipped with NDS. It also introduces you to the administrative tools needed to manage and maintain your NDS database—ConsoleOne, ConsoleOne Web Edition, and NetWare Administrator—and includes instructions on creating NDS objects with these utilities.

Chapter 6, "Controlling Network Access," introduces Novell's new security infrastructure and steps through the configuration of all the necessary components, including NICI, PKIS, SAS, and SSL. It then discusses the various protocols used to access NDS, including internal protocols such as NCP, as well as external protocols such as LDAP. It also illustrates the configuration of LDAP services for use with NDS and the use of Catalogs and NDS 8 indexes to improve LDAP performance.

Chapter 6 finishes with a review of NDS authentication and access control principles and mechanisms such as inheritance, security equivalence, groups, IRFs, ACLs and explicit assignments, and how they all work together to determine a user's effective NDS rights.

Chapter 7, "Administering Workstations," includes information about managing workstations with ZENworks, including creating and managing workstations, desktops, and application distribution by creating and implementing ZENworks policy packages. It also discusses other features of ZENworks such as workstation inventory, help requester and remote control. The features of ZENworks allow you to reduce the costs associated with administering the network by reducing the time spent troubleshooting and administering individual workstations.

Chapter 8, "Administering Printing," discusses Novell Distributed Print Services and how it is an integral part of NDS. The chapter explains how to set up and administer NDPS objects in NDS. It includes information on troubleshooting printing problems.

Chapter 9, "Managing the NDS Environment," discusses the primary administrative tasks, such as partition and replica administration, time sync administration, and NDS tree modification, involved in the day-to-day operation of an NDS tree. It also introduces the various tools available for performing these tasks. Chapter 9 also explains how to backup the NDS database, as well as perform other periodic maintenance procedures through the use of DS Repair.

Chapter 10, "Advanced NDS Tools," starts with a discussion of the various database integrity technologies available in NDS such as self-healing and roll-forward logs, as well as functional features such as External References, DRLs, and Subordinate References. Chapter 10 then discusses additional utilities you can use to monitor and repair your NDS environment such as DS Trace, DS Maint and DS Diag, including tools developed by Novell and other third-party software makers. It also looks at some NDS mapping utilities that are available to help administrators create visual maps of the NDS environment.

Chapter 11, "Troubleshooting NDS," discusses three general categories of NDS problems and provides general troubleshooting tips for each type of problem. It also introduces tools for identifying and interpreting NDS errors, including the use of protocol analyzers and Novell's LogicSource. Finally, it discusses different sources for additional information and when it is most appropriate to contact Novell Technical Services to resolve some more difficult NDS problems.

Chapter 12, "Customizing NDS," explains what the NDS Schema is and how it can be extended to include additional functionality. This chapter also includes a discussion of snap-ins for NetWare Administrator and ConsoleOne that are necessary to properly manage Schema additions. It also includes a brief discussion of creating customized NDS snap-ins for specific company needs. Finally, it presents information on several NDS-enabled utilities and applications that can add provide the NDS administrator with more power and flexibility for managing the network infrastructure.

Chapter 13, "Using NDS to Manage Your Internet Presence," explains how the latest version of NDS creates greater opportunities for companies involved in the Internet. It includes a discussion of how companies are currently leveraging NDS to do successful e-commerce transactions and create sources of revenue. This section also discusses why and how companies, such as Internet Service Providers, can create *digital identities* that can be used multiple times across the Internet using NDS.

What This Book Does Not Cover

This book assumes that you have at least some limited knowledge about networks. It also assumes that you have done at least some network administration. If you do not have this experience or knowledge, you might want to read one or more books on networking in general as a companion to this book.

This book concentrates on the administrative tasks necessary to successfully administer an NDS directory. Except for brief explanations or for specific utilities available on the server, it does not cover administering network servers, specific platforms, or other databases such as Oracle, PeopleSoft, LotusNotes, GroupWise and others that can be integrated into the NDS directory. It also does not cover hardware issues or general principles of networking. This book does provide explanations of industry standards where applicable, but it does not include lengthy discussions of these standards. When such information is important to understanding NDS, we provide you with references to sources for information on the Web and in printed materials.

For More Information

Although this book is designed to cover all the basic principles of NDS 8 and to provide advanced administrative information, NDS touches so many areas of networking that it would be impossible to cover all topics in a book of this size. As we compiled the outline for this book, we quickly realized that to cover all the necessary topics in an in-depth manner would take about 1,200 pages. For example, this book only covers basic installation options for NetWare 5. It does not cover other versions of NetWare or troubleshooting your NetWare 5 server.

There are other books that do an excellent job of covering topics that we can only briefly cover in this book. There are also Web sites that provide additional information and resources. Novell Documentation also provides additional insight into technology that you might want to read more about. Finally, one of the best resources on current issues and solutions with current Novell products is the Novell Technical Support *Technical Information Document* (TID) database. At the end of each chapter, we suggest books, articles, Web sites, documentation, and TIDS that pertain to the chapter's topics. We encourage you to read these sources for more information on specific topics.

Because networking and NDS administration is very flexible, do not be concerned if you feel that you cannot know everything there is to know about NDS. The more experience you gain with NDS, the easier it will be to take in new concepts and understand new applications of the core NDS technology. Good luck and welcome to the world of NDS and directory-enabled networks!

ACKNOWLEDGMENTS

The authors would like to thank the following individuals. Writing a book of this size would not have been possible without their help and insight.

Thanks to Kevin McLelland, Maurice Smulders, Jay Patton, Eddy Pulido, Jim Short, and Cydni Tetro for sharing their technical expertise and helping us to better understand the administrative tools used with NDS.

Thanks to the FLAIM development team, including James Davis, Andy Hodgkinson, Scott Pathakis, Brian Jensen, and Daniel Sanders for providing a neophyte's view into the mystical world of directory databases.

Thanks to Kenny Bunnell and Jared Walter in the NTS Lab for helping to configure an environment appropriate for testing NDS eDirectory and Corporate Edition.

And finally, many thanks to John Tippetts for offering his UNIX expertise so that we didn't have to become UNIX administrators before being able to describe NDS on the Solaris platform.

We hope this book brings insight and information to NDS administrators everywhere. You have the ability to make your company a better and more effective organization by getting the most out of your NDS environment. We wish you well in all your endeavors.

Understanding NDS

One of the most important tasks a network administrator has is making sure that users have access to the files, resources, and services that they need on the network. This task often can consume most of an administrator's time, because without the correct access, the network is useless. The ability to manage the directory—the database of all resources, services, and users on the network—is critical, because the directory provides users with access to what they need on the network. This chapter provides you with an overview of what a directory is and how *Novell Directory Services* (NDS) implements the concept of the directory. This chapter also explores how NDS stacks up against other directories available today and those promised in the near future and how NDS is emerging as the premiere directory.

What Is NDS?

The heart (maybe a better metaphor would be the brains) of the network is the directory. It is the central point at which everything comes together. The directory is the central database where vital information about all network resources is kept. It is responsible for receiving and responding to requests for access to resources or services available on the network. The resources and services requested may come from any one of multiple servers running different network operating systems, such as NetWare, Windows NT, UNIX, and soon even Linux. The NDS database works with the servers to provide navigation to resources.

Some people confuse the NDS database with the file server. Although NetWare file servers, Windows NT file servers, and UNIX file servers may provide the services that the directory manages, the directory is not the same as the file server. The *directory* is the database that stores information about the entire network, such as which users exist on the network and what rights they have to work on the network. In contrast, the *file system* is a collection of files, such as data files and applications, that are stored on the network and which a user might need. The directory and the file system have separate security systems. The directory controls which network resources and services users can access. The file system controls access to data and programs. In some instances, these security rights overlap. For example, the directory can control access to certain volumes that store file server data.

NDS is the world's most advanced network directory. It has been a cornerstone of Novell's networking products for more than six years. When NDS was developed in 1993, few people understood the power and capabilities that this technology would bring to the world of networking. In fact, its advanced capabilities probably have taken many people inside Novell by surprise. According to the Aberdeen Group, "Any enterprise executive wanting to harness the power of the net—Inter-, Intra-, Virtual or Private—for competitive advantage cannot do so without a powerful directory to manage all the connections. In Aberdeen's opinion, NDS is the most powerful directory available today." Many industry experts feel that any directory database must do the following four things in one form or another. Novell has taken them further:

- *Discovery*.   You should be able to browse, search, and retrieve the information you need from the directory. You should be able to search for specific object types, such as users, printers, and application objects, or search their specific properties, such as user's name, phone number, address, and network number. NDS takes advantage of the *Lightweight Directory Access Protocol* (LDAP) protocol for fast search and retrieval.

- *Security*.   You should be able to control access to all the information stored in the directory. You should be able to grant rights to the users for the information in the directory. You should also be able to control the flow of information within your company, across networks of partners, and even among your customers. In NDS, security also means managing the electronic transactions between companies and across the Internet through the cryptographic and key management systems. The *Public Key Infrastructure* (PKI) available in NDS today provides security for Internet data integrity and privacy across public networks, including both public-key cryptography and digital certificates for checking the authenticity of keys used in a public session.

- *Storage*.   You should be able to save information in the database for future reference. The database is indexed, cached, and guarded from data corruption. In addition to storing the data, the NDS database enables you to automatically control the type of data by applying classifications to the data structures. These classifications are flexible and extensible to provide future representations in the database. Also, the NDS database can be split into physical pieces and distributed or placed on multiple servers (partitioning and replication previously mentioned). This enables you to place a portion of the data close to the users and resource that needs it and to make multiple copies of the data for fault protection and load balancing.

- *Relationships*.   You should be able to build associations between the people, network devices, network applications, and information on the network. NDS has taken relationships to a new height. NDS makes the associations between the people, network devices, network applications, and information on the network globally available on the network. Instead of storing the user's profile information on the local machine, it is stored in NDS in a user profile. The profile information becomes global, and the user can access the profile information from anywhere in the network. This means that no matter where Bob Smith logs in to the network, he receives the same profile. In addition, no one but Bob Smith can access his user profile because he is the only one with the proper credentials. Thus, the integrity of profile information is protected and secure, and the user can access it globally and easily.

Although all directories manage discovery, security, storage, and relationships to some extent, NDS takes the management of these functions to a higher level and makes advanced directory services possible. And, the press have noticed. A recent article in the *Boston Globe* proclaimed that "Microsoft Corp., IBM Corp., Oracle Inc., and Sun Microsystems Corp. are all taking their shots at the [Directory] market. But for now the leader is Novell Inc."

NDS maintains information about services and resources in a directory database—often referred to as the *Directory*—in a logical, hierarchical design called the *Directory Tree*. This information is stored in NDS objects. When a user or some other network entity needs access to a resource or service, a request is made, and rights associated with the user's object are checked before access is granted. The network services and resources in the NDS database may be represented by one Directory Tree or by many, depending on the company's internal layout and network design. However, NDS is powerful enough to enable users access to all the resources they need, even if these resources are on different trees, with one login password. More specific information about the creation of the Directory Tree is located in Chapter 2, "NDS Design Issues." Information about creating NDS objects is discussed in Chapter 5, "Administering NDS Objects."

For many years, NDS has been recognized by companies, industry analysts, and the press for its ability to reduce management costs by providing a single point of administration, strong security, and cross-platform support for user account management. By releasing products that leverage NDS and partnering with ISVs with directory-enabled applications, Novell has shown how NDS can help you ease management tasks like the following:

■ Manage network protocols

■ Manage firewalls

- Manage desktops
- Distribute applications
- Gather information about workstations in the enterprise
- Enable a single sign-on to directory-enabled applications
- Control workstations from a remote location
- Manage Windows NT domains and users
- Manage Solaris users
- Manage LDAP-enabled applications
- Manage physical infrastructure, such as routers and switches

This is just a short list of some of the things you can do with NDS.

NDS also provides the means by which you easily can distribute the Directory to key locations in your network to increase response time. Because the Directory is organized in a logical, hierarchical manner, it even enables you to distribute only parts of the Directory that are relevant to a specific segment of the network. This is called *partitioning the directory*. These smaller segments are still a part of the logical whole and can be updated and maintained with relative ease.

Partitions can be copied out to multiple file servers in the network. This process is called *replication,* and the specific copy of the partition is called a *replica*. These replicas can be stored on multiple file servers, which gives NDS a very high level of fault protection and load balancing in addition to quick access. Periodically, these replicas must all be updated so that each one has the same information. This process is called *synchronization* and ensures that the latest data is always available. NDS synchronization occurs automatically when changes are made to the database. More information about partitions and replicas is discussed in Chapter 2.

What Is SKADS?

You may have heard about SKADS recently. It has been discussed in the press widely and touted at Novell's 1999 BrainShare conference. What does it really mean for your network? SKADS stands for *Scaleable Kick-Ass Directory*, which is the internal Novell code name for NDS version 8, the newest version of NDS for NetWare Networks. This version of NDS, also called NDS Corporate Edition, is so revolutionary and has caused so much discussion because it increases the number of objects that can be located in the Directory Tree. Novell has demonstrated a Directory Tree with more than a billion objects in it without sacrificing directory performance. Others have reported passing even this staggering number with no end in sight. What's more, NDS Corporate Edition can support large object sizes of up to 50K. These capabilities have also been made available on Windows NT and Solaris servers.

Your first concern might be that putting so many objects in the Directory would cause a performance hit, but that has not been an issue for NDS Corporate Edition. NDS Corporate Edition performs LDAP version 3 search queries with consistent speed, even after a billion objects are added to the directory. Competing directories lose significant LDAP search query capabilities in direct proportion to the number of users in the directory. No matter how many objects you put in the Directory, the performance is still the same. The one caveat to the statement that NDS Corporate Edition can handle a billion objects is that it must be running in a pure NetWare 5, a pure Solaris, a pure Windows NT 4.0 environment, or a mix of these three specific platforms to support that many objects. In an environment with NetWare 4.x or NetWare 3.x servers, NDS will be limited by the lowest common denominator on the network (NetWare 4.x or NetWare 3.x), because these servers will not be running NDS version 8 or later.

NDS Corporate Edition can store so many objects and maintain a consistent search query speed because the underlying database technology has been replaced by a new database, *FLexible Adaptive Information Manager* (FLAIM), that works with indexed values (see Figure 1-1). This database, you might say, is the magic maker. The advantage of indexing is that it improved the performance and speed of directory access. The values that have been indexed will affect the speed of look ups and NDS background processing. More information about the FLAIM database is discussed in Chapter 2.

NDS Corporate Edition also uses persistent caching so that changes being made to a server are held in a vector. If the server crashes in the middle of changes, NDS will load faster and synchronize the changes in seconds when the server is brought back up. Also, NDS Corporate Edition no longer uses Novell's Transaction Tracking System to make sure that all transactions are completed. It now uses a rollback model with a log file to roll forward transactions in the event of a system failure. Details about this model are discussed in Chapter 10, "NDS Administration Tools."

NDS Corporate Edition has been touted as the next evolutionary step for the Directory because it is the first database that enables companies to merge their internal and external databases into one. It is the first Directory that can easily support an enterprise network and still enable a company to establish an Internet business using the same directory database. Companies now have the ability to implement e-commerce initiatives, consolidate human

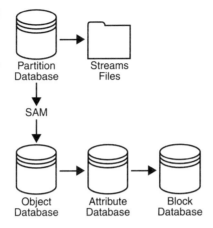

Figure 1-1

The new database structure in NDS

resources data, unify their network-management consoles, and integrate multiple, heterogeneous platforms with one directory while reducing total cost of ownership. And for those companies not interested in redirecting existing databases, NDS eDirectory allows them to use NDS in Windows NT and Solaris environments. More information on NDS eDirectory is available in Chapter 13.

NDS is also the first directory that successfully integrates both application and resource management into one database. NDS is the market leader in the NOS-integrated directory services market space. However, NDS also enables Novell to take a chief spot in the application directory market. Until NDS, competing with Netscape's Directory Server and other LDAP products has been difficult, chiefly because of performance and scalability. Now, NDS brings the two directory worlds together with one solution.

NDS is centered on scalability, performance, LDAP version 3, and management. NDS offers the following enhancements:

- Increased performance for directory reads, writes, and searches
- Enhanced directory scalability, so that trees can have millions of objects
- ConsoleOne Management
- Improved LDAP version 3 functionality
- LDIF support for adding, modifying, and deleting directory objects
- Extended DNS naming support
- LDAP version 3 controls, such as server-side sorting, paged results, and virtual lists

Because of its scalable performance and proven replication capabilities, NDS works for both centralized Internet and highly distributed enterprise applications. NDS now enables companies to solve their immediate needs, grow their businesses without disruption, and build the necessary infrastructure required for e-commerce. *Internet Service Providers* (ISPs), telephone companies, global companies, and small businesses can bring all of their customers and supply-chain partners online today while preparing for tomorrow.

NDS enables you to maintain your existing technology investments because it integrates most Internet standards. This means that you can keep what you have running in your network without ripping it out to use NDS. For example, NDS natively supports LDAP v3, which means any application written to use LDAP is an NDS application. Market analysts expect the industry-standard LDAP protocol to dominate directory access through 2002, so you are set into the next century. You can easily integrate any open standards-based application with NDS. Use what works with what you already own. You don't have to rely on one company or use products you are not happy with because your operating system dictates them.

NDS's standards-based infrastructure provides easy, flexible control over your company's security policies. PKI, cryptography, and authentication services are tightly integrated with NDS, so you can centrally manage policies and control access across the entire network. Because NDS provides a flexible foundation for user-authentication support, ranging from passwords to X.509 v3 certificates to smart cards and biometrics, NDS is an excellent choice for companies with evolving or varied security needs. NDS also has a flexible access control architecture that provides granular control over customer data. These features become more and more important as companies set up e-commerce and other Internet-based services.

One example of how NDS can be used in the wild and fast-paced world of emerging Internet and e-commerce is being explored by a third-party company called Bowstreet Software. This company is working on framework software that will make it faster, easier, and less expensive to create business-to-business applications. You will be able to build customized e-commerce applications on the fly instead of hard coding programs for each business partner. By using NDS in conjunction with *Extensible Markup Language* (XML), Bowstreet pulls disparate systems together to build applications without the need for extensive technical expertise or expensive data-interchange applications. This means that a customer can log on to buy a car. Using the Directory, Bowstreet would first authenticate the customer. Then once the security checks are run, other distributed back-end systems, such as financing, pricing, inventory, and credit checks, would be brought up. Bowstreet would gather all the information that the customer needed and present it on a single screen. The real power in this software is that the code can be reused for multiple applications and for multiple business partners.

This is just one example of the power of NDS and the Directory. In overall capabilities, NDS far outpaces all competing directories. Although it still has some weak spots, it is the only directory to provide so much flexibility and scalability.

How Does NDS Compare to Other Directories?

NDS is not the only directory on the market today. Currently viable directories are being offered by Netscape, Oracle, Microsoft, ISOCOR, and others. Some of these directories originally were created for single purposes but have grown to serve more general directory needs. Because so many different directories have specialized purposes, some companies choose to implement and maintain more than one directory in an attempt to meet varying needs in an organization. However, several studies, including a recent one by the Burton Group suggests that the cost of managing multiple directories is far greater than the cost of implementing one enterprise directory.

Even if your company has decided to go with an enterprise directory strategy, which one should you implement? Because we don't have time to delve into all the possible directories or network configurations, let's just take a look at the most common directories and how they compare to NDS.

How Does NDS Compare to Windows NT 4.0?

Windows NT technology uses the domain as its basic unit of centralized administration and security. The domain structure is well-suited for small workgroup structures and works well in small offices of 5–20 employees. But as technology has evolved and the network has become more integrated, managing domains has become a complex task. When an office has a larger number of employees, multiple servers, and many network devices, such as printers, storage devices, and fax machines, managing it all through domains becomes more complex. In addition, Windows NT has several drawbacks that make it even harder to use in a heterogeneous enterprise network:

- Difficulty integrating with applications, even though applications like Exchange require domain functionality
- No way to manage or delegate administration easily
- No integration of network resources
- No rights inheritance (rights that flow down to all objects)
- No ability to move objects between domains without deleting and recreating the object, which leaves more room for human error

Using Windows NT has meant maintaining multiple databases for domains and applications (like Exchange) and creating complex trust relationships between domains so that users have access to the resources they need (see Figure 1-2).

This creates a difficult administrative situation because as the number of domains grows, so does the number of possible trust relationships needed to provide users with necessary resources. For example, only 10 NT servers have the possibility of having up to 90 different trust relationships that must be administered. If you have 100 servers, this number jumps to 9,900 trust relationships. In addition to the trust relationships you must manage, if you have a heterogeneous network with NetWare servers as well as NT servers, you must create usernames and passwords for each user in both databases. Another problem that you might face is that you must replicate the entire domain on multiple servers. This means that you must choose between high replication overhead or complex trust relationships. Neither of these choices is a good choice, and no one would willingly choose such a complex setup.

The NDS for NT Solution   NDS for NT enables you to easily administer mixed Windows NT, Solaris, and Novell networks from a single access point

Figure 1-2

Example of domain relationships

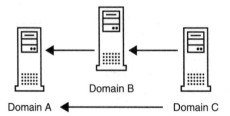

Domain B

Domain A

Domain C

Trust relationships are not transitive

and without the complexity of trust relationships. Or, you can choose to administer your native Windows NT network with NDS. With NDS for NT, you can move Windows NT domain information into your NDS database. You then manage domains as NDS group objects. If you have a heterogeneous network, you no longer have to create and maintain separate Windows NT and NetWare user accounts to give users access to resources. With NDS for NT, users log in only once to access all the resources they need on both NetWare and Windows NT servers. If you have a native Windows NT network, you no longer have to deal with the complexity of domain structures, and you can choose to give users rights where they need them instead of where the domains dictate they can have access. Your level of security increases, and your time to administer the network decreases.

How NDS for NT Works   In a Windows NT domain, all applications on the NT Server or NT workstations needing access to the NT domain make requests to the SAMLIB.DLL. The SAMLIB.DLL then communicates to the SAMSRV.DLL using *Remote Procedure Calls* (RPC). For applications that run on the server, this is all done internally. For requests originating from a workstation, the RPC requests are received at the server via the network. When the server RPC receives the request, the request is passed to the SAMSRV.DLL. The SAMSRV.DLL then accesses the Windows NT *Security Accounts Manager* (SAM) where the domain namebase is stored and performs the requested operation (see Figure 1-3).

NDS for NT integrates Windows NT domains into NDS by replacing the NT SAMSRV.DLL with a new DLL that redirects domain access calls to NDS (see Figure 1-4). The new SAMSRV.DLL directs all requests from the domain to NDS through the Novell Client. NT User, Computer, and Group objects then can be migrated to NDS where both NT and NDS resources can be managed.

DOMAINS MIGRATED TO NDS   In NDS, each Windows NT domain is represented by a Domain object that behaves similarly to a Group object. The Domain object not only holds information about the domain and users that are members of the domain, but it also contains a list of Member objects, such as computers and groups, just as an actual domain would have (see Figure 1-5).

The Domain object acts as a group with a list of domain members. The computers and groups associated with the domain are represented as objects contained within the NDS Domain object. Because objects are linked to the domain as members of the domain rather than as integrated parts of the domain, the objects can be moved anywhere in the tree and still have membership in specific domains.

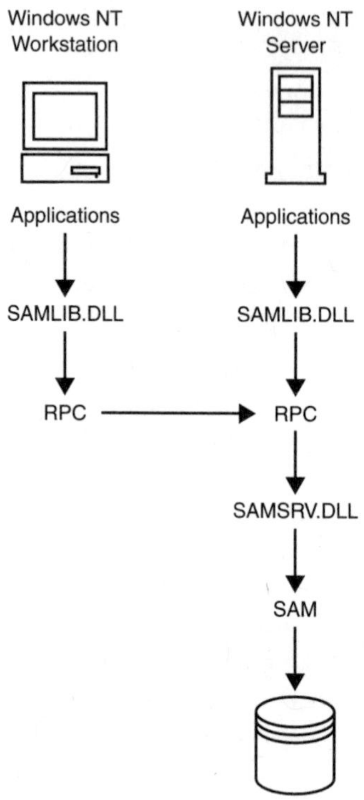

Figure 1-3
Windows NT Server
domain architecture

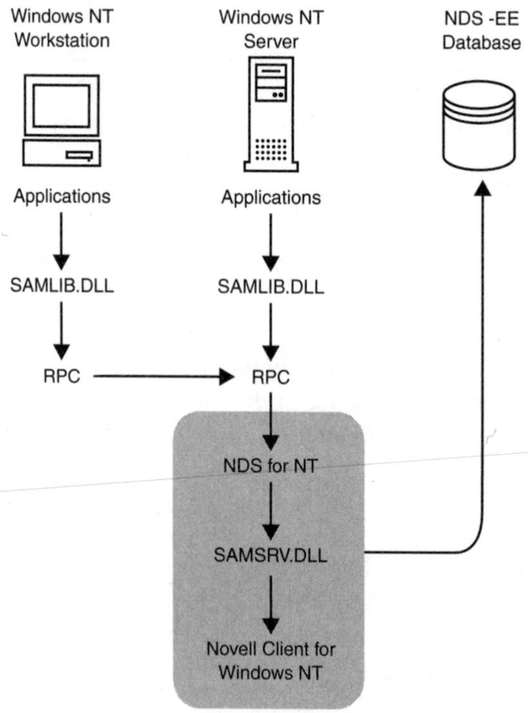

Figure 1-4
NDS for NT
architecture

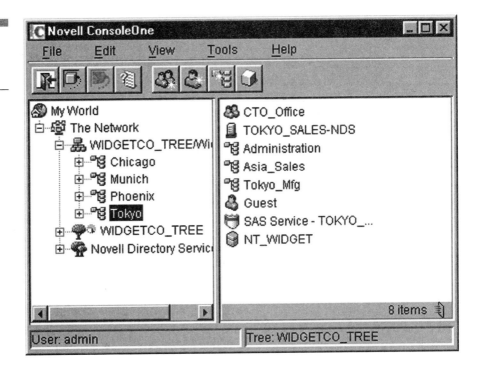

Figure 1-5
Domain objects in
NDS viewed with
Console One

Because NDS for NT stores each user's *Relative Identifier* (RID) in the NT Domain object and not as part of the User object, one NDS User object can be a member of more than one NT Domain object. This provides a way for a single NDS user to access resources in multiple domains without having to set up complicated trust relationships.

During the migration of objects to NDS, you have several options:

■ You can create a new object in NDS that represents the Domain object.

■ You can associate the Domain object with a corresponding object that already exists in NDS. This option is useful if you are combining two databases.

■ You can choose not to move objects that are unused. This eliminates any access by these objects to either NDS or NT.

After the NT objects have been moved to NDS, you have the power of NDS to control your NT and NetWare resources. You can associate the objects with other network resources, including NetWare and Solaris severs. You also can grant additional rights or restrictions through NetWare Administrator. You can group users into groups or assign users to organizational roles. You can eliminate trust relationships and thus free yourself from administrative hassles.

SAM REQUESTS REDIRECTED TO NDS The Windows NT Security Accounts Manager is the database where the NT domain namebase is stored. A number, the *Security Identifier* (SID), uniquely identifies an NT domain across a network. A SID that is created by combining the domain SID with a RID also identifies objects in the domain. This object SID is used throughout the Microsoft network to identify the object and its access to system resources. In NDS for NT, these requests are just redirected to NDS and not eliminated.

LOCAL REPLICAS INSTALLED ON THE NT SERVER In addition to migrating NT objects to NDS, NDS for NT enables you to maintain copies (replicas) of the NDS tree on the local NT Server (either a PDC or a BDC). These replicas make sure that users always have quick access to the resources they need, and changes to the NDS tree can be made quickly without having to contact the PDC.

NDS on a Native NT Network NDS for NT can also be installed in a native NT environment to help ease the burden of managing multiple databases and user information across these databases. Because NT requires different databases for certain applications, such as Exchange and SQL, it is difficult to keep the user information across these databases in synch. The solution is to manage all these databases from one central location—the NDS Directory. NDS also gives native NT environments the opportunity to split domains into smaller partitions that can be replicated across the network where they will do the most good. It increases the strength, speed, and capabilities of your network.

NDS for NT provides Novell's own Directory, modified to incorporate NT's flat domain architecture. NDS for NT enables you to administer a network from a single point with ease. NDS removes headaches like trust relationships and repetitious domain management. NDS allows for a great deal of scalability and a more intuitive form of network management, simplifying administration and reducing cost. What's best is that users need only one password, which will be easier to remember than the three passwords they need with other directories, and they probably won't need to write their passwords down, so your network will be more secure. Chapter 3, "Installing NDS," discusses how to install NDS for NT and migrate your domains to NDS.

How Does NDS Compare to Windows 2000?

Microsoft's current NT 4.0 Server technology is based on the LAN Manager domain technology introduced in 1987. At that time, the domain structure worked well for the administration of small workgroups. However, as networking has evolved and as our workgroups have grown, many limitations have emerged:

- *Limited object types.*   You cannot add new object types or information to an NT database.
- *Flat structure.*   Names do not indicate where a person is located in the tree, and each domain must be managed as one large workgroup.
- *Few applications can integrate with domains.*   Two distinct databases must be maintained to run applications like Microsoft Exchange.
- *All-or-nothing management.*   Users or administrators cannot be given rights to manage specific resources, such as printers, or specific information, such as phone numbers.
- *Complex trust relationships.*   Trust relationships are not transitive and require a lot of administrative time.
- *Unscalable domain synchronization.*   Because all updates must be sent to and received from the PDC, synchronizing the database takes a long time and uses precious band-width.
- *Difficulty moving objects between domains.*   To move an object, you must delete the object in the first domain and recreate it in the second domain. Then you must reassign all rights and resources to the object.

Microsoft 2000 and Active Directory solve some of these problems, but not all of them.

Currently, NT Server 4.0 domain information is stored in a relatively secure portion of the NT Registry that was designed to store small amounts of machine-specific information, such as software configurations and hardware settings. However, it is not well suited to store large numbers of users and groups because the registry does not incorporate important database features, such as indexing and advanced replication. Because the current domain database is not able to understand anything but what was predefined with NT Server, applications such as Exchange cannot store their application-specific information in the domain. These applications must place the needed information in application-specific databases.

Microsoft 2000's Active Directory no longer uses the registry for storing domain accounts. It uses a JET database based on the Exchange JET

Figure 1-6
The new JET
database

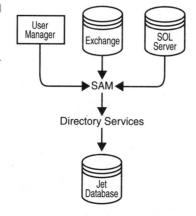

database for all Active Directory information (see Figure 1-6). This resolves registry and scalability problems and enables the database to understand new objects and attributes. The Security Accounts Manager remains to provide backwards compatibility for all applications that use the SAM APIs.

Active Directory addresses significant limitations of the current NT domain structure with the addition of an Organizational Unit. The Organizational Unit provides hierarchical naming, allowing more descriptive names like `mseller.salesdept.orm.firstfederal`, instead of just `mseller`. Hierarchical naming for users and resources simplifies locating resources because the name includes information about the user or resource, such as a department, division, or geographic location.

The Active Directory organizational unit also allows for greater administrative rights delegation. With the current NT 4.0 domain, administration is granted by object type, such as printers, accounts, and servers, for the entire domain. Active Directory enables you to delegate domain administration rights by object type at a lower level for the entire organizational unit.

In addition, Active Directory's container hierarchy is important because it gives administrators the ability to grant privileges to users based on the specific functions they must perform within a given scope. Administrative scope can include an entire domain, a subtree of organizational units within a domain, or even a single organizational unit.

Although it solves some hierarchy problems, Active Directory still requires trust relationships (see Figure 1-7). In fact, the trust relationship is an integral component of Active Directory, because trust relationships are the links

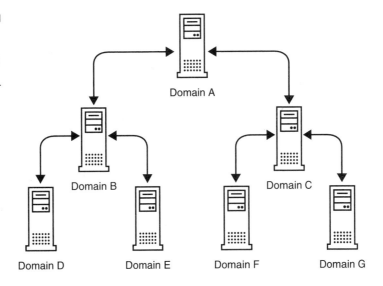

Figure 1-7
The new trust
relationships required
by Windows 2000

Domain A

Domain B

Domain C

Domain D   Domain E   Domain F   Domain G

Trust relationships are transitive

that build the Active Directory tree. Active Directory improves the trust relationship by making trust relationships automatic and transitive. Unlike NT Server 4.0, which requires administrator intervention for trust-relationship management, Active Directory handles most trust-relationship management. For example, if you have five NT Server domains, you can connect them with as few as four trusts. In the older trust-relationship model, it would have taken 20 trust relationships to connect the domains. Trust relationships are automatically created to parent domains when new domains are added to the Active Directory tree.

Partitioning, Replication, and Synchronization Active Directory introduces multimaster replication to the NT domain. Multimaster replication permits updating the domain at any NT server that holds a Domain Controller—a read/write copy of the domain database. Domain updates occur as long as a read/write copy of the domain is available. Active Directory uses a concept known as *Update Sequence Numbers* (USNs), which is very similar to NDS timestamps in that both determine which objects or attributes should synchronize between directory databases.

Moving Objects between Domains In the Active Directory world, objects are assigned to logical workgroups or other organizational units rather than to individual servers. Therefore, users won't have to change how they find and name objects like files when administrators move them to different physical servers. This should eliminate the need to delete and recreate objects as changes occur in the corporate structure.

Active Directory's Limitations Even though Active Directory improves many of the limitations that administrators face today, it still has limitations of its own. Four of the largest drawbacks are limited application integration, limited distributed management, static inheritance, and limited partitioning capabilities.

LIMITED APPLICATION INTEGRATION Because Active Directory uses the JET database instead of the registry for storing information, the database's capabilities can be extended, and objects within the Active Directory domain may include additional attributes not found in the current NT 4.0 domain. For example, the domain user object could be extended to include a new attribute for email addresses or fax numbers. However, extensions to the domain database are available only to Active Directory-enabled applications. Applications that use old-style SAM APIs for accessing the domain database cannot access new Active Directory domain extensions.

LIMITED DISTRIBUTED MANAGEMENT It is possible to grant a user administrative rights over an entire organizational unit. However, you cannot grant a user administrative rights over a single object within the organizational unit, such as an individual server, printer, another user, or a single object attribute. In addition, the delegation of administrative rights cannot include multiple domains, and administrative rights do not pass through trust relationships. In other words, it is not possible to grant administrative rights or rights to resources to the top of an Active Directory tree and expect administrative rights to flow to lower domains through trust relationships.

STATIC INHERITANCE AND RIGHTS Both Active Directory and NDS use *Access Control Lists* (ACLs) in their respective directories to determine who can do what to an object or its attributes. The ACL determines who has rights to manage the directory and who has rights to access resources, such as printers, file servers, email servers, and database servers. However, in Active Directory, inheritance is static. This means that directory management and resource rights granted to higher container objects permit management or access to subordinate objects but require updating all subordinate objects' ACL lists.

For example, suppose that you have 3,000 objects in the directory tree and need to grant Sally rights to manage all objects in the tree. With Active Directory, you drag and drop Sally to the top of the Active Directory domain. The client utility then must locate and individually update the ACL list on all 3,000 objects. As a consequence of granting this right, the directory database grew by at least 3,000 ACL updates; namely, Sally's object is now in the ACL list for every object in the tree. If we assume that each of the 3,000 ACLs are 512 bytes in size, the directory database increased by a minimum of 1,536,000 bytes.

By using static ACL inheritance, the Active Directory database quickly grows because redundant ACL information is added to multiple objects. Active Directory doesn't store the management information in the Active Directory hierarchy. Instead, Active Directory requires that every single object in the directory be updated.

Active Directory's static inheritance also increases replication traffic on the network, which is especially problematic for slower *wide area networks* (WAN) links. When granting global management rights, Active Directory updates all the directory objects with a new ACL list, generating a tremendous amount of directory synchronization traffic. Consider the previous example in which Sally needed management rights over all 3,000 users in the Active Directory tree. Because Active Directory requires that all 3,000 ACL be updated, 1,536,000 bytes must be replicated to 12 servers, which means 18,432,000 bytes of data must be passed.

LIMITED PARTITIONING, REPLICATION, AND SYNCHRONIZATION The smallest unit of replication in Active Directory is the entire domain. It is not possible to partition the domain into smaller units for replication, such as partitioning the domain at an organizational unit and replicating just those objects within the organizational unit instead of replicating the entire domain. Rather than implement one large Active Directory domain, customers may choose to create multiple domains linked by transitive trust relationships into a larger Active Directory tree. However, each Windows 2000 Server may hold only a domain replica of a single NT domain. This one domain per domain controller limitation will increase the number of Windows 2000 servers required for domain fault tolerance.

NDS Delivers Now Several features that will be a part of Active Directory have long been a part of NDS. In addition, NDS solves many of the limitations that still exist with Active Directory.

EXTENDING THE DATABASE The NDS database is completely extensible and allows the addition of custom information for object attributes and object types. This is the entire reason why products like NDS for NT and ZENworks are possible with NDS. NDS has what it takes to have a robust, extensible directory that can facilitate today's networking needs and that is ready for the future of your network.

DYNAMIC, HIERARCHICAL NAMING Dynamic naming has always been a part of NDS. With user names like `.mseller.salesdomain.orm.` `firstfederal`, you know just where the user is located. And, if you have users with the same name in different parts of the tree, you can easily identify who they are and where they belong.

DISTRIBUTED MANAGEMENT NDS provides the capability to delegate administrative rights to a subset of objects. Like Active Directory, NDS enables you to grant a specific user rights to manage objects in a single organizational unit. Unlike Active Directory, NDS also provides the capability to grant finer administrative rights, such as the ability for a user to manage individual objects (like users, printers, and servers) or attributes (like email addresses and phone numbers). The flexibility of NDS enables you to grant rights to resources by either groups or organizational units and enables the rights to be as specific as a single object or as an object's individual attributes.

NDS organizational units provide much more functionality that greatly simplifies network management. Many of the important labor-saving NDS organizational unit features are missing from Active Directory. Because the organizational unit often reflects geographical locations or departments and divisions within a corporation, leveraging the organizational unit simplifies network management.

NO COMPLEX TRUST RELATIONSHIPS Even though Active Directory has improved many of the difficulties of trust relationships, they still exist and must be managed. In NDS, you do not have to worry about trust relationships because all resources in the same tree already trust one another. That way, it does not matter to users where the resources they need are located. You can place necessary restrictions on sensitive data or on specific network resources to which you do not want all users to have access. For example, if you have a color printer that you want only your graphic designers to have access to, you can limit that access. In this way, you can decide quickly and easily how access is handled for your integrated network.

INHERITANCE AND RIGHTS NDS uses dynamic inheritance, which allows NDS to store directory management information in one location in the directory. NDS directory logic then determines the flow of management rights throughout the directory, eliminating the need for storing redundant management information. With dynamic inheritance, the NDS database remains lean, fast, and efficient. In the scenario presented previously, NDS would enable you to drag and drop Sally to the top of the tree. As a result of dynamic inheritance, Sally now has rights to manage all objects in the tree because Sally's management rights flow down to subordinate objects. Only Sally's object was added to the ACL of the corporate container object, and if we assume that each ACL is 512 bytes in size, the directory database increased by only 512 bytes. Because NDS requires only one ACL update (512 bytes) to be replicated to all 12 servers, the change generates only 6 kilobytes of network traffic in comparison to more than 18 megabytes of network synchronization traffic generated by Active Directory.

PARTITIONING, REPLICATION, AND SYNCHRONIZATION NDS enables you to determine the size of your partitions and then store those partitions on multiple servers wherever they are needed. Each partition contains a set of container objects, all the objects contained in them, and the data about those objects. And, you can share multiple partitions on one NDS server, thus eliminating the need for many additional servers for fault tolerance. When you have created your partitions, you can replicate and distribute them to increase your NDS performance. You can, for example, locate a partition of the NDS tree on an NT Server in a remote office so that users can log in to the partition and do not have to wait to log in across the WAN. As updates to the database are made, the changes can be made to the local read/write partition and then synchronized with the NDS database on a scheduled basis. You, as the administrator, schedule when these updates (synchronization) occur. So, you can schedule them during off-peak times.

NUMBER OF OBJECTS IN THE TREE NDS can hold more objects than any directory. This means that you do not need to have multiple databases or complex domain relationships. With NDS, you can have at least one billion objects and their file size can be as large as 50M. Even though you have increased the number of objects in the Directory, your performance and speed will not degrade. You can now combine your Internet and enterprise networks in to one.

With all the hype about Windows 2000, NDS still provides the best and most proven directory. If you find that you can't do without Windows 2000, Novell has announced that it will support Windows 2000. However, because of the changes in the way that Windows 2000 directs calls to the database, it will take some re-engineering and some time to overcome Microsoft's attempt to run Novell out of the directory arena.

How Does NDS Compare to Solaris?

Sun SPARCstations running Solaris are noted for their high vertical scalability in delivering mission-critical applications and Web services from a single server to many users. However, they are not well known for their sophisticated implementation of user access or directory. NDS enables you to take advantage of the power of Solaris to deliver applications effectively while having the ease of NDS user administration. NDS for Solaris enables the network user administration to scale in relation to an organization's Solaris application needs. NDS provides a simplified and distributed way to administer users for applications that scale across the network. Only one user object needs to be created and managed, so it is simple to give users access to resources across the network, on multiple operating systems and networking devices.

NDS helps administer users without being obtrusive or noticeable to users. NDS runs seamlessly in the background so that most users will never know that NDS for Solaris is on the network. However, you will notice that you have more time to perform tasks that improve the network and business process instead of responding to support calls. By decreasing support calls, improving user access to the network, and decreasing the cost of owning and operating a network, NDS for Solaris can benefit everyone on the network.

SUMMARY

NDS is the leading directory available today. It enables you to take advantage of the technologies and platforms you need. It is flexible and scalable. NDS maintains information about services and resources in NDS objects that are arranged in a Directory Tree. When someone needs access to a resource or service, NDS is powerful enough to allow users access to all the resources they need—even if these resources are on different trees—with one login password.

With NDS, the Directory can now manage more than a billion objects and provide companies with the capacity to manage their enterprise network while creating new opportunities in the Internet and e-commerce arenas. NDS also enables you to maintain your existing technology investments and to integrate any open standards-based application. NDS is an excellent choice for companies with evolving or varied security needs because the PKI, cryptography, and authentication services are tightly integrated with NDS. These features become more and more important as companies set up e-commerce and other Internet-based services.

NDS is the most mature and developed directory available today. It can integrate the competition into its infrastructure, making the added cost and frustration of maintaining multiple databases unnecessary. Whether you have a mixed environment with any combination of NetWare, Windows NT 4.0, and Solaris, or you have a native environment, NDS is ready. NDS overcomes the shortcomings of its competition and provides a better administrative environment for you and a better experience for your users.

For More Information

Here are some additional resources for information on NDS.

Web Sites

Novell Directory Services Web site: `http://www.novell.com/products/nds/index.html`

NDS Cool Solutions Web site: `http://www.novell.com/coolsolutions/nds/`

NDS Reviewer's Guide Web site: `http://www.novell.com/products/nds/nds8_rg.html`

NDS competitive information: `http://www.novell.com/advantage/nds/`

NDS Solutions Toolkit Web site: `http://www.novell.com/passport/soltoolkit/ptk_nds.html`

Web Articles

"NDS v8: The Future of Novell Directory Services" `http://developer.novell.com/research/appnotes/1999/march/a1frame.htm`

"Introduction to NDS v8" `http://developer.novell.com/research/devnotes/1999/march/a1frame.htm`

"NDS 8 Update" `http://www.developer.novell.com/research/devnotes/1999/july/a4frame.htm`

"An Introduction to NDS for NT v2.0" `http://www.developer.novell.com/research/appnotes/1999/january/a3frame.htm`

"Overview of NDS for NT 2.0" `http://www.developer.novell.com/research/devnotes/1999/may/a3frame.htm`

"NDS for NT Q & A" `http://www.developer.novell.com/research/devnotes/1999/april/a3frame.htm`

"NDS for Solaris: An Overview" `http://www.developer.novell.com/research/devnotes/1999/may/a7frame.htm`

"An Introduction to NDS for Solaris 2.0" `http://www.developer.novell.com/research/appnotes/1999/april/a1frame.htm`

"Managing Mixed NetWare and Solaris Networks with NDS for Solaris 2.0" `http://www.developer.novell.com/research/appnotes/1999/june/a2frame.htm`

NDS Design
Issues

Planning the design of a directory is like creating an outline before writing a term paper or reading the instructions before assembling a barbecue. It may not be the most engaging part of network implementation, but nothing promises to do more to eliminate mistakes and make the whole process easier. I, for one, never read the assembly instructions for my barbecue, and I still have spare parts stashed in the bottom of my toolbox. I would hate to have my enterprise directory assembled in the same fashion. A thoroughly planned and well-designed directory tree is more efficient, more secure, and more fault tolerant.

As the importance of network directories increases, their influence will touch nearly every aspect of modern information infrastructure. NDS offers tremendous value, but that value is directly proportional to the quality of the design. This chapter will provide an overview of NDS architecture and administration. It also will present a set of general design rules that will result in a stable, efficient NDS implementation. Our goal here is to provide only an overview of the design process. This material must be understood before we can effectively approach the administrative issues that will be discussed in later chapters. Because the focus of this book is more on presenting information on administrative processes and tools rather than on uncovering the intricacies of directory design, every design eventuality will not be covered. However, we will endeavor to address the most significant issues and then recommend sources for a more in-depth treatment of NDS design issues.

NDS Architecture

NDS architecture has three main aspects:

- The physical NDS database
- Rules governing NDS data
- Organization of data in NDS

Physical NDS Database

At its lowest physical level, NDS is simply a database. A typical database comprises a dataset together with methods of searching and retrieving specific data from the dataset. NDS is an object-oriented, hierarchical database. A hierarchical database maintains data (objects) in a logical tree structure, as in Figure 2-1. Specific objects are located by traversing (walking) the tree. Each object in the NDS database is identifiable through a unique name that includes an identifier together with information describing the location of that object within the hierarchical tree structure. Figure 2-1 also shows the relationship between object name and logical position within the directory.

NDS introduces a completely new database technology from that used in previous versions of NDS. This database technology provides the tremendous scalability and performance in NDS. The *FLexible Adaptive Information Manager* (FLAIM), is a breakthrough in database technology that combines the best of the relational and object-oriented database models. Novell acquired this database technology as part of its acquisition of WordPerfect Corporation. FLAIM initially was used in Novell's GroupWise collaboration product. They have since been awarded four patents related to FLAIM with more patents currently pending.

Figure 2-1

Sample directory name (location determines name)

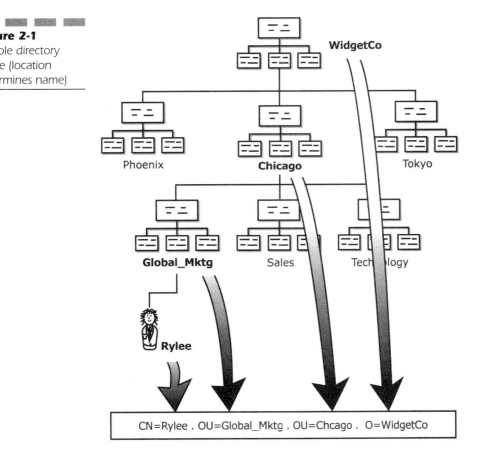

FLAIM was developed to support datasets that required a high degree of flexibility, such as genealogical information. In this situation, database fields can exist, which need to track multiple values such as multiple potential first names. To provide this data flexibility, FLAIM concerns itself primarily with data collection. The specific data model, be it relational, object-oriented or some combination of the two, is provided as a layer on top of the FLAIM datastore.

The actual FLAIM database is organized as a B-Tree, a well-known type of data structure. The B-Tree provides the tremendous scalability to NDS. B-Trees are ordered—or sorted—trees in which the root node functions as the middle of the tree. A B-Tree node contains multiple elements. In the case of NDS, an element corresponds to a directory object. This means that values lower than those stored in the root node occupy the "left" branches of the tree while values greater than those stored in the root node occupy the "right" branch of the tree as in Figure 2-2. The B-Tree is also what is known as a *Bushy* tree, meaning that a large number of nodes can occupy a single level of the tree.

The result of these two characteristics is a data structure in which a huge number of elements can be stored. Furthermore, each element can be located very quickly.

The incredible search performance, which characterizes NDS, is also a product of FLAIM. The FLAIM database makes extensive use of indexing. This means that the data in the FLAIM datastore is sorted in a variety of different ways in order to further decrease the time required to locate a given piece of information. Each index is a smaller B-Tree structure that is automatically updated whenever any relevant piece of the database is added, changed, or deleted. When a query is received by NDS, internal logic determines what index, if any, should be used to most efficiently respond to the query. Table 2-1 lists the default indexes implemented by NDS.

Figure 2-2
Simple B-Tree

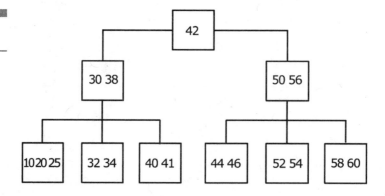

Table 2-1	**Index Type**	**Description**
Index Types Included with NDS	Operational	Internal indexes used by NDS to look up an object; indexed on internal object IDs
	Display	Used by client to speed display of container or tree contents
	Obituary	Speeds location of deleted directory entries marked by obituaries
	Name Substring	Provides wildcard search indexes for the "Common Name" and "UniqueID" attributes
	Domain Container	Indexes on the LDAP dc= attribute
	LDAP and ConsoleOne	Indexes all User objects based on CN=, uniqueID, Given Name, and Surname
	List	Indexes objects with a large number of values for the same attribute, such as a Group object

Note that using indexes is not a silver bullet. NDS essentially trades update speed for search speed. In other words, maintaining indexes increases the time it takes to perform an update when some object or attribute is changed, added, or deleted. It also decreases the time it takes to find a given object or attribute.

Chapter 10, "Other NDS Administration Tools," discusses the IXEdit utility that can be used by administrators to create custom indexes for use with NDS.

Rules Governing NDS Data

Rules defining valid object types—where they can be stored and what can be done with each of the object types—are maintained within the NDS schema. The schema provides the structure to the NDS tree. The schema is comprised of a set of object classes. Object classes define the types of objects that can be created within an NDS tree. Each object class contains a set of attributes that specifies the type(s) of data that can be stored within each object. In this way, the schema creates the logical view of the NDS data, which network administrators and users use every day.

Novell provides a base set of object classes in NDS but has recognized that they cannot account for every possible use of the directory. To address this, the NDS schema is fully extensible. This means that third parties are free to define new object classes and attributes in order to customize NDS capabilities. One neat example of this is a product called ScheMax from Netoria. ScheMax provides the ability to add classes and attributes to NDS without doing any programming. It also automatically creates management snap-ins that enable NDS management tools to interact with those new classes and attributes. ScheMax is discussed in more detail in Chapter 12.

Data Organization in NDS

NDS organization has two aspects, the physical organization and the logical organization. The physical organization of data in NDS revolves around its distributed nature and the need to provide fault tolerance for the NDS database. Each piece of the total NDS database is known as a *partition*. In order to make the data contained in a given partition more secure and accessible, multiple copies of that partition can be stored across the network. This process of creating and maintaining multiple partition copies is known as *replication* (see Figure 2-3). Replication is an extremely powerful capability, and Novell has designed NDS with a complex set of checks and balances in order to maintain the integrity of directory data across the distributed environment. The partition and replication process are discussed in more detail later in this chapter.

The logical organization of data in NDS determines how the data stored in NDS will be presented to users and administrators. The logical organization is what you *see* when you look at NDS. This logical NDS organization is controlled by the schema. The schema essentially defines the types of data that can be stored in NDS and the acceptable set of operations that can be performed on that data.

First, the NDS schema defines a class of objects that can store other objects. These are known as *container objects*, or simply containers. Containers are the building blocks used to create the structure of the NDS tree. Objects that cannot hold other objects are known as *leaf objects*. Leaf objects define the actual network resources available in the NDS tree. Leaf objects will be discussed in more detail in Chapter 5, "Administering NDS Objects."

Each class of leaf object contains a unique set of attributes that describes the data and functionality associated with that object. Leaf objects might include users, printers, network routers, applications, or

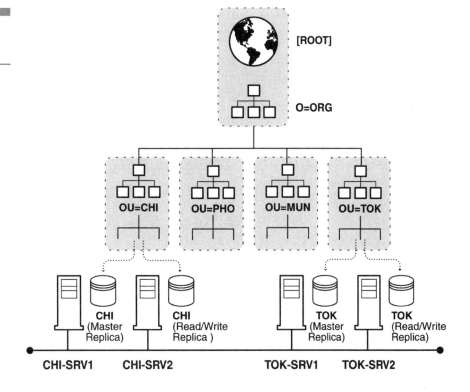

Figure 2-3
NDS partitions
and replicas

even other databases. Because the NDS schema is fully extensible, new object classes can be defined and created within NDS by anyone who might need them. Novell independent application developers or organizations that use NDS might choose to extend the schema in order to incorporate new functionality.

With this brief introduction to NDS architecture, we are ready to move into the issues that surround the planning and design of an effective NDS tree.

High-Level NDS Planning

When planning an NDS tree, as with most projects, it is best to start with the general and work toward the specific. Before anything else, those ultimately responsible for NDS should be assembled to discuss the general goals of the NDS implementation. This discussion should take into account the organizational structure, administrative philosophy, and management goals. Getting this information up front will prevent having to make significant structural changes to the NDS tree after it is in production. NDS is extremely flexible and adaptable to many organizational needs, but it cannot simultaneously support conflicting strategies. Department heads and IS management must come together and agree upon (or mandate) an overall design strategy.

Upper management may or may not be involved in these meetings, but they must sign off on all resulting decisions. Often, the preparation and design of an enterprise directory can uncover inefficiencies in organizational structures and processes. Rather than implement the inefficiencies into the directory, it might be a good time to consider modifications to the structures and processes of the organization. Obviously these types of decisions can affect the dynamics of the organization as a whole, so network administrators will not make them alone. However, because the organization and structure of the directory will mirror that of the organization, it is appropriate to examine potential flaws in organizational structures and process while considering the design of the directory.

Decisions involving the transition of responsibility, the centralization of administration, or the elimination of duties are often met with significant resistance. This is why upper management must be supportive of the directory initiative and remain informed of the issues confronting the directory design team. If they are not supportive of the goals of the directory implementation, then this type of resistance cannot be overcome.

These high-level design meetings should result in—when coupled with an NDS tree design that follows a few simple rules—a directory implementation plan for the organization. A directory planned and executed in this way will yield a highly stable and reliable information infrastructure. All final results of these planning meetings should be formally recorded in a directory design document that will guide the directory implementers and serve as a bible of organizational strategy with regards to the directory infrastructure.

A good directory design document will include the following:

- Current network resource map
- Current organizational chart
- Defined administrative model (centralized versus decentralized)
- Definition of administrative responsibilities
- Defined directory naming standards
- Defined time synchronization strategy
- Server/replica map

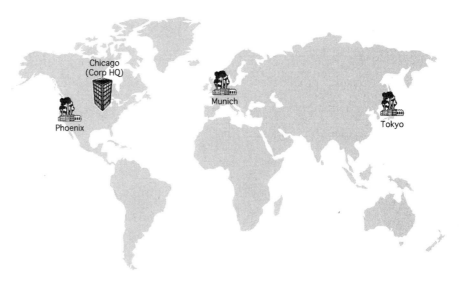

Figure 2-4
WidgetCo worldwide
operations

At this point, we would like to introduce our own multinational corporation, WidgetCo. WidgetCo will be used throughout the remainder of this book to demonstrate the various design and administration principles that we will be discussing (see Figure 2-4).

WidgetCo has decided to enter the modern computing era by implementing a corporate NDS tree as a full-service directory infrastructure. They hope this NDS implementation will result in a common structure for network administration, security, and resource access and control. WidgetCo maintains multiple network platforms, including NetWare, Windows NT, and Sun Solaris. Each has its place, but WidgetCo would like to centrally manage access and resources across these platforms seamlessly.

Network Resource Map

A network map will be critical when determining a partitioning and replication strategy for NDS. The network map will contain a complete list of sites and resources located at each site along with descriptions of any WAN links connecting the various sites. Network protocols in use at each site also should be identified. Each resource, such as a file server or printer, should be associated with the group that comprises the primary users of that resource. The WidgetCo network resource map is shown in Figure 2-5.

Current Organizational Chart

A current organizational chart is often very elusive, but it is critical for developing the lower levels of the NDS tree (see Figure 2-6). Try to get copies of organizational charts for every department that will be affected by the NDS rollout. The lower levels of an NDS tree should be created based upon the organization structure. Placement of containers, users, and resources should mirror the organizational chart wherever possible.

Figure 2-5
WidgetCo network
resource map

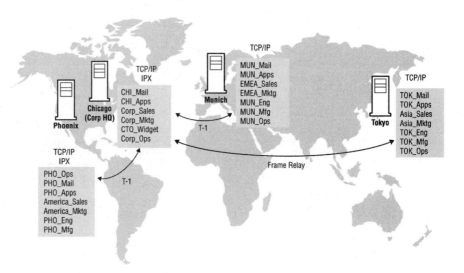

Figure 2-6
WidgetCo
organizational chart

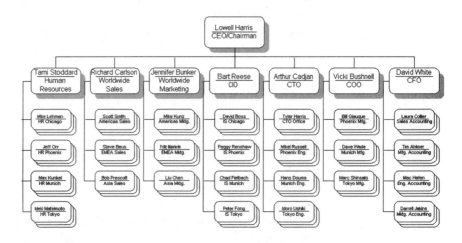

Administrative Model

The choice of an administrative model is one area where it may be prudent for departments to sacrifice some autonomy and power for the sake of organizational consistency and efficiency. If each department or division is managed as an island, then it becomes much more difficult to define the processes for communicating between those islands. This does not mean that each department or division cannot have its own administrators, but some standard policies should define acceptable behavior when that behavior can affect more than a single department or division. Some administrative tasks also are much more efficient if they are performed at a higher level.

Centralized administration is the recommended method for managing NDS because it showcases the strengths of the directory model. In many ways it is more efficient than a decentralized model. In the centralized model, administrative users are created at higher levels of the directory tree, where they are naturally afforded more control. The centralized administrative model is commonly implemented as a *Help Desk* in larger organizations. The Help Desk is an IS department responsible for the administration and maintenance of a large portion of the network infrastructure. Multiple departments or divisions may fall under their responsibility. Typically, the Help Desk will maintain the network at a large organizational site, such as a corporate headquarters, while small branch offices may not fall directly under their control. The effectiveness of a Help Desk is diminished when operating across a WAN link because access to physical resources is restricted.

The decentralized model is less efficient than centralized administration but may be preferable in those situations where departments need to be compartmentalized for security reasons.

In this scenario, each department or division will have its own administrator or administrative group. To maintain separation, *Inherited Rights Filters* can be installed at the container to prevent upper level administrators from having any control at the lower levels. This model should be used only when absolutely necessary because it sacrifices efficiency and consistency for local control. In most cases, this is exactly what organizations are trying to avoid.

These two models lay at opposite extremes of an administrative continuum. For most organizations, some processes and data are best controlled locally and some should be managed centrally. For example, departments may be given the task of maintaining employee information, such as phone numbers and addresses, while a central IS staff will control the timing of system upgrades. The key is determining how to organize administrative tasks so that the organization operates as efficiently as possible. NDS is making it possible to integrate these administrative styles through the use of role-based administration, which will be discussed in detail in Chapter 6, "Controlling Network Access."

Definition of Administrative Responsibilities

This definition of administrative responsibilities is an extension of the preceding section's discussion, but it goes beyond the overall administrative philosophy to determine what types of control each layer of administration will possess. This discussion also serves to define the degree of responsibility assigned to each administrator within the system. For example,

- What will a regional administrator do as opposed to a departmental administrator?
- Will role-based administration be implemented?
- What types of role-based administrative tasks will be specifically assigned?
- Will roles be defined at the organizational or departmental level?
- Will administrators at the same level of the tree, but in different branches, have similar responsibilities?

These types of questions will be the most difficult to answer because they get back to the underlying management and operational processes. You may find during the design process that the current decision-making process for certain issues is very inefficient. Perhaps responsibility for these types of decisions should be moved up (or down) in the organization. These issues will have to be addressed if the NDS design is to be efficient. It makes little sense to perpetuate organizational inefficiencies in the directory design.

The goal of this examination process is to let the Directory help build process efficiency that will enable the organization to function more efficiently as a unit while still maintaining the local control necessary for day-to-day operations.

Naming Standards

The purpose of creating naming standards for directory objects is to make it easier to browse the tree and recognize the resources that are available. Unfortunately, this means that more creative names such as Server1, Socrates and Jupiter may have to be relegated to the Lab environment and not installed into the production network. Although these creative names may be entertaining, they do little to provide information about what that resource does, who should have access to it, or who is responsible for it.

Directory names should be descriptive. Because the directory tree is a logical construct, object names provide the only mechanism to overlay information about physical or organizational location onto the directory itself. In other words, if containers and resources are not named properly, then it becomes much more difficult to determine who should have control of that resource or how it should be managed. It also makes it much more difficult for users to know who has access to a given printer or to know what is stored on a given file server. For example,

■ *Container objects*: Name derived from physical location, organizational structure, or a combination of both (e.g., Houston, ATL_Sales, or Engineering).

■ *Printer objects*: Name should give information regarding physical location or department(s) that make use of the printer (e.g. Sales_Laser, Floor1_Color, or Admin_Canon.

In the NDS design document, create a naming section that lists all object types that will be created within the tree and enumerate the rules governing the naming of each class of object. For example, the naming standards should outline how a User object name is determined (e.g., first initial + last name).

This section might look like Table 2-2. After naming standards have been defined, they must be followed religiously.

	NDS Object Type	Name Definition
Table 2-2	User	First initial + middle initial + full last name
		Ex. JLHARRIS
WidgetCo Naming Standards		Note: Use middle initial if it exists
	Organization	Name of organization
		Ex. WidgetCo
	Organizational unit	City location and/or division/dept. name.
		Ex. TOKYO, Global_Mktg, PHO_Eng.
	Server	Three-letter location code and description of primary user or primary function. If multiple servers provide the same function, add number to end of name.
		Ex. CHI_Sales, MUN_MAIL2, TOK_APP1
	Printer	Printer type and location. Use Mail stop to identify physical location.
		Ex. HP5MP_CHI-331, Tek550_PHO-122

Time Synchronization

Time synchronization is an interesting topic. Although time synchronization is vital to the proper function of NDS, NDS does not implement time synchronization. NDS relies on the underlying *Network Operating System* (NOS) platform to provide a fully time-synchronized environment within which NDS can operate.

Because NDS was originally released as a component of NetWare, Novell chose to implement a proprietary time sync model that ran over on the IPX protocol. However, because NDS is now being offered as a cross-platform directory solution, NetWare-based networks need to be able to synchronize time with non-NetWare servers and/or networks. To do this, Novell has extended the NetWare time sync modules to support an industry standard time synchronization protocol known as *Network Time Protocol* (NTP).

NTP is exhaustively described in RFC 1305, which can be found on the IETF Web site at `http://www.ietf.org/rfc/rfc1305.txt`. Although NetWare still does not use NTP directly, it is possible to integrate NetWare-based time synchronization with platforms running NTP as their time sync protocol. This makes it possible to synchronize time across heterogeneous networks running NetWare, Solaris, and/or Windows NT.

NOTE: *NDS does not care what method is used to synchronize time as long as it is done. NDS will run equally well under a NetWare time sync model or an NTP time sync model—or some combination of the two.*

The following section provides an overview of the NetWare time sync model as well as the NTP model. It also describes how these two methods can be used together to achieve cross-platform time synchronization. Administration of time synchronization is covered in Chapter 9, "Administering NDS."

NetWare Time Synchronization   Three strategies provide time synchronization:

- *Voted Time*. Participating systems each provide input and arrive at a consensus time that is used throughout the network.

- *Forced Time*. This strategy defines a single master time source, which distributes the official network time. All other systems are slaves that receive the network time and set their clocks accordingly.

- *Hybrid Time*. This strategy is a combination of the previous two in which a small group of systems determine a consensus network time and then distribute that time to all other systems.

NetWare time synchronization can be configured to operate under the Forced Time or the Hybrid Time strategies depending upon the size and complexity of the network environment.

Four types of timeservers can be defined in an NDS environment:

- *Single Reference*. This timeserver uses its own internal clock, or an external time source, to determine network time. This NDS time then is communicated to secondary timeservers and network clients. The Single Reference timeserver is the master source for network time.

- *Reference*. This timeserver uses its own hardware clock, or external time source, to determine network time. Reference servers replace the Single Reference timeserver in more complex network environments. The Reference server participates with other timeservers in a voting process to determine a consensus time. When a reference server is used, NetWare uses a Hybrid time sync strategy. However, as will be seen, other participants in the time-synchronization process will converge toward the Reference server time.

- *Primary*. Name notwithstanding, a Primary timeserver does not generate network time. Primary timeservers participate in a polling process with other Primary servers and the Reference server. During the polling process, each Primary timeserver votes on the correct network time. From this process, a consensus network time emerges. Each Primary timeserver synchronizes its internal clock to the consensus network time and helps distribute that time to all interested parties.

- *Secondary*. Secondary timeservers receive network time from Single Reference, Reference, Primary, or other Secondary timeservers. Secondary timeservers are slaves that do not participate in the time-polling process, but simply receive and pass on the consensus network time.

The choice of a time-synchronization strategy is largely dependent on the size of the network. You have your choice of a default strategy that is appropriate for smaller networks or a more complex Time Provider Group strategy that will be more efficient in a large network environment.

DEFAULT TIME SYNC   The default time-synchronization strategy is suitable for smaller networks with fewer than 30 servers in the network and no WAN connections. The default time-synchronization strategy utilizes SAP in an IPX environment and SLP in an IP environment to locate and query the Single Reference server.

Under the default strategy, the first server installed into an NDS tree is designated as a Single Reference timeserver (see Figure 2-7). All subsequent servers installed into the tree are designated as Secondary timeservers. In this scenario, the Single Reference server defines the network time and responds to all queries regarding network time. Obviously, as the network grows and/or WAN links are added, this single source for network time will become a bottleneck. If this Single Reference server has to be contacted across a WAN link, this time-synchronization method will also add unnecessary traffic to expensive WAN links.

TIME PROVIDER GROUP More complex environments should implement a *Time Provider Group* (TPG), or groups. A TPG consists of a centrally located Reference server and between two and seven Primary servers that will distribute the network time to all servers in the network, as shown in Figure 2-8. This strategy spreads the task of distributing network time out across multiple servers. It also makes it possible to limit the amount of time-synchronization traffic that needs to traverse costly WAN links.

In a well-designed network environment, it is easy to determine the optimal locations for the various timeservers. The Reference server should exist at the hub of the network, perhaps at a corporate headquarters to which all satellite or branch offices are connected. The Reference server will normally receive its time from a highly accurate external time source such as an atomic clock, radio clock, or Internet time source. These time sources may be contacted through dial-up connections or across the Internet.

Figure 2-7

Default time-synchronization configuration

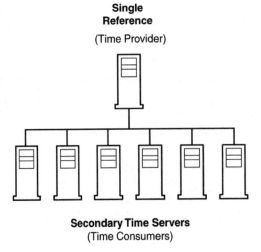

Single
Reference

(Time Provider)

Secondary Time Servers
(Time Consumers)

Figure 2-8
Time Provider group

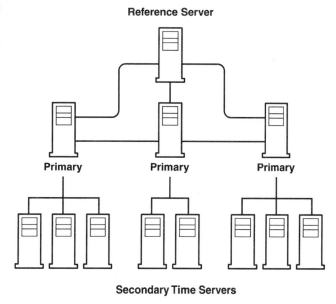

Primary servers should be strategically placed at the largest branches, and they distribute time information to secondary servers at their own site as well as any small satellite sites in their area.

Network Time Protocol   NTP uses a hierarchical master/slave model to distribute time across a network. NTP operates under the idea of a *Universal Time Constant* (UTC), which is the number of seconds that have elapsed since January 1, 1990. A single authoritative UTC time source is defined as the *Stratum 1 timeserver*. There are 16 possible NTP strata. Each successive stratum indicates another level removed from the authoritative time source. Stratum 16, the highest stratum, indicates that the server is not communicating with any trustworthy time source. Stratum 2 timeservers receive time from the Stratum 1 server, adjust their own clocks to match network time, and then propagate network downward to other level(s) of time consumers on the network.

The NTP hierarchy is self-configuring, meaning that a built-in NTP algorithm determines the optimal flow of time information across the network and designates timeservers as Stratum 2, Stratum 3, etc. NTP utilizes UTP port 123 to distribute network time.

Because NTP is tied to real time through the UTC, several features of NTP are designed to do things like correct clock *drift* and add in leap seconds.

A full NTP implementation is a fairly heavyweight protocol due to all these extra features.

Using NTP and NetWare Together TIMESYNC.NLM is the primary module responsible for the management of time synchronization within a NetWare environment. To provide compatibility with NTP, TIMESYNC.NLM has been modified to be able to accept time from an NTP source and/or provide time in a format suitable for an NTP environment. However, TIMESYNC.NLM offers a lightweight NTP implementation because it is used specifically for NDS consumption. This means that a NetWare server or servers can be integrated with NTP to synchronize time across both types of systems. A network administrator can choose to have his or her NetWare environment receive time from an NTP network or vice versa (see Figure 2-9). At this point, the random mixing of NetWare and NTP servers is not recommended.

For more information on the specifics of configuring time synchronization in a mixed NetWare/NTP environment, see Chapter 9, "Administering NDS."

Figure 2-9
NetWare/NTP time-synchronization environment

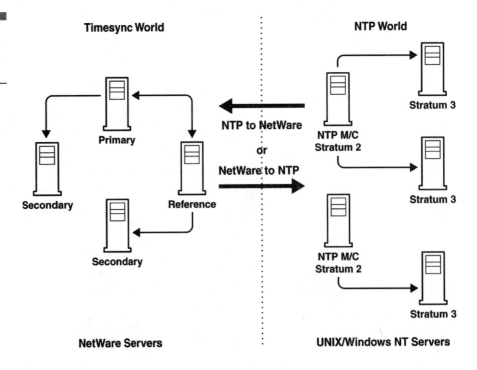

	Partition -> Server	[Root]	CHI	PHO	TOK	MUN
Table 2-3 *WidgetCo Server/Replica Map*	Global_Sales	Master	Master			
	Global_Mktg		Read/Write			
	CTO		Read/Write			
	Americas_Sales			Master		
	PHO_Mfg			Read/Write		
	PHO_Eng			Read/Write		
	Asia_Sales	Master			Master	
	TOK_Mfg				Read/Write	
	TOK_Eng				Read/Write	
	EMEA_Sales	Master				Master
	MUN_Mfg					Read/Write
	MUN_Eng					Read/Write

Server/Replica Map

The Server/Replica Map is a good way to keep track of what servers hold copies of the NDS database. The site administrator should maintain the Server/Replica Map, which contains a list of all replicas stored on each server at the site.

The Server/Replica map is simply a table that lists all servers on one axis and all partitions on the other axis. The cells show the type of replica stored on that server for that particular partition, as in Table 2-3.

The Server/Replica Map enables administrators to quickly isolate the servers involved in a given partition operation in order to troubleshoot more effectively.

NDS Design Considerations

The whole purpose of implementing a network directory is to make the operation of the network more efficient and simpler. Unfortunately, this means that the directory cannot be rolled out without any consideration for the environment into which it is being inserted. A few basic rules should be followed when designing an NDS tree:

- Design the top of the tree to reflect physical network layout.
- Design the bottom of the tree to reflect organizational structure.
- Place objects in the tree to facilitate access and administration.
- Partition and replicate to achieve scalability and fault tolerance.

We will not present every possible design option as part of this chapter. Our goal is to present the basic rules that can be universally applied to any NDS design and to demonstrate the use of those rules in creating an NDS tree. As network administrators or IS managers, it is your responsibility to understand basic design principles and apply them to your specific organizations.

Design the Tree Top to Reflect Physical Network Layout

The top one or two levels of an NDS tree form the foundation for everything that will come later. If these levels are not configured properly, the whole tree will suffer. Similar to the construction of a house, the NDS tree foundation needs to be stable and not prone to changes in structure. (I don't know about you, but I have always avoided building my houses on sandbars!)

The same is true for NDS. Given the constantly shifting structure in today's modern organizations, basing the directory architecture entirely on organizational structure would be very unwise. The stable part of a modern organization is its capital assets (i.e., plant(s) and equipment). The organizational structure might change, but the organization is still located in the same corporate headquarters as before. Make use of this stability by designing the foundation of the NDS tree around physical locations.

Four main items should be determined when designing the top levels of the NDS tree:

1. Name the Tree [Root].
2. Determine use of Country and Locality objects.
3. Define the Organization object.
4. Define location-based Organizational Unit objects.

When you name your NDS tree, you are naming the [Root] object. Make the name short, descriptive, and unique. Many use the following tree name convention:

```
Organization Name_TREE
```

For WidgetCo, that means that `[Root]` is named `WidgetCo_TREE`.

Next, you have to decide how to create the first level in your NDS tree. This involves determining whether or not you are going to incorporate the use of *Country* (C) or *Locality* (L) objects into your NDS tree design (see Figure 2-10).

In most cases, the use of Country and Locality objects does not make sense. However, if it is important to comply with X.500 naming syntax to interact with external X.500 directories, then these objects can be used to adhere to X.500 naming standards. Other than that, it is best to start with the *Organization* (O) object and define geographical regions under the Organization as *Organizational Units* (OU) (see Figure 2-11).

Next you must determine the name of your Organization object. Normally, this is the first level of the tree, and simply using the organization name—WidgetCo—is a good way to go.

Finally, define subsequent levels of the tree around the physical network infrastructure currently employed (or planned) by the organization. For WidgetCo, this means that regional sites are defined as level-two Organizational Units. Organizations larger than WidgetCo also could designate level-three Organizational Units as branch offices. In most cases, three levels dedicated to the geographical structure of the organization will accommodate even the largest organizations.

The opposite is true for smaller companies. When the company is located at a single site, the physical levels can be eliminated altogether, if desired. However, this strategy is not recommended if the company will grow into multiple sites in the future. The lack of containers based upon physical sites will make it much more difficult to expand the NDS structure as the organization grows.

Figure 2-10
WidgetCo tree if using Country and Locality objects

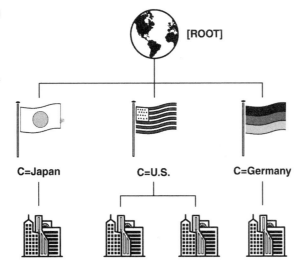

[ROOT]

C=Japan   C=U.S.   C=Germany

Figure 2-11
Actual WidgetCo tree

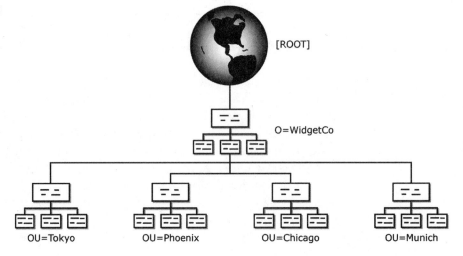

Design the Bottom of the Tree to Reflect Organizational Structure

The bottom portion of the tree is where all the action will be. Unlike the top of the tree, we fully expect adaptation and evolution to occur over time at the lower levels of the tree. This means that we need to design flexibility into the system.

For this reason, the lower levels of the NDS tree will grow based not on physical locations, but on organizational structure (see Figure 2-12). The best way to visualize the NDS tree at this point is to look at a current copy of the organizational chart. This is why we mentioned having current organizational charts as part of the NDS design document. If you can't find copies of current charts, take the time to survey the organization and assemble a view of the organizational structure. You will need to understand the divisions and/or departments that operate at each physical site to create the lower levels of the NDS tree. This information doesn't need to go all the way down to the individual employee, but you do need to understand how departments and divisions are organized at each physical site.

The reason that organizational containers are so useful at this level is that they enable us to group resources together. We can put the users in the marketing department together with their printers, servers, and applications. Then those users and resources can be managed together. As we will see in the next section, this grouping also enables us to minimize the overhead associated with maintaining replica integrity and currency.

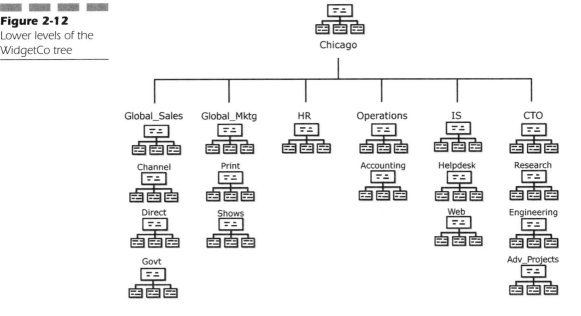

Figure 2-12
Lower levels of the
WidgetCo tree

Place Objects in the Tree to Facilitate Access and Administration

Now that you have the general tree design and containers created, how should you organize all the leaf objects that will populate the NDS tree? The two primary considerations are as follows:

1. Make it as easy as possible for users to access the resources they need.

2. Make it as easy as possible to centrally control and administer the network resources

In most cases, you will be able to place resources, such as servers, printers, and departmental applications, in the same container with the users who will need access to those resources. However, if users in multiple containers will share resources, place those resources one level above the user containers. This makes the resource much easier to locate.

By using organizational containers for the bottom of our NDS tree, we can group users based upon common sets of resources. This means that things like access controls, login scripts and policies can be managed from the container level, rather than having to create each of these things individually. Only the exceptions to the general container rules need to be specifically managed. Management by exception is tremendously powerful as a tool for reducing complexity and increasing efficiency.

One last consideration when designing the bottom levels of your NDS tree is the use of *Bindery Services*. Bindery Services provides compatibility between NDS and applications written for older versions of Novell NetWare (i.e., v2.x and v3.x). These older versions of NetWare maintained a server-specific database of user and resource information known as the *Bindery*. Our first recommendation is to eliminate the need for Bindery compatibility by upgrading these legacy applications if at all possible. Bindery compatibility inherently reduces the efficiency of NDS and increases the complexity of the network.

If it is not yet possible to eliminate these older applications, they can be installed on newer versions of NetWare by creating Bindery Contexts on the NetWare 5 servers on which they will run. A Bindery Context allows access to the objects stored in a specific NDS container through the Bindery *Application Programming Interface* (API). Basically, NDS data is mapped to the old Bindery model so that legacy applications will know how to access that data.

The Bindery Context can be set through the NetWare MONITOR utility (see Figure 2-13). Up to 16 Bindery Contexts can be set on each NetWare server.

The problem with Bindery Contexts arises from the fact that the server on which the Bindery Context is set must hold a replica of the Bindery Context container. If several Bindery Contexts are defined for legacy applications used throughout the organization, this will increase the number or replicas (and the overhead required to maintain them) dramatically. So, if Bindery Contexts must be used, it is best to consolidate all Bindery applications on a few servers. Users who will make use of those applications also

Figure 2-13
MONITOR Bindery
Context screen

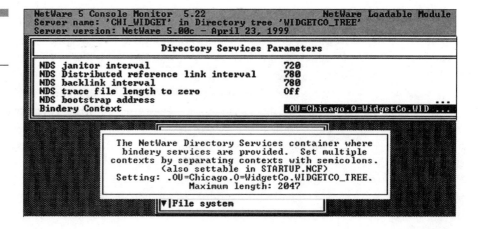

should be grouped together. This can be done either by putting them in the same container(s) or by creating special group objects and placing the group in the Bindery Context containers. Groups will be discussed further in Chapter 6, "Controlling Network Access."

The goal is to limit as much as possible the number of additional replicas necessary to support legacy Bindery applications.

Partition and Replicate to Achieve Scalability and Fault Tolerance

Partitions   NDS allows the creation of partitions to distribute the directory database across the network. A copy of a given NDS partition is known as a *replica*. By creating multiple replicas of a given partition, you build fault tolerance into the directory architecture. If a server holding a partition replica fails, the partition is still available from the other replica servers.

Locating those portions of the NDS database close to those users that make use of it will dramatically increase the performance of the directory. It will also greatly reduce the network traffic associated with directory interaction. This is particularly important when multiple sites are connected by costly WAN links. The last thing we want to do is promote WAN traffic for background operations like searching for a server or printer.

This section does not detail the utilities available for partition and replica manipulation. These utilities will be discussed in detail in Chapter 9, "Administering NDS." Here, we confine ourselves to discussing the strategy behind partition and replica creation and placement.

When the first NDS server is installed, a [Root] partition is automatically created, and a replica of that partition is stored on the NDS server. After [Root] exists, the rest of the directory can be built by adding the necessary container and leaf objects.

As other NDS servers are installed, replicas of [Root] should be created to provide the fault tolerance already mentioned. If you maintain a small network at a single site, the [Root] partition may be all you need. Chapter 3, "Installing and Upgrading NDS," will discuss a special case when using NDS for Solaris. Replicate it to two or three servers for fault tolerance, and you are done. However, if your network environment is more complex, as is the case for WidgetCo, more work must be done to create an efficient NDS environment.

Planning your NDS partition strategy is similar to planning the top levels of the NDS tree. Partition creation should follow the physical network infrastructure. WAN links should always be considered boundaries between partitions. This eliminates the need to pass background NDS traffic across expensive, low bandwidth links. Consider the WidgetCo partition boundaries in Figure 2-14.

WidgetCo should create four child partitions (see Figure 2-15). Child partitions are created from the container level. The name of each child partition is determined by the name of the container used to start that partition. This container is known as the partition root object. Partitions cannot overlap in any way (i.e., the same object cannot exist in multiple partitions). Essentially, child partitions are discrete portions of the [Root] partition.

Each child partition then should be replicated to multiple servers at the site that partition is serving.

After partitions have been created based upon the physical network structure, the bottom levels of the NDS tree can be examined. In most cases, you will not need to partition the bottom layers of a tree unless you want to reduce the number of objects in a given child partition. On older versions of NDS, it was recommended that the number of objects per partition be kept down to a few thousand for best performance. Today, NDS has completely removed that limitation. NDS can now maintain millions of objects per partition with negligible impact on performance.

A child partition might also be further partitioned to limit the number of partition replicas that exist across the network. Remember our discussion of Bindery Services. Each Bindery Context server requires a replica to support

Figure 2-14
WidgetCo partition boundaries (using a map representation)

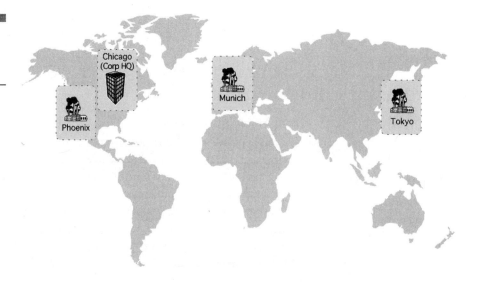

Figure 2-15
WidgetCo partitions

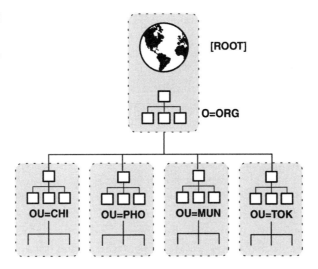

Bindery-based applications and services. Large numbers of partition replicas increase the background traffic required for replica synchronization and complicate partition repair operations that may be necessary. A good rule of thumb is to limit the total number of replicas of a given partition to 10 or fewer.

The result of your partitioning efforts should be a small [Root] partition and a child partition for every physical site in the network. The [Root] partition should end up containing only [Root] and the Organization object. The reason for this is explained in the following section.

Replicas   A replica is a physical copy of an NDS partition. Four types of NDS replicas exist:

- *Master replica*. By default, the first replica created is designated as the Master replica. Each partition will have one, and only one, Master replica. Other replicas will be designated as Read/Write, Read-only, or Subordinate Reference.

  The Master replica contains all object information for the partition. Objects and attributes maintained in the partition can be modified from the Master replica. These changes are propagated to other servers holding replicas of this partition. Furthermore, all changes to the partition itself, such as creating other replicas or creating a child partition, must be performed from the perspective of the server that holds the Master replica.

- *Read/Write replica*. A Read/Write replica contains the same information as the master replica. Objects and attributes maintained in the partition can be modified from the Read/Write replica. These changes are propagated to other servers holding replicas of this partition. Any number of read/write replicas can be created. However, for the sake of overall directory performance, it is recommended that the total number of partition replicas not exceed 10. This type of replica cannot initiate partition operations.

- *Read-only replica.* The Read-only replica contains all the same information as the Master and Read/Write replicas. Users can read, but not modify, the information contained in these replicas. The replica is updated with changes made to the Master and Read/Write replicas. In practice, Read-only replicas are seldom used because they are unable to support login operations. The login process requires updating some directory information. Because a Read-only replica does not support directory updates, it cannot provide login services. One potential use is maintaining a backup copy of a partition. The Read-only replica receives all partition updates but will not participate in the update process in any way.

  These replica types exist primarily to eliminate the single point of failure in an NDS environment. A recommended design goal is three replicas, one Master and a combination of Read/Write and/or Read-only replicas. As stated, the Read-only replica is seldom used, so most NDS implementations will focus on Master and Read/Write replicas in their production environments.

- *Subordinate Reference.* Subordinate References are special replica types that provide connectivity between the various partitions that exist in an NDS environment (see Figure 2-16). Subordinate references are internally used replicas that are not visible to end-users or configurable by administrators. A Subordinate Reference contains a copy of the root partition object of a child partition. The root partition object contains a Replica attribute. The *Replica attribute* is a list of all servers that hold replicas of that partition. NDS uses this list to locate the nearest replica of a child partition so that it can walk down the tree when searching for an object. Remember that NDS always starts an object search from [Root].

A partition's Subordinate Reference is stored on all servers that hold a replica of that partition's parent. Subordinate References effectively point to child partition(s) that are not stored on that particular server. The distributed nature of NDS allows servers to hold replicas of the parent partition but not all of the corresponding child partitions.

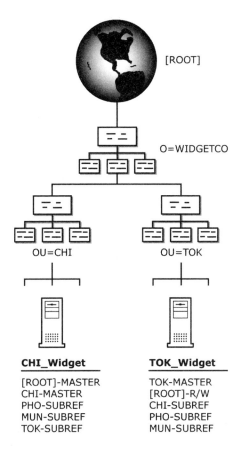

Figure 2-16
NDS Subordinate
References

[ROOT]

O=WIDGETCO

OU=CHI   OU=TOK

CHI_Widget   **TOK_Widget**

[ROOT]-MASTER   TOK-MASTER
CHI-MASTER   [ROOT]-R/W
PHO-SUBREF   CHI-SUBREF
MUN-SUBREF   PHO-SUBREF
TOK-SUBREF   MUN-SUBREF

Now that we understand the various replica types, we will turn our attention to those considerations that affect the overall replication strategy. The NDS replication strategy is a balancing act between the need to provide consistency across the directory and the limitations of network hardware and bandwidth. Some rules that should be followed when creating your replication strategy include the following:

- Don't replicate across WAN links if at all possible.
- Replicate to limit subordinate references.
- Replicate to improve NDS performance.

WAN links represent one of the most costly network resources. To clutter up these links with unnecessary NDS traffic would be a terrible mistake. To avoid this, all copies of a given partition should be maintained locally. The one situation where this rule might not apply is the case of a small satellite office with only one server. In that case, it is more important to protect the NDS database by placing a replica across a WAN link than it is to preserve the WAN link bandwidth itself. Fortunately, a partition that contains only one server will not usually generate a great deal of NDS-related traffic.

With the release of NetWare 5, Subordinate References no longer participate in the normal NDS replica update process, because they contain only small, relatively static portions of the total partition data. This does not limit the capability of NDS to function in any way. However, from a pure design perspective, it is still valuable to limit the number of Subordinate References to reduce overall NDS complexity. You can do this in two ways:

1. Limit the number of child partitions that are created.

   This number is only partially controllable because we always want to define WAN links as partition boundaries. However, this consideration does argue for limiting the number of additional partitions that are created within a single site.

2. Store both parent and child partition's replicas on the same server wherever possible.

   If multiple partitions are going to exist at a single site, try to distribute replicas so that parent and child partition replicas are stored together.

The final reason to replicate is to provide the best possible performance for network users. If the partition and replication guidelines in this chapter are followed, a user will find most of his or her resources within the local partition. Occasionally, it may be necessary to access a resource on the other side of the world. These situations require NDS to traverse, or *walk* the tree to locate the requested resource. As we previously noted, these searches start at [Root] and proceed down the tree until the requested object is located. Placing replicas of [Root] at strategic locations, such as communications hubs, can facilitate these searches. To do this without significantly increasing the overall replication burden, the [Root] partition must be small (only the [Root] object and the Organization object), and the number of [Root] replicas should not exceed three or four.

HOW REPLICATION OCCURS   Replication is an event-driven process, meaning that it is initiated by the occurrence of some external trigger. A few of these trigger events include adding, deleting, and moving directory objects as well as modifying object attributes. Each trigger event is flagged as *being high convergence* or not. High convergence means that NDS considers this event to be more significant, and these events should be replicated as quickly as possible.

High-convergence events are scheduled for *Fast Synchronization* (Fast Sync). Fast Sync occurs every 10 seconds by default. Other events are replicated using *Slow Synchronization* (Slow Sync). Slow Sync occurs every 30 minutes by default. Both of these Sync processes serve to send the changed information out to each server that maintains a replica of the affected partition. Because only the actual database changes are replicated, as opposed to sending the entire partition, replication operations are generally small.

Because each directory operation is time stamped, the synchronization process relies heavily on the time-synchronization processes described earlier. During the NDS synchronization process, each operation will be ordered based upon its timestamp and will be applied to the NDS database in that order.

Understanding NDS Security

Prompted by the explosion of interest in the Internet as a tool of commercial activity, the ability to positively identify the parties involved in an electronic transaction is critical. With the ability to centralize the administration of security, directories offer tremendous value by reducing the complexity of developing electronic relationships. NDS provides a framework within which a complete security strategy can be created and managed. One of the keys to maintaining strong network security is making the system as simple as possible to use. NDS hides the complexities of network security from the user and makes the security environment much easier to manage for the administrator.

With the release of NetWare 5, Novell provided (for the first time) a comprehensive security infrastructure. This infrastructure provides the foundation for integrating advanced security technologies into NDS. As NDS has been separated from the underlying operating system, the security components have been integrated into the NDS product offering, because it is most logical to manage a security policy from the Directory rather than from the network operating system. Included with NDS is a comprehensive cryptographic platform, *Novell International Cryptographic Infrastructure* (NICI), and a set of *Public Key Infrastructure Services* (PKIS).

NICI

NICI is a modular security framework that incorporates three main layers (see Figure 2-17):

- Cryptographic Services (Services layer)
- Policy Manager (Policy layer)
- Cryptographic Engine (Xeng) (Engine layer)

The Services layer provides controlled access point(s) to the cryptographic features of NICI. NICI ships with the *Controlled Cryptographic Services* (CCS) library by default. This library provides access through a set of CCS APIs. This layer enables applications to access the features of NICI automatically.

The Policy layer provides the management of the cryptographic infrastructure. Policies can be defined that specify the type of encryption to be used for the various objects and containers within the directory tree. This layer provides the simplified management and powerful modularity to NICI. Different objects can be configured to use different levels or types of encryption, based upon their needs and the local laws governing security and encryption for that object.

The Engine layer provides the actual cryptographic engines used to encrypt communications on the network. By default, Novell includes an RSA-based cryptographic engine. RSA is widely recognized as one of the preeminent cryptography providers available on the market today. Novell

Figure 2-17
NICI architecture

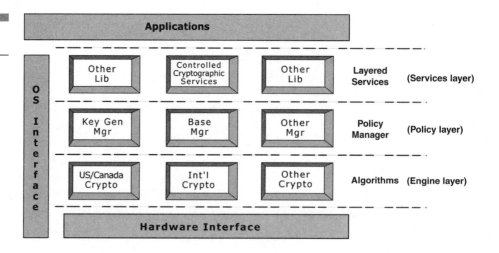

has maintained a relationship with RSA because they started using proprietary PKI technology with NetWare 4 in 1995.

The advantage of using NICI as a security foundation is that it eliminates the need to build cryptographic functionality into each application. Because of varied export laws across countries, applications would have to be written in several different versions if they were to be used worldwide.

NICI consolidates all cryptographic functionality into NDS. Applications leverage the existing cryptographic infrastructure and do not have to worry about multiple versions. It also means that all security management can take place from the standard NDS management tools. The modular nature of NICI allows for the support of varied cryptographic export laws through the policy manager in NICI. NICI prevents the insertion and use of cryptographic modules that would violate export laws. Because of this, NICI has received export approval from the United States. All applications that leverage NICI for their cryptographic functions will need to pass only a cursory export review, rather than having to endure the whole process.

PKIS

PKIS is Novell's name for a set of services that implements a *Public Key Infrastructure* (PKI) to create key public key pairs, generate certificates, import externally generated certificates, and revoke PKIS generated certificates.

PKI is also referred to as *asymmetric encryption*. Asymmetric encryption algorithms were developed in the 1970s as a way to avoid having to transmit cryptographic keys to those who needed to be able to decrypt secure messages. Previous to this, the world used symmetric encryption. *Symmetric encryption* algorithms are those with which most of us are familiar. The same key is used to both encrypt and decrypt the message. Most of us as children—and perhaps as adults too—have used some type of character-replacement algorithm to pass *secure* messages in class. Think back to when you did that. How did your partner know how to decode your message? Generally, you created a system for encoding the message and then had to pass the system to the person who needed to be able to decode your important messages. They, in turn, would commit the system to memory or keep the code key in a safe place. This is the same problem that exists for the complex symmetric encryption algorithms today. How should the key be transmitted to those who need to be able to decrypt the message? This problem becomes much more complex when a new key is used to encrypt each and every message, and the two parties lie on opposite sides of the globe (see Figure 2-18).

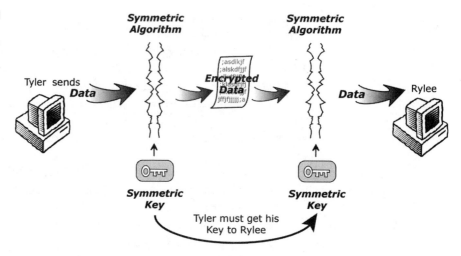

Figure 2-18
Symmetric encryption
problem

Asymmetric encryption, or PKI, eliminates this problem entirely by utilizing a mathematically related key pair instead of a single key to provide the encryption and decryption capabilities. When a message is encrypted using an asymmetric key, it can be decrypted only using the other half of the key pair. You can't even decrypt using the same key over again!

So what does this mean? One of the keys can be publicly distributed to provide cryptographic capabilities. Each person is assigned a key pair, and one of those keys is published as the public key. The other is carefully guarded as the private key. If I want to send you a secure message, I encrypt it using your public key and send it out (see Figure 2-19). I know that the only person who can decrypt that message is the person with the other half of that key pair—you!

Now let's switch to the receiving end of that secure message. I decrypt the message using my private key and find out that it is a note from you, except that I can't be sure that you were actually the person that authored it. What if someone is attempting to impersonate you by sending me this forged message? Well, PKI also solves this problem by providing the ability to electronically sign a message (see Figure 2-20).

Assume that, before you encrypt the message, you include a certificate that you have encrypted with your private key. This certificate contains your name and possibly some other vital information. I receive the message and decrypt it using my private key—just like before—except now I also go out and get your public key. If I am able to successfully decrypt the certificate, I am assured that you were actually the person who sent this message. This ability to prove the origin of some piece of information is known as *non-repudiation*.

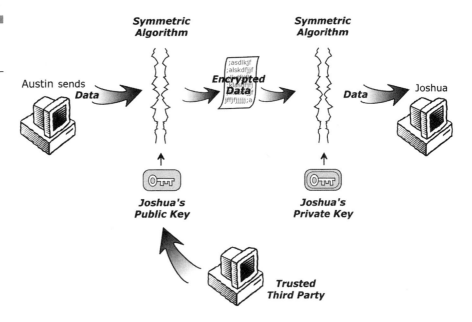

Figure 2-19
PKI with asymmetric
encryption

So, PKI offers two levels of protection by providing both encryption and non-repudiation. The implications for e-commerce are staggering! PKI provides the foundation for safe electronic transactions. As such, the world is going crazy trying to establish a standard PKI environment within which electronic commerce can take place.

One major piece of this e-commerce puzzle is creating repositories for all of the public keys that are going to be floating around out there. Public keys are stored, together with vital statistics about the owner, in a standard certificate format known as X.509. These certificates then can be stored in large databases known as *Certificate Authorities* (CA). Some of the public CAs out there today include Verisign and Entrust. One major obstacle confronting these public-key repositories is the assignment of responsibility if private keys are stolen and used improperly. The major obstacle still confronting the creation of an e-commerce infrastructure revolves around the assigning—and acceptance—of blame when something goes wrong. Just how secure are the cryptographic keys that are being offered? Who is responsible if an encrypted communication is broken or forged? Who is responsible when a private key is stolen? All of these issues will have to be resolved before a universal e-commerce infrastructure is anything more than a grand dream. More on the issue of key strength will be presented in Chapter 6, "Controlling Network Access."

PKIS provides organizations the ability to use NDS as a Certificate Authority. Cryptographic keys and certificates can be created and/or managed by

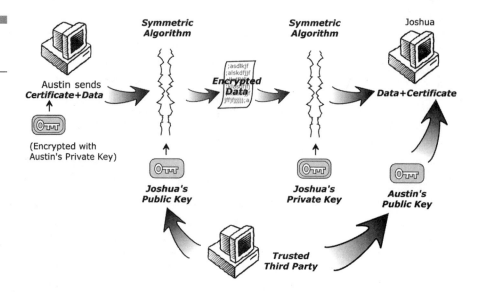

Figure 2-20
How electronic
certificates work

NDS. PKIS also can interact with external entities such as Verisign or Entrust through the use of standard communication protocols and certificate formats. PKIS supports the dominant standards in the security space, including X.509 certificates, PKCS#10 certificate-signing requests, and SSL (for communicating with the certificate authority and securing LDAP communications). Organizations can make NDS the hub for all of their security needs from secure authentication and resource access to secure communications with external parties and the non-repudiation of business-critical communications.

More information on these Internet security standards can be found at

- `X.509: http://www.ietf.org/rfc/rfc2459.txt`

- `PKCS#10 (and all other PKCS standards):`

- `http://www.rsa.com/rsalabs/pubs/PKCS/`

- `SSL: http://home.netscape.com/eng/ssl3/draft302.txt`

Novell is beginning to offer a more complete set of security services that build upon the foundation of NICI and PKIS. These will include a Secure Single Sign-On service and advanced authentication services that support multiple authentication methods such as Smart Cards and Biometrics in addition to the traditional username/password option. This security foundation is also pulling Novell toward strong support for Internet security standards. The advantage for business managers and network administrators is that they can feel confident that as network security progresses, NDS will be able to support the advanced security features that organizations will demand.

Overview of Security Concepts

In addition to the more recent Internet security issues, Novell is also an expert in the area of traditional network security. However, today's network security involves a lot more than assigning passwords to network users. Today's complex computing environments require advanced techniques for ensuring that only those persons required to access network resources are able to do so. These advanced techniques can be divided into two areas:

- *Authentication.* This refers to the system's capability to properly identify the person who is requesting access to the system. Processes must be in place to ascertain that users really are who they say they are.

- *Authorization.* Once authenticated, authorization refers to the ability to restrict a user's access to a specific subset of total available resources. Processes must be in place that regulate the actions of users after they have been granted access to the system.

The last section of this chapter focuses on the general concepts behind more traditional network security. NDS provides a robust architecture for accomplishing both of these security tasks. This discussion lays the groundwork for upcoming chapters, which discuss the administration of NDS security.

Authentication   Authentication is perhaps the most critical operation performed by NDS. Authentication provides the doorway for access to network resources. Without a strong authentication mechanism, sensitive network resources are essentially laid bare for anyone to access. The primary authentication method currently used with NDS is the username/ password combination. The effectiveness of this method can be argued, but until very recently it was the only viable authentication method suitable for large-scale deployment.

Initially, Novell's authentication method was centered on the server. However, with the separation of NDS from the underlying operating system, NDS has had to acquire a complete set of authentication services. This has been accomplished with the release of NDS for the NetWare, NT, and Solaris platforms. A common set of security mechanisms can now control access to networks built on each of these differing platforms.

To provide a strong authentication mechanism, Novell has turned to PKI. NDS has used PKI authentication since 1995. Because the original Novell implementation of PKI predates the standards we have today, Novell created a proprietary environment for authenticating users to NDS.

Novell Directory Access Protocol (NDAP) is the proprietary protocol that provides access to NDS. NDAP is currently supported by Novell client software to provide directory access. However, NDS is quickly moving toward a standards-based authentication mechanism based upon PKIS and X.509 certificates. X.509 eventually will replace NDAP as the authentication protocol of choice, and NDAP will be maintained solely for backward compatibility.

Authenticating in a NetWare directory environment consists of two processes:

■ *User login.* The first step is for users to present themselves to the directory to establish their identity. The user offers a network identity, or distinguished name, coupled with a password. NDS uses the distinguished name to search for a copy of that user's object. The user object will exist within a replica of the user's partition. As noted in the section on partitions and replicas, the user object must be retrieved from a writeable replica (a Read-only replica will not suffice) because object attributes are updated as part of the login process. After the user object has been located, NDS retrieves the private key from that user object.

NDS uses a combination of random number generation and hash functions, along with the password value stored in NDS, to perform a comparison against the user-supplied password value. If the comparison is successful, the client is passed a timestamped session key based upon their private key. The client subsequently uses this key to prove his or her identity when requesting access to specific network resources.

■ *Background authentication.* To authenticate to actual network resources, the client sends the distinguished name in a handshake message encrypted with their session key to the server holding the requested resource. If the resource server can successfully decrypt the handshake message using the user's public key, the server knows that the message was sent from an already-authenticated user, and appropriate access will be granted to the requested resource.

NDS and the NDS client software accomplish the entire background authentication process without any user intervention. In addition to users, this process also can be used by external services that need to authenticate themselves to NDS.

Authorization Authorization has to do with the degree of access offered a given user after a successful authentication. Three important concepts must be understood to design an NDS authorization strategy. Those concepts are Access Control Lists, Inheritance, and Inherited Rights Filters.

ACCESS CONTROL LISTS Each object in an NDS tree maintains two types of access rights. The first set of rights is *Object rights*. Object rights define how an object can be manipulated by other directory entities. NDS Object rights are described in Table 2-4.

The second set of rights is *Property rights*. Property rights define how the attributes associated with an object can be manipulated. NDS Property rights are described in Table 2-5.

When object and/or property rights are conferred to an NDS entity, that entity becomes a trustee of the conferring object. The list of trustees and the

Table 2-4

NDS Object Rights

Object Right	Description
Browse	Enables a trustee to discover and view the object in the NDS tree
Create	This right applies only to container objects. It allows the trustee to create objects within the container.
Delete	Enables a trustee to delete the object.
Rename	Enables a trustee to rename the object
Supervisor	Enables a trustee full access to the object and its attributes.

Table 2-5

NDS Property Rights

Property Right	Description
Compare	Enables a trustee to compare or see whether an attribute contains a given value.
Read	Enables a trustee to read an attribute value. This right confers the Compare right.
Write	Enables a trustee to add, delete, or modify an attribute value. This right confers the Add or Delete Self right to the attribute.
Add Self (Delete Self)	Enables a trustee to add or delete its name as an attribute value (if applicable).
Supervisor	Assigns a trustee all attribute rights.

specific object and property rights they have been granted is maintained in an ACL associated with each NDS object. For an object to have access to itself, other than the Browse object right, an object must be made a trustee of itself.

The ACL contains three pieces of information about a trustee assignment: Trusted ID, Protected Attribute ID, and Privilege Set.

Trustee ID   This field identifies the object that is being granted rights. It can also contain one of the special entry references outlined in Table 2-6.

Protected Attribute ID   This field specifies the type of right that is being granted. It also specifies how that right is to be applied. Rights can be assigned to a specific property, to all properties, or to the object itself.

Privilege Set   This field lists the right(s) that have been granted. In the NDS schema, most object classes specify a default access template that is used to create an ACL attribute for a new object. This default template provides basic access control for the new entry, enabling it to function in the Directory. Different object classes have different default ACL templates to reflect their different needs. For example, the default ACL template for the User object grants the Write right to its own login script attribute. This enables users to change their personal login scripts as necessary.

INHERITANCE   Inheritance is one of the most important administrative features of NDS. It allows rights granted higher in the tree to flow down to all objects lower in the tree. Inheritance allows rights to be granted at the

Table 2-6	**Reference**	**Description**
ACL Special Reference Values	Inherited Rights Filter	NDS uses this reference to mask or filter privileges rather than granting rights.
	Public	NDS uses this reference to grant rights to all entries in the NDS tree.
	Root	NDS uses this reference to grant all rights to all authenticated entries.
	Creator	NDS uses this reference to grant all rights to the client that created the object.
	Self	NDS uses this reference to enable objects to add or delete themselves as values of attributes and to grant the object rights to its own attributes.

Organizational Unit (OU) or Organization (O) level and to have those rights automatically applied to all objects below that OU or O. Rights that flow down through the tree are known as Inherited rights.

NDS uses what is known as a *Dynamic Inheritance Model*. In this model, the effective rights a user possesses to a given NDS object is calculated in real time when the access is requested. Therefore, changes to Inherited rights will be reflected immediately, rather than having to wait for updates to static ACLs to be updated. This model also eliminates the need to store Inherited rights' information redundantly on every object inheriting the access from higher in the tree. The NDS database is much more compact as a result.

One critical aspect of Inherited rights concerns their interaction with explicitly assigned rights. Inherited rights are pre-empted by an explicit rights assignment. They are not additive. If a user inherits the Write right to a given object and is then explicitly assigned the Read right for that same object, the Write right will be eliminated.

INHERITED RIGHTS FILTERS   *Inherited Rights Filters* (IRF) are used to stop the flow of Inherited rights down the tree. Explicit rights assignments are not affected by an IRF.

This combination of object and property rights, managed through ACLs, allows tremendous flexibility in establishing access controls for each object in the NDS tree. Administrators can be granted a virtually limitless degrees of control, from full tree administration all the way down to access to a single attribute of a single object.

Those individuals who require full NDS rights (view, modify, delete, etc.) across the entire tree are granted supervisory access at the [Root] object. Inheritance enables these rights to automatically flow through the entire tree structure unless an IRF is placed lower in the tree to block the flow of rights.

If another individual requires full NDS at their location or within their department, full NDS rights can be granted at their container object, which would then grant them control over all the objects in their branch of the tree. Versions of NDS available after the release of NetWare 5 have been enhanced to allow Role-based administration. This enables an administrator to be granted access to a single attribute or several select attributes of all objects in the tree or subtree. In this way, an email administrator can be granted access just to those fields that are email specific, or a password administrator can be created that can set passwords and nothing further.

NDS provides the flexibility to tailor the network access controls to match the needs of the organization. After these concepts are understood, a strategy can be developed that will offer the necessary access to network users while making it as easy as possible to administer those access controls. In fact, if the design methods outlined earlier in this chapter have been followed, most users and resources already are grouped in such as way that they will share many access needs. This is where the design of the bottom levels of your NDS tree becomes so important. That design directly affects the ease with which the network can be administered.

Some other administrative tools can be used to customize NDS access and administration. These tools include Group objects, Aliases, and Organizational Roles. These will be discussed in detail in Chapter 6.

SUMMARY

We have presented a great deal of background information in this chapter. It is intended to provide a foundation upon which the many NDS administrative tasks can be discussed. For those of you who have worked with NDS previously, you already understand much of this information. However, for those who are new to directories in general and NDS specifically, this background information is critical as you move forward with your NDS implementation plans.

A key argument of this chapter is that no NDS rollout should proceed without first specifically defining the goals of the proposed implementation. A high-level design phase should first answer the important political and structural questions as well as assemble the information necessary to properly plan the NDS environment. Some of the questions that will be answered by this high-level design include the following:

How will NDS be managed?

What does the physical network look like?

What does the organization look like?

What is the partition and replication strategy?

How will objects be named in the NDS tree?

How will time synchronization be accomplished?

These questions need to be answered before NDS is ever installed—at least in a perfect world. For those of you who are tasked with redesigning or managing an existing NDS environment, find out whether this work has been done. If it has, get a copy of the design document, and most of the difficult questions will already be answered. If it has not been done, make the effort to get it done as soon as possible. Managing a complex NDS environment without any of these tools is a guaranteed road to long hours, budget overruns, and general frustration.

NDS has the potential to reduce administrative overhead and to increase network efficiency tremendously. However, if the design homework is not done up-front, the best you can expect is a continuation of the status quo.

For More Information

Novell has published a great deal of information concerning proper NDS design and implementation. Obviously, it is in their best interest to have people implement NDS correctly to enjoy the maximum possible benefit. If you would like to dig a little deeper into NDS design issues, we recommend the following resources:

Books

- *Four Principles of NDS Design*, by Jeffrey Hughes and Blair Thomas, IDG Books, 1996.

  This is probably the seminal work on NDS design. It was published in 1996, so some of the specific administrative tools mentioned are dated, and performance recommendations like "number of objects per partition" are no longer applicable. Also, it was written entirely from the perspective of NetWare 4.1, so it will not provide any cross-platform information for those of you implementing NDS on NT or Solaris. However, the high-level design principles presented in this text will apply to any NDS implementation.

- *NDS Design and Implementation*, Novell Education Course 575, Novell Part # 100-004149-001

  This student manual prepares you for the NDS Design and Implementation test toward CNE certification. The information is similar to that found in *Four Principles of NDS Design* but is not as well written. However, this title has been updated to take into account changes in NDS as it shipped with NetWare 5. This manual is also focused on NetWare-based implementations of NDS.

Web Sites

NDS Web site: `http://www.novell.com/products/nds/index.html`

NDS Cool Solutions Web site: `http://www.novell.com/coolsolutions/nds/`

NDS Security Web site: `http://www.novell.com/corp/security/index.html`

Web Articles

"Planning a NetWare 4.0 Directory Tree" `http://developer.novell.com/research/appnotes/1993/april/a3frame.htm`

"NDS Technical Overview" `http://developer.novell.com/research/devnotes/1998/april/a3frame.htm`

"Design Rules for NDS Replica Placement" `http://developer.novell.com/research/appnotes/1997/january/a1frame.htm`

"Designing NetWare 4.x Security" `http://developer.novell.com/research/appnotes/1993/november/a2frame.htm`

"NDS Database Operations" `http://developer.novell.com/research/devnotes/1998/may/a3frame.htm`

"Learning and Applying the Rules of NDS Security" `http://developer.novell.com/research/appnotes/1997/august/a2frame.htm`

Technical Information Documents

Novell Technical Support provides further information on Novell products. The following is a *Technical Information Document* (TID) that can be located at `http://support.novell.com/servlet/Knowledgebase`:

2946878   *DS Design, Replication, and Partition Strategy*

Installing and Upgrading NDS

How you will be installing or upgrading to NDS Corporate Edition depends entirely on the server operating systems your company uses. If your company has standardized on NetWare or if you use NetWare as your main network operating system, you have several options and must consider several things, depending on the version you are currently running. If your company has standardized on a different operating system, such as Windows NT or UNIX, or if you have a mixed environment, your options for installing and implementing NDS differ slightly. However, the end result—a unified database that manages all network resources—is the same.

This chapter discusses the different installations and issues associated with various platforms. If you currently have NDS installed and are using it to manage the Directory, this chapter also covers reasons why and issues surrounding upgrading to NDS Corporate Edition. It includes complete instructions to upgrade to NDS Corporate Edition.

NDS Corporate Edition Server Requirements

Various server requirements exist for installing NDS Corporate Edition, depending on which operating system you are using. Table 3-1 provides all the requirements for NetWare Windows NT and Solaris.

Note that you cannot currently install NDS Corporate Edition on NetWare 3.x or NetWare 4.x servers. You first must upgrade them to NetWare 5 and then upgrade NetWare 5 to NDS Corporate Edition. This upgrade process will change in future versions of NetWare 5 but is the situation for the first and probably the second version of NetWare 5.

Installing NDS with NetWare

Adding the NetWare operating system to a server-class PC turns it into a high-performance network server, providing connectivity among personal computers, printers, mass storage devices, and other networks, such as the Internet. Because it can integrate with other network operating systems, NetWare provides you with the tools you need to create an integrated, manageable network, whether your network has a single NetWare server or thousands of NetWare, NT, and UNIX servers located at sites around the world.

The latest and greatest version of NetWare is NetWare 5. If you have used or are currently using previous version of NetWare and you want to use NDS Corporate Edition, you must upgrade to NetWare 5 before

Table 3-1

Server hardware
requirements
for NDS Corporate
Edition

Operating System	Processor	Additional Requirements
NetWare 5 with Support Pack 2 or higher	Pentium server class processor with at least 64M of RAM (128 is recommended) and 550M of disk space	▪ DSREPAIR download (if the first installation of NDS Corporate Edition is on a server that does not hold a replica of the [Root] partition) ▪ Administrative rights to [Root] to modify the schema ▪ An administrator's Pentium Pro 200 workstation (or better) with a minimum of 64M of RAM (128 is better), 125M of disk space, and the latest Novell Client (IP-enabled) ▪ For ephemeral key support for SSL connections, you need the Novell Cryptography Support Modules (NICI 1.2 or later)
Windows NT 4.0 with Service Pack 1, 3, or 4	Intel-based processor with 64M RAM and 90M of disk space	▪ Assigned IP Address on the Windows NT server ▪ Monitor Color Palette set higher than 16 colors ▪ An NTFS partition (NDS for NT will not install on a FAT partition) ▪ Admin rights to the NT server and all portions of the NDS tree that will contain user objects that are domain-enabled. (If this is the first installation of NDS for NT, you also will need Admin rights to the root of the tree so that you can extend the schema)
Solaris 2.6/7	SPARCstation Ultra 5 with at least 64M of RAM (128 is recommended for LDAP), 25M of disk space, and 3M per 100 User objects in the Replica	▪ An administrator's Pentium Pro 200 workstation (or better) with a minimum of 64M of RAM (128 is better), 125M of disk space, and the latest Novell Client (IP-enabled)

upgrading to NDS Corporate Edition. Currently, no straight path exists to NDS Corporate Edition. After you have NetWare 5 installed, you can download NDS Corporate Edition or get it from the combined NDS Corporate Edition CD-ROM that ships with NDS for NT and NDS for Solaris.

NOTE: *An update to NetWare 5 is planned for release sometime in 2000. If your timetable permits, you might consider purchasing this version instead. It includes additional installation utilities and features along with other fixes and additional services.*

Migration from previous versions of NetWare to NetWare 5 has been greatly simplified, making the cost of deploying this version of NetWare in time and resources much less than many companies anticipate. NDS is installed as part of a NetWare 4.x or 5.x server install. If you are installing for the first time or you are migrating data from a bindery database, you should read Chapter 2, "NDS Design Issues," before installing the NetWare servers so that you are sure what naming conventions you are using for the NDS tree and volumes that are created during installation.

WARNING: *Although it is possible, changing the tree name after you have created the NDS database is not recommended. After you create drive mappings, users, and login scripts relative to this tree name, it is difficult, if not impossible to make sure that the tree name has been changed in all the places it should be. This means that users will have problems authenticating and accessing resources on the network. Be sure you have considered the tree name and structure before you begin installing NetWare or NDS Corporate Edition on native platforms, such as Windows NT and Solaris. You will be prompted for this information during installation.*

Before you install the NetWare 5 server, several decisions must be made about the server. You will want to read the documentation provided by Novell and pay close attention to how you configure your server and volumes. Review Chapter 2, and make sure that you understand the directory structure before beginning.

Because this book is focused more on NDS Corporate Edition than on NetWare, we will not discuss the details of installing a new NetWare 5 server. We do, however, discuss several issues as they relate to NDS that you will want to consider. Novell provides excellent Step Guides and an entire library of online documentation to help you install the server correctly. In addition, Novell maintains a NetWare Deployment Toolkit Web site that contains additional information about integration, installation, and even about competitive analysis and strategies for getting upper management to buy off on NetWare. This Web site is located at www.novell.com\deployment. You also should have received a *NetWare 5*

Overview and Installation manual along with the NetWare 5 CD-ROM and license disk. This manual is an excellent guide to installing NetWare 5 and deciding which additional Novell networking products and services you want to install during a NetWare 5 server installation. These services include

- *Novell Distributed Print Services* (NDPS) (discussed in Chapter 8, "Administering Printing")
- LDAP Services for NDS (discussed in Chapter 6, "Controlling Network Access")
- NDS Catalog Services (discussed in Chapter 6)
- WAN Traffic Management Services (discussed in Chapter 9, "Administering NDS")
- Secure Authentication Services (discussed in Chapter 6)
- Novell Public Key Infrastructure (PKIS) (discussed in Chapter 6)
- Novell Internet Access Server 4.1
- Storage Management Services
- Novell DNS/DHCP Services

Because upgrading an existing server involves more NDS issues, we will later discuss in more detail the upgrade process.

Things to Consider When Installing NetWare 5

Before you install NetWare 5, you need to know the following information:

- The current version of DS.NLM running on your network: If you will be installing a NetWare 5 server in a network that already has NetWare 4.x servers, you need to make sure that all NetWare 4.x servers are running DS.NLM version 5.99 or higher. This is the main NDS module. To see what the DS.NLM version number is, run the MODULES DS.NLM at the server console. If you are not running DS.NLM version 5.99 or higher, you must update the existing servers before you can install NetWare 5. Version 5.99 is included on the NetWare 5 CD-ROM, but you should check the Novell corporate download page for later versions or additional patches.
- *The server's time zone*   You will need to know what time zone you want to use on the server and whether it supports Daylight Savings Time.

■ *The name of the directory tree*   You will need to know the name of the directory tree into which the server will be installed.

■ *The server's name and context in the directory tree*   Make sure that you understand NDS and how your tree is laid out. You will need to specify to which Organization object or Organizational Unit object this server belongs. For more information, read Chapter 2 to give you a better idea about how NDS is structured.

■ *Your Admin fully distinguished username and password*   If this is the first server in the tree, you will specify this information during the installation. If you are installing into a tree that already exists, you will need your full username and context to complete the install.

■ *The server's type of time synchronization*   By default, the installation makes the first server in the tree a Single Reference server and all others Secondary timeservers. However, depending on how many servers you have in your network, you might be using a different strategy. For more information on time synchronization, see Chapter 2 and Chapter 9.

■ *Whether you are using NDPS for printing services*   When you install the NetWare 5 server, you can install the NDPS Broker and additional pieces that enable you to manage your printers through NDS. However, if you are not going to use NDPS, you should not install the NDPS Broker. For more information, see Chapter 8.

You must install NetWare 5 Support Pack 2 or the latest Support Pack available on Novell's Web site at www.novell.com/download.

Additional services are also installed and configured during the installation of NetWare 5. If you have specific questions or just want to review what all the options are before installing, the *NetWare 5 Overview and Installation* manual has brief descriptions of each of the options. More detailed information on configuring each service is provided in Novell's online documentation at www.novell.com/documentation or at the NetWare Deployment Toolkit Web site at www.novell.com\deployment. You also need to upgrade NDS to NDS Corporate Edition. For more information, see "Upgrading Existing NetWare Servers to NDS Corporate Edition" on page 95.

NOTE: *If you are installing the next version of NetWare 5, you still have to upgrade to NDS Corporate Edition after the installation is complete. However, in the next version, the NDS Corporate Edition upgrade is a part of the installation process in the Other Products and Services option at the end of the NetWare 5 installation.*

Upgrading a NetWare Server

Depending on what type of server you currently have, you can use several methods for upgrading your servers (see Table 3-1). Before you decide to upgrade your server, you should take all the issues just discussed into consideration. You need to know the information covered in the preceding section before you begin the upgrade. If you are upgrading a NetWare 4.1x server to NetWare 5, you can use three methods to install the server:

- In-place upgrade
- Novell Upgrade Wizard
- Accelerated Upgrade (for advanced administrators only)

Note that if you are upgrading a server from NetWare 3.x to NetWare 5 to take advantage of NDS, you need to take a few more steps than when upgrading from NetWare 4.x to NetWare 5, because your directory is a bindery and you need to create an NDS database in which the objects may reside.

To upgrade from NetWare 3.1x to NetWare 5, you must first plan your NDS tree. Planning your NDS tree is covered in Chapter 2. Make sure that you have read and understand how to plan your NDS tree before you start upgrading from NetWare 3.x to NetWare 5. You can upgrade your NetWare 3.x servers in two ways:

- In-place upgrade
- Novell Upgrade Wizard

The Accelerated Upgrade does not work because it assumes that you already have NDS on your server.

IMPORTANT: *At this time, Novell does not have a direct path from NetWare 3.x or NetWare 4.x to NDS Corporate Edition. After you migrate to NetWare 5, you need to update NDS to NDS Corporate Edition. (See "Upgrading Existing NetWare Servers to NDS Corporate Edition" later in this chapter.)*

Table 3-2

NetWare 5 server
requirements

Component	Requirement
Computer	A server-class PC with a Pentium or higher processor
Monitor	A VGA or higher resolution display adapter (SVGA recommended)
Disk Space	550M of available disk space (50M for a boot partition, 500M for a NetWare partition)
Memory	64M of RAM (128M recommended to run Java-based applications)
Network Boards	One or more network boards
CD-ROM	A CD-ROM drive that can read ISO 9660-formatted CD-ROM disks
Mouse	A PS/2 or serial mouse (not required)

Using an In-Place Upgrade An in-place upgrade upgrades the operating system to NetWare 5 if your existing server meets the hardware requirements necessary for NetWare 5 (see Table 3-2). Upgrading retains all your server data, such as files, directory structures, partitions, and volumes. If you are upgrading a NetWare 4.x server, the upgrade preserves your NDS Directory and file system as they are. If you are upgrading a NetWare 3.x server, you are prompted during the installation to select a new name for the Directory Tree, volumes, and certain objects. User objects probably will not need to be renamed unless duplicates will be in the same container object. Bindery objects are then migrated to NDS with these names and their access rights. If duplicate names exist, you will be prompted to either delete or rename the bindery object. You can run an in-place upgrade from the NetWare 5 CD-ROM or from files copied to the network.

Before upgrading the server, make sure that you have the following

- NetWare 5 Operating System CD-ROM
- DOS CD-ROM drivers to access the server's local CD-ROM
- NetWare 5 License disk
- A valid, static IP address

Make sure that you check to see that all computer hardware components, such as storage devices, are functioning properly and that you have backed up all your data including the directory containing the server startup files. If the upgrade is not successful, you may need to restore this directory.

▬▬ ▬▬ ▬▬ ▬▬ ▬▬ ▬▬ ▬▬ ▬▬ ▬▬ ▬▬ ▬▬ ▬▬ ▬▬ ▬▬ ▬▬ ▬▬ ▬▬ ▬▬ ▬▬ ▬▬

WARNING: *Because the in-place upgrade copies over some files, make sure that you have a backup of the server in case the upgrade fails.*

The installation occurs in two parts. First, the hardware is set up, and the SYS volume is created. This is a text-based DOS program. When the video drivers are installed, the second part of the installation occurs. The second part sets up the server's environment using a Java-based installation program. To begin the server upgrade, complete the following steps:

1. Notify users that the server will not be available until after the upgrade is complete.

2. Make sure that you have commented out all third-party NLMs and incompatible NLMs from the STARTUP.NCF and AUTOEXEC.NCF files. A complete list of these is available from the Novell Technical Support Web site at www.support.novell.com.

3. Make sure that you have the DOS CD-ROM drivers installed.

4. Bring down the server and reboot it in DOS.

5. Insert the NetWare 5 Operating System CD-ROM. You also can log in to the network from a DOS workstation and map the root to the directory where the installation files reside on the network.

6. Type INSTALL.

7. Select the language and accept the License Agreement if you have an international version of NetWare 5.

8. Select Upgrade from 3.1x or 4.1x.

9. Select Continue. At this point in the installation, you are prompted to set up the server hardware. Because the NetWare 5 upgrade program auto-detects the existing server hardware, you probably can accept the default. If the server was using multiple processors running SMP, it automatically is upgraded along with NetWare

10. Follow the on-screen instructions to do the following:

   ■ Select the mouse and video type. The mouse type and video type are not auto-detected by the install program.

   ■ Select a platform support module (if required), PCI Hot Plug module (if required), and storage adapter.

- Select a storage device. The NetWare 5 upgrade program automatically replaces DSK drivers with *host adapter modules* (HAMs) and *custom device modules* (CDMs), if available.

- Select a network board.

11. After the GUI part of the install begins, you can create additional volumes (if you have space on your server). These volumes can be traditional or *Novell Storage Services* (NSS) volumes. Click the free space and then click Create to create additional volumes. If you are creating an NSS volume, you must allocate at least 10M of free space to create it.

12. You should add the IP protocol stack in addition to the IPX protocol the server originally had. When your network no longer requires IPX, you can remove it. To add the IP protocol stack, click the network adapter and click IP.

13. Enter the IP address, the subnet mask, and the router gateway.

14. Enter your admin name and password to log in to NDS.

15. Insert the License disk and select the drive where the licenses are located.

    If an NDS tree already exists, you can install the server into the existing NDS tree. If this is the first server you are upgrading from NetWare 3.x to NetWare 5, you need to set up NDS, including creating the NDS tree. During the upgrade, all NetWare 3.x bindery objects will be automatically converted to NDS objects. If duplicate names exist, you may be prompted to rename the object or move it to a different location in the tree.

    To set up NDS and migrate bindery objects to NDS, complete the following steps:

    - Choose the type of NDS installation (new or installing into an existing tree).

    - Enter an NDS tree name—an existing name or a new one if you are creating a new NDS tree.

    - Enter the Organization and Organizational Unit container object where the server will reside.

    - Enter the Supervisor username and password. If you are creating a new NDS tree, enter a username and password for the user who will have Supervisor rights to the server's container object. If you are installing into an existing NDS tree, enter the full context username and password of a user with Supervisor rights to the server's container object.

■ You may be prompted to modify the schema. When prompted, you must provide the full context administrator name and password for the [Root] of the NDS tree.

16. Make sure that you record the administrator name, password, and other relevant information before proceeding.

17. After you have created the NDS tree or moved objects into an existing tree, you will need to install NetWare 5 licenses. The NetWare 5 License disk is included as part of your NetWare 5 installation package. When prompted, insert the License disk provided.

At this point in the install, other Novell networking products and services can be installed during a NetWare 5 server upgrade. These services include the following:

■ *Novell Distributed Print Services* (NDPS) (discussed in Chapter 8, "Administering Printing")

■ LDAP Services for NDS (discussed in Chapter 6)

■ NDS Catalog Services (discussed in Chapter 6)

■ WAN Traffic Management Services (discussed in Chapter 9, "Administering NDS")

■ Secure Authentication Services (discussed in Chapter 6, "Controlling Network Access")

■ Novell *Public Key Infrastructure* (PKI) Services (discussed in Chapter 6)

■ Novell Internet Access Server 4.1

■ Storage Management Services

■ Novell DNS/DHCP Services

After upgrading to NetWare 5, some products will require additional configuration or will need to be completely reinstalled before they will function. Extensive information on these services is provided in the online documentation at www.novell.com/documentation. You also will need to upgrade NDS to NDS 8. See "Upgrading Existing NetWare Servers to NDS 8" later in this chapter.

Using the Novell Upgrade Wizard The Novell Upgrade Wizard enables you to copy your directory files across the network from a source server and to place them in an existing NDS tree on a destination server. The previous version of the Upgrade Wizard (2.3) enabled you to upgrade from a NetWare 3.x source server to a NetWare 4.x or NetWare 5 destination server. With version 3.0, you also can upgrade from a NetWare 4.x source server to a new NetWare 5 destination server. You will want to use the Novell Upgrade Wizard if your server does not meet the minimum hardware requirements for a NetWare 5 server. Note that the Upgrade Wizard is not a replacement for backing up your NDS database and file system before upgrading your servers. Even though the files still exist on the source server, reversing the migration process and making the server viable again can be very difficult. Make sure that you back up your data before doing any type of upgrade.

NOTE: *The next version of NetWare contains a new Novell Upgrade Wizard utility that provides additional features. For example, it runs* DSREPAIR *before files are migrated. It also enables you to restore trustees to the older NetWare 4.x server so that you can more easily recover in the event of migration problems.*

The new NetWare 5 destination server replaces and assumes the identity of the old NetWare 3.x or NetWare 4.x source server on the network. With NetWare 4.x, no drive mappings or other changes need occur. You can edit the configuration files on the destination server automatically. After the files are copied and the configuration files modified, the Upgrade Wizard copies the NDS files from the source server to the destination server. They are then restored and upgraded to NetWare 5 DS files. Licenses are automatically installed, the schema upgraded, and file trustees are restored. The Upgrade Wizard automates a process that previously entailed many manual steps.

IMPORTANT: *If you are using the IP protocol and you want to use the same IP address on the destination server when the migration is complete, you will want to make sure that you change the IP address when the Upgrade Wizard prompts you to modify the configuration files. If you forget to do so, you can copy the address and enter it by hand in the destination server's* AUTOEXEC.NCF *file, or you can modify the IP Address in the* INETCFG.NLM *on the destination server.*

The Upgrade Wizard version 3.0 is available from the Novell corporate Web site at http://www.novell.com/download/. The Novell Upgrade Wizard files come compressed in a self-expanding file that must be copied to and installed on the local drive of a Windows 95/98 or Windows NT workstation running Novell Client software. You can either choose to download one file or four separate files (for slow or bad Internet connections). If you choose to download the four files, double-click each one to expand the files. When this is done, double-click INSTALL.BAT to unpackage the Upgrade Wizard. Both downloads include a response file that automates the installation of a dummy NetWare 5 server you can use to migrate your NetWare 4.x server.

When these files are downloaded, complete the following steps:

1. Double-click NUW30.EXE to unpack the Upgrade Wizard files. (If you choose the four-part download, this step is completed for you when you unpackage the files using INSTALL.BAT.)

2. Select the language, then click OK.

3. Click Next.

4. Click Yes to accept the license agreement.

5. Select the destination folder where you want the Upgrade Wizard installed, and then click Next. By default, the files are installed in the PROGRAMFILES\NOVELL\UPGRADEWIZARD directory.

6. When the file copy is finished, click Finish.

As a part of the Upgrade, you will need to have an existing NetWare 5 server in the tree, or you will need to install one. Before beginning the upgrade, make sure that you purchase hardware that meets the minimum requirements for NetWare 5 (see Table 3-2). We suggest that you buy additional memory. Novell suggests a minimum of 64M of RAM. However, this amount barely covers the basic processes. You should use at least 72M of RAM—128M of RAM if you want to run Java applications. After you have the correct hardware on the new server box, you can do one of the following:

- Install NetWare 5 from the CD-ROM or files located on the network (briefly covered previously). If you are installing the first NetWare 5 server and you are migrating NetWare 3.x to this server, this is your best option. You can set up the tree and other NDS objects the way you want them, and then you will be ready to migrate objects to them during the upgrade.

- Install NetWare 5 using the automated response file included with the Novell Upgrade Wizard 3.0 in the PROGRAMFILES\NOVELL\UPGRADEWIZARD directory. You can use this file to set up a NetWare 5 server with a temporary tree name and server name. During the migration, the NetWare 5 server name and tree name change to the name of the NetWare 4 server. If you are migrating to a NetWare 3 server, the server name and tree name will not be updated during migration. You must change the name of the server and the name of the tree in the response file to the correct server name and tree name. Therefore, it is better to install a NetWare 5 server from CD-ROM when you are upgrading a NetWare 3 server. In either case, the files on your NetWare 3.x or 4.x server will be moved to the NetWare 5 server, and your objects will be moved into the NDS tree.

To use a response file to automate the server installation, complete the following steps:

1. Copy the response file to a floppy disk, hard disk, or network directory accessible by the PC on which you are installing NetWare 5.

2. If you are using the response file to set up a NetWare 5 server that will receive bindery data from a NetWare 3 server, the server name and tree name will not be updated during migration. You must change the name of the server and the name of the tree in the response file to the correct server name and tree name. Make the appropriate changes and save the file. You do not need to make these changes if you are migrating a NetWare 4 server because that server's tree and directory will replace the temporary tree and directory created by the response file.

3. Type INSTALL /RF=<Response File DOS path\filename>. Then press Enter to start the server installation. For example, if you are installing NetWare 5 from the CD-ROM and the Response file is on a disk, you would type INSTALL /RF=A:\RESPONSE.TXT at the CD-ROM DOS prompt. Then follow the on-screen instructions.

The response file automates the install and creates the user Admin (user=admin.wizard) with a password (password=Novell). You are now ready to upgrade your servers to NetWare 5. If you are more interested in the response file and want to learn about response file syntax, file selections, and keys, see the December 1998 AppNote "Automating NetWare 5 Installation with a Response File" at http://developer.novell.com/research/appnotes/1998/a9812.htm.

Whether you install the server manually or use the response file to set up your NetWare 5 server, make sure of the following:

- The server has enough disk space to accommodate the files and directories moving from the source server.
- The server is running the IPX protocol.
- The server is running *Storage Management Services* (SMS).
- The server is not running products other than Storage Management Services.

■ A volume SYS on the destination server is at least as large as volume SYS on the source server.

■ Other volumes are at least as large as the volumes you will migrate from the source server. For NetWare 4.x, volume names on the destination server must be the same as volume names as on the source server.

You also should load `DSREPAIR` and run Unattended Full Repair on both the new NetWare 5 destination server and the old source server. Make sure that Unattended Repair, Time Synchronization, and Report Synchronization Status finish with no errors. Also, make sure that you back up NDS and all data.

UPGRADE FROM NETWARE 3.X TO NETWARE 5 It is relatively easy to move your NetWare 3.x source server to a NetWare 5 destination server using Novell Upgrade Wizard because you create a project—a model that enables you to place the NetWare 3.x bindery objects anywhere in the NDS tree. Creating a project enables you to try out different configurations so that the bindery objects transition smoothly to NDS. The utility enables you to drag-and-drop bindery objects to desired locations in the NDS tree. You can even add or delete objects, assign rights, and many other things without affecting the actual NDS tree. When you have created a model of what you ultimately want your NDS tree to look like, you then can migrate the bindery objects and the file system into the NDS tree.

When the bindery objects get migrated, all the information previously contained in them also gets migrated including user accounts, properties, printing objects, login scripts, print configurations, and any trustee assignments. You probably will want to modify some of this information after objects are migrated or create additional objects to accommodate new features of NDS. For example, if you are taking advantage of Novell Distributed Print Services, you will need to set up NDPS objects in NDS.

Novell Upgrade Wizard requires the following system and software configuration to upgrade from NetWare 3 to NetWare 5:

■ A Windows 95/98 or Windows NT (4.0 or later) workstation with 25M of available disk space and running the latest Novell Client using the IPX protocol.

■ A source server running the NetWare 3.11, 3.12, or 3.2 operating system and the latest updates running on a common LAN segment with an IPX external network number.

- A destination server running the NetWare 4.11, 4.2, or NetWare 5 operating system, and the latest updates running on a common LAN segment with an IPX external network number. (If you are installing NDS Corporate Edition, however, you must upgrade to NetWare 5.)

- Supervisor or supervisor equivalent rights, including Console Operator rights, to both the source and destination servers.

Before you use the Upgrade Wizard, you need to do the following:

1. Back up the NDS database and volumes to which you will be migrating NetWare 3.x files and data. This ensures that you have a copy if you need to restore the files due to a failed migration.

2. If you are upgrading several servers to the same NDS context, make sure that you consolidate names of users who exist under different names on different servers.

3. If you are upgrading several servers to the same NDS context, make sure that you change the names of users with the same names on different servers that are upgraded to the same context.

4. Make sure that you have sufficient rights. You will need Supervisor rights on the NetWare 3.x server and on the NetWare 5 server (called admin rights in NetWare v 5). You must also have console operator rights in NDS.

5. If you have SAP filtering on your network, disable it.

6. Make sure that any third-party NLMs and incompatible NLMs have been updated with more recent versions. Working versions of these NLMs are found in the `PRODUCTS\NW3X` subdirectory where you installed the Novell Upgrade Wizard. Copy any newer NLMs in the `PRODUCTS\NW3X` subdirectory to the `SYS:SYSTEM` subdirectory of the NetWare 3.1x or 3.2 server.

7. Unload the following NLMs in the order indicated.

   - `TSA311.NLM` or `TSA312.NLM`
   - `SMDR.NLM`
   - `SMDR31X.NLM`
   - `SPXS.NLM`
   - `TLI.NLM`
   - `AFTER311.NLM`
   - `CLIB.NLM`
   - `A3112.NLM`
   - `STREAMS.NLM`

8. Load TSA311.NLM or TSA312.NLM to automatically load the newly copied NLMs.

9. Load and add appropriate name spaces if any of the volumes you are going to upgrade contain files with Macintosh or NFS naming conventions. You must load the appropriate name spaces on the destination volumes and then add the name spaces to the volume prior to the upgrade. The Macintosh name space is loaded through MAC.NAM. The NFS name space is loaded through NFS.NAM.

10. Determine what objects to migrate. You can upgrade the entire NetWare 3.1x or 3.2 bindery and/or the contents of the individual NetWare 3.1x or 3.2 volumes. In most cases, you will want to upgrade both the bindery and the contents of the server volumes. However, on occasions where you want to upgrade only the bindery (for example, to quickly add users in a Directory tree) or the contents of an individual volume.

Make sure that you know the following information before you begin migrating your NetWare 3.x bindery information to NetWare 5:

■ The name of the tree to which you will be migrating

■ The appropriate NDS context for the server

■ The administrator name (either ADMIM or another username with Supervisor rights to this context)

■ The administrator password to NDS

To complete the NetWare 3.x upgrade to NetWare 5, complete the following steps:

1. Update the source server with new NLM programs.

2. On the Windows workstation, change to the directory where you installed Novell Upgrade Wizard.

3. Copy the files from the PRODUCTS\NW3X directory to the SYS:SYSTEM directory on the NetWare 3 server.

4. Bring down and restart the NetWare 3 server.

5. Back up all data.

6. Verify that you have Supervisor rights on the source server.

7. Disable SAP filtering.

NOTE: *To disable SAP filtering, load INETCFG at the server console and follow the on-screen prompts. If SAP filtering cannot be disabled, ensure that the default server (preferred server) for the workstation is on the same LAN segment as the destination and source servers.*

8. Log in to the source server from the Windows 95/98 or Windows NT workstation.

9. Click Start.

10. Select Programs and then select Novell.

11. Select Novell Upgrade Wizard and then select Novell Upgrade Wizard.

12. Click Create a new project and then click OK (see Figure 3-1).

13. Select the type of upgrade you are performing and then click OK (see Figure 3-2).

Figure 3-1
Novell Upgrade
Wizard Startup
dialog box

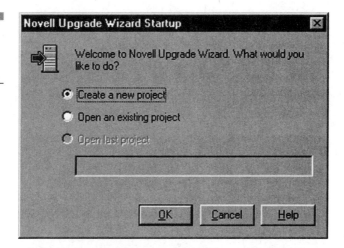

Figure 3-2
Select a NetWare 3
to NetWare 4 or
NetWare 5 upgrade.

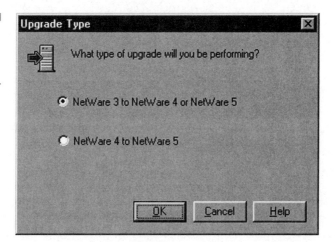

14. Make sure that your NetWare 5 server meets the requirements indicated and then click Next to continue.

15. Name the project.

NOTE: *The upgrade project file contains all the commands, successes, and failures relating to copying files and objects to the destination server.*

16. Select the source server and destination NDS tree.

17. Drag the bindery and volume objects from the source server and drop them into containers (folders) on the destination NDS tree (see Figure 3-3).

NOTE: *To create a new container, right-click on the parent of the container.*

Figure 3-3
Drag the bindery and volume objects.

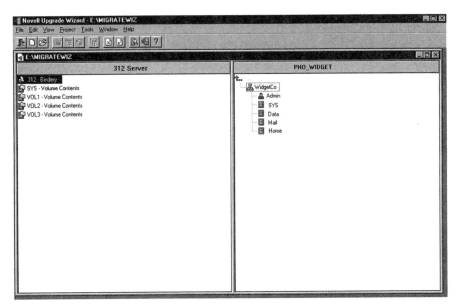

18. Verify that the data can be copied by clicking Project and then click Verify Project.

19. Follow the instructions to correct any warnings or errors. All errors must be corrected before migrating. Although you have selected the containers where the NetWare 3 data will be copied, no data has yet been migrated. When migrated, the bindery data is converted to NDS objects and placed in the NDS tree on the destination server.

20. Click Project and then click Migrate.

After migrating the files and objects, you should do the following:

1. Run DSREPAIR on the destination server to make sure that no errors occurred.

2. Modify the server's print configuration if you are upgrading to NDPS. If you are using queue-based printing, you should check to make sure that your queues and print servers are still functioning.

3. Make sure that all of your applications have migrated correctly. You may need to reinstall applications that may not have correctly migrated to the destination server.

4. Make sure that user information has migrated correctly.

5. Modify login scripts so that they take advantage of NDS. Login scripts are discussed in Chapter 6.

After you have completed the migration, the NetWare 3.x server will still function. However, it is best not to return to NetWare 3.x, because you will loose the added functionality and opportunities that are available in NDS. You now want to upgrade your NetWare 5 server to NDS 8. See "Upgrading Existing NetWare Servers to NDS 8."

UPGRADING FROM NETWARE 4 TO NETWARE 5   Upgrading from a NetWare 4.x source server to a NetWare 5 destination server requires you to install a new NetWare 5 server in a temporary NDS tree. Then you copy the files and data from the NetWare 4 source server to the NetWare 5 destination server. Finally, you transfer the NDS information to the NetWare 5 destination server. After the NetWare 4.x NDS is transferred to NetWare 5, the source server will be brought down automatically, and the NetWare 5 server will reboot. The NetWare 5 server will appear in the same NDS container with the same name as the NetWare 4.x source server. If the upgrade was not successful, you can return the server to its premigration configuration. However, the process of reversing the migration is not simple. You should not rely on this as a way to back up your database or file system. Instead, you should back up all files and data before you begin any upgrade so that you can restore them if something doesn't work properly.

When you have completed the upgrade to NetWare 5, you will need to upgrade NDS to NDS Corporate Edition. This procedure is described on page 95. See "Upgrading Existing NetWare Servers to NDS Corporate Edition."

Novell Upgrade Wizard requires the following system and software configuration to upgrade from NetWare 4 to NetWare 5:

- A Windows 95/98 or Windows NT (4.0 or later) workstation with 25M of available disk space and running the latest Novell Client using the IPX protocol.

- A NetWare 4 source server running the NetWare 4.10, 4.11, or 4.2 operating system and the latest updates running on a common LAN segment with an IPX external network number. The NetWare 4.x source server must be running long namespace support on all volumes to be copied.

- A destination server running the NetWare 5 operating system and the latest updates running on a common LAN segment with an IPX external network number. NetWare 5 requires Support Pack 2 (NW5SP2.EXE) or later. If the destination server will be the first NetWare 5 server in the NDS partition, the NetWare 4 source server must have a read/write or master NDS replica prior to migrating.

- Supervisor or supervisor equivalent rights, including Console Operator rights, to both the source and destination servers.

To complete the upgrade, do the following:

1. Verify that you have Supervisor rights on the source server.
2. If the destination server will be the first NetWare 5 server in the NDS partition, make sure that the NetWare 4 source server has a read/write or master NDS replica.

NOTE: *To verify supervisor rights from a Windows workstation, run NetWare Administrator from the* SYS:PUBLIC *directory.*

3. Update the source server with the latest software:

- **NetWare 4.11**

  ```
  LIBUPI.EXE
  DS411P.EXE
  TSA410.NLM
  ```

- **NetWare 4.10**

  ```
  410PT8B.EXE
  DS410N.EXE
  LIBUPI.EXE
  SMSUPG.EXE
  ```

4. Make sure that long namespace support is running on all volumes to be copied. To add long namespace support to a NetWare 4.11 or NetWare 4.2 server, enter the following at the server console:

```
LOAD LONG
ADD NAME SPACE LONG TO volumename.
```

To add long namespace support to a NetWare 4.10 server, enter the following at the server console:

```
LOAD OS2
ADD NAME SPACE OS2 TO volumename.
```

5. Load `DSREPAIR` and run Unattended Full Repair. Make sure that Unattended Repair, Time Synchronization, and Report Synchronization Status finish with no errors.

6. Back up NDS and all data in case difficulties arise during the migration.

7. Load `INETCFG` at the server console and follow the on-screen prompts to disable SAP filtering. If SAP filtering cannot be disabled, you should make sure that the default server (preferred server) for the workstation is on the same LAN segment as the destination and source servers.

8. Log in to the source server from the Windows 95/98 or Windows NT workstation.

9. Click Start.

10. Select Programs and then select Novell.

11. Select Novell Upgrade Wizard and then select Novell Upgrade Wizard again.

12. Click Create a new project and then click OK

Figure 3-4
Select a NetWare 4 to
NetWare 5 upgrade.

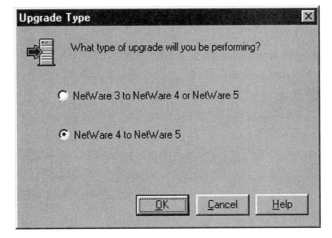

Figure 3-5
Select the NDS tree.

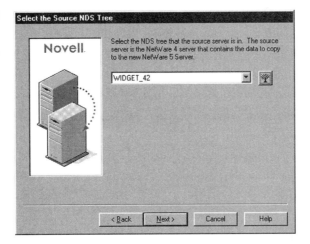

13. Select the type of upgrade you are performing and then click OK (see Figure 3-4).

14. Make sure that your NetWare 5 server meets the requirements indicated and then click Next to continue.

15. Name the project. The upgrade project file contains all the commands, successes, and failures relating to copying volumes and NDS to the destination server.

16. Select the NDS tree in which the source server resides (see Figure 3-5). If you are not logged in, you will be prompted to log in. Make sure that you log in as admin with all rights to this server. Then Click Next.

17. Select the source server and then click Next (see Figure 3-6).

Figure 3-6
Select the
source server.

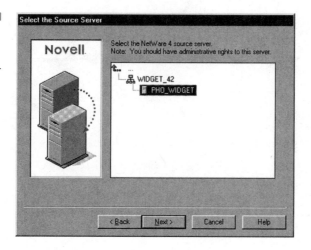

18. Select the NDS tree in which the destination server resides. If you are not logged in, you will be prompted to log in. Make sure that you log in as admin with all rights to this server. Then Click Next.

19. Select the destination server and then click Next.

20. Click Create to create the project.

21. Click Perform Pre-Upgrade Tasks and make sure that you have done everything suggested there (see Figure 3-7). It is important that you run DSREPAIR so that your migration will go smoothly. All servers also must be synchronized before a migration can take place.

22. Click Copy Volumes and proceed to copy volumes. You do not need to copy all the volumes at once. You can select volumes to copy now and copy other volumes later by reopening the project file (see Figure 3-8).

23. Click Edit Configuration Files and make any changes necessary to the configuration files. The Novell Upgrade Wizard creates an AUTOEXEC.NCF and STARTUP.NCF file for the NetWare 5 destination server with default LOAD statements and parameters. If the source server was running an NLM program or application and you want to run it on the destination server, you must copy the commands from the configuration file on the source server to the appropriate configuration file on the destination server.

24. Click Migrate NDS to migrate the NDS information from the NetWare 4 source server to the NetWare 5 destination server. After clicking Migrate NDS and completing all the steps required to migrate NDS, the

Figure 3-7
Novell Upgrade
Wizard Migration
window

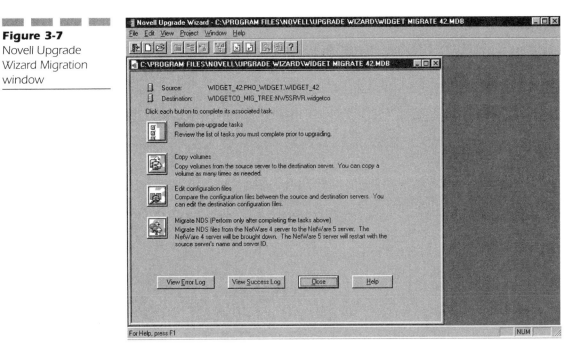

Figure 3-8
Select Volumes to
Copy dialog box

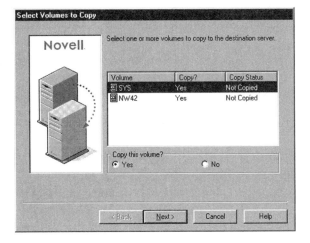

NetWare 4 server will be brought down, and the NetWare 5 server will restart with its new server name and NDS tree.

25. Make sure that the NetWare 5 destination server has restarted.

After migrating the server, you should do the following

1. Run DSREPAIR on the destination server and select Unattended Full Repair.

   ■ Type DSREPAIR at the server console and select Time Synchronization to make sure that time is in sync on the NetWare 5 server. If time is not synchronized, enter SET TIMESYNC RESTART FLAG=ON at the NetWare 5 server console.

   ■ Type DSREPAIR at the server console and select Report Synchronization Status to make sure that NDS is synchronized on the NetWare 5 server. If the destination NetWare 5 server does not contain a Read/Write or Master replica, you must check NDS synchronization by running DSREPAIR on a server with another server in the NDS tree that has a Read/Write or Master replica.

   If NDS is not synchronized, enter the following commands at the server console:

   ```
   SET DSTRACE=*U
   SET DSTRACE=*H
   SET DSTRACE=+SYNC
   ```

   ■ Type EDIT SYS:SYSTEM/NUW30/NUW.ERR at the server console to view the error log file. You must resolve any Novell Licensing Service errors recorded in the NUW.ERR error log file.

2. Modify the server's print configuration if necessary.

3. Make sure that user information migrated successfully.

4. Make sure that applications have migrated correctly. Reinstall applications that may not have correctly migrated to the destination server.

5. Make sure that user information has migrated correctly.

6. Modify login scripts.

You will now need to update NDS to NDS Corporate Edition. See "Upgrading Existing NetWare Servers to NDS Corporate Edition" on page 95.

Using the Accelerated Upgrade to Upgrade NetWare 4.x Servers
If you have an extensive knowledge of scripting and you have several servers to upgrade, you might want to look at using the Novell Accelerated Upgrade. This utility enables you to customize the installation through advanced scripts and to take advantage of the features and benefits of NetWare 5 as quickly as possible. The Accelerated Upgrade was

developed when Novell's *Information Systems and Technology* (IS&T) department was faced with the challenge of rapidly upgrading its own NetWare 4.11 servers to NetWare 5 because Novell had a goal to have every server in the company migrated to NetWare 5 before the product shipped. To achieve this goal, the needed to be able to upgrade multiple servers in a single evening, and they needed to upgrade many of these servers from remote locations. They accomplished this using the Accelerated Upgrade. The Accelerated Upgrade is available from the Novell download page at `http://www.novell.com/download/`. The Web site includes all the documentation you will need to set up the Accelerated Upgrade. When you have completed the Accelerated Upgrade, make sure that you update your server to NDS Corporate Edition.

Upgrading Existing NetWare Servers to NDS Corporate Edition

If you already have existing NetWare 5 servers, you can upgrade them to NDS Corporate Edition. A new data store enables NDS Corporate Edition to accommodate millions of objects in a directory tree. NDS Corporate Edition offers the following features:

- Increased NDS capacity—NDS Corporate Edition can contain one billion objects in a single tree.
- Increased performance for directory reads, writes, and searches
- A new ConsoleOne utility that runs on the workstation instead of on the server (You can even manage some objects through a browser with the new ConsoleOne utility. This makes administration possible from any workstation—even an Apple workstation.)
- Increased *Lightweight Directory Access Protocol* (LDAP) version 3 performance
- Improved DSREPAIR utility
- New BULKLOAD utility for adding, modifying, and deleting NDS objects in a batch process
- Extended naming support, including "dc=" naming and uniqueID
- In-place upgrade of existing NDS database

Note that the NDS tree cannot contain servers running NetWare versions earlier than 4.10. You will need to upgrade these servers before installing NDS Corporate Edition.

Before you upgrade your existing NetWare 5 servers, make sure that they meet the following minimum requirements:

- NetWare 5 Service Pack 2 or later
- DSREPAIR download (if the first installation of NDS Corporate Edition is on a server that does not hold a replica of the [Root] partition)
- Administrative rights to [Root] to modify the schema
- A ConsoleOne administrator's workstation must be a Pentium Pro 200 or better with a minimum of 64M of RAM running the latest Novell Client software
- A NetWare 5 serial number (required before you download NDS)

To get NDS Corporate Edition, you can purchase an NDS Corporate Edition CD-ROM with all versions of NDS Corporate Edition on it. Or, if you already have NetWare 5, you can download either the single product file or smaller multiple files from www.novell.com/download. When you download this file, you need to have your NetWare 5 serial number handy. This serial number will be verified before continuing with the download process. This may take a few seconds.

Before upgrading your existing NetWare 5 server to NDS Corporate Edition, do the following:

1. If you are upgrading your hardware in conjunction with the NDS upgrade, install the new hardware and test it with the existing network operating system and NDS version before upgrading NDS. To take advantage of the performance and scalability of NDS Corporate Edition, consider upgrading all servers in a replica ring with comparable server hardware (RAM, disk space for volume SYS, and processor speed) and fast network connections (100 Mbps Ethernet, for instance).

2. If your first installation of NDS Corporate Edition is to a server that does not hold a replica of [Root], download DSREPAIR from the product download page and copy it to the SYS:SYSTEM directory of a server holding a replica of the [Root] partition. To check the DS.NLM version, run NDS Manager (NDSMGR32.EXE), click the Server object, and then click Information

NOTE: *If your first installation of NDS Corporate Edition is on a server holding a replica (master or read/write) of the [Root] partition, you don't need to prepare the NDS tree; proceed with Upgrade Servers. It doesn't matter which [Root] server you upgrade first.*

3. At the server console, run DSREPAIR and select Advanced Options Menu, then Global Schema Operations, and then select Post NetWare 5 Schema Update. You will be prompted for your Admin name and password.

4. Make sure that all users are logged out during the upgrade. The installation scripts automatically restart the server during the upgrade process.

5. If you install the product using RCONSOLE, make sure that you include the following commands in the server's AUTOEXEC.NCF file:

```
REMOTE [password]
RSPX
```

6. If you are using the Java-Based Remote Console, make sure that you include the following commands in the AUTOEXEC.NCF file:

```
SPXS
RCONAG6 [password] [TCP port] [SPX port]
```

When your server is prepared and you have checked that you have the necessary patches and files, complete the following steps:

1. Download the NDS Corporate Edition files and expand them to a single directory on the NetWare 5 server.

2. At the server console, start NWCONFIG.NLM again.

3. Select Product Options.

4. Select Install a Product Not Listed.

5. Press F3 (F4 if you're using RCONSOLE).

6. Specify the path to the expanded NDS Corporate Edition files in the dialog box. The file copy process will begin, and when the files are copied, the server will automatically reboot.

7. Make sure that all volumes are mounted. Trustee assignments to the volumes are upgraded as part of the NDS Corporate Edition installation process. If you're not sure whether all volumes are mounted, type MOUNT ALL at the server console.

8. Press Ctrl+Esc and then select the number corresponding to the screen to switch to the NWConfig Screen.

9. Enter you admin name (with context) and password.

10. Press Esc to close the upgrade status log.

11. When prompted to reboot the server, select Yes, Restart Now.

After the server has rebooted, you have completed the NDS 8 upgrade on this server. You will want to repeat this procedure for each NetWare 5 server you want upgraded to NDS Corporate Edition.

You will want to set up some other things when you are finished with the upgrade. You can set up ConsoleOne on a workstation running the latest Novell Client. This is explained in Chapter 4, "Installing Novell Client." Also, if you have sufficient RAM to increase the NDS cache size, you can increase NDS performance considerably for large databases by allocating more RAM to the NDS cache. By default, NDS Corporate Edition uses 8K of RAM for cache.

You can set the cache size by typing

```
SET DSTRACE = !m[hexadecimal KB]
```

or

```
SET DSTRACE = !mb[bytes]
```

at the server console. The smallest tested cache size is 0, and the largest is 2G. NDS runs with either amount. However, determining the proper cache size for your server depends on the memory needs of other processes running on the same server and on the amount of disk cache required. You should test a variety of cache sizes to find a good balance. If NDS is essentially the only application, give it as much cache as possible. All allocated cache eventually will be used. NDS performance on highly volatile data is improved with more cache. Very low cache-to-file size ratios noticeably degrade NDS performance.

Installing NDS for NT

NDS for NT brings all the benefits of NDS to the NT Server and alleviates or even eliminates the pain of managing domains and trusts. This means that you can choose the operating system that is best for each part of your network without incurring additional management time and costs. With NDS, you get true integration between diverse operating systems while keeping the ease, flexibility, and stability of the NDS directory database.

Before you can install NDS for NT, you must meet the minimum requirements listed in Table 3-1.

WARNING: *Make sure that you first install NDS for NT on the PDC before installing it on the BDCs.*

To install NDS for NT, complete the following steps:

1. Insert the NDS Corporate Edition CD-ROM.
2. Locate the NT directory.
3. Double-click SETUP.EXE.
4. Check all the checkboxes in the startup screen to install the management utilities and the Novell Client software and to run the migration wizard. You can choose not to install part of the NDS for NT package, but you will be missing key functionality. We suggest you install all components at the same time unless you do not have Microsoft Exchange; in that case, you should not check this checkbox (see Figure 3-9).
5. Click Install.

Figure 3-9
The NDS for NT
Installation screen

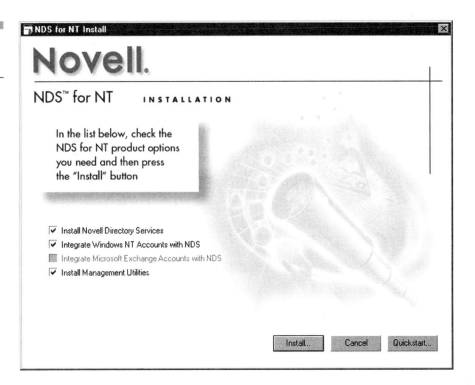

6. Click Yes to install the Novell Client. If you want to customize the installation of Novell Client, click Custom. However, typical should work fine. More information about installing Novell Clients is available in Chapter 4, "Installing Novell Client." Remember that you will have to install the latest Novell Clients on all workstations after the NDS for NT installation if you want to take advantage of all the features available with NDS for NT.

7. Click OK to reboot. When the workstation reboots, you can install the Management Utilities.

8. Click Next.

9. Click Yes to accept the license.

10. Click Yes to install NT server Management Utilities.

11. Click Next to accept the default shared folder.

12. Click Next to accept the default folder location.

13. Review the Summary and then click Next.

14. Click OK to create a share called SYS.

15. Click OK. You are now ready to install ConsoleOne.

16. Select the language you want for ConsoleOne and then click OK.

17. Click Next.

18. Click Yes to accept the license agreement.

19. Click Next to accept the default destination folder.

20. Click Next to accept the default program folder.

21. After reading the summary, click Next. It may take a while to copy all the necessary files.

22. Click Finish. The installation now continues on to install NDS for NT and migrates NT users to NDS. This part of the installation is a Java installation and may take some time to begin.

23. Click Next to begin installing NDS for NT (see Figure 3-10).

24. Click Accept to accept the license agreement.

25. Click Next to accept the default installation destination or browse to a different location. This location must be on an NTFS partition. NDS for NT cannot be installed on a FAT partition.

26. Select the desired languages and then click Next.

27. Insert or locate the license disk and then click Next.

Figure 3-10

Novell NDS for NT
Product Installation
screen

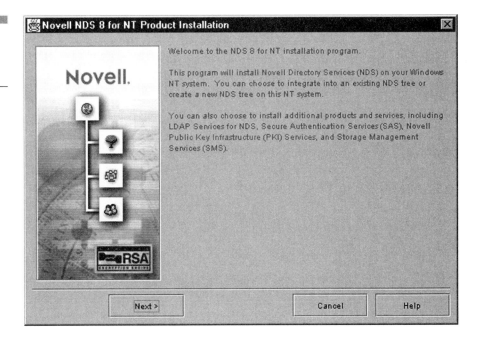

NOTE: *Additional information on NICI is provided in Chapter 6, "Controlling Network Access."*

28. Choose the type of NDS installation and then click Next (see Figure 3-11). If you already have an existing tree, choose Install Directory Services in an existing tree. If you do not have an existing tree, click Create a new NDS Tree.

29. If you are installing into an existing tree, do the following:

   ▪ Enter the NDS information about the tree where you want to install the domain and your fully distinguished admin username and password. Then Click Next.

   ▪ Select the components you want to install and then click Next.

   ▪ Read the product summary.

30. If you are creating a new tree, enter the NDS information to create a new tree and then click Next.

31. Click Finish. You have now installed NDS and are ready to migrate your users and workstations to NDS.

Figure 3-11
Choose the type
of installation.

Figure 3-11
Choose the type
of installation.

32. Click Close. The server reboots, and you must log in again as the NDS admin. The Domain Object Wizard automatically starts (see Figure 3-12).

33. Click Next.

34. Select the NDS tree to which you want to move the domain and then click Next (see Figure 3-13).

35. Click Next.

36. Log into NDS as an administrator, who has right to extend the schema, and then click Next.

37. Specify the NDS context where you want to create the Domain object and the context where you want to create users (see Figure 3-14). If you want to force the NT and NetWare passwords to sync or if you want to force users to enter new passwords after the migration, check the appropriate checkbox.

38. Click Next.

39. Choose whether or not to search for duplicate users in the NDS tree and then click Next. If you choose to search, the Wizard will locate any users in the NDS tree with the same names as NT users to be migrated. This process is recommended because NDS cannot accept duplicate names in the same context.

40. Select the containers you want to search for duplicate users and then click Next (see Figure 3-15).

Figure 3-12
Domain Object
Wizard screen

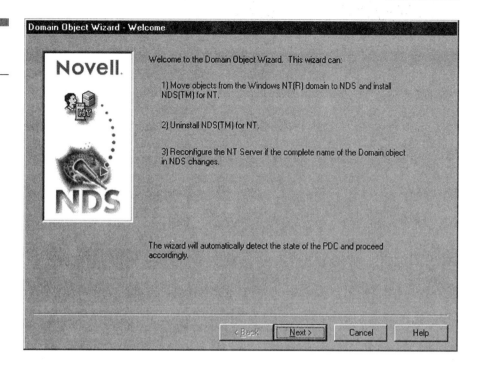

Figure 3-13
Select the NDS tree
where you want the
domain migrated.

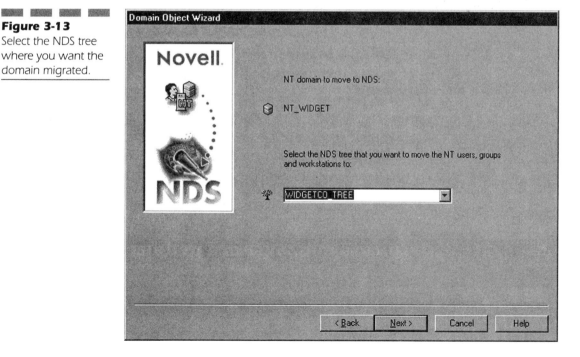

Figure 3-14
Specify Domain
object context and
default user context.

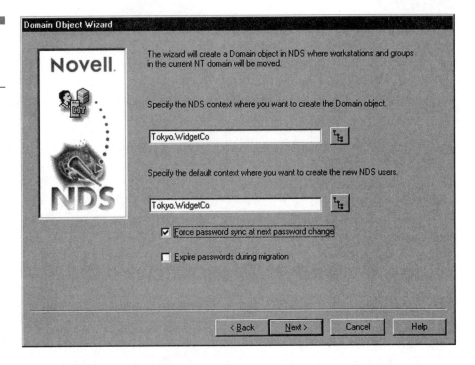

Figure 3-15
Select the containers
to search for
duplicate user
names.

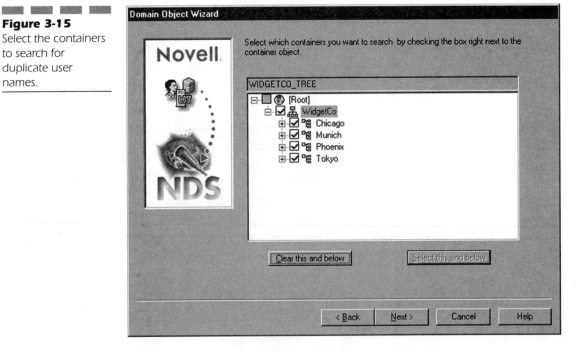

41. Click Search to begin the search. When it is complete, click Next.

42. In the Summary window, check the information for the users being migrated. You must reconcile any problems with users before the Domain Object Wizard can be completed. For instance, if users have duplicate names, you must do one of the following:

- Associate the two users with each other if they are the same person.
- Don't move the NT user.
- Create the NT user with a different NDS name.

You also can choose to associate other users, such as Admin and Administrator, so that there is only one user object. The passwords for associated users are combined, and the NT password is used (see Figure 3-16).

43. When you have finished checking the migration summary, click Next.

44. Click Move to move the users. The Moving Status window then shows the results of the migration (see Figure 3-17). Errors are also detected and must be resolved before you can continue. You can click Back to resolve any errors.

NOTE: *The Domain Object Wizard enables you to stop and resume at a later time (called multipass migration). However, no objects are migrated to NDS until you resolve all errors and complete the Wizard. You cannot migrate part of a domain and then return and migrate other users later. If you migrate only part of the users, the users left in NT will lose all access to the network.*

Figure 3-16
Associate users during the migration

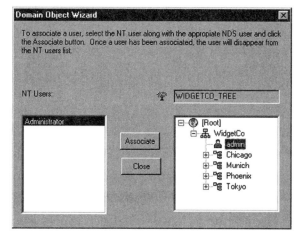

Figure 3-17
Domain Object
Wizard Moving
Status window

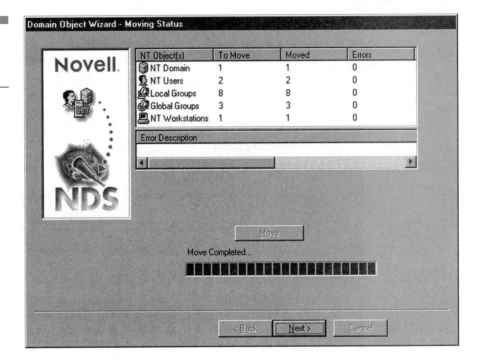

Figure 3-17
Domain Object
Wizard Moving
Status window

45. Click Next when all errors are resolved.

46. Click Finish. The computer reboots, and the users are migrated to NDS.

You can now check that these users and the domain have been migrated to NDS in NetWare Administrator or ConsoleOne.

Upgrading Existing NDS for NT Servers to NDS Corporate Edition

If you have previously installed NDS for NT, you can use the same utility to upgrade to NDS Corporate Edition. You can use this utility to upgrade the Novell Clients, the administration utilities, and to upgrade NDS. Select the components of NDS for NT you want to upgrade to NDS Corporate Edition and follow the on-screen instructions. The installation will prompt you and tell you that an additional copy of NDS for NT cannot be installed, and it will lead you through the upgrade process.

Installing NDS for Solaris

NDS for Solaris enables you to scale in relation to an organization's Solaris application needs. Many mission-critical applications and Web services are designed to run on Solaris. NDS give you a simplified and distributed way to administer users for these applications, which scale across your entire network. Because only one user object exists to create and manage, a simple point-and-click gives the user access to resources across the network, on multiple operating systems, and on networking devices. They now need only one password to access all network resources. They will never even know that NDS is running in the background. However, you will notice the reduction in administrative time, because you will have to administer only one database.

NDS for Solaris deploys Novell's directory service, NDS, on Solaris systems. Solaris systems now can belong to an NDS tree, along with NetWare 5 systems. This enables you to manage Solaris user accounts through NDS and authenticate to NDS locally by placing an NDS replica on the Solaris server. NDS for Solaris can place replicas of the NDS database on a Solaris server. These replicas utilize the same directory services provided on NetWare 5 servers. The capability to add replicas provides local access to NDS on Solaris servers, enabling greater speed and accessibility on remote networks.

NDS for Solaris includes a migration tool that migrates existing Solaris users in the /etc/passwd, NIS, and NIS+ databases to NDS. Passwords are also migrated. However, you should note that unlike the Novell Upgrade Wizard, the NDS for Solaris migration tool does not check for the uniqueness of the Solaris user being migrated. You will need to check that no duplicate user names exist across the entire NDS tree. After NDS for Solaris is installed, an NDS replica is installed on the Solaris system. This enables you to install Read/Write or Read-only replicas of the NDS database on the Solaris server to provide local access and greater speed and accessibility on remote networks. The master replica should always reside on a NetWare 5 server, for greatest reliability and access to NDS management and repair utilities. NDS for Solaris also includes a new *Pluggable Authentication Module* (PAM), which redirects authentication requests to NDS.

When you install an NDS replica on a Solaris System, the Solaris system becomes an NDS Server object in NDS. NDS for Solaris is an IP application. It works with other Novell products over IP only. You can use ConsoleOne and NetWare Administrator to manage NDS objects and NDS Manager to manage NDS partitions. The replicas on NDS for Solaris 2.0 and NetWare 5 can synchronize over IP. NDS for Solaris and NetWare 4.11 (DS version 6.00) servers can coexist in the same tree as long as the master replica of the root partition is on NetWare 5. Both servers should not contain replicas of the same partition. If partitions have replicas on NetWare 4.11 servers only, you need to put the master replica on a NetWare 5 server if NDS for Solaris needs to access objects in those partitions. NDS for Solaris also works with NDS for NT and ZENworks (when it is installed on a NetWare server).

Before you begin the actual installation, decide whether you want to install NDS User Account Management (User Account Manager), NDS Server, or both. NDS User Account Manager needs to be installed on all the Solaris systems whose users need to be in NDS. NDS Server needs to be installed on all Solaris systems on which you want to place an NDS replica if there is a NetWare server. If this will be installed in a native Solaris environment, you should definitely install both NDS Server and User Account Manager.

Before you install User Account Management, make sure that you identify the NDS tree into which you want to install NDS User Account Manager. If you have a NetWare Server, the master replica for this NDS tree should be on the NetWare 5 server. If not, it will reside on the Solaris server. You will need to know the following:

- NDS context of the root of the NDS partition into which you want to install NDS User Account Manager
- NDS context where the UNIX workstation object that represents the Solaris system should be created
- Which NetWare 5 servers you will have the NDS for Solaris snap in for NetWare Administrator (if you have NetWare 5)
- NDS tree into which you want to install the NDS Server. NDS Server and NDS User Account Manager share the same NDS tree.
- NDS context where you want to add the Solaris system as a NDS server object

NOTE: *If you are installing in a native Solaris environment, you will specify the name of the tree to be created during installation. Make sure that you name the tree correctly. Changing tree names is not suggested. You might also want to review Chapter 2, "Designing NDS," so that you understand how and where containers should be created.*

Also make sure that time is synchronized on the servers in the network. You can synchronize the time by using *Network Time Protocol* (NTP). If you want to synchronize NetWare servers with Solaris servers, use TIMESYNC.NLM version 5.12. More information about time synchronization is located in Chapter 9, "Administering NDS."

To install NDS for Solaris, you will need the NDS Corporate Edition CD-ROM. Then complete the following steps:

1. At the Windows 95/98 or Windows NT system, run `Winsetup.exe` from the `solaris/windows` directory.

2. Select the administration utility you want to use. ConsoleOne is the new administration utility and is Java-based. However, because all functionality has not been ported to ConsoleOne, you may need to install both utilities. More information about ConsoleOne and NetWare Administrator is located in Chapter 5, "Administering NDS Objects."

3. Follow the on-screen instructions for these installations.

4. When prompted, enter the name of the tree into which the product should be installed and the name of the NetWare 5 server into which the NDS for Solaris snap-in for Net-Ware Administrator should be installed. If you have not logged into the NDS tree or the account with which you have logged in does not have administration rights to the root of the NDS tree, you will be prompted for the name and password of this user. The Windows setup program extends the NDS schema of the NDS tree to support Solaris accounts and installs the NDS for Solaris snap-in for NetWare Administrator.

5. Install the Client DLLs. To do this, run `setup.exe` in the `public\ mgmt\consoleone\1.2\install` directory.

6. At the Solaris system, log in as root.

7. Change to the Solaris directory on the CD-ROM. Then open the next Solaris directory.

8. Run `nds-install`. The Installation program provides the option of installing the NDS User Account Manager component, the NDS Server component, or both components. You will be asked for your approval before adding each package.

9. Enter the configuration information using the default editor invoked by `nds-install`. The information you need to enter will be placed where asterisks currently exist (`********`). Depending on the option selected in the preceding step, you need to provide different inputs. Examples are provided to show you what type of information you need to enter and how to format it. If you select to install NDS User Account Manager only, you need to enter the name of the NDS tree, the NDS context of the root of the NDS partition, and the NDS context for the UNIX workstation object. If you select to install NDS Server only, you need to enter the name of the NDS tree, and the NDS context where the NDS server object should be added.

10. When prompted, enter the password of the user with administration rights to the NDS partition.

11. In the ndscfg.inp file (which opens automatically), make sure that you have entered all the configuration parameters necessary.

12. To create a partition (if it doesn't exist), change the Create Partition parameter to Yes.

13. To install LDAP Services for NDS, change the LDAP Services for NDS parameter to Yes.

14. Save the information and close the editor.

15. When prompted, insert the disk with the NIC foundation key.

16. Enter the admin name and password.

You have now completed the installation and configuration. If the NDS Master on NetWare 5 system carrying the master replica is separated geographically, create a read/write or read-only replica on the Solaris system using NDS Manager.

You also need to migrate Solaris user accounts to NDS using the /usr/sbin/migrate2nds tool. You need 128M of RAM on the server (NetWare 5 or Solaris) hosting the NDS replica into which you will be migrating a large number (about 15,000) of users. After migrating the accounts to NDS, you can configure the Solaris systems to use NDS authentication by modifying the /etc/pam.conf and /etc/nsswitch.conf files. You can use the NDS entries in /etc/pam.conf.nds and /etc/nsswitch.conf.nds files. These files are copied into the Solaris system during product installation. Both the pam.conf and nsswitch.conf files should be modified together.

Before you begin the migration, you should do the following:

■ Make sure that the passwords and groups entry in the /etc/nsswitch.conf file are sent only to files, files nis or files nisplus. If accounts are being migrated from files, run the pwconv command to update the entries.

■ Make sure that no invalid entries are in the files or in the databases.

■ Consolidate Solaris user accounts so that each person has only one account across all Solaris systems. This resolves duplicate uids and gids. If duplicate names appear during the migration, the utility will prompt you to choose to map the duplicate to an existing account, migrate it with a different name or not migrate it.

To migrate users to NDS, complete the following steps:

1. Create or edit the `migrate2nds.inp` file. When the installation completes, this file should appear. This file is located in the `/var/ndsuam` directory. You must include the name of the administrator of the NDS tree and the users that are to be migrated.

2. Specify other settings you want to use during the migration. You can specify several other settings to be used during the migration such as the User Context, Group Context, Workstation Access, Force Password Expire, Set Search Context, Unattended Migrate, and others. These are explained in the file and in the accompanying documentation.

3. Run `migrate2nds` from the root of the NIS master server. This will delete the migrated accounts from NIS.

4. Follow the prompts. If duplicate names exist, you will be prompted to deal with each name individually. During the migration, Groups are migrated first, then User accounts, and finally Group Member lists. Because NDS does not allow multiple users with the same name in the same context, you will need to decide how to migrate these accounts.

5. When the migration is complete, modify the `/etc/pam.conf` file to use the NDS authentication and copy it to the Solaris system.

NOTE: *If you are running the Unattended Migrate, you will not be prompted for input. Passwords will not be updated on accounts that have been mapped to an existing account. If the user account has been locked in Solaris, the account will be migrated and disabled. User accounts with No Password will also be disabled.*

WARNING: *migrate2nds does not check for unique uids or gids.*

SUMMARY

You can install NDS Corporate Edition in several ways, depending on what server operating systems you have. If your company has standardized on NetWare or you use NetWare as your main network operating system, you have several options and things to consider based on the version you are currently running. If your company has standardized on a different operating system, such as Windows NT or UNIX, or you have a mixed environment, your options for installing and implementing NDS differ slightly. This chapter discussed various ways to install NDS Corporate Edition or upgrade existing NDS databases to NDS Corporate Edition. Remember that before any installation or upgrade is attempted, you should make sure that your server is already running correctly and that NDS is replicating correctly. This will avoid many problems during the upgrade.

For More Information

Here are some additional resources for information on installing NDS on NetWare, Windows NT, and Solaris.

Books

Administering NetWare 5 by Dorothy Cady. This book contains extensive information on NetWare 5.

Web Articles

"What's New in the NetWare 5 Operating System?" http://www.developer.novell.com/research/appnotes/1998/septembe/a1frame.htm

"Installing NetWare 5: Tips and Tricks" http://www.developer.novell.com/research/appnotes/1998/septembe/a2frame.htm

"Migrating to Pure IP with NetWare 5" http://www.developer.novell.com/research/appnotes/1998/septembe/a3frame.htm

"Compatibility Mode Installation and Configuration" `http://www.developer.novell.com/research/appnotes/1998/septembe/a4frame.htm`

"Automating the NetWare 5 Installation with a Response File" `http://www.developer.novell.com/research/appnotes/1998/december/a1frame.htm`

"More About Automating the NetWare 5 Installation with a Response File" `http://www.developer.novell.com/research/appnotes/1999/february/a3frame.htm`

"Upgrading an Enterprise Using the NetWare 5 Accelerated Upgrade" `http://www.developer.novell.com/research/appnotes/1999/april/a2frame.htm`

Technical Information Documents

Novell Technical Support provides further information on Novell products. The following is a list of Technical Information Documents that can be located at `www.support.novell.com`.

2942687	NetWare 5 Documentation and Technical Info
2947852	NDS Update for NetWare 5
2943750	Understanding NetWare 5 Licensing
2944797	NW5 Installing MLA License Certificates
2947186	Troubleshooting NW5 Licensing Summary
2940793	How to configure Contextless Login in NW5
2940703	NT 4.0 Migration to NetWare
2913292	DS Health Check Procedures
2929065	Valid File Server Names for NW3.x–5.x
2943060	NW5 Upgrade Wizard Issues
2934033	4.x or 5.x Migration/DSMaint Procedure
2920601	DSMaint–PSE
2940514	3.1x or 4.1x upgrade option in NetWare 5
2942263	Upgrading to NetWare 5 Print Services
2947308	Backreving NW5 Versions and Service Packs
2943060	Upgrade Wizard Issues
2944438	NetWare Server Setup Checklist

Installing Novell Clients

To authenticate to the NDS tree and gain access to network resources, you must install client software on all workstations. The Novell Client consists of software that makes it possible for users to do the following:

- Log in and authenticate to the network
- Locate network resources
- Gain access to network resources (through authentication)

The Novell Client is the key to ensuring that only authorized users have access to the network. It also helps to manage the flow of data to and from the workstation. After the Novell Client is installed, you can browse the network and see what resources are available.

This chapter explains how to install the Novell Client on Windows 95 and Windows NT workstations. It also explains how to install multiple clients across the network without having to install the software on each workstation individually. Finally, this chapter covers information about the new Novell Client for Macintosh version 5.12.

NOTE: *This chapter does not cover the installation and configuration of the Novell Client for DOS and Windows 3.1x, because it has not been updated to support many of the new features of NDS. However, this software still works with NDS Corporate Edition and is the best option if you must support DOS or Windows 3.1x on your network. Novell provides extensive documentation on the Novell Client for DOS and Windows 3.1x at its documentation Web site at* www.novell.com/documentation. *This chapter also does not cover any client software for OS/2 because Novell no longer supports this platform.*

After you have installed and configured the Novell Client, you also will need to make sure that users have correct access to the network and its resources. You need to create User objects for them. This process is covered in Chapter 5, "Administering NDS Objects." Setting up access (passwords), creating login scripts, and other logging-in tasks are covered in Chapter 6, "Controlling Network Access." Then, Chapter 7, "Administering Workstations," provides additional suggestions on how to minimize the overhead of managing client workstations.

How the Novell Client Works

The Novell Client is the software that resides on a workstation. It enables a network user to communicate with a file server on the network. The Novell Client establishes a connection to the network when a user logs in to the network and provides a valid username and password. After NDS has found the user's object and verified that the user and the password are valid, the user is logged in to the network. Information about creating User objects is located in Chapter 5.

Then, when the workstation needs access to a network resource, it sends a request to the server for services or data. The request is processed at the server, and the NDS database validates the user's right to access that information or service. The Novell Client waits to get approval back from NDS. When this is acquired, the network resources or data are released to the workstation. This happens in a matter of seconds.

Requirements

Before you install the Novell Client software, you should make sure that the client workstations have sufficient resources and the required software.

Network Connection

First check for a valid network connection. If you have never installed a client or created a network connection, you might not have access to the network. If this is the case, you must install the client software from CD-ROM. This installation process is explained later in this chapter. To check for a valid network connection from a Windows 95/98 or Windows NT workstation, do the following:

1. Double-click Network Neighborhood.
2. Check that the servers and trees that you expect to see actually appear in the Network Neighborhood window.

Long Filename Support

The Novell Client for Windows 95/98 and Novell Client for Windows NT require long filename support. This is included on all NetWare 5 servers. If users need to access NetWare 3.x and NetWare 4.x servers, you must install and load the appropriate name spaces.

Hardware and Software Requirements

Make sure that all your workstations meet the following hardware and software requirements for Windows 95/98:

- 486 processor or better
- Minimum 28M free disk space
- Minimum 16M RAM (more is always better)
- Windows 95/98 Service Pack 1 or later installed
- Windows 95 or Windows 98 CD-ROM or the Windows CAB files for the appropriate operating system

The .CAB files might be requested during the Novell Client installation. In all cases, it is best to copy these files to the same directory if you are doing a network install or have the files on CD-ROM or on the local workstation if you are doing a local install.

For Windows NT, workstations must have the following:

- Windows NT 4.0
- Service Pack 4 or later installed
- Minimum 20M RAM

You can get the Service Packs from Microsoft's corporate Web site at www.microsoft.com.

You also must have a network card and cabling to connect the workstation to the network. Novell Client for Windows NT and Novell Client for Windows 95/98 support *Network Driver Interface Specification* (NDIS) drivers. *Open Data-Link Interface* (ODI) drivers are not installed on Windows 95/98 or Windows NT. However, if you are upgrading an older version of the client and you have ODI drivers currently installed, these drivers are still supported. If you are installing for the first time, NDIS drivers will be installed. If you do not already have the necessary NDIS driver, you might need to obtain it from the Windows 95 or Windows 98 CD-ROM or from the network board manufacturer. Because the installation of network boards differs slightly between manufacturers, you should refer to the board manufacturer's instructions for information about installing the network board.

If you will be installing the workstation locally, make sure that the workstation has a CD-ROM drive. You cannot install the Novell Client for Windows 95/98 or Windows NT from disk. If absolutely necessary, you can install the Novell Client for DOS and Windows 3.1x from floppy disk if your network is using the IP protocol stack. A read-me file on the CD-ROM explains how to create a disk for installation. After you have used this client to connect to the network, you should upgrade to the Novell Client for Windows 95/98 or Windows NT.

The Novell Client can work in an IP-only, an IPX-only, or a mixed IP and IPX environment. During the installation, you need to specify which protocol to use. If you have installed the Novell Client previously, the Novell Client Installation auto-detects the current protocols you are using and selects these as the default. If you have never installed a Novell Client and are unsure which protocols to use, choose IP and IPX. This might cause some unnoticeable slowing in the connection, but it will ensure that you will be able to access the network.

Installing the Clients

If you are installing the Novell Client software on a small number of workstations or if the workstations are not yet connected to a network, you will need to install the Novell Client from the Novell Client CD-ROM. If you plan to install the Novell Client on several workstations on the network, you should consider using a network installation option. A network installation can upgrade existing client software or install new client software. Later, this chapter discusses one of the network installation options. If you have ZENworks installed, you also can install the Novell Client using ZENworks application distribution. More information about ZENworks is located in Chapter 7, "Administering Workstations."

Installing Clients on a Local Workstation

The Novell Client Setup utility helps you install Novell Client software on Windows-based workstations. You can select the platform to which you want to install from a list of available platforms. To install from a local CD-ROM drive, do the following:

1. Insert the CD-ROM. If the Novell Client Setup utility does not automatically launch, run `winsetup.exe` from the root of the CD-ROM.

2. Click on a language you want to use.

3. Select a platform—Windows 95/98 or Windows NT (see Figure 4-1).

4. Click Install Novell Client to start the installation utility for that software.

Figure 4-1
Select the platform you want to use to install the Novell Client.

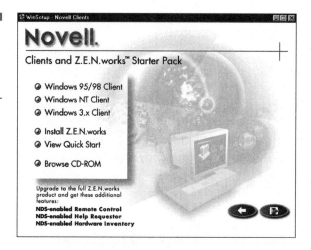

Figure 4-2
Novell Client network protocol screen

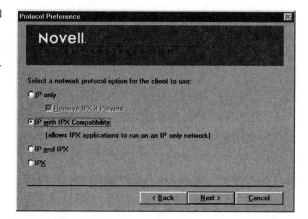

5. Read the license agreement and then click Yes.

6. Click Custom and then click Next. The order of the following steps varies slightly between Windows 95/98 and Windows NT, but the same information is requested in each installation.

7. Select the protocol you want to use (see Figure 4-2).

8. Choose whether you want to log in to NDS or to the Bindery (NetWare 3.x). If you plan to use this client to log in to NDS 8, you must choose NDS.

9. Select the optional components you also want to install (see Figure 4-3). A short description of each option appears when you select it. If, for example, you are using *Novell Distributed Print Services* (NDPS) in your network, you will want to select NDPS.

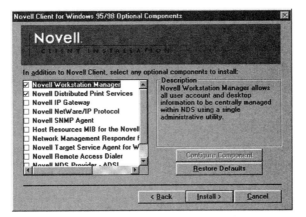

Figure 4-3
Optional
components installed
during the Novell
Client installation

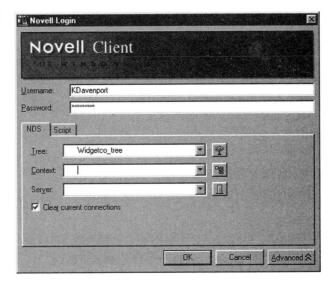

Figure 4-4
Novell Client
Login screen

10. Click Install.

11. If the Novell Client cannot detect your network board, it will prompt you to select the appropriate card. You may need to provide a disk with the LAN drivers.

12. When the installation is complete, click Reboot to restart the workstation. For help during the installation, refer to the online help that accompanies the software.

    When the workstation restarts, you should see the Novell Client Login screen (see Figure 4-4).

    You can enter your username and password to log in to the network.

Configuring the Novell Client Software

After you have installed the Novell Client for Windows 95/98 or Windows NT, you might need to configure the software to work in your network. The Novell Client is configured by modifying the Novell Client Property Pages. You can access the Novell Client Property Pages through the following:

- *Network Neighborhood* Right-click the Network Neighborhood icon and then click Properties. In the network components list, click Novell NetWare Client and then click Properties. The Novell Client Property Page appears.

- *Network Control Panel* Click the Start button. Click Settings and then click Control Panel. Double-click the Network folder. In the network components list, click Novell NetWare Client and then click Properties. The Novell Client Property Page appears.

- *N Icon* Right-click the red N icon in the system tray and then click Properties. The Novell Client Properties Page appears (see Figure 4-5).

The Novell Client Property Page enables you to set specific information, such as the preferred server and preferred tree. It also enables you to set up

Figure 4-5

Novell NetWare Client Properties page

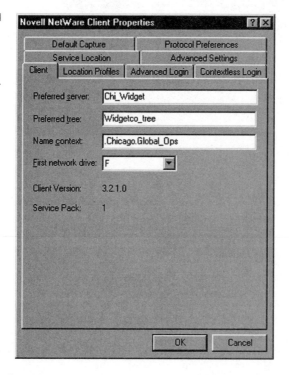

protocol preferences, default capture settings, network message timeout, and many other features.

If you have never installed the Novell Clients or are adding new users, you also need to set up access (passwords), create login scripts, and generally set up the user environments. These tasks are covered in Chapter 6, "Controlling Network Access," and Chapter 7, "Administering Workstations."

Installing the Novell Client across the Network

If you are installing several workstations, you probably don't have the time to visit each workstation. You also probably have users of varying technical abilities in your network, who might or might not be comfortable installing the software on their own. Or, maybe you do not have a CD-ROM because you downloaded the Novell Client from the Novell corporate Web site. You probably soon found out that the client software will not fit on a floppy disk and does not include a disk install method.

You can eliminate the need to install the Novell Client on individual workstations by installing it over the network. Installing across the network is easy. However, it works only for workstations that are already connected to the network either by Novell's client software or the Microsoft client software. If you have workstations that are not connected to the network, you need to use the CD-ROM installation described previously. The latest Novell Client CD-ROM can be ordered for a nominal fee. The client software might also have been shipped with other software that you purchased from Novell, such as the NetWare 5 CD-ROM or the NDS Corporate Edition CD-ROM.

Even if your network has workstations on multiple platforms, you can install and upgrade the client software on multiple Windows platforms when users log in. The process requires you to create a folder on the NetWare server and to copy the Novell Client files and other required files to this folder (workstations then can read the files during login). After you have created the folder, you need to give users rights to the new folder. You can do this by creating a Group object in NDS and adding these users to the group. Then you will need to create or update the appropriate configuration file located in these directories for each platform-specific client. This configures the Novell Client during installation so that you or the network user will not have to manually configure the client at each workstation.

When this is done, you need to create or modify the appropriate login script. Finally, make sure that you tell users in advance about the upgrade so they understand what is happening when they log in to the network and when the installation is launched. You can choose to run the installation either with user input or in silent mode without user intervention. In either case, you should notify users so that they understand what is happening.

NOTE: *Because the Novell Clients are updated on a regular basis, you should download the latest Novell Client from the Novell corporate Web page at* www.novell.com/download. *Changes in the client mean that some features may not be documented here. For example, a future version of the Novell Client reportedly uses a configuration file that enables you to bypass additional installation issues and even further customize the installation. These instructions were written for Novell Client for Windows 95/98 version 3.1 and Novell Client for Windows NT version 4.1. Read the accompanying documentation and note changes that might have occurred. The documentation that accompanies the Novell client will contain information on any changes.*

Also check for Novell Client Service Packs that are soon to be released on a regular basis. Service Packs contain changes that need to be made for functionality between the Novell Client and specific products. For example, ZENworks might add some functionality that requires the Novell Client to do something a little differently or add a function. Rather than make people download and install totally new clients, the Service Packs can be distributed easily through ZENworks software distribution and management with the least effect to the workstation and the users. These changes are always included in the next version of the Novell Client software.

To set up the Novell Client network installation, do the following:

1. Log in to a server as Admin or as a user with Admin equivalence. You need rights to copy files to a network folder that all users can access and rights to modify login scripts.

2. Create a folder called CLIENT in the SYS:PUBLIC network folder.

3. From the Products directory on the Novell Client CD-ROM, copy the Winnt, Win95, Doswin32, and Adm32 directories to the new folder. If you are downloading the Novell Client software from www.novell.com/download, follow the download instructions and expand the client software files in this network folder.

4. If you are installing the client in only one language or if you do not have enough space to accommodate multiple language directories, you can delete the language directories you do not need from the NLS

directory under each client directory. To ensure that you have all necessary files, copy the entire client directory and then delete only the extra language directories.

5. If you are installing the Novell Client for Windows 95/98, you also need to copy Windows 95 or Windows 98 CAB files from the appropriate operating system CD-ROM to the Win95 directory.

6. In NetWare Administrator, create a Group object called Client in the NDS tree and add the users whose workstations need to be installed or upgraded to that object. Make sure that the group has Read and File Scan rights to the new folder you created. If you created the new folder in SYS:PUBLIC, the new folder should have Read and File Scan rights already associated with it, but make sure that these rights have not been changed.

7. Start the Novell Client Install Manager (NCIMAN.EXE). For Windows 95/98. The Install Manager is located in the SYS:PUBLIC\CLIENT\ WIN95\IBM_LANGUAGE\ADMIN directory you copied to the server.

   For Windows NT, the Install Manager is located on the in the SYS:PUBLIC\CLIENT\WINNT\I386\ADMIN directory you copied to the server. The Novell Client Install Manager (NCIMAN) is a GUI-based utility that helps you to configure the client properties. Using Novell Client Install Manager eliminates your having to configure each workstation manually. After you have created the configuration file with Install Manager, use the /U command line parameter in the login script to call the configuration file and set the properties. If you are using the default settings to install the clients, you do not have to create or modify the configuration files.

8. Click File and then click New File and select the appropriate platform.

9. Modify the installation options as needed. In the Installation options list box, double-click the configuration option you want to modify. In the Property Pages, set the parameters and then click OK. The values you set appear in the right list box.

▬ ▬

NOTE: *You can set up one workstation the way you want all of the workstations set up and then use Novell Client Install Manager to import the settings from that workstation's registry. Then save them to the configuration file you use during the installation. After you set up the workstation, click File and then click Open Registry to import the settings into the Novell Client Install Manager.*

10. Click File and then click Save. Save the file with any filename that is descriptive of the platform. For example, you could rename the file `unatt_95.txt`.

11. Copy this file to the `SYS:PUBLIC\CLIENT\WIN95\IBM_LANGUAGE` directory (for Windows 95/98) or to the `SYS:PUBLIC\CLIENT\WINNT\I386` directory (for Windows NT)

12. In NetWare Administrator, select the object whose login script you want to create or modify.

13. Click Object and then click Details.

14. Click the Login Script page (see Figure 4-6).

15. Enter the login script commands and information into the login script text box. Login scripts are discussed in Chapter 6.

NOTE: *A sample login script is also available in a text file called* `inst_log.txt` *on the CD-ROM or in the download. If you choose to use the sample login script, make sure that you edit the sample login script to match the server names, directory paths, and specifications of your network.*

16. To save the login script and close the Details dialog box, click OK.

You're finished, and the client software will be installed or updated the next time the users log in. You also can set more advanced configuration

Figure 4-6
Login Script Page
in NetWare
Administrator

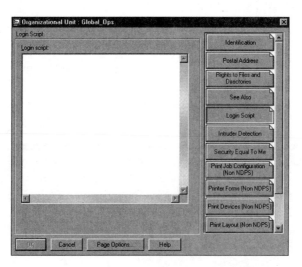

parameters in the Windows 95/98 SETUP.INI file. For example, you can set up the installation to run without prompting the user for input.

When the users log in to the network the next time, the installation will run. Users might see system messages as their workstations are upgraded, depending on how you set up the installation. You can set the installation to ask for as much or as little information as you want users to deal with. If workstations already have current client software, the client login runs as usual.

Other Network Installation Methods

There is more than one way to install the Novell Client. The network installation just discussed is simple and straight-forward. However, you might want to investigate another installation method. If you want to install the Novell Client and the operating system at the same time, you might try the MSBATCH method. This can be achieved by using a batch file process. Although this process does not work for all platforms, it can be an easy way to get workstations configured quickly. The current Novell Client documentation does not discuss this option because it was not supported on Windows 98 for some time. It is currently being supported, and several TIDs are available from the Novell Technical Support Web site at www. support.novell.com.

If you are using ZENworks in your network, you can use Application Launcher and application distribution to push the Novell Client out to your workstations. ZENworks is a powerful use of the NDS directory that enables you to manage your workstation's desktops, distribute applications, and troubleshoot problems on the workstation from a central administrative workstation. ZENworks and application distribution are discussed in Chapter 7, "Administering Workstations."

Using the NetWare Client for Mac OS

Although Novell stopped developing the Mac client a few years ago, it has recently been picked up by a third-party vendor called Prosoft Engineering.

They have the exclusive right to develop the NetWare Client for Mac OS. The NetWare Client 5.12 for Mac OS enables Mac OS users to log in to the network. It seamlessly integrates these Mac OS clients into your NetWare network, enabling you to manage them just like any other client. You manage the User objects in NDS like you would manage User objects for Windows users. This new version of the Macintosh client also eliminates the need for NetWare for Macintosh on the server (although it is compatible), because users can now authenticate to any IPX server from the Mac OS Chooser (see Figure 4-7).

NetWare Client for Mac OS is optimized for the Mac OS 8.x and Apple's G3 processors. As with the Windows client software for Windows 95/98 and Windows NT, the NetWare Client for Mac OS can be installed locally by CD-ROM or over the network, making it easier to distribute across your entire site. You can even customize the software to meet your network's specifications.

One large difference exists between the Mac client provided by Prosoft Engineering and the Windows clients provided by Novell—you have to pay for the Prosoft Engineering Mac client. NetWare Client 5.12 for Mac OS comes at a cost of $49.95 per client. However, Prosoft Engineering offers direct volume discounts for buying directly from Prosoft Engineering's online store or customer order center. Prosoft Engineering probably release new versions every six to eight months. To reduce the cost, they offer upgrade protection, which gives you the right to install and use future versions of the product released during the coverage period. Upgrade protection annual licenses start at $49.95 for five users and goes up to $5,994 for a site license. You currently must purchase the software directly from Prosoft Engineering. However, in the future, your company will be able to purchase Mac client support as a part of an overall NetWare package from Novell.

Figure 4-7
The Macintosh
Chooser

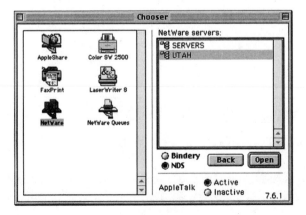

Requirements

You can run the NetWare Client for Mac OS software on a system that meets the following requirements:

- Mac OS-based workstation with a 68030 processor or better
- 5M of available RAM
- 7M of free hard disk space
- System 7.6.1 or later
- The LaserWriter 8 driver, version 8.6 or later, included with System 8.5 (required for MacIPX printing)
- NetWare 4.11 or NetWare 5 server
- IPX loaded and bound to the Network Interface Card
- Macintosh Namespace on a NetWare Server (added through INSTALL.NLM)

Installing the NetWare Client for Mac OS

To install NetWare Client for Mac OS on a single workstation, use the NW Client Installer on the CD-ROM and complete the following steps:

1. Mount the NetWare Client for Mac OS CD.
2. Double-click the NW Client Installer icon at the root of the CD.
3. Click the Continue button to view the Release Notes.
4. Click the Continue button to view the license agreement.
5. Click the Agree button to indicate your acceptance of the terms of the license agreement and to continue with the installation.
6. Enter your registration information, including a serial number. The serial number can be found either on the box or on a registration card.
7. Click the Register button to continue.
8. Choose the Install button or the Custom button from the NW Client Installer window. If you want to install all of the necessary software for your workstation, click the Install button. If you prefer to install only selected portions of the software, select the Custom option.
9. Follow the on-screen instructions for the installation type you chose.
10. When prompted, click the Restart button.

Configuring the NetWare Client for Mac OS

The NetWare Client for Mac OS includes two tools used to configure client workstations for access to NDS:

■ NetWare Client Configuration window
■ MacIPX Control Panel (see Figure 4-8)

These tools automatically configure NetWare Client for Mac OS, so users are not required to use them. However, complications might occur with the automatic configurations, in which case you must use the tools to manually configure NetWare Client for Mac OS.

The NetWare Client Configuration window enables you to configure your Directory Services preferences so that you can use the Directory Services login menu. The NetWare Client Configuration window stores its settings in the NetWare Prefs file, located in the Preferences folder. The NetWare Prefs file contains all the information you set using the NetWare Client Configuration window. The file also contains the context cache. To open the NetWare Client Configuration window, click Configure from the NetWare Tree menu (see Figure 4-9).

Figure 4-8
Mac IPX control panel

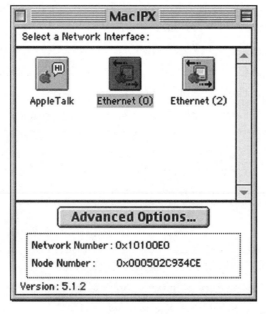

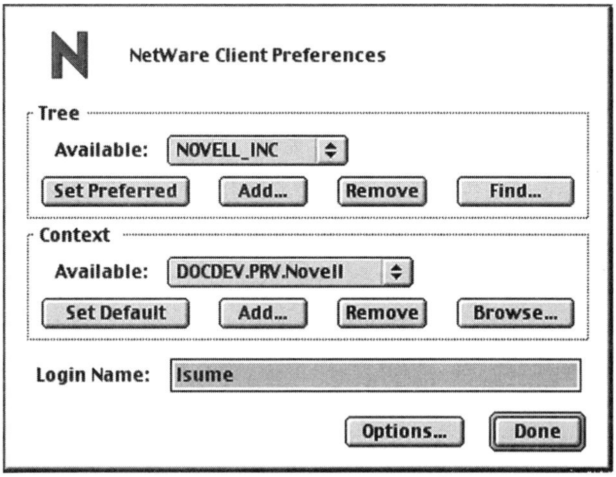

Figure 4-9
Mac Client
Configuration
window

In this window, you can set the following options:

- Preferred Tree
- Context
- Login Name

You also can set Advanced Settings such as packet signing, messaging, packet size, and checksum.

You can copy a specific configuration to several workstations on the network if you want several people on the network to use the same NetWare Client Control Panel settings. You do not need to configure each individual Mac workstation. To copy the NetWare Client Configuration window settings from one workstation to another, complete the following steps:

1. Configure NetWare Client in the NetWare Client Configuration window as described previously.

2. Leave the Login Name field in the NetWare Client Configuration window empty. Otherwise, the name in the Configuration window will appear on all workstations and will have to be changed manually.

3. Close the NetWare Client Configuration window to save the NetWare Preferences file.

4. Copy the NetWare Preferences file from the Preferences folder in the System Folder to a server or floppy disk. Copying the file to a server

makes it unnecessary for you to go to each workstation individually. However, you must make sure that you copy the file to a server that all of the workstations can access.

5. Copy the NetWare Preferences file from the server or disk to each workstation that should use the configuration. If a previous NetWare Prefs file exists, delete it. Place the new NetWare Prefs file in the Preferences folder in the System Folder.

SUMMARY

The Novell Client software is the key to getting connected to the network. The Novell Client software resides on a workstation and enables you to communicate with a file server on the network by establishing a connection to the network through a valid username and password. After NDS has verified that the username and the password are valid, you are logged in to the network.

When you install the client, you can authenticate to the NDS tree and gain access to network resources. The Novell Client makes it possible for users to log on and authenticate to the network, locate network resources, and gain access to network resources (through authentication). The Novell Client is the key to ensuring that only authorized users have access to the network because it works with NDS to check user rights. It also helps to manage the flow of data to and from the workstation. The Novell Client is available on all Windows platforms and for the Mac. If you are installing the software on a small number of workstations, you can install it from the CD-ROM. If you have downloaded the software or you need to install it on several workstations, you have various options for installing it across the network. For more information on the Novell Client for DOS and Windows 3.1x, see Novell's documentation Web site at `www.novell.com/documentation`. OS/2 is no longer supported by Novell but may work with your network.

After you have installed and configured the Novell Client, you will need to create User objects for them. This is covered in Chapter 5, "Administering NDS Objects." Setting up access (passwords), creating login scripts, and other logging in tasks are covered in Chapter 6, "Controlling Network Access." Chapter 7, "Administering Workstations," provides additional suggestions on how to minimize the overhead of managing client workstations. Chapter 8, "Administering Printing," explains how to administer printing through NDS and provide the correct printer drivers to the users' desktops. These four chapters are essential to completing the end-user setup.

For More Information

Here are some additional resources for information on installing and configuring the Novell Client.

Web Sites

Novell Client for Windows 95/98 Web site `http://www.novell.com/catalog/qr/sne14370.html`

Novell Client for Windows NT Web site `http://www.novell.com/catalog/qr/sne14320.html`

Novell Client for DOS and Windows 3.1x Web site `http://www.novell.com/catalog/qr/sne14385.html`

NetWare Client for Mac OS at the Novell Web site `http://www.novell.com/catalog/qr/sne14351.html`

NetWare Client for Mac OS at the Prosoft Engineering Web site `http://www.prosofteng.com/netware.htm`

Web Articles

"Disconnecting NetWare Clients That Have Automatic Reconnection Enabled" `http://developer.novell.com/research/appnotes/1997/february/a3frame.htm`

"Understanding the Advanced Settings in the Novell Client for Windows 95/98 `http://www.developer.novell.com/research/appnotes/1999/april/a3frame.htm`

Technical Information Documents

Novell Technical Support provides further information on Novell products. The following is a list of TIDs that can be located at `www.support.novell.com`.

2942195	NW5 Client common questions
2948684	NW5 IP Discovery Options in Protocol Preferences
2944038	Configuring a Client to Login IP across a Router

2942990	Configuration of Remote IP Clients
2946397	Optimizing NW5 clients in a NetWare 4.x environment
2942060	*Automatic Client Upgrade* (ACU)
2943427	ACU Step-By-Step Process with NCIMAN
2948052	Troubleshooting IP Login Issues
2942867	No Login to NW5 IP only server

Administering NDS Objects

A recent Gartner Group study revealed that 79 percent of the total cost of owning a network is incurred in administration costs alone. Without a directory-enabled network, you are often required to perform the same operations multiple times, either for each user or each server. NDS eliminates the need for redundant administration by providing a single point of administration for your entire enterprise and a choice of a Java or Windows administrative tool—ConsoleOne or NetWare Administrator. NDS reduces the total cost of managing and maintaining networks.

The main benefit of integrating the network infrastructure with the directory service is the reduced administrative cost that results from integrated network-wide management. The directory service enables you to centralize management of your network and avoid redundancy of management tasks. This integrated management approach lets you accomplish several beneficial administrative tasks:

- Eliminate redundancies of managing the services (DHCP, DNS, RADIUS, Quality of Service, authentication, etc.) in your network
- Realize time/management efficiencies by using directory-aware applications that leverage directory services (and by relying on the directory service to complete certain tasks)
- Centralize authentication and authorization for applications and services
- Implement policy-based management to simplify distribution of network privileges

You can take advantage of the administrative benefits of NDS only if you create NDS objects that represent the network resources and users you want to manage in the Directory. Each NDS object contains information about a specific resource or user. This information can be used to manage and locate network resources. In addition to objects about resources and users, NDS also contains different types of logical or organizational objects that enable you to group users into Groups, which then can have specific rights assigned to them. Other objects also enable you to create policies that can be applied to specific workstations, operating systems, or users to enforce standard network or desktop software or environments. In addition to the dozens of standard types of NDS objects, you can add objects if you need to represent other types of resources in your network, or you can add custom information to already existing object types (extending the schema and customizing NDS is discussed in Chapter 12, "Customizing NDS"). NDS is flexible enough to contain all the information about your network.

Creating and managing NDS objects is quite simple. You can use either ConsoleOne or NetWare Administrator. NetWare Administrator (otherwise known as NWAdmin) has been the NDS administrative tool of choice since NDS was first shipped. However, with the release of NetWare 5, Novell has created a new Java-based utility called ConsoleOne. Over time, ConsoleOne will replace NetWare Administrator as the administrative utility of choice, and it has several additional features added for NDS 8. However, during the transition time, you probably will find it useful to understand and use both utilities, because each utility currently has some functionality not found in the other. This chapter discusses ConsoleOne and NetWare Administrator as well as various types of NDS objects and how to create and use them. Because NDS objects are at the heart of the NDS database, different NDS objects and their properties are discussed throughout the book. For example, setting rights, restricting access, and creating security objects, such as certificates, are discussed in Chapter 6, "Controlling Network Access." ZENworks policy packages, another kind of NDS object, and managing workstations are discussed in Chapter 7, "Administering Workstations."

Understanding ConsoleOne

ConsoleOne was developed for use on the new NetWare 5 GUI server desktop. In previous versions of NetWare, no GUI desktop was at the server, and all utilities that ran on the server and were accessed at the server were text-based. ConsoleOne is a Java-based utility that enables you to graphically manage your NDS database from the server console or the workstation. The first version of ConsoleOne was very slow and clunky due to the underlying *Java Virtual Machine* (JVM). This version runs on the server and is installed as part of the original NetWare 5.

However, the version of ConsoleOne (1.2b) that ships with NDS Corporate Edition has increased speed and functionality. It can be run on the NetWare or Windows NT server or from a Windows workstation. If you are running NDS for Solaris, you must run ConsoleOne from a Windows workstation. No version of ConsoleOne runs on the Solaris server. If you have Netscape FastTrack Server on your NetWare 5 server, you can use a version of ConsoleOne called ConsoleOne Web Edition. This version of ConsoleOne enables you to perform basic tasks through an Internet browser, such as Netscape Navigator or Internet Explorer.

ConsoleOne v1.2b includes new features for managing additional NDS object types, customizing the NDS schema, configuring NDS for LDAP-based access, and managing properties of files and folders on NetWare volumes. In fact, some new NDS administration features are available only in ConsoleOne, because NetWare Administrator updates are being slowly phased out in favor of using ConsoleOne (see Figure 5-1).

NOTE: *ConsoleOne is shipping updates on a regular basis. You should check for the latest version at* www.novell.com/download. *Toward the end of 1999 or the beginning of 2000, a new version of ConsoleOne will ship, which has even more functionality including a role creation feature that enables you to assign a role object rights to specific properties. Also, as other Novell products release newer versions of their software, they will ship snap-ins for ConsoleOne that will enhance its capabilities to manage your entire network.*

NOTE: *If you have installed an earlier version of ConsoleOne, you should consider using version 1.2b, which ships with NDS Corporate Edition. It enables you to run ConsoleOne on the server or the workstation. Earlier versions of ConsoleOne had large limitations. For example, the snap-in components included in ConsoleOne version 1.2 require the latest Novell client software, effectively limiting you to using ConsoleOne on a 32-bit Windows workstation. ConsoleOne also requires Java 1.1.7, which could further restrict your platform choice at first.*

Figure 5-1
ConsoleOne running on the workstation

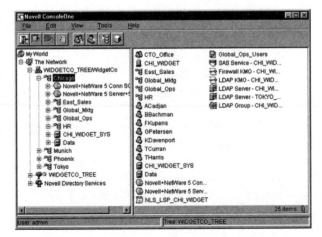

ConsoleOne also encompasses some of the administrative features of other text-based server administration applications, such as MONITOR. Depending on the composition of your network, you will see a particular set of features. For example, if NDS is installed on your network, you see features for browsing NDS trees and administering NDS objects. If NetWare 5 is installed, you see features for accessing NetWare server consoles and managing server resources.

Like its counterpart, NetWare Administrator, ConsoleOne is a modular utility that can have additional modules or snap-ins added as they are developed. Third-party companies as well as Novell itself are working on future snap-ins and enhancements. Also, because it is Java-based, ConsoleOne can be run on the workstation or in a browser in addition to being run at the server GUI desktop.

You can use ConsoleOne to do the following:

- Create NDS objects
- Modify the properties of existing NDS objects
- Delete NDS objects
- Search for objects by a particular property
- Rename objects
- Edit server configuration files
- Access another server's console using the Remote Console J utility
- Execute Java applets
- Browse huge NDS containers
- Search or customize views
- Configure LDAP services
- Extend the NDS schema
- Set up user accounts by template
- Control NDS rights inheritance
- Manage NetWare file services

You can use ConsoleOne to create most objects, such as User, Group, Organization, Organization Unit, and Template objects. In future upgrades, you will be able to create additional objects such as ZENworks Policy Packages. You can identify properties for the objects, but rights assignments must still be made through the NetWare Administrator utility. ConsoleOne also enables you to use NDS to browse the network's resources. Because it is Java-based, you can use ConsoleOne to add users from any workstation on the network that is Java-enabled. When ConsoleOne launches, the left window displays the NDS tree you connected to during login. The right window contains the leaf objects in the selected container.

Note that not all of these functions are currently available for the browser version of ConsoleOne. The browser version is much more limited and only enables you to create, delete, modify, and disable User objects and to manage passwords.

To run ConsoleOne on a workstation, you must have a Windows 95/98 or Windows NT workstation with a 200 Mhz or faster processor, 64M RAM, and an equal amount of virtual memory (disk swap space). If you have more RAM, you will get improved performance. You must be running the Java1.1.7 (included with ConsoleOne), the latest Novell Client software, and new versions of a few Novell client DLL files (also included with ConsoleOne).

To configure a Windows 95/98 or Windows NT workstation to run ConsoleOne, you must install a few required Novell Client DLL files on the workstation, which do not ship with the latest Novell Client. These are installed during the regular installation process. Because new Novell Client DLL files are installed, you must restart after installing ConsoleOne. After you have completed the installation process and have restarted your workstation, a ConsoleOne program icon is added to the to the Windows desktop.

NOTE: *You can install ConsoleOne program files locally on a workstation. If you download the latest version of ConsoleOne from* www.novell.com/download, *you will be asked whether you want to install it locally or on the server. The following instructions explain how to install it from the server.*

Installing ConsoleOne from the NetWare 5 Server

To set up a Windows workstation to run the latest version of ConsoleOne, make sure that you have at least one NetWare 5 server and then complete the following steps:

1. Map a drive to volume SYS on the server. This must be a persistent drive mapping so that it can be used later to run ConsoleOne from the workstation.

2. Browse to SYS:\PUBLIC\MGMT\CONSOLEONE\1.2\INSTALL.

3. Double-click SETUP.EXE to run the ConsoleOne setup wizard.

4. Double-click SETUP.EXE to run the ConsoleOne setup wizard and install the new DLL files needed to run ConsoleOne.

5. Click Next.

6. Click Yes to accept the license agreement.

7. Click Next to accept the default program folder and then click Next again.

8. Click Finish.

9. Restart the workstation.

After you have installed the program, you can run it by double-clicking the ConsoleOne icon on your Windows desktop.

 NOTE: *If you do not create a persistent map drive, the ConsoleOne icon on your desktop will not be able to find the files. You will need to reinstall the software. However, the second time, you will not need to restart the workstation.*

Installing ConsoleOne in a Windows NT-Only Environment

If you choose all options during the NDS for NT installation, ConsoleOne is installed as part of the installation process. If you need to re-install ConsoleOne or if you skipped it during the initial installation, you can install it by completing the following steps:

1. Insert the NDS Corporate Edition CD-ROM.

2. Locate the NT directory.

3. Double-click SETUP.EXE.

4. Check the Install Management Utilities checkbox and then click Install.

5. Select the language you want for ConsoleOne and then click OK.

6. Click Next.

7. Click Yes to accept the license agreement.

8. Click Next to accept the default destination folder.

9. Click Next to accept the default program folder.

10. After reading the summary, click Next. It may take a while to copy all the necessary files.

11. Click Finish.

ConsoleOne, NetWare Administrator, and NDS Manager are all installed.

Installing ConsoleOne in a Solaris-Only Environment

To set up a Windows workstation to run the latest version of ConsoleOne, you should complete the following steps:

1. Insert the NDS Corporate Edition CD-ROM on your Windows workstation.

2. In the Solaris directory, double-click NDS8WIN.EXE. This program expands all the necessary files you need to install ConsoleOne, NetWare Administrator, and NDS Manager on the Windows workstation. The installation defaults to the C:\WINDOWS\TEMP directory.

3. In the C:\WINDOWS\TEMP directory (or the specified directory you chose during installation), double-click WINSETUP.EXE.

4. Select the language you want to install.

5. Click ConsoleOne.

6. Click Next.

7. Click Yes to accept the license agreement.

8. Enter the destination drive for the ConsoleOne installation and then click Next (see Figure 5-2). The program then installs the files you need on that drive.

9. Click Next. The files you need to update the Novell Client DLLs are copied to the destination drive you specified and are placed in the PUBLIC directory.

10. Click Finish.

11. Browse to the PUBLIC\MGMT\CONSOLEONE\1.2\INSTALL directory located on the destination drive you specified during the setup.

12. Double-click SETUP.EXE to run the ConsoleOne setup wizard and install the new DLL files needed to run ConsoleOne.

13. Click Next.

14. Click Yes to accept the license agreement.

15. Click Next to accept the default program folder and then click Next again.

16. Click Finish.

17. Restart the workstation.

The ConsoleOne icon appears on your workstation desktop. You can now run ConsoleOne by double-clicking the icon.

Figure 5-2
Select a destination
drive for the
ConsoleOne
installation on a
Windows workstation
(Solaris-only
environment).

Understanding ConsoleOne Web Edition

ConsoleOne Web Edition is the perfect alternative for those times when you are not at a workstation with ConsoleOne loaded and you need to make a quick change. ConsoleOne Web Edition is a set of Java servlets that extend your Web server (Netscape FastTrack Server included with NetWare 5) so that you can perform NDS administration tasks through a Web browser. No client software is required. If your servers are running NetWare 5 with Netscape FastTrack Server and you have a browser, you can use Web Edition.

You can perform a subset of the tasks available in the full ConsoleOne utility. ConsoleOne Web Edition is installed on a Web server and accessed through a Web browser using an URL established during installation (see Figure 5-3).

If you have the correct rights, you can complete the following tasks after connecting to the URL and logging in:

- Create users
- Delete users

Figure 5-3
ConsoleOne running in a browser.

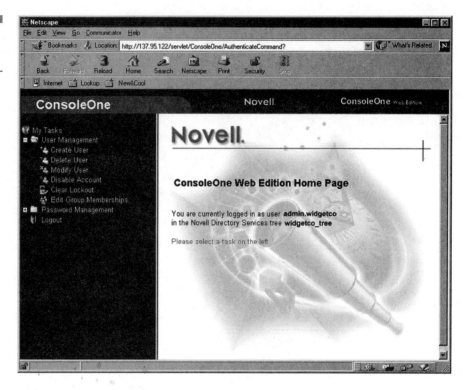

- View or edit basic user information
- Disable login for users
- Unlock user accounts that were locked due to intruder detection
- Edit users' group memberships
- Set user passwords

For example, you might be at a workstation and need to reset the user password. If the workstation has a browser, you can use ConsoleOne Web Edition.

Setting Up the Server to Run ConsoleOne Web Edition

To install the ConsoleOne extensions on the Netscape FastTrack server (NetWare 5 only), complete the following steps:

1. Configure the Web server that you will install ConsoleOne Web Edition on to use *Secure Sockets Layer* (SSL). This is important to ensure

security for ConsoleOne Web Edition transactions, which include transmitting NDS login passwords. For information on configuring your Web server to use SSL, see your Web server documentation.

2. Unload the Web server by typing NVXWEBDN at the NetWare server console.

3. Unload Java by typing JAVA -EXIT at the NetWare server console.

4. From a Windows workstation, map a drive to the SYS volume of the target NetWare server.

5. In a Web browser, go to www.novell.com/download.

6. Click ConsoleOne Web Edition and proceed to download the software.

7. On the download page, choose the option to download the Full File and save it to a temporary location.

8. Run the installer by double-clicking the file that you just downloaded.

9. Follow the instructions on-screen to complete the installation. When the installer prompts you for the location to install the product, select the drive that you mapped to the SYS volume. When the installer displays the results of the installation, at the bottom of the screen, enter the Web server IP address and port number and indicate whether the Web server is using SSL connections. This information is required to create a ConsoleOne Web Edition shortcut on your desktop and to configure the ConsoleOne Web Edition welcome page. If you cancel without specifying the correct Web server information, the shortcut and welcome page won't be configured correctly.

NOTE: *If the Web server is using the default port, you can leave the Port field blank.*

10. If more than 10 simultaneous users of ConsoleOne Web Edition are anticipated, configure the Web server to accomodate the higher usage load when the installation is complete. To do this, open the OBJ.CONF file located on the Web server in SYS:NOVONYX\ SUITESPOT\HTTPS-nwservername\CONFIG\ in a text editor and increase the value of the REQUESTTHREADS parameter (located on the line that begins with Init fn="ServletGateInit"). Then save the file. If you have questions about this, refer to the Novell online documentation at www.novell.com/documentation.

11. Configure and restart the Web server by typing C1WCFG at the NetWare server console.

12. Use NetWare Administrator or the full ConsoleOne utility to set up the Rights for ConsoleOne Web Edition users as needed.

Setting the Number of Web Edition Users   One thing that is different about Web Edition is that a limited number of people can use one single ConsoleOne Web Edition installation simultaneously. You set that number by configuring the servlet gateway of the Web server that is hosting the ConsoleOne Web Edition software. The servlet gateway is a Web server component installed with the ConsoleOne Web Edition software. By default, the servlet gateway is configured to support about 10 simultaneous users well. If significantly more users start to use the system simultaneously, they might see "service not available" messages. In such cases, you can reconfigure the servlet gateway to accommodate the higher usage loads by increasing the value of the REQUESTTHREADS parameter. Extensive instructions on setting these parameters are discussed in the Novell online documentation for Web Edition available at www.novell.com/documentation.

Setting Rights for Web Edition Users   If you will be giving access to users other than those that have explicit admin rights to administer the NDS tree, you need to set up these rights. For more information about setting user rights, see Chapter 6, "Controlling Network Access." Here is a quick synopsis of the rights that users will need to perform specific tasks:

- *Create users*   Read and create object rights to the container in which you want to create the new user.

- *Delete users*   Read and delete object rights to the container that holds the user object.

- *View or edit basic user information*   Read and write rights to the specific user properties you want to modify.

- *Disable login for users*   Read and write rights to the Login Disabled property of the User object (Account Disabled property in NetWare Administrator).

- *Unlock user accounts that were locked due to intruder detection* Read and write rights to the Locked By Intruder (Account Locked in NetWare Administrator), Login Intruder Attempts (Incorrect Login Count in NetWare Administrator), and Login Intruder Reset Time (Account Reset Time in NetWare Administrator) properties.

- *Edit users' group memberships*   Read and write rights to the Group Membership property of the user object and to the Members property of the group object.

- *Set user passwords*   Read and write rights to the Password Management property of the user object.

Accessing and using ConsoleOne Web Edition is described in "Creating and Managing NDS Objects with ConsoleOne Web Edition," later in this chapter.

Understanding NetWare Administrator

For several years, the main tool for creating and modifying NDS objects has been NetWare Administrator—previously called NWAdmin (see Figure 5-4). It is a utility that you run on a Windows 95/98 or Windows NT workstation. From NetWare Administrator, you can do the following:

- Create NDS objects
- Modify the properties of existing NDS objects
- Delete NDS objects
- Search for objects by a particular property

Figure 5-4
NetWare
Administrator screen

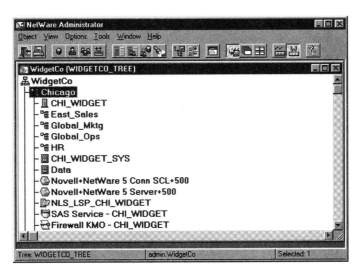

- Rename objects
- Create and manage NDS rights
- Create user templates
- Create user and workstation policies to be used in ZENworks
- Manage NetWare file services
- Extend the NDS schema

In this chapter, we discuss some of these capabilities. Others are covered in later chapters of this book.

The NetWare Administrator utility that ships with NetWare 5 (NWADMIN32.EXE) resides in the SYS:PUBLIC/WIN32 directory and is run from your Windows 95/98 or Windows NT workstation. The easiest way to access NetWare Administrator is to create a shortcut on your desktop. If you are using NDS for NT, NetWare Administrator was installed during the NDS for NT installation. After the installation is complete, you can easily access NetWare Administrator from the Start Menu (Start > Programs > Novell (Common) > NetWare Administrator). If you are using NDS for Solaris, you must install several Windows components on a Windows workstation. After you install these components, you also can access NetWare Administrator from the Start Menu (Start > Programs > Novell (Common) > NetWare Administrator) on a Windows 95/98 or Windows NT workstation.

Installing NetWare Administrator in a Windows NT-Only Environment

If you choose all options during the NDS for NT installation, NetWare Administrator is installed as part of the installation process. If you need to reinstall NetWare Administrator or if you skipped it during the initial installation, you can install it by completing the following steps:

1. Insert the NDS Corporate Edition CD-ROM.
2. Locate the NT directory.
3. Double-click SETUP.EXE.
4. Check the Install Management Utilities checkbox and then click Install.
5. Select the language you want and then click OK.
6. Click Next.
7. Click Yes to accept the license agreement.

8. Click Next to accept the default destination folder.

9. Click Next to accept the default program folder.

10. After reading the summary, click Next. It may take a while to copy all the necessary files.

11. Click Finish. ConsoleOne, NetWare Administrator, and NDS Manager are all installed.

You can access NetWare Administrator from the Start menu (`Start > Programs > Novell (Common) > NetWare Administrator`).

Installing NetWare Administrator in a Solaris-Only Environment

Because you cannot install NetWare Administrator directly on the Solaris server, you must install it on a Windows workstation. To set up a Windows workstation to run the latest version of ConsoleOne, you should complete the following steps:

1. Insert the NDS Corporate Edition CD-ROM on your Windows workstation.

2. In the Solaris directory, double-click `NDS8WIN.EXE`. This program expands all the necessary files you need to install ConsoleOne, NetWare Administrator, and NDS Manager on the Windows workstation. The installation defaults to the `C:\WINDOWS\TEMP` directory.

3. In the `C:\WINDOWS\TEMP` directory (or the specified directory you chose during installation), double-click `WINSETUP.EXE`.

4. Click the language you want to install.

5. Click Admin Utilities.

6. Click Next.

7. Click Yes to accept the license agreement.

8. Click Yes to install on the Windows workstation.

9. Click Next to accept the default destination folder.

10. Click Next to accept the default program folder.

11. Review the summary and click Next.

12. Click Finish.

NetWare Administrator and NDS Manager are installed. They can be accessed from the Start menu (`Start > Programs > Novell (Common) > NetWare Administrator`).

Creating and Managing NDS Objects

Each network resource or user in the NDS tree must be represented by an NDS object that corresponds to that type of object. For example, printers have a specific NDS NDPS Printer object that differs from NDS User objects. Some objects represent logical groups or roles. For example, you can create a Group object to group a set of users that need access rights to the same set of resources. You also can define specific roles and the resources that the particular role needs to access. Then you can assign one or more users to that role. And, you can even have NDS objects that represent specific services available on the network such as SAS or *Novell Licensing Services* (NLS).

Each object contains properties or pieces of information about the object. This information can be customized. For example, a User object contains the users first and last name, title, location, telephone number, employee identification number, email address, and so on (see Figure 5-5).

These properties also can be called attributes. They define the specifics of the object. Other objects have a different set of object properties. For example, Several objects also contain name and location like the User object, but they also contain other information not related to User objects, such as net address and status information (see Figure 5-6).

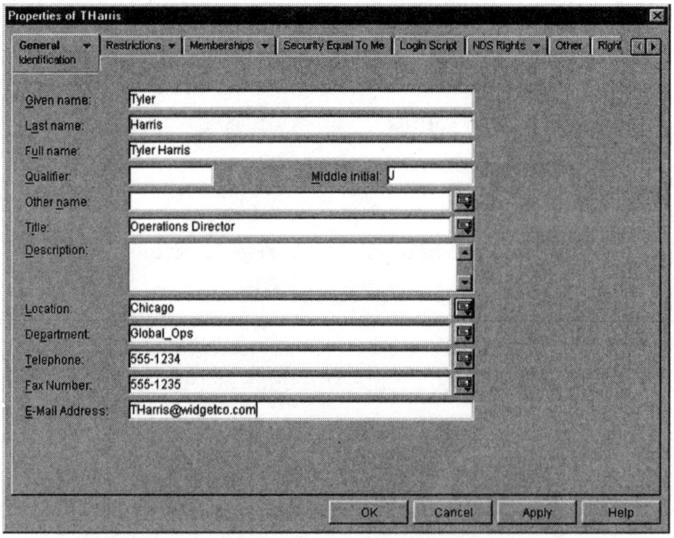

Figure 5-5

An NDS User object property page in ConsoleOne

Figure 5-6
A Server object
property page in
ConsoleOne

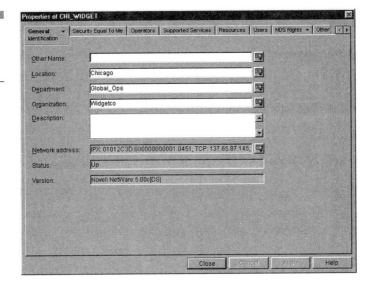

Understanding NDS Objects

NDS objects come in three classes:

- *Root object* Only one Root object exists, and it is located at the very top of the Directory tree.

- *Container object* Container objects hold other objects, such as users. For example, the Training Container object could hold the User objects for all the users who worked in the Training department. It could also hold all their Workstation objects, the Printer objects associated with the printers they use, and any other objects associated with network resources accessed by the Training department.

  Several types of container objects exist. You may or may not use all the container object types, depending on your Directory tree structure and on your company's size and structure.

  - *Country* (C) If you have a multinational company, you might want to use the Country container. You can have only one level of country objects, and these objects must reside directly below the Root of the Tree. These objects are named with a standard two-letter code such as US, UK, DK, or DE. The Country object is required only when connecting to certain X.500 global directories. If you do not need it to support X.500, you might consider using Organization objects instead to group your countries, because the Country object can contain only Organization objects.

- *Locality* (L)   Locality designates the location of a specific part of the network. For example, you might distinguish part of your US division as East or West. This object is always placed under the Country object. As with the Country object, you can achieve the same division by using Organization objects, which have more flexibility. This object is required by only X.500 specifications and is not necessary.

- *Organization* (O)   This object type is the most common container type in an NDS tree. You create an Organization object during the installation. You can also add other Organization objects at a peer level to represent geographical divisions in your organization. These objects are located under the Country object if available or directly under the Root if there is no Country object. You must have at least one Organization object.

- *Organizational Unit* (OU)   Most NDS trees also have Organizational Unit objects. These objects help you subdivide the NDS tree to represent divisions or departments within the company. You can create more than one level of Organizational Unit objects so that your tree structure more closely resembles your corporate structure. Organizational Unit objects then hold all the objects to which a specific division or department needs access, including User objects, Printer objects, Volumes, and Application objects. If your network is small, you probably do not need multiple levels of Organizational Unit objects. You may find that the Organization object is sufficient for your needs.

- *Licensed Product container*   Licensed Product containers are a special type of NDS Container object that are used with applications, which are using *Novell Licensing Services* (NLS) technology. At least one Licensed Product Container object is created when you install or create a license certificate from applications that are NLS-enabled. These containers then hold the specific licenses for these software applications. For example, you could have an NLS Licensed Product container object that holds all your NetWare licenses.

- *Leaf Objects* (CN)   Leaf objects are the most basic objects in NDS. They represent individual services, users, and resources available on the network. Leaf objects cannot contain other objects. Leaf objects are distinguished by the abbreviation CN, which stands for *Common Name* (this is required by X.500 specifications). New leaf objects are added to NDS all the time. Your company may purchase third-party software that adds types of leaf objects by extending the schema.

Using these three types of object classes, you should be able to represent your company's structure and layout an excellent organization for locating resources and users in the network. Table 5-1 describes the basic objects available in NDS.

Object Name	Description
Address Range	Defines a range of IP addresses used by DHCP.
Administrator Group	Represents a group of users who have access to DNS/DHCP Locator objects. Users in this object can use the DNS/DHCP Administrator utility to create and manage DNS and DHCP objects.
Alias	Points to the actual location of an object in the directory. Aliases enable you to place duplicate icons for the same object in several places in the tree so that the resources they represent can be accessed from a user's current context.
Application	Points to an application installed on the network. The Application object can be created and then associated with User objects or Container objects so that users in that container have access to the application. Using Application objects simplifies the tasks of assigning rights, customizing login scripts, and launching applications. The Application object is also used with ZENworks Application Launcher (discussed in Chapter 7, "Administering Workstations").
Application Folder	Contains several Application objects. Application folders are used with ZENworks Application Launcher (also discussed in Chapter 7).
Bindery object	Used when a Bindery object was upgraded but the object could not be converted to a corresponding NDS object.
Bindery queue	A print queue not located in the NDS tree (probably on a NetWare 3.x server). Having this object in the NDS tree means that you can manage the queue using NDS, even though it is not a part of your NDS tree.
Certificate Authority	Stores a certificate authority that is used in PKI security (discussed in Chapter 6, "Controlling Network Access").
Computer	Represents a computer on the network. The Computer object plays a significant role in ZENworks desktop management and workstation inventory.
Country	Represents the country where part or all of your company resides. This object is required only by X.500 specifications. If you do not need to meet these specifications, it is best not to use this object.

Table 5-1

Basic objects available in NDS

continues

Table 5-1

continued

Object Name	Description
DHCP Server	Represents a DHCP server. It contains a list of subnet ranges the server can service.
Directory Map	Points to a specific directory or path in the file system. It simplifies drive mapping and login scripts by reducing the complex file system paths to a single name.
Distribution List	Contains a list of email addresses used by your *Message Handling Services* (MHS).
DNS Resource Record Set	Represents an individual domain name in a DNS zone.
DNS Server	Represents a DNS server. It contains object properties like the server's IP address.
DNS/DHCP Group	Represents a group of DNS/DHCP servers.
DNS/DHCP Locator	Contains DNS/DHCP information such as DNS servers, global defaults, subnets, zones, DHCP options, and so on.
Group	Contains a list of all users associated with the group. These users are given the same set of rights to certain network resources.
IP Address	Represents an IP address used with a DNS/DHCP server.
Key Material	Stores server security information, such as a public key, private key certification, or a certificate chain, so that security applications can access the information.
LAN Area	Lists all servers that use the same WAN Traffic Policy.
LDAP Group	Contains configuration information for servers that provide NDS information to LDAP clients.
License	Stores a license for NLS-enabled applications or metered certificates.
License Catalog	Provides information about licenses on the network.
License Certificate	Represents a product license certificate and contains information about the application and its licenses, including the product name, version number, and how many licenses are available.
List	Contains a list of other objects (list members do not have security equivalence to the List object).
Locality	A container object that represents a location (optional and not recommended).
LSP Server	Contains information about a License Service Provider (part of NLS).

Object Name	Description
Message Routing Group	Represents a group of messaging servers that route email directly between them (used with MHS).
Metered Certificate	Records software usage.
NDPS Broker	Controls three NDPS printing services: *Resource Management Services* (RMS), *Event Notification Services* (ENS), and *Service Registry Service* (SRS).
NDPS Manager	Represents the software that controls all printer agents.
NDPS Printer	Provides information on an NDPS printer. You can stop and re-arrange print jobs from this object.
NetWare Server	Contains information about the NetWare Server.
Organization	Container object that represents an Organization.
Organizational Role	Represents a specific role in the company to which certain rights are assigned.
Organizational Unit	Container object that can form subdivisions under the Organization object to logically arrange your NDS database.
Policy Package	Contains information about ZENworks policy packages.
Print Queue	Represents a queue in queue-based printing.
Print Server	Contains information about Non-NDPS print servers used in queue-based printing.
Printer	Represents a printer attached to the network and used in queue-based printing.
Profile	Provides a login script that can be used by several User objects in the same container to simplify the login process.
Root	The highest object in the tree. It cannot be deleted.
Security Container	Contains all security objects.
SLP Directory Agent	Manages how services are advertised and located via SLP on the network.
Subnet Container	Contains configuration information that applies to all IP Addresses and Address Range objects in the Subnet container (DNS/DHCP).
Subnet Pool	Provides support for multiple subnets (DNS/DHCP)
Template	Defines characteristics common to all User objects created with the template.

continues

Table 5-1

continued

Object Name	Description
Unknown	Represents objects that the schema does not recognize. This may be because the objects were imported from an NDS schema that had been extended to include other objects.
User	Contains information on a specific network user, such as name, telephone number, location, and title.
Volume	Represents a NetWare volume.
Workstation	Contains information about workstations that were registered and imported into the NDS tree by ZENworks. These objects are used in desktop management, application management, and workstation inventory.
Zone	Contains the information about a DNS zone.

Creating and Managing NDS Objects with ConsoleOne

ConsoleOne has matured gracefully since its first inception as a Java utility that ran only on the NetWare 5 server. You can now create most basic types of objects with ConsoleOne, and it is much easier to manage object attributes than it was in previous versions.

NOTE: _Because ConsoleOne ships updates often, you will want to check out the latest version at_ www.novell.com/download.

Creating Objects in ConsoleOne   To create an object, you must complete the following steps:

1. Right-click the container in which you want to create the object.

2. Select New and then click the type of object you want to create.

   If you selected User, Group, or Organizational Unit, proceed to step 4. If you selected Object, proceed to step 3.

3. From the Object Class list, select the type of object you want to create and then click OK (see Figure 5-7).

4. In the Name field, enter a name for the object (see Figure 5-8).

Figure 5-7
Object list in
ConsoleOne

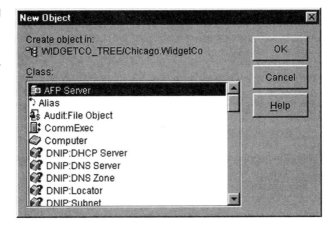

Figure 5-8
New User dialog box
in ConsoleOne

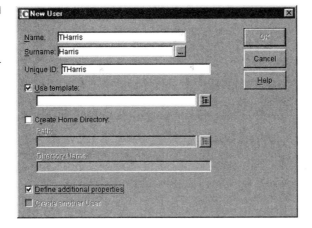

5. Specify any other information requested in the dialog box. Whether you have to specify other information besides the name depends on the type of object you are creating. You should enter as much information as possible about the object as possible.

6. If you have previously created templates for this type of object, click Use Template and specify which template to use.

TIP: *Creating templates for objects with similar properties saves time and ensures that the correct information is entered each time. For example, if all the users in a container have the same department name, post office box, and fax number, you can create a template that automatically adds that information to the User object.*

7. If you want to define additional properties, check the Define Additional Properties checkbox and then enter the information in this window.

8. After you are done adding information about the object, click OK.

Creating Template Objects in ConsoleOne Template objects are an excellent way to cut down on the time it takes to administer objects in NDS. A template provides a set of properties for created new user accounts. When a new object is created using the templates, the properties of the Template object are copied to the new User object. For example, if everyone in a specific department uses the same fax number, has the same postal address, the same group memberships, the same login time restrictions, and the same password restrictions, you can set these up in a template and use this template to create users. If you create User objects using the Template object feature, you can later make modifications to all the User objects created with this template instead of having to make changes on each User object. See Modifying Object Properties later in this section.

To create a template object, you must complete the following steps:

1. Right-click the container in which you want to create the object.

2. Select New and then click Object.

3. From the Object Class list, select Template, and then click OK.

4. Type the name of the template.

5. If you have already created a user or template that has most or all of the correct information, check the Use Template checkbox, and enter the object name.

TIP: *You might have created a user that has some but not all of the properties that you want to set up in the template. You can check the Define Additional Properties checkbox and modify these properties before saving the template.*

6. Check the Define Additional Properties checkbox and click OK.

7. Enter the information that you want to become a part of the template standard (see Figure 5-10). Remember that the more standard information you include here, the fewer times you will need to enter it in the future.

8. When you are finished entering template information, click Apply and then click Close.

Figure 5-9
Creating a new
template in
ConsoleOne

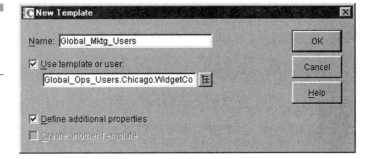

Figure 5-10
Template window
in ConsoleOne

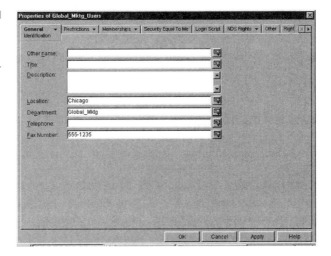

You can now use this template to supply standard information when creating new User objects.

Creating Group Objects in ConsoleOne After you have created several objects, you may need to group them so that you can apply rights and give them access to a set of resources. Group administration is a simple and easy way to cut down on your administration overhead. To create a Group object, complete the following steps:

1. Right-click the container where you want to create the Group and then click Group.

2. Type the name of the Group.

3. Check the Define Additional Properties checkbox and click OK.

4. Click the Members tab.

5. Click Add.

6. Select the objects you want to add to this group.

7. When you have finished selecting objects, click OK

8. Define additional properties as needed.

9. Click Apply and then click Close.

Locating Objects in the Directory Using ConsoleOne Sometimes once an object has been created, it is difficult to remember where it was created and where it is currently located. ConsoleOne makes it easy to locate objects. You can either search for objects by type, property, or name.

To find an object by its name, complete the following steps:

1. Browse to and select the container that you think holds the object.

2. Click anywhere in the right pane.

3. Start typing the object name. The letters appear in the lower righthand corner of the ConsoleOne screen. If you know the full name, you can type it or you can just type part of the name. If there is more than one object with the partial name, it will locate the first object.

4. Press Enter to jump to the object.

Or, if the object is in an NDS tree, you don't have to browse to the container first. You can use the Go To or Find command (see Figure 5-11). Just click the Edit menu and then click either Go To or Find. Type the object name and click OK.

NOTE: *Make sure that you have selected the correct container when searching for an object. In ConsoleOne, it is quite easy to select a container without even knowing that you have done so. If your search does not work, check to make sure that you have the intended container selected.*

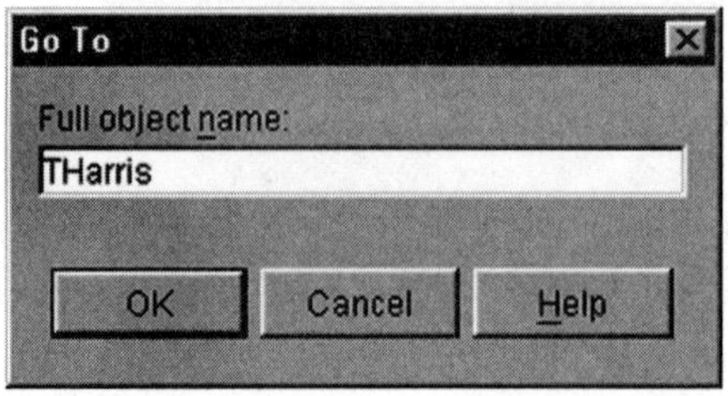

Figure 5-11
Go To window in
ConsoleOne

Go To

Full object name:

THarris

OK   Cancel   Help

If you have problems locating an object by its name, it might be because when the right pane contains more than 1,000 NDS objects, typing an object name finds the object only if it is the first type of object listed. For example, if you are trying to jump to a User object but several Group objects are at the top of the list, the system only searches the Group objects. This is due to a limitation in the JNDI Service Provider currently used by ConsoleOne. In this situation, it is more useful to do the following:

1. Click the Edit menu and then click Find (see Figure 5-12).

2. Enter information about the object such as its name, type, and the container where it is located.

3. Click Find.

TIP: *If you want to set up even more advanced search criteria, select Advanced from the Find Type drop box. You can now do more advanced boolean searches (see Figure 5-13).*

Modifying Object Properties After you have created objects, you might need to modify one or more of their properties. To modify an object's properties, complete the following steps:

1. Browse to and right-click the object and then click Properties (see Figure 5-14).

2. Edit the Property pages as needed.

3. When you are finished, click Apply to make the changes permanent.

Figure 5-12
Find window in
ConsoleOne

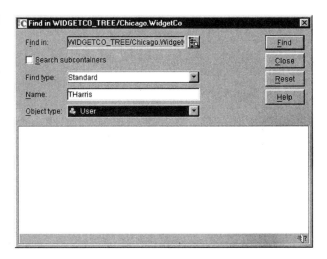

Figure 5-13
The Advanced Search
window in
ConsoleOne

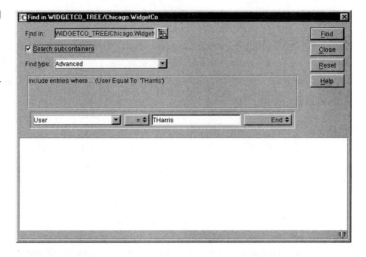

Figure 5-14
User Object
Properties page in
ConsoleOne

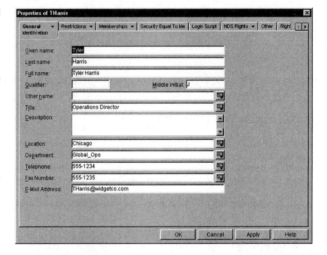

TIP: *One of the ways that ConsoleOne differs from NetWare
Administrator is how you access Properties. If you are used to using
NetWare Administrator, it might take you some time to locate properties in
ConsoleOne. Instead of being accessed from buttons on the right-hand side
of the screen, in ConsoleOne some Property pages are accessed by clicking a
down arrow on the tab that relates to that property page (see Figure 5-15).
You might not think to look there. For example, a user's home directory
information is located in the Environment section. Properties are found on
the same pages as in NetWare Administrator. However, the procedure for
finding these pages differs slightly.*

Figure 5-15
The down arrow on
the ConsoleOne
Property pages

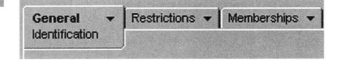

TIP: *Sometimes ConsoleOne has a problem accepting changes when the OK button is clicked instead of Apply. So, to be safe, always click Apply.*

4. Click Close to close the Property page.

You may sometimes need to modify the same properties on several objects of the same type. You can do this in several ways. You can modify multiple objects, a Group or Template object (so that it modifies the members of this object), or a container to modify its subordinate objects. To modify the properties of multiple objects, complete the following steps:

1. Select the objects you want to modify. You can Shift-click or Ctrl-click to select multiple objects of the same type; you can click a Group or Template object to modify its members; or you can click a Container object to modify its subordinates.

2. Click the File menu and then click Properties of Multiple Objects.

NOTE: *If you modify the Template object properties without selecting Properties of Multiple Objects, these changes apply only to objects created with the template after the change has been made. Objects created with the template prior to the change retain the previous properties.*

3. Select the type of object you want to modify and then click OK (see Figure 5-16).

4. Make sure that only the objects you want to modify are listed in the Objects to Modify window.

NOTE: *If objects appear that you do not want to modify, click Remove. If an object that you want to modify does not appear in the Objects to Modify window, click Add to add it. It will be modified with the group, but it will not be added to the group permanently. If you want to make this object a permanent member of the group or container, you will have to modify the original Container or Group object to add that object to the membership list.*

Figure 5-16
Multiple objects to
modify in
ConsoleOne

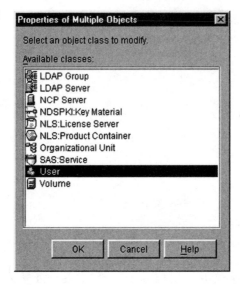

5. Specify the properties you want on the Property pages.

6. When you are finished setting the properties, click Apply.

7. Click Close.

Renaming Objects   In rare instances, you may need to rename an object. However, you should try not to do this in case this object is the member of a group or has an alias in another container. Changing names causes orphan objects and problems with membership lists. To rename an object, complete the following steps:

1. Browse to and right-click the object

2. Click Rename.

3. In the New Name field, type the new name.

4. Specify any other properties you want to change and then click OK.

TIP: If you think that other users will look for this object under its old name, click Save Old Name. This saves the old name as an unofficial value of the Name property and enables users to search for the object by its old name. You can view the old name in the Other Name field.

Deleting Objects   If you need to delete an object from the tree, complete the following steps:

1. Browse to and right-click the object.

2. Click Delete.

3. Click Yes.

Customizing ConsoleOne Views While you are working in ConsoleOne, you can customize the views in both the left and right pane in various ways. For example, you can adjust the column width in the right pane, or you can filter objects from view in the right pane. You can even reset the top object in the left pane so that if you often access a particular part of the NDS tree, you can start your ConsoleOne view there instead of at the Root. The one drawback is that all customizations to the left and right pane are lost when you exit ConsoleOne.

SETTING AN OBJECT AS THE TOP OBJECT IN THE LEFT PANE If you have a large network or you manage only one part of the network, you may want to set a different container object or other NDS object as the top object in the left pane. This makes it easier to navigate the NDS tree. If you want a different object to appear as the top object in the left pane, complete the following steps:

1. Click the object, such as a container object, that you want as the root in the left pane.

   This object is highlighted, and the objects that appear in the container are shown in the right pane (see Figure 5-17).

2. Click the Set As Root button.

Figure 5-17
Highlighted
container object
in ConsoleOne

This object now becomes the top object (see Figure 5-18), and an arrow appears so that you can still access the objects above it in the tree.

If you need to put My World back at the top of the left pane, just click the Show My World button (see Figure 5-19).

You can also right-click the arrow at the top of the left pane and then click Show My World.

FILTERING OBJECTS FROM THE RIGHT PANE Sometimes so many objects are in the Directory that you need a way to filter down to the objects you want to see. ConsoleOne enables you to filter objects by type or by name. To filter objects from the right pane, complete the following steps:

1. Click the View menu and then click Filter (see Figure 5-20).

2. To sort by object type, select the object types you want shown and deselect those you want hidden. If you want to filter by name, enter the name of the object. You can also use a wildcard pattern with an asterisk (*) to apply as a filter on the object names. For example, the wildcard pattern abc* filters out all objects but those names that start with "abc".

3. When you are done, click OK.

Figure 5-18
Container object in Set as Top object in ConsoleOne

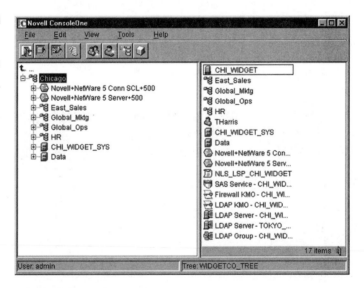

Figure 5-19
The Show My World button in ConsoleOne

Figure 5-20
Filter window in
ConsoleOne

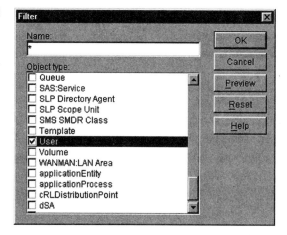

After you have set up the ConsoleOne environment to your liking, you can create, modify, delete, and rename NDS objects.

Creating and Managing NDS Objects with ConsoleOne Web Edition

ConsoleOne Web Edition is the perfect alternative for those times when you are not at a workstation that has ConsoleOne loaded and you need to make a quick change. If you have a browser, the URL to the ConsoleOne Web Edition, a valid username and password, and if you have the correct rights, you can use Web Edition. For example, you might be at a Macintosh workstation working with a user and need to reset the user's password. If the workstation has a browser, you can use ConsoleOne Web Edition.

Or, you can also assign a role to a specific user, who will modify only certain attributes of object information and enable them to access these objects through ConsoleOne Web Edition. For example, you might assign an administrative assistant to keep all the department phone numbers current. She can do this from the browser on her workstation using ConsoleOne Web Edition.

Accessing ConsoleOne Web Edition   To access ConsoleOne Web Edition from any browser, complete the following steps:

1. Enter the Web address for ConsoleOne in the browser. The address should be something like `https://webserverIPaddress:port/ConsoleOne` if your Web server has SSL enabled or `http://webserverIPaddress:port/ConsoleOne` if your Web server doesn't

have SSL enabled. If your Web server is using the default port, you can omit the port number.

2. On the welcome page, click the picture of the computer monitor (see Figure 5-21).

3. On the login page, enter your fully distinguished NDS username, your login password, and the name of the NDS tree you want to manage (see Figure 5-22).

4. Click Login.

You are now ready to administer the NDS tree from your Web browser. When navigating in ConsoleOne Web Edition, use only the buttons in the left and right frames. Do not use the Back and Forward buttons of your Web browser.

WARNING: *As a note of caution, do not leave the computer unattended. Even though this information is located in a browser, you will want to make sure it is secure. If you access Web Edition from a user's workstation, make sure that you log out and exit the browser before leaving the workstation. If you leave ConsoleOne Web Edition idle for more than 10 minutes, you will be prompted to log in again before continuing.*

Figure 5-21
The ConsoleOne
Web Edition
welcome page

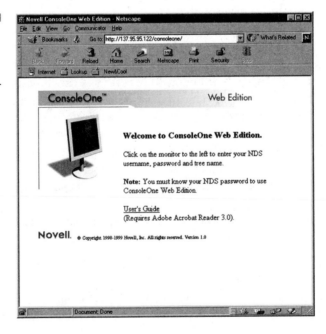

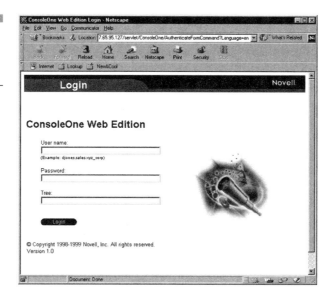

Creating Users in ConsoleOne Web Edition   Creating user accounts is quite limited in ConsoleOne Web Edition. You cannot set up all the properties that you can set in ConsoleOne or in NetWare Administrator. You can specify only the username, last name, and the container in which the user will be created. In later releases, you will be able to specify more properties.

To create a user in ConsoleOne Web Edition, complete the following steps:

1. Click Create User in the left pane (see Figure 5-23).

2. In the right pane, enter the container where the user will be created.

3. Enter the username.

4. Enter the user's last name.

TIP: If you are unsure if the username is being used or if you cannot remember the exact name of the container, you can search for this information in the middle pane.

5. Click Create.

You will receive confirmation that the user has been created. If you want to add information on other properties, you can modify the user information in Web Edition.

Figure 5-23
Create User page in
ConsoleOne Web
Edition

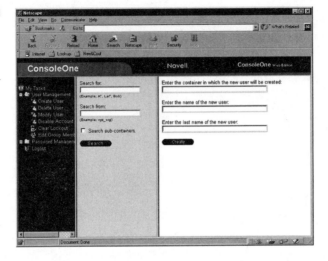

Figure 5-24
Modify User page in
ConsoleOne Web
Edition

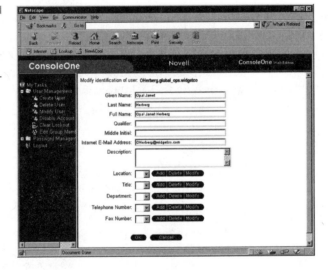

Modifying User Information in ConsoleOne Web Edition   Modifying
user information enables you to modify things like full name, given name,
middle name, email address, telephone number, and so forth. To modify a
user's information, complete the following steps:

1. Click Modify User.

2. Enter the name of the user to modify and then click OK (see Figure 5-
   24).

TIP: *The usernames in ConsoleOne Web Edition must be fully distinguished names. In other words, they must supply the entire context for the user. For example, you cannot just type msellers. You must type* msellers.training.nyc.widgetco.com *to get the correct user object. If you are not sure, use the search pane to search for the username and context.*

3. Modify the information in the right pane.

4. Click OK.

You will receive confirmation that the change has been made.

Deleting Users in ConsoleOne Web Edition   To delete a user account, complete the following steps:

1. Click Delete User in the left pane (see Figure 5-25).

2. Enter the username. Remember to use the complete context.

3. Click Delete.

You will receive confirmation that the user has been deleted.

Disabling User Accounts in ConsoleOne Web Edition   You may need to disable a user account. To do this, complete the following steps:

1. Click Disable Account in the left pane (see Figure 5-26).

Figure 5-25
Delete User page in ConsoleOne Web Edition

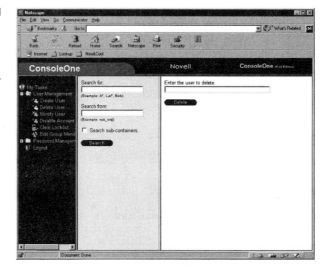

Figure 5-26
Disable Account
page in ConsoleOne
Web Edition

2. Enter the username in the right pane. Remember to use the complete context.

3. Click Disable.

You will receive confirmation that the user has been disabled.

Editing Group Membership in ConsoleOne Web Edition You can also edit group membership from ConsoleOne Web Edition.

To add a user to a group, complete the following steps:

1. Click Edit Group Membership in the left pane.

2. Enter the username in the right pane. Remember to use the complete context.

3. Click OK. The group memberships for that user are displayed (see Figure 5-27).

4. Click Add.

5. Enter the name of the group in the right pane. Remember to use the full context.

6. Click Add.

7. You will receive confirmation that the change has occurred; then click Continue. You can now edit other group memberships for this user.

8. When you are done changing group memberships, click Done.

Figure 5-27
Edit Group
Membership page in
ConsoleOne Web
Edition

To delete a user from a group, complete the following steps.

1. Click Edit Group Membership in the left pane.
2. Enter the username in the right pane. Remember to use the complete context.
3. Click OK. The group memberships for that user are displayed.
4. Click the group from which you want to delete the user.
5. Click Delete.
6. Click Delete again to confirm that you want to delete this user.
7. You will receive confirmation that the change has occurred; then click Continue. You can now edit other group memberships for this user.
8. When you are done changing group memberships, click Done.

Although ConsoleOne Web Edition is a huge step in the right direction, it still needs some refining and development. In the future, its capabilities will be expanded, and it will become quite useful for role-based administration. You can assign certain users the rights to administer certain objects, and they will be able to administer them from a browser using ConsoleOne Web Edition. For now, it is a good tool to use if you are at a user's workstation and they have forgotten their password and need to have it reset. Information on Managing Passwords with ConsoleOne Web Edition is available in Chapter 6, "Controlling Network Access."

Creating and Managing NDS Objects with NetWare Administrator

NetWare Administrator has long been the standard tool for administering NDS. Even though it is slated to be replaced by ConsoleOne, you will need to use it to configure many objects in NDS. Development on ConsoleOne snap-ins continues but lags behind all the snap-ins currently available for NetWare Administrator. For example, the snap-ins for GroupWise administration will be available with the GroupWise 5.5 Enhancement Pack. However, as with general NDS administration, only a subset of the tasks available in NetWare Administrator will be provided in this first release of snap-ins. Over time, and as the number of snap-ins increases, NetWare Administrator will become more obsolete. But, for now, you need to use both tools.

TIP: *Several of the objects that cannot be created in ConsoleOne can still be administered in ConsoleOne after they have been created with NetWare Administrator. For example, even though you cannot create ZENworks Policy Packages in ConsoleOne, you can administer them after they are created. If you have already created these objects in your NDS tree, you might not need to use NetWare Administrator as often.*

Creating an Object in NetWare Administrator   Creating an object in NetWare Administrator is easy. To create an object, complete the following steps:

1. Start NetWare Administrator. NetWare Administrator is located in the Sys/Public/Win32 directory.

2. Right-click on the container where you want the new user created and then click Create.

3. In the Class of new Object list, select the type of object you want to create (see Figure 5-28).

4. Click OK.

5. Enter a name for the object.

6. If you want to use a template to create the user information, check the Use template checkbox and select the template.

7. Specify any other information requested in the dialog box. Whether you have to specify other information besides the name depends on the type of object you are creating. You should enter as much information about the object as possible.

Figure 5-28
New Object list
in NetWare
Administrator

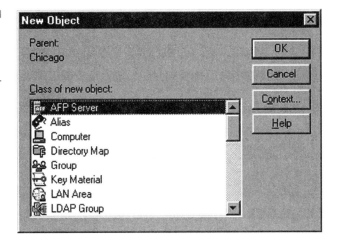

NOTE: *Templates are useful for information, such as department fax numbers, that may be common for many users. For more information on creating templates, see the following section.*

8. Click OK to create the object.

You can now view the new object in the NDS tree in the container you selected. You can assign specific rights to the user and customize access to network resources.

Creating Templates in NetWare Administrator   Creating templates is an excellent way to cut down on the time it takes to administer objects in NDS. A template provides a base set of properties and setup procedures for created user accounts. When a new object is created using the templates, the properties of the Template object are copied to the new User object. For example, if everyone in a specific department uses the same fax number, has the same postal address, the same group memberships, the same login time restrictions, and the same password restrictions, you can set these up in a template and use this template to create users. Also, if you need to modify properties of several User objects that you previously created with templates, you can modify them once, and the properties are updated. See "Modifying Objects in NetWare Administrator" in the next section.

NOTE: *You cannot use templates to apply new properties to existing accounts.*

To create an object in NetWare Administrator, complete the following steps:

1. Right-click the container where you want to create the template and then click Create.

2. From the Object Class list, select the Template object, and then click OK.

3. Type the name of the template (see Figure 5-29).

4. If you have already created a user or template that has most or all of the correct information, check the Use Template checkbox and enter the object name.

TIP: *You might have created a user that has some but not all of the properties that you want to set up in the template. You can check the Define Additional Properties checkbox and modify these properties before saving the template.*

5. Check the Define Additional Properties checkbox and click Create.

6. Enter the information that you want to become a part of the template standard (see Figure 5-30). Remember that the more standard information you include here, the fewer times you will need to enter it in the future.

7. When you are finished entering template information, click OK.

You can now use this template to supply standard information when creating new User objects.

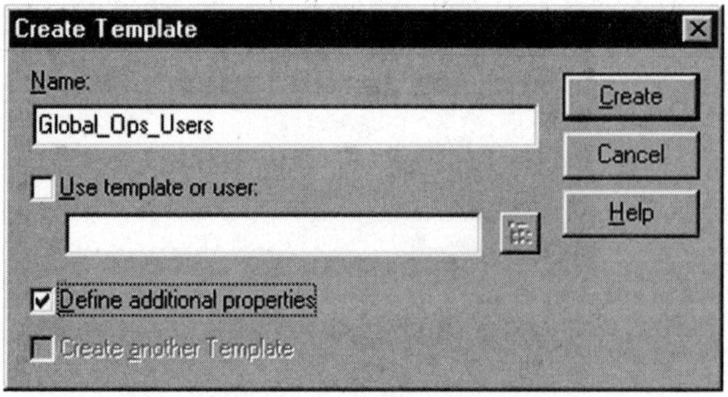

Figure 5-29
Create Template window in NetWare Administrator

> **Create Template** ☒
>
> <u>N</u>ame:
> `Global_Ops_Users`   [<u>C</u>reate]
>   [Cancel]
> ☐ <u>U</u>se template or user:
> `_____` 🔲 [<u>H</u>elp]
>
> ☑ <u>D</u>efine additional properties
> ☐ Create another Template

Figure 5-30

Template window in NetWare Administrator

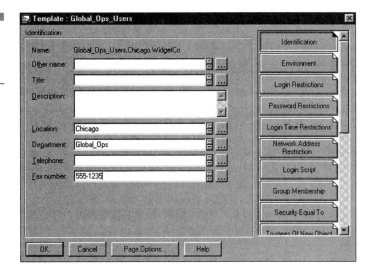

Creating Group Objects in NetWare Administrator After you have created several objects, you may need to group them so that you can apply rights and give them access to a set of resources. Group administration is a simple and easy way to cut down on your administration overhead. To create a Group object, complete the following steps:

1. Right-click the container where you want to create the Group and then click Create.
2. Select the Group object and then click Create.
3. Type the name of the Group.
4. Check the Define Additional Properties checkbox and click OK.
5. Click the Members tab.
6. Click Add.
7. Select the objects you want to add to this group.
8. When you have finished selecting objects, click OK
9. Define additional properties as needed.
10. Click OK.

Modifying Objects in NetWare Administrator After you have created objects, you might need to modify one or more of their properties. To modify an object's properties, complete the following steps:

1. Browse to and right-click the object and then click Details (see Figure 5-31).

Figure 5-31
User Object
properties page in
NetWare
Administrator

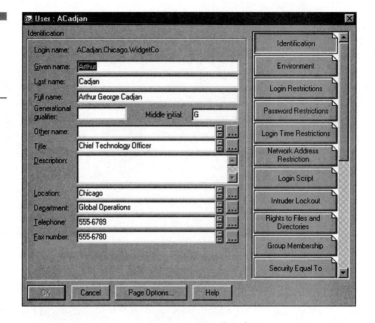

2. Edit the Property pages as needed.

3. When you are finished, click OK to make the changes permanent.

You may need to modify the same properties on several objects of the same type. You can do this in several ways. You can modify multiple objects, a Group or Template object (so that it modifies the members of this object), or a container to modify its subordinate objects. To modify the properties of multiple objects, complete the following steps:

1. Select the objects you want to modify. You can Shift-click or Ctrl-click to select multiple objects of the same type; you also can click a Group or Template object to modify its members; or you can click a Container object to modify its subordinates.

2. Click the Object menu and then click Details on Multiple Objects (see Figure 5-32).

NOTE: *If you modify the Template object properties without selecting Details of Multiple Objects, these changes apply only to objects created with the template after the change has been made. Objects created with the template prior to the change retain the previous properties.*

3. Make the changes to the properties and click OK.

Figure 5-32
Details on Multiple
Users page in
NetWare
Administrator

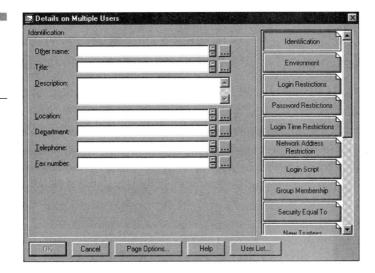

4. Click OK to confirm that you understand this operation may take some time.

If you are modifying a Group object and you do not want all members of that group to receive the changes, you can exclude members of the Group object from receiving the changes without deleting them from the group. If you want some users to have the same changes, but they do not belong to this Group object, you can add them to the list, and then changes will occur in their properties as well. Properties will be modified with the group, but the User object will not be added to the group permanently. If you want to make this object a permanent member of the group or container, you have to modify the original container or Group object to add that object to the membership list.

To change the users in the Group that will receive the modified property rights, complete the following steps:

1. Click the Group object whose properties you want to modify.

2. Click the Object menu and then click Details on Multiple Users.

3. Click User List (see Figure 5-33).

4. Modify the list of User objects that will receive these changes. You can add or remove User objects for the purposes of this property modification. This does not mean that these users are added to or deleted from this Group object permanently.

5. When you are finished modifying the list, click OK.

Figure 5-33
User List in Details
on Multiple Users
window

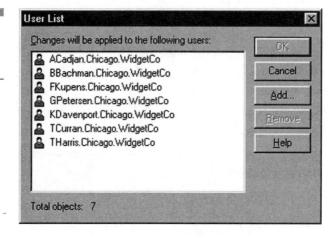

6. Make the necessary changes to the properties and then click OK.

7. Click OK to confirm that you understand this operation may take some time.

Renaming Objects   You may need to rename an object. However, you should try not to do this in case this object is the member of a group or has an alias in another container. Changing names causes orphan objects and problems with membership lists. These objects might also have subordinate or external references that would be broken if the name was changed. More information on subordinate and external references is located in Chapter 10, "Other NDS Administration Tools." If you have considered these problems and still need to rename an object, complete the following steps:

1. Click the object.

2. Click the Object menu and then click Rename.

3. In the New Name field, type the new name.

TIP: If you think that other users will look for this object under its old name, click Save Old Name. This saves the old name as an unofficial value of the Name property and enables users to search for the object by its old name. You can view the old name in the Other Name field.

4. Click OK.

Deleting Objects   If you need to delete an object from the tree, complete the following steps:

1. Browse to and right-click the object.
2. Click Delete.
3. Click Yes.

Creating NDS Objects with UIMPORT

You may want to use UIMPORT to create NDS objects. UIMPORT is a DOS-based utility that enables you to take an existing database of user information that you want to import to NDS and create NDS objects. As long as you can create a delimited ASCII text file, you can use UIMPORT to import user data. UIMPORT is not the easiest tool to use to create User objects. It cannot put information in to the User object that does not already exist in the database file. You may have to go back and add user information later. If this is the case, you might try modifying the properties of multiple objects at once to save yourself the headache of opening and modifying each object. To use UIMPORT, you must do the following:

- Create a user information delimited database file from an existing database of user information.
- Create a control file to specify the format and field sequence for the data you are importing.
- Set certain parameters to restrict whether UIMPORT creates user objects or just updates existing NDS objects.
- Specify the context into which these user objects will be created in the Tree.

Novell documentation provides information on creating User objects using the UIMPORT utility. For more information on using UIMPORT, see NetWare 5 documentation Reference set the Novell documentation Web site at www.novell.com/documentation. After you have located the Utilities Reference Set, search for UIMPORT in the left pane.

Creating NDS Objects with BULKLOAD

NetWare 5 also has a new utility called BULKLOAD.NLM that enables you to create, modify, and/or delete NDS objects in a batch process. It uses *LDAP Directory Interchange Format* (LDIF) files for batch processing.

NOTE: *The performance of* BULKLOAD *is affected considerably by cache size (more is faster). You can set the cache size by typing*

```
SET DSTRACE = !m[hexadecimal KB]
```

or

```
SET DSTRACE = !mb[bytes]
```

at the server console. The smallest tested cache size is 0 and the largest is 2G.

To use BULKLOAD.NLM, you must have already created your LDIF file. After you have created the LDIF file, do the following:

1. Copy the LDIF file to the SYS:SYSTEM directory of a server running NDS.

2. At the server console, type BULKLOAD.NLM.

3. When prompted, log in as a user with Admin rights.

4. Select Apply LDIF File to run the batch process.

If any errors occur, they are written to a log file named after the LDIF file. For instance, if the LDIF file is NEWEMPLY.LDIF, the log file will be NEWEMPLY.LOG. Additional instructions and specifications on LDIF and BULKLOAD.NLM are available from the Novell Documentation Web site at www.novell.com\documentation.

SUMMARY

The most time-consuming thing you will do as a network administrator is manage network resources and users. It is by far the highest cost in owning a network. NDS eliminates the need for redundant administration by providing a single point of administration for your entire enterprise. With NDS, you will need to use either a Java or Windows administrative tool—ConsoleOne or NetWare Administrator.

NDS enables you to centralize management of your network and avoid redundancy of management tasks so that you can:

- Eliminate redundancies of managing services.
- Realize time/management efficiencies by using directory-aware applications that leverage directory services.

■ Centralize authentication and authorization for applications and services.

■ Implement policy-based management to simplify distribution of network privileges (discussed in Chapter 6).

To take advantage of the administrative benefits of NDS, you must create NDS objects that represent the network resources and users you want to manage in the Directory. These objects contain specific information about resources or users. NDS also contains different types of logical or organizational objects that enable you to group users into Groups that can then have specific rights assigned to them. Other objects also enable you to create policies that can be applied to specific workstations, operating systems, or users to enforce standard network or desktop software or environments

You can use either ConsoleOne or NetWare Administrator to manage your NDS tree. NetWare Administrator has been the NDS administrative tool of choice since NDS was first shipped. But, with the release of NetWare 5, Novell has also created a new Java-based utility called ConsoleOne, which will replace NetWare Administrator as the administrative utility of choice in the future. For now, you probably will need to use both programs since each utility currently has some functionality not found in the other. Whenever possible, this book will show how to use ConsoleOne to complete a task. When it is necessary to use NetWare Administrator, we will use it instead.

Managing NDS Security

This chapter builds on the introductory information provided in Chapter 2, "Designing NDS," by describing the tools and methods available for implementing security throughout your NDS environment. One of the most important features promised by NDS is the capability to centralize the authentication of users to the network environment and the control of access to all network resources under the NDS umbrella. A thorough understanding of the access control features of NDS, together with an understanding of how they interact and how they can be managed, will go a long way in helping the administrative staff create a stable NDS environment.

First, we describe the relatively new cryptographic infrastructure Novell has built into NDS as well as the tools necessary to manage that security environment on NetWare, Windows NT, and Solaris. Then we will look at the installation and configuration of the various protocols that can be used to communicate with NDS, both internally and externally. Finally, we will discuss the specific issues surrounding authentication and authorization within the NDS infrastructure and present the tools that will enable you to assemble a coherent security strategy.

NDS Security Services

With the release of NetWare 5, Novell introduced a new set of security components that serve as the foundation for a whole new breed of NDS security. The most basic of these features already have been released, and many more exciting enhancements to NDS authentication and authorization techniques are coming down the road. The following sections describe the major components of the NDS security services.

Novell International Cryptographic Infrastructure

The *Novell International Cryptographic Infrastructure* (NICI) provides the cryptographic foundation for NDS security. It is installed on all three platforms as part of NDS. The NDS license disk contains the NICI Foundation Key. The NICI Foundation Key, as its name implies, provides the foundation for all cryptographic keys and certificates that will be created under your NDS tree. Novell maintains a B3-rated secure system that churns out the key pairs distributed with NDS licenses. These keys form the basis for subsequent tree and server keys that will be used to configure your own PKI.

Installing NICI on NetWare   One of the options during the latter stages of the NetWare 5 server installation is to install NICI v1.0. This option installs the initial release of NICI that shipped as part of NetWare 5. An update to NICI v1.0 was released in February, 1999. If you are upgrading the version of NDS on the NetWare 5 platform, upgrade NICI prior to the installation of the NDS software to have access to the latest functionality. The latest version of the NICI update includes NICI v1.31 and is available from the Web site at `www.novell.com/products/cryptography/`. You should check this site periodically and watch for future updates.

The download process for NICI updates is a little odd so it has been included here for reference:

1. From the `/cryptography` URL mentioned, select either the Worldwide or the US/Canada version of NICI. This selection determines the cryptographic strength of the crypto-engine used by NICI. The U.S. Department of Commerce has restricted the export of cryptographic technology stronger than 56-bit. The 128-bit version available for use in the United States and Canada can be exported only under special license from the Department of Commerce.

2. Page down and click Proceed to Download.

3. Click I Accept at the bottom of the Strong Encryption Software Eligibility Declaration.

4. Fill in your vital statistics and click Click Here to Submit Your Order.

5. After a brief wait, you order will be accepted. Then page down and click Click Here.

6. A Save File dialog box will pop up. Select the desired directory and save the file to a local directory. This process will save the SmartCert utility to your local directory. SmartCert is a secure download tool used to protect the transfer of the NICI update utility. This type of protection is required due to the export-restricted nature of NICI.

7. Run SmartCert. A new download utility will start and tell you what you are about to download. See Figure 6-1. Click Download.

8. Review the licensing agreement and click Accept Terms.

9. Select the directory where you want to store the NICI update file and click OK. The NICI update will be saved to the specified directory.

10. You will get a Successful Download message when the transfer is complete. You will be asked whether you want to run the extraction utility now. The update file—`NICI-U?` for the U.S./Canada version or `NICI-W?` for the worldwide version, where ? is a number—is a self-

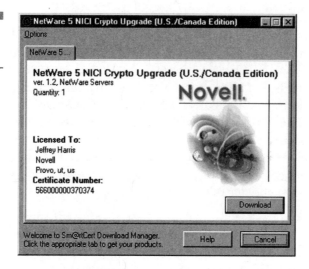

Figure 6-1
SmartCert download screen

extracting ZIP file you can extract at any time. Extract the file to a file server directory for safekeeping.

11. After the file has been extracted, the NICI update can be applied via the NetWare 5 NWCONFIG utility—either from the server console or remotely via RCONSOLE. You will need to restart the server after the update, so time your update accordingly.

After the NICI update has been applied, you are ready to update the NetWare 5 version of NDS. This version of NICI provides support for ephemeral keys, which are required for specific types of *Secure Sockets Layer* (SSL) operations. Ephemeral keys are short-term session keys generated by the server to support SSL sessions with clients that may not support the same cryptographic strength as the server. For example, a U.S./Canada strong cryptographic server connects with an International grade cryptographic client.

Installing NICI on NT Because NDS for NT was created as a self-contained unit, the current version of NICI is installed by default when NDS for NT is first installed. All you have to do is supply the NICI Foundation Key—on the NDS license disk—when prompted for it during the NDS installation program. See Chapter 3, "Installing and Upgrading NDS," for more information on installing NDS for NT.

Installing NICI on Solaris Because NDS for Solaris was created as a self-contained unit, the current version of NICI is installed by default when NDS for Solaris is first installed. All you have to do is supply the NICI

Foundation Key—on the NDS license disk—when prompted for it during the NDS installation program. See Chapter 3, "Installing and Upgrading NDS," for more information on installing NDS for Solaris.

Public Key Infrastructure Services

After NICI has been installed, we are ready to start adding security services to NDS. The first of these is *Public Key Infrastructure Services* (PKIS). As mentioned in Chapter 2, "Designing NDS," PKIS gives NDS the capability to function as a PKI Certificate Authority. PKIS is an installation option when installing NDS on all three currently supported NDS platforms. For information on the NDS installation process, refer to Chapter 3.

After PKIS has been installed, it needs to be configured as a Certificate Authority. A few things need to be done to make this happen:

- Install a tree *Certificate Authority* (CA)
- Install Server Certificates, also known as *Key Material Objects* (KMO)
- Export tree certificate to browsers for use in establishing SSL connections to the NDS server.

Creating the Tree CA   After NICI and PKIS have been installed, load ConsoleOne, and you will see a Security container off the [Root] of the NDS tree.

The Tree CA will be created within the Security object. To do this, complete the following steps:

1. Right-click on the Security object and select New and then Object (see Figure 6-2).

Figure 6-2
Object creation options in Security object

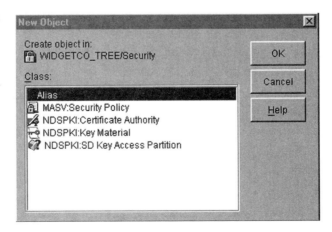

NOTE: *You will note a couple of objects in the list that will not be discussed much in this book. The first is the MASV: Security Policy object. Mandatory Access Control Services (MASV) exists to support Graded Authentication (GA) features within NDS. However, because Novell has yet to release a GA product, no management tools are associated with MASV objects.*

The second object is the Key Access Partition (KAP). The KAP contains a copy of the Partition Key object—shown as WO in Figure 6-2. The partition key is distributed to each server onto which PKIS or Single Sign-On Services (SSOS) is installed. The partition key is used to encrypt sensitive user authentication materials. Because each PKIS and SSOS server uses the same partition key, it doesn't matter which server a user attaches to on any given day. Their authentication secrets and private keys will always be accessible.

2. Select the Certificate Authority icon and click OK. This brings up the wizard that will walk you through the creation of the Tree CA.

3. First select the server that will host the Tree CA. The server you specify will hold the Tree CA cryptographic keys. In most cases, it makes sense to place these keys on a server that is in a central location. WidgetCo has chosen, in Figure 6-3, to put the Tree CA on a server in Chicago because that is the corporate headquarters.

Figure 6-3
Creating a Certificate
Authority object

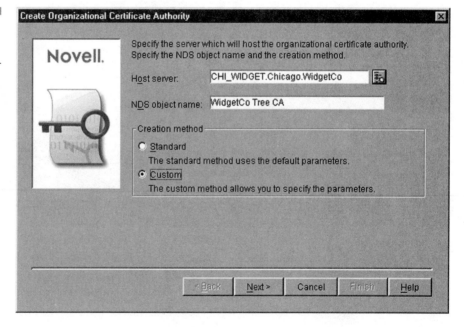

4. Specify the name of the Tree CA object and select either a Standard or Custom creation method; then click Next. The standard option won't ask for any more information—it will just apply default values to each of the Tree CA properties. To examine each of the Tree CA options, we will walk through the Custom installation process.

5. Specify the size of the Tree CA cryptographic key pair, as shown in Figure 6-4, and then click Next. Here, larger is better because it is harder to crack. However, any key size more than 512 bits is export restricted, so only the U.S./Canada version enables you to select key sizes higher than that.

NOTE: *Don't confuse the key sizes listed here with the 56- and 128-bit key sizes we are used to seeing in client applications, such as Internet browsers. The strength associated with any given key size is dependent upon the underlying cryptographic algorithm. Those smaller keys are used with secret key—or symmetric—cryptography, and 128-bits offer extremely strong protection.*

The 2048-bit key we are selecting here is used with public key— or asymmetric—cryptography that, because of the underlying algorithm, requires a much larger key to offer the same level of

Figure 6-4

Selecting the Tree CA key size

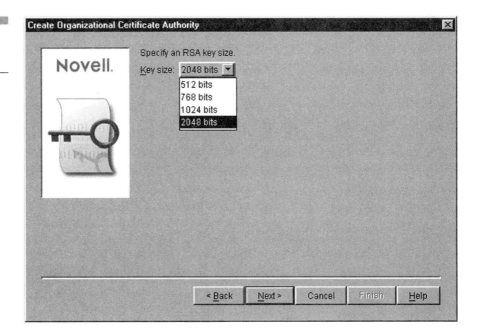

protection. Generally, a 1024-bit asymmetric key is judged to be of equivalent strength to a 128-bit symmetric key.

Because this key size is dependent upon the version of NICI that is installed, PKIS will query NICI on the server you have chosen to see what key sizes it will support. Default for the U.S./Canada version is 2048 bits.

6. Provide the following certificate parameters: Subject Name, Encryption and Hash algorithms, and Certificate Lifespan (see Figure 6-5). Then click Next. These parameters are used when generating the X.509 public key certificate that will be created for the Tree CA.

The Subject Name specified here will be entered in the Subject line of the public key certificate. The default is the name of your NDS tree, but you can put anything here that you would like. The important thing is that the resulting certificate has a unique subject line. You may want to consider adding a country value to the subject name. The country selection is useful if you are concerned with maintaining compatibility with X.500 directory-naming standards. Some external directories and applications may require X.500 naming, so including the country information is not a bad idea.

The encryption and hash algorithms are used to create the signature for your Tree CA. At this time, RSA is the only encryption algorithm

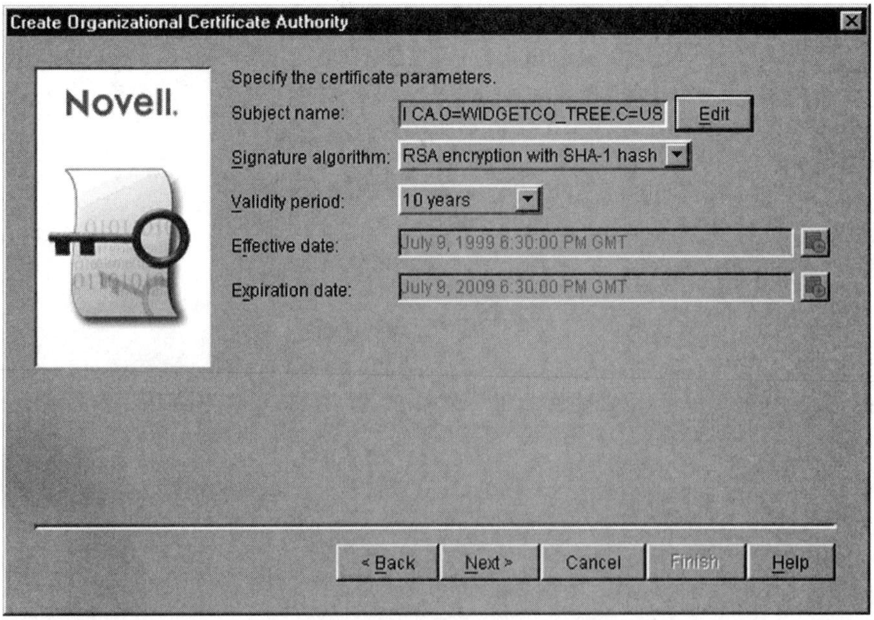

Figure 6-5
Tree CA certificate parameters

Create Organizational Certificate Authority

Novell.

Specify the certificate parameters.

Subject name:	I CA.O=WIDGETCO_TREE.C=US Edit
Signature algorithm:	RSA encryption with SHA-1 hash
Validity period:	10 years
Effective date:	July 9, 1999 6:30:00 PM GMT
Expiration date:	July 9, 2009 6:30:00 PM GMT

< Back   Next >   Cancel   Finish   Help

supported by NICI, but in the future, more encryption mechanisms may exist to be selected in this area.

The hash signature is the most important part of the Tree CA certificate. A hash function is a mathematical algorithm that creates a fixed-length fingerprint of some block of data—regardless of the length of that block of data. This fingerprint—known as the hash digest—is appended to the message before it is sent. Upon receipt, the hash digest can be recalculated using the same hash algorithm. If the resulting hash value is the same, then the message has not been modified during transmission.

NOTE: *MD5 and SHA-1 are the most popular hash functions currently used in PKI systems. SHA-1 is the default selection. Some say that SHA-1 has a lower collision rate than MD5—meaning that two different data strings are less likely to hash to the same digest value. At any rate, unless you are really plugged in to the world of cryptography and have a specific reason for changing this value, the default selection is probably the way to go.*

The certificate lifespan determines the amount of time that this certificate will be valid. The default is 10 years. You can also choose to specify a specific effective date and expiration date, if so desired. The value you select here is a compromise between the degree of assurance you want—where a shorter time period is better—versus the effort required to update all the entities that are making use of the Tree CA certificate.

After the certificate expires and is recreated, or renewed, it will again have to be exported to all applications that use the Tree CA certificate. In addition, the Server certificates will need to be re-signed using the new Tree CA certificate in order to remain valid. Because the whole PKI structure of the NDS tree is built upon this certificate, replacing it can entail a significant amount of overhead.

7. Review the summary information for accuracy and click Finish (see Figure 6-6). This summary will outline the selections you have made in order to create the Tree CA certificate.

At this point, NICI will generate the cryptographic key pair of the length specified and generate a Tree CA public key certificate.

The resulting certificate is created under the Security object in NDS. To view it, double-click the Security object and then double-click the Tree CA object itself. When the certificate object is open, a lot of information is

Figure 6-6

Tree CA details
summary

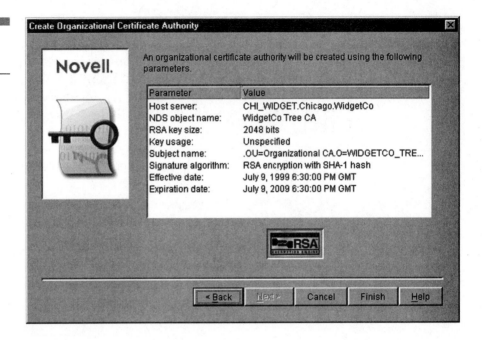

available. Fortunately, most of it is simply informational, because an attempt to decipher some of the entries would be pretty involved. However, a few details are interesting:

■ Click the Certificates tab and select Public Key Certificate. The Issuer Name field identifies the signer of the Tree CA certificate. In this case the Machine-Unique CA signs it (see Figure 6-7). The Machine-Unique CA is created when NDS is installed on a server. The Machine-Unique CA was signed, in turn, by the NICI Licensed CA. The private key for the NICI Licensed CA ships on the NDS license disk from Novell. You can see what is happening here. The degree of assurance associated with a PKI comes from a hierarchy of Certificate Authorities—each signed by its superior—that traces back to some Root Certificate Authority. The Root CA is self-signed because it comprises the first CA in the chain. It is theoretically possible to trace up the certificate chain and identify each CA that participates. A user or organization then can examine the participating CAs and decide whether or not to trust certificates spawned from this chain.

Proponents of PKI believe that vertical industries, such as banking or insurance, will unite to create a common Root CA that is trusted by all participants. These Trusted Roots will allow trusted PKI systems to operate across organizational boundaries. The tricky part of this process

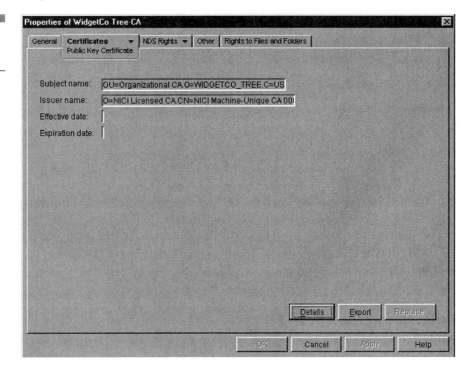

Figure 6-7
Tree CA certificate issuers

is defining the degree of liability that each link in the certificate chain must bear if some problem should arise under that CA's area of influence.

Companies like Verisign, Entrust, Novell, or even national governments are most likely not the organizations that will need to function as Trusted Roots. These organizations likely will aid in the establishment of a common PKI but lack the worldwide support and/or financial means necessary to become a Trusted Root. Most expect that Trusted Root(s) will have to arise from the Banking and Financial institutions, in whom we already place a great deal of trust. Only those types of organizations will inspire a sufficient level of trust in those who will be using certificates for critical electronic transactions. The Novell certificate hierarchy (see Figure 6-7) is there to serve as a hierarchy for creating organizational PKI, not for uniting the world under a universal Trusted Root.

■ Note that there is a difference between the Issuer of a key pair and the signer of the public key certificate. The key issuer determines the strength and level of confidence associated with the cryptographic keys themselves. The certificate signer, on the other hand, is responsible for verifying that the public key contained within the certificate actually belongs to the entity described by the certificate. The certificate signer makes no comment about the strength of the key itself, the signer purports only to identify the key's owner.

- The Export button is used to export the Tree CA certificate. This certificate is used by clients to validate the whole certificate chain, rather than just a given server certificate. The Tree CA certificate can be exported in standard DER or B64 formats. The certificate then is imported into any browser or application that needs it.

- To see the X.509 certificate information, click Details on the Public Key Certificate page. Then select the X.509 Certificate tab (see Figure 6-8). The X.509 certificate includes all the information we specified while creating the Tree CA.

- Click Extensions in the Certificate Details page. Then highlight the Novell Security Attributes entry and click Details. This page lists Novell-specific attribute extensions that provide more specific information regarding key strength, cryptographic module strength, and process quality (see Figure 6-9). This is more information that can be used to judge the level of assurance that should be associated with this particular certificate.

Figure 6-8

Tree CA X.509 certificate

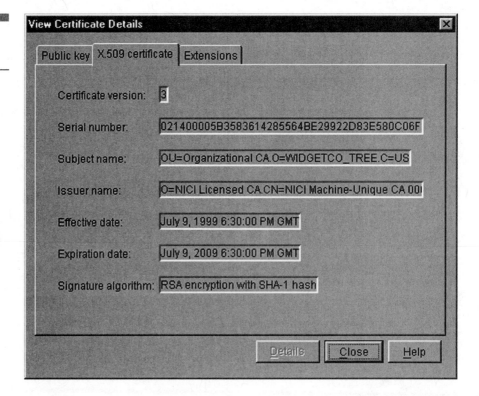

View Certificate Details		
Public key	X.509 certificate	Extensions

Certificate version: 3

Serial number: 021400005B3583614285564BE29922D83E580C06F

Subject name: OU=Organizational CA.O=WIDGETCO_TREE.C=US

Issuer name: O=NICI Licensed CA.CN=NICI Machine-Unique CA 00I

Effective date: July 9, 1999 6:30:00 PM GMT

Expiration date: July 9, 2009 6:30:00 PM GMT

Signature algorithm: RSA encryption with SHA-1 hash

Details   Close   Help

Figure 6-9
Novell Security
attributes

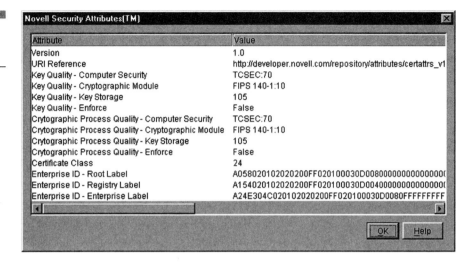

At the bottom of the list, you will note three Enterprise ID entries. The Enterprise ID is Novell's solution to the problem of assigning responsibility in a CA hierarchy. Enterprise IDs are still in the development stage at this time so they are seldom used.

Creating the Server Certificate   Now that the Tree CA is created, you are ready to create another link in the certificate hierarchy—the server certificate. The server certificate is referred to as the *Key Material Object* (KMO) in NDS. The KMO is primarily used in securing server communications through SSL. Novell expects that the use of server certificates will grow as new features are added to Novell's security services.

The KMO is like a personal check you write for groceries. The cashier often will ask for proof of identity in the form of a driver's license. The driver's license symbolizes the due diligence that your state's government has gone through to positively identify you. In the same way, the Tree CA certificate is used to sign the KMO as a symbol of the due diligence performed to identify the holder of the KMO.

The KMO must be created in an NDS container that also contains a PKIS server, because the KMO contains the key pair and certificate associated with a specific server. Eventually, Novell expects all KMO functionality to be accessible through the server object itself. To create a KMO, complete the following steps:

1. Right-click on the Container object and select New. Then select Object. Select the Key Material object type and click OK to open the KMO creation wizard (see Figure 6-10).

Figure 6-10
KMO naming page

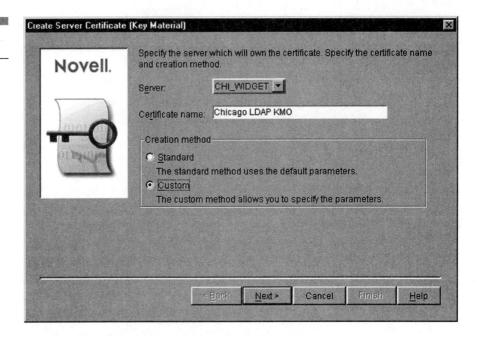

Figure 6-10
KMO naming page

2. Specify the name for your KMO key pair and the server that will use it; then click Next. The Certificate Name and the Server fields will be combined to create the KMO object name in NDS.

If you choose the Standard creation routine, you will not have to specify any further information. The following steps are those associated with the Custom creation routine.

NOTE: *You will want to create a separate key pair for each security application that runs on the specified server, so the key pair name should describe the application that will use it. In this case, we will be using the KMO for LDAP services so the name will reflect that.*

3. Specify how the KMO certificate will be signed, then click Next. By default, the KMO certificate will be signed by the Organizational CA— the Tree CA—you just created. However, you may choose to have the certificate signed by an external entity such as Verisign (see Figure 6-11).

You might choose to sign some KMOs externally, such as those that will be used by Internet browsers, while others are signed internally, such as the certificate used by the corporate firewall software.

If you choose to sign the KMO certificate internally, complete the following steps:

Figure 6-11

Select internally or externally signed KMO.

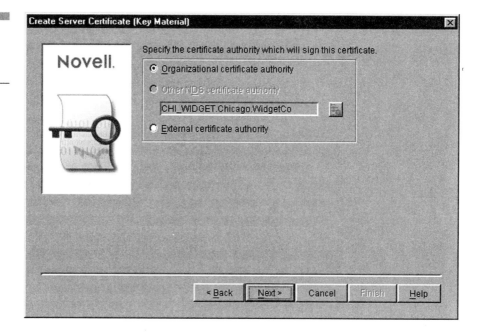

1. Specify the KMO Key size and how it will be used and click Next. The key types listed in this page are defined by the X.509 certificate standard (see Figure 6-12). Because the internally signed KMO we are creating for WidgetCo is for use by firewall software, we will choose the SSL option, which supports key usage for both key encipherment and digital signature.

   This usage parameter is managed through the NICI policy layer, which prevents keys specified for use in digital signature only from being used for data and/or key encryption. This feature has allowed Novell to gain export approval for digital signature keys of greater strength—1024 bits—than that normally allowed for export. Keys for data encryption are still limited to 512 bits.

TIP: *Any time you set an X.509 certificate extension to critical by checking the Set The Key Usage Extension To Critical checkbox, it means that applications making use of the certificate must be able to interpret, and abide by, the requirements specified by that extension. Because the whole PKI world is still relatively new, this can be a dangerous assumption. Don't do it unless you are absolutely sure that you understand how that extension will affect the usage of the KMO key.*

Figure 6-12
Specify key size
and type.

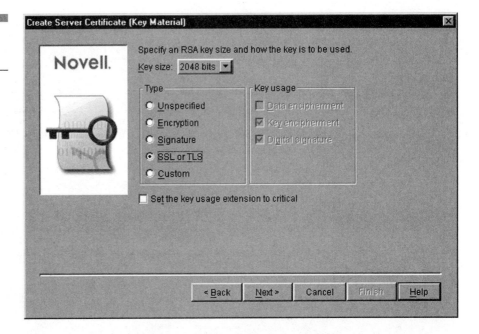

Figure 6-13
KMO certificate
parameters

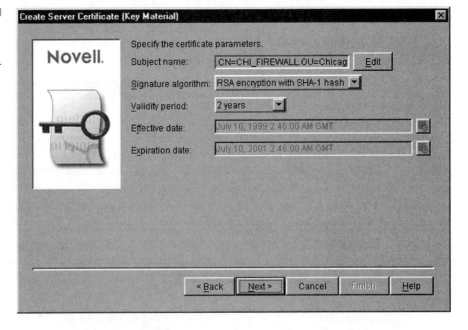

2. Specify the Subject name for the KMO certificate, the cryptographic
and hash algorithms, and the lifespan (default is two years) for the
KMO certificate and click Next (see Figure 6-13).

TIP: *Some secure clients require DNS information in the subject field of the certificate before they will accept the certificate as valid, such as* www.widgetco.com.

3. Select how your KMO will be internally signed and click Next. You can choose to select your organization's internal Tree CA as the Trusted Root, or you can choose Novell's Global Root as your Trusted Root (see Figure 6-14). Novell's Global Root is an option for those organizations who want to create a PKI that is not completely rooted within the organization. This may provide some increased sense of assurance for external entities that need to decide whether or not to trust the certificates generated within the organization. However, the Novell Global Root is not a liability assuming Root; meaning that Novell makes no guarantees that its certificates are any more secure than those from the organization, even though they probably are. Because of this, it is unlikely that the Novell Global Root will get widespread use.

If you choose Novell's Global Root, the application that will use this KMO must be able to recognize and use Novell Registered Attributes. For example, if you choose Novell BorderManager as your firewall solution, you could choose to chain your KMO certificate to the Novell

Figure 6-14

Select a local root or the Novell Global Root.

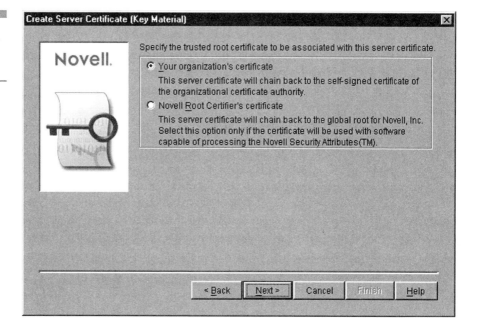

Global Root. BorderManager understands the Novell Registered Attributes.

NOTE: *If you are using non-Novell products, we do not recommend chaining to the Novell Global Root at this time. You should check with Novell to make sure that the product you are contemplating will support chaining to the Novell Global Root. There is just not enough support for Novell Registered Attributes yet. For more information on Novell Registered Attributes, see the preceding Tree CA discussion.*

4. Review the information for accuracy and then click Finish.

5. The newly created KMO will appear in the right pane of ConsoleOne. Double-click on the KMO and select the Certificates tab. The screens available in the KMO are similar to those discussed in the Tree CA process. However, if you select the Certificates tab, you will note that the Issuer name is the Tree CA we previously created rather than the NICI License CA. This indicates another link in the certificate chain.

If you choose to sign the KMO certificate externally, complete the following steps:

1. Specify the key size and click Next.

2. Enter the Subject name for the KMO certificate and select the cryptographic and hash algorithms to be used in creating the KMO certificate; then click Next.

3. Review the summary information for accuracy and click Finish to create the KMO certificate.

   NICI generates the key pair and a PKCS#10 *Certificate Signing Request* (CSR). For more information on PKCS#10, see Chapter 2, "Designing NDS."

4. Choose how you want to save the CSR and click Save (see Figure 6-15). The CSR can be saved to either the clipboard or to a file depending on how you want to deliver it to the external authority for signing. Save it to the clipboard if you are going to deliver the CSR as the subject of an email message. Save it to disk if you are going to send the CSR as an email attachment or deliver it by disk to the external authority.

   Send the CSR to the external signing authority. They will perform whatever due diligence they determine appropriate in order to make sure you are who you say you are. When satisfied, the external authority will sign your KMO certificate and send it back to you.

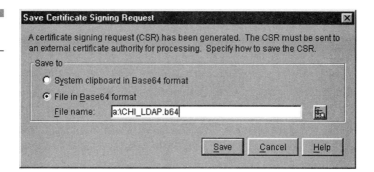

Figure 6-15

Saving the KMO CSR

NOTE: *Both of these transactions should be encrypted for privacy and protection. You can encrypt the CSR with the public key of the external authority to ensure that only they will be able to decrypt it.*

Similarly, the external authority can encrypt the signed certificate with your public key to be sure that you are the only person, or organization, that can decrypt it. The external certificate authority will deliver the signed certificate in another standard format known as PKCS#7.

5. Double-click on the newly created KMO in the right pane of ConsoleOne and select Certificates. Note that no certificates are present for this KMO. When you receive the signed certificate from your external authority, click Import Certificates and then click Read From File. Browse to and select the file you have received. The certificate contents will be copied into the Import Server Certificates page (Figure 6-16). Click Next to import the certificate.

6. Double-click on the KMO object and select the Certificates tab again to see the details on the newly imported certificate.

Using the Server Certificate   Now that PKIS is configured within NDS it would be nice if clients could make use of it. To demonstrate this, we will show how Netscape Internet browsers can be configured to use secure connections to communicate with the PKIS server. With our KMO configured, we can configure SSL communications. The KMO makes it possible to establish SSL connections to its host server. More information on SSL is provided later in this chapter.

Before starting with the browser, make sure that LDAP is configured on the KMO host server. If you selected LDAP services as an optional product when you installed NDS 8, then you are ready to go. If not, refer to Chapter 5, "Administering NDS Objects," for information on installing NDS 8 and its

Figure 6-16
Importing an
externally signed
server certificate

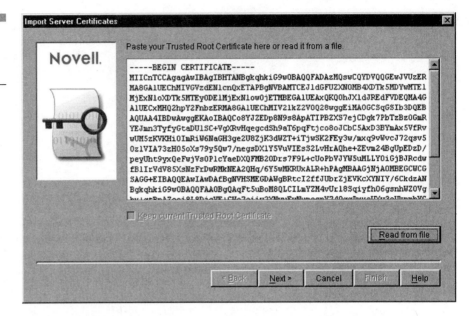

Figure 6-16
Importing an
externally signed
server certificate

optional services. See "Configuring LDAP Services," later in this chapter. To check the status of LDAP on your NDS server, complete the following:

1. Look in the container where your NDS 8 server is located. When LDAP services are installed, some new LDAP objects will be created in NDS.

2. Double-click on the LDAP Server object.

3. Click the Browse button next to the SSL Certificate field and select a KMO that has been created (see Figure 6-17). You also may want to check the box next to Disable TCP Port. This prevents unsecured communications over port 389—forcing the browser to use a secure SSL connection if they want to communicate with this LDAP server.

TIP: *The changes you have just made will not be active until you click the Apply button. For more information on LDAP with NDS, see "Configuring LDAP Services" later in this chapter.*

4. Click Refresh NLDAP Server Now. This will restart LDAP Services on the NDS server with the new information you have provided. Now the LDAP server is ready to accept SSL sessions from clients.

Before an SSL client can communicate with our newly configured LDAP server, we have to export the certificate used by the LDAP server to the client software so it can validate the SSL connection process.

Figure 6-17
LDAP Server General
Properties page

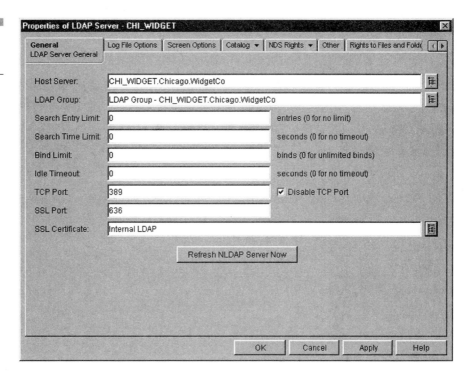

Figure 6-17
LDAP Server General
Properties page

NOTE: *In the following example, we are using Netscape Communicator v4.51. Keystrokes may vary slightly on different versions of the software. However, you must have version 4.03 or newer to have support for LDAP connections. This same type of operation can be performed on current versions of Microsoft's Internet Explorer.*

To export the LDAP server certificate to a Netscape browser, complete the following:

1. Open ConsoleOne and double-click on the KMO whose certificate you would like to export (see Figure 6-18). Select the Certificates tab and click the Export button.

2. Select the format for the certificate file. DER is a binary encoding scheme that results in a more compact certificate file. Base 64 encoding is a text-based scheme that is not as efficient as DER but is more durable. If you are going to be sending this file by email, the Base 64 file will survive a transfer across an old text-based email system. In most cases, this is probably not a problem, but it is something you should think about.

Figure 6-18
Export a server
certificate.

3. Specify a location and filename for the certificate file and click Export. A certificate in the specified format will be created. Transfer the file to the workstation that will be running the Internet browser.

4. Open Netscape Communicator. In the Location field, specify the path and name of the certificate file. After reading the file, Netscape will bring up a message about accepting a new Certificate Authority. Click Next.

5. Another informational message will then be displayed. Click Next. You will see a page displaying the certificate owner and the signer of that certificate—in this case WidgetCo.

6. Click the More Info button to see the details of the certificate (see Figure 6-19).

   The Certificate Fingerprint is the hash digest that was discussed earlier in this chapter. The accuracy of the data contained in this certificate can be confirmed by rerunning the hash algorithm and comparing the result with what is listed here.

7. Click OK to return to the previous screen.

8. Click Next.

Figure 6-19
Certificate
Information including
Hash value

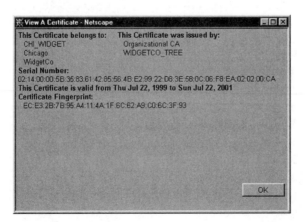

9. Check the boxes that correspond to the type of certification that can be performed by this CA and then click Next (see Figure 6-20).

   Each checkbox corresponds to an increased level of assurance. By the time you are ready to certify software developers with this CA, you had better be very comfortable with the quality and security of the CA, because of the damage that can be caused by letting a malicious developer sneak in with a forged certificate.

10. Specify whether or not you want to be warned before sending any information to site(s) certified by this CA and then click Next. Because WidgetCo is importing its own CA, it chooses not to be warned.

11. Specify a nickname for this CA that will be used to identify it in the Netscape CA list and click Finish (see Figure 6-21).

NOTE: You can automate the distribution of these server certificates through the use of Novell's ZENworks desktop management product. For more information on ZENworks, see Chapter 7, "Administering Workstations."

12. To confirm the import of the new CA certificate, click Security on the Netscape tool bar.

13. Click Signers and look for the nickname you just assigned to your Trusted Root certificate (see Figure 6-22).

14. (Optional) Click Verify to check the format, not the quality, of the certificate that is highlighted.

Figure 6-20

Specifying how to use this Certificate Authority

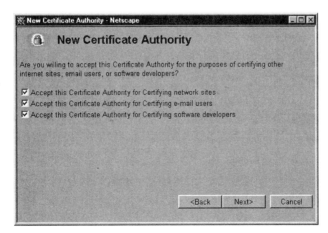

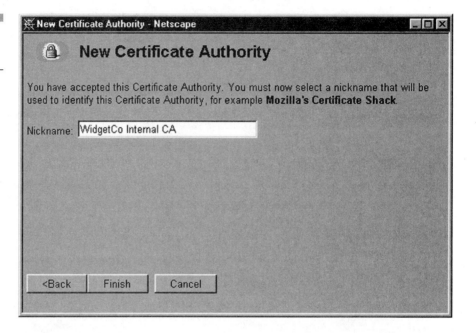

Figure 6-21
Nickname for
new CA

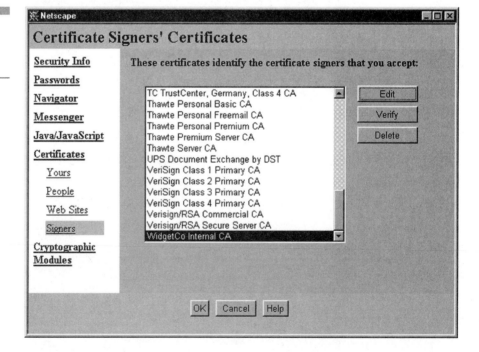

Figure 6-22
Verifying import
of Trusted Root
certificate

15. (Optional) Click Edit to display the certificate information, which enables you to change any of the options that were selected while importing the certificate.

With a server certificate installed in a browser, it is possible to create secure connections to the server that hosts that KMO.

The Trusted Root certificate is used to set up an SSL session through which LDAP communications can be protected. SSL is discussed in more detail later in this chapter. Using the same browser from the previous examples, it is possible to connect to the WidgetCo NDS tree and browse the objects contained in that tree.

To set up an SSL session between the Netscape browser and the LDAP server, complete the following:

1. Configure our NDS tree as a valid directory in the Netscape browser. To do this, click the Communicator drop-down menu and select Address Book. Remember that Communicator defines a directory as a White Pages database that can be used to locate user information. The Novell view of directories is considerably more ambitious, but NDS can still do this type of mundane user search.

2. In the Address Book utility, click the File drop-down menu and select New Directory.

3. Specify a name for the directory and the location of the LDAP server— either Domain Name or IP address. You can also restrict the container in which to search for objects by specifying the distinguished container name in the Search Root field (see Figure 6-23).

4. Check the Secure checkbox and click OK. The default is the unsecured LDAP port 389. Note how it changes to port 636, the default port for secure SSL communications.

--- --- --- --- --- --- --- --- --- --- --- --- --- --- --- --- --- --- --- ---

TIP: *You may need to close and re-open the Address Book in order to see the new directory (see Figure 6-24).*

5. Highlight the new directory that was just created, and the browser will open an SSL session with the LDAP server. You can now use the search field in the Address book to perform LDAP searches on the NDS tree.

Figure 6-23
Configuring a new
directory

Secure Authentication Services

As with NICI and PKIS, *Secure Authentication Services* (SAS) is an optional feature when installing NDS. Except for managing SSL connections for NDS, SAS provides limited functionality in this release. If you view the properties of the SAS object, you will find that only the default NDS object properties are provided. No configuration options exist for SSL at this time. However, this will likely change over the next few months as SAS functionality is exposed for use. In fact, Novell recently announced the release of a new version of their BorderManager product line, which supports strong authentication via tokens and smart cards. This functionality is provided by SAS.

NDS Communication Protocols

Because NDS is a distributed enterprise directory, Novell dreams of NDS being the top dog of the network. All other network resources will consult with NDS to learn about and interact with all other network resources. Although this is still a dream in progress, NDS supports several different protocols for communicating both internal and external information.

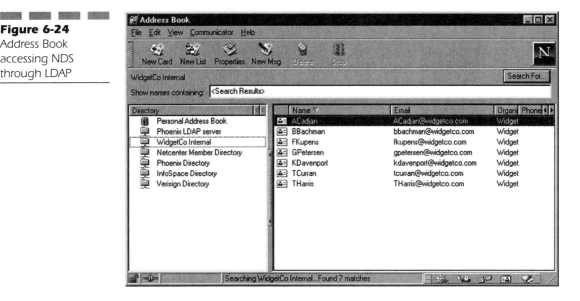

Internal Communication Protocols

Internal communication protocols are the unseen workers in an NDS network. By internal, we mean that these are proprietary protocols created by Novell to serve specific purposes within their network products. Novell uses these protocols in a variety of different ways to provide communication between clients, servers, applications, and directories. Not a lot of configuration or maintenance is necessary to manage these protocols. Because of this, you might be wondering why we should discuss these things if they just do their job without any interference on our part? The answer, as we will see in more detail in Chapter 11, "Troubleshooting NDS," is that the capability to recognize and understand how these protocols are used provides us with important information for troubleshooting network problems and bottlenecks that might relate to NDS.

NetWare Core Protocol   One of the most important communication protocols for internal NDS communications is the *NetWare Core Protocol* (NCP). NCP is a proprietary communications protocol designed by Novell to enable clients to request the various services available through a NetWare server.

   The release of NetWare 5 brought some changes to NCP as Novell began to prepare NDS for life on other network platforms. NCP is now completely independent of the network-layer protocol being used on the network. Formerly, NCP relied on interaction with Novell's IPX protocol to function. Now NCP runs equally well, perhaps better, on IP. NCP is a higher level protocol that combines aspects of the Transport, Session, Presentation, and Application layers of the seven-layer OSI communications model. As such, it is transmitted across the network within packets created by lower level protocols.

Each of the types of requests that can be made to NDS has been assigned a number. When an NDS client needs to submit a request, it places the number—as well as any additional information that might be needed—in the service code field of the NCP packet. Depending on the type of request, the NCP might provide additional fields for the client to provide specific instructions to NDS. NDS also can use these fields to report any problems or errors that might have occurred while processing the request in these additional fields. Figure 6-25 shows the format of a typical NCP packet. This packet would ride in the data area of an IPX or IP packet as it is transmitted across the network.

Novell Directory Access Protocol The *Novell Directory Access Protocol* (NDAP) is a proprietary protocol developed by Novell to provide an authentication mechanism for NDS. NDAP is a specific form, or subfunction, of NCP, so when NCP was modified to become protocol independent, NDAP was able to take advantage of this new functionality.

NDAP manages the primary and background authentication processes described in Chapter 2, "Designing NDS."

External Communications Protocols

External Communications Protocols are those that Novell is now supporting to provide compatibility with the outside world. It would be naïve to

Figure 6-25
NCP Packet format

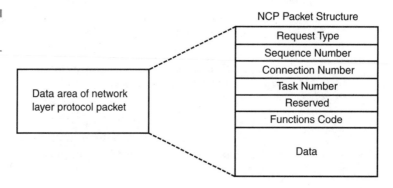

assume that the rest of the world would run to Novell's proprietary protocols when creating products that might need to communicate with NDS. Unfortunately, because of its proprietary origins, many still view NDS as a directory for NetWare. The latest version of NDS is intended to change that perception by bringing a standards-compliant version of NDS to those market segments that have the greatest need for large directory implementations—namely *Internet Service Providers* (ISPs).

As residents of the Internet, ISPs require that the products they use be fully compatible with those protocols and standards in use on the Internet. Novell has actively targeted this market by moving NDS away from its proprietary roots and toward full integration with Internet standards. Following is a description of the primary Internet protocols that NDS 8 has embraced as well as descriptions of the installation and configuration processes for those protocols.

Lightweight Directory Access Protocol   The *Lightweight Directory Access Protocol* (LDAP) is perhaps the most widely recognized Internet standard. LDAP provides a standard mechanism for querying directories and accessing their content.

LDAP was born from the X.500 directory standard. However, because X.500 was so complex and required so much overhead to implement, engineers at the University of Michigan decided to split off some of the X.500 functionality and publish it as a separate standard that did not require all the X.500 overhead. The *Internet Engineering Task Force* (IETF) is now maintaining LDAP under *Request for Comment* (RFC) numbers:

- 2251: Lightweight Directory Access Protocol (v3)
- 2252: Lightweight Directory Access Protocol (v3): Attribute Syntax Definitions
- 2253: Lightweight Directory Access Protocol (v3): UTF-8 String Representation of Distinguished Names
- 2254: The String Representation of LDAP Search Filters
- 2255: The LDAP URL Format
- 2256: A Summary of the X.500(96) User Schema for use with LDAPv3

Complete copies of these RFC documents can be found at the IETF Web site at www.ietf.org/rfc/.

It is important to recognize that LDAP first emerged as a standard in RFC 1777, which was published in 1995. This was a full two years after NDS was initially released to the public. Novell recognized, as did those engineers at the University of Michigan, that the X.500 *Directory Access Protocol* (DAP) would not be appropriate for PC-based network environments. In fact, an X.500 DAP client would require as much as 500K of resident memory space in order to load. Given the DOS limitation of 640K conventional memory, it is easy to see that the X.500 directory implementation was unworkable. Because of this, Novell had to create its own solutions to these problems. Hence, the emergence of NDAP as described. However, as LDAP began to catch on, Novell recognized that NDS would have to support LDAP if it was ever to grow in usage beyond the Novell NetWare LAN environment.

Secure Sockets Layer   SSL provides the ability to encrypt a channel between two parties to provide secure communications. NDS now provides support for SSL through its cryptographic infrastructure. In most cases, SSL is valuable because it can secure requests from a user to a server and prevent sensitive information, such as passwords from being passed across the network—or Internet—in plain view. This eliminates the need to build specific cryptographic functionality into client applications.

NDS LDAP Implementation

Now that you understand a little why these protocols are important, let's look at how NDS implements its support for these protocols.

The first attempt at LDAP support came in the form of an LDAP gateway that was offered for NetWare 4.11. The gateway provided basic LDAP interoperability but was much slower than a native LDAP implementation. The LDAP gateway was improved tremendously with the release of NetWare 5. LDAP Services for NDS v3 was based on the IETF RFC 2251 LDAP v3 protocol. This meant that LDAP clients could perform an LDAP v3 bind as described in the specification. LDAP Services for NDS fully understands the LDAP v3 protocol and could respond to the following requests:

- Discovery of available features (authentication mechanisms, controls, schema)
- Demand or request controls
- Support for extended requests

LDAP v3.0 compliance also means that the Novell implementation supports the following LDAP features that were not supported in previous versions of the LDAP Services for NDS:

- Limited support for Auxiliary Classes. In this initial release, Novell chose to limit this support to those classes required by Netscape and Entrust.

- Modified distinguished name requests that enable users to rename an object or move it to another place in the NDS tree
- UTF8 support for internationalization
- Referrals in the LDAP v3 format

With more robust support for LDAP now available for NDS, Novell turned its attention to speeding up the performance of LDAP queries to NDS. To increase this performance, Novell's LDAP support was integrated with a catalog service. A catalog is essentially an external index. NDS Catalog services runs only on the NetWare server platform, so native NT and Solaris environments cannot use this option. Catalog Services can be installed as part of the NetWare 5 server installation or at a later date through the NWCONFIG utility. After it has been installed, Catalog Services can be configured to compile an index of directory objects. The catalog uses a dredger that periodically rebuilds the catalog by searching the NDS database for updated objects. The dredger can be configured to run at specific intervals. It is important to strike a balance between having up-to-date information on the catalog and limiting the overhead associated with running the dredger. This is one of the drawbacks of using a catalog to speed up directory queries.

Because the catalog is just another NDS object, it is no longer necessary to traverse the NDS tree to search for specific objects. Just consult the catalog. The catalog can be configured to index on specific types of objects and on specific attributes.

Configuring Catalog Services   Catalog Services is still available for use with NDS running on the NetWare 5 platform, but because NDS now offers full indexing capabilities, Catalog Services is necessary only for those who are currently running applications that use NDS Catalog Services. The main use of catalogs at this point is for contextless login. To configure NDS catalogs for contextless login, complete the following steps:

1. Load DSCAT.NLM from the server console. This starts the catalog service. To automate the loading of Catalog Services, you can insert the DSCAT load statement in the AUTOEXEC.NCF.

NOTE: *Because catalogs are not going to survive, no snap-in exists for managing them via ConsoleOne. You can actually create the object in ConsoleOne if you would like, but you won't be able to configure or manage the catalog object(s).*

2. Load NetWare Administrator to create the Master Catalog. The master catalog is configured to store the objects and/or attributes you define. It receives updates from the dredger and then sends those updates to any Slave catalogs that might exist.

3. Right-click on the container object in which you want to create the master catalog and select Create.

4. Highlight the NDSCat: Master Catalog object type and click OK.

5. Enter a name for the catalog and check the Define additional properties box; then click OK (see Figure 6-26).

6. Select a Host server. The host server will run the dredger that will populate and update the catalog. The Description, Location, Department, and Organization fields are optional fields that enable you to specify more information about the catalog.

7. Click New and enter the primary and secondary labels; then click OK. The labels are identifiers used by applications and administrators to assign the catalog for use. A catalog can be shared by multiple applications.

TIP: *Because these are simply identifiers, you can use anything you would like, but as with any object, it is wise to define a naming standard for these objects. One option might be to use the organization or container name as the primary identifier and a description of what the catalog is used for as the secondary identifier.*

Figure 6-26
Master Catalog
properties page
in NetWare
Administrator

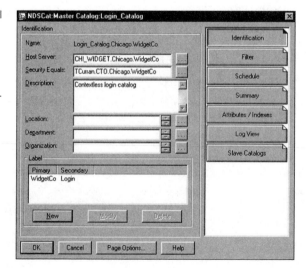

8. Click Filter. Specify the types of objects and/or attributes stored in the catalog. Because this is a login catalog for user objects, we will specify Object Class=User. In the Filter field, we specify the NDS schema classes and attributes that should be pulled into the catalog (see Figure 6-27).

9. The Context Limits field is used to specify where the dredger should start searching in order to populate the catalog. This enables you to create catalogs of different branches of the tree, if desired. Because a login catalog is global, this field is left blank. The Search Subtree radio button should be selected.

10. Click the Schedule tab to define how the dredger will operate. You can use manually initiated or automatic modes. We have decided to use an automatic update and run the dredger once a day at 2:00 A.M. (see Figure 6-28). You can configure these parameters any way you see fit.

11. Click the Attributes/Indexes tab and specify the object attributes that should be maintained in the catalog. For our purposes, we will catalog all attributes, but you can use the Select Attributes button to pull up a list of all attributes in the NDS schema and select the specific attributes you need.

12. Click the Select Indexes button. The Indexes field enables you to identify how the catalog will be indexed. Because the catalog will be used for user login, it is indexed on the Full Name attribute (see Figure 6-29).

13. Click OK to save the master catalog configuration.

Figure 6-27
Configuring the catalog filter in NetWare Administrator

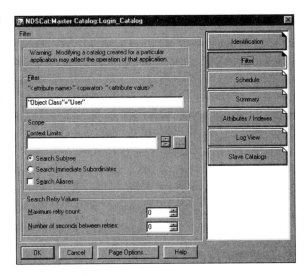

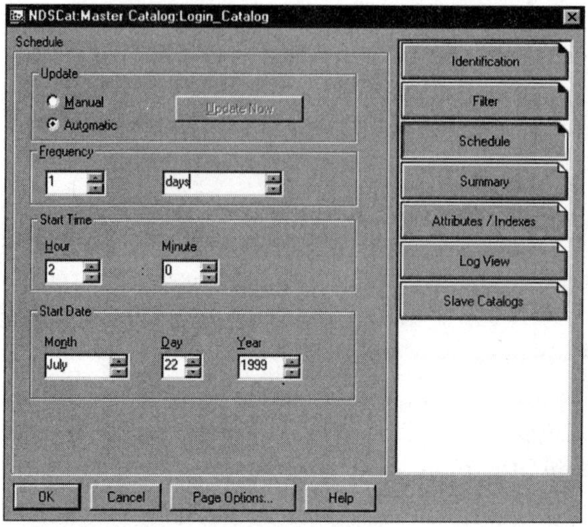

Figure 6-28
Schedule dredger
operation in NetWare
Administrator

Figure 6-28
Schedule dredger
operation in NetWare
Administrator

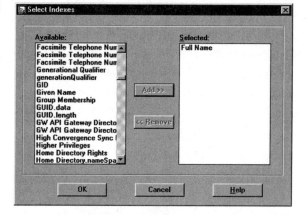

Figure 6-29
The Select Indexes
dialog box

The Slave Catalogs tab can be used to identify other catalogs that will be
fed information from the master catalog. If you have a distributed environment, like WidgetCo, it is not a bad idea to publish the Master catalog to
multiple sites to increase performance and prevent catalog access over
WAN links. To create slave catalogs, complete the following steps:

1. Identify the container in which you want to place the slave catalog and
   create the objects using NetWare Administrator.

2. In the Slave Catalog Properties screen, select the master catalog (see
   Figure 6-30). The primary and secondary labels will be taken from the
   master catalog configuration.

Figure 6-30
Slave catalog
configuration
in NetWare
Administrator

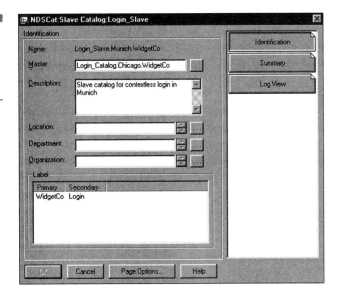

3. After creating the slave catalogs you need, re-open the master catalog object properties and select Slave Catalogs. Note that the slave catalogs now appear in the list box.

Configuring LDAP Services   This section gives an overview of configuring LDAP services using ConsoleOne. When LDAP services is installed on a NetWare server, two new objects are installed in the container where the LDAP server resides:

■ *LDAP Server object*   This object is used to configure the LDAP environment for your LDAP server.

■ *LDAP Group object*   This object is used to configure LDAP client access to NDS.

The LDAP Server object is always created in the same container as the server on which LDAP services are installed. Five pages of configuration information are provided for the LDAP Server object. Figure 6-31 show the LDAP Server General Properties page, and Table 6-1 describes the configuration options available from the General Properties page.

The Log File Options page enables you to configure a log file for LDAP and to define the types of events that are recorded in it (see Figure 6-32). The logging process consumes processor cycles on the LDAP server. For best performance, keep logging activities to a minimum.

Log File Options are described in Table 6-2.

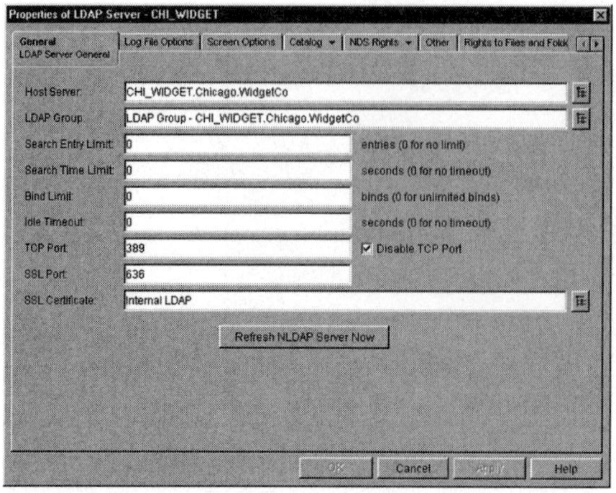

Figure 6-31
LDAP Server General
Properties

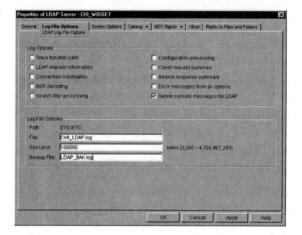

Figure 6-32
LDAP Server Log
File page

Table 6-1	Field Name	Description
LDAP Server Object General Properties	Host Server	Stores the name of the server that is hosting LDAP Services for NDS.
	LDAP Group	Indicates the LDAP Group object that specifies the configuration settings used by this LDAP server. By default, an LDAP Server object is created with its own LDAP Group. Otherwise, you can use the Browse button to locate the LDAP Group object you want to associate with this LDAP server.
	Search Entry Limit	Defines the maximum number of objects that will be returned for any given search: Default is 500; Minimum is 1; Maximum is 2,147,483,647. When this limit is reached, the LDAP server will terminate the search request. This limit is independent of any potential limits set by the LDAP client.

Field Name	Description
Search Time Limit	Defines the maximum amount of time spent on any given request in seconds: Default is 3600; Minimum is 1; Maximum is 2,147,483,647. When the limit is reached, the request will terminate.
Bind Limit	Defines the maximum number of simultaneous connections supported by the LDAP server: Default is 0 (no limit); Minimum is 1; Maximum is 4,294,967,295. The number of connections a server can support is dependent largely upon the available server memory. Each LDAP request requires approximately 160K of memory, and one client can make multiple requests.
Idle Timeout	Defines the maximum amount of time, in 10-second increments, that an LDAP connection can be inactive: Default is 900; Minimum is 0 (no limit); Maximum is 4,294,967,290.
TCP Port	Defines the TCP port used for LDAP Services on this server: Default is 389 (the well-known LDAP port); Minimum is 0; Maximum is 65,535. This value should be changed only if another TCP service on the server is already using port 389.
SSL Port	Defines the TCP port used for SSL connections on this server: Default is 636 (the well-known SSL port); Minimum is 0; Maximum is 65,535. This value should be changed only if another TCP service on the server is already using port 636.
SSL Certificate	Specifies the KMO that stores the SSL certificate for this LDAP Server. Each LDAP server will have only one SSL certificate associated with it.
Refresh NLDAP Server Now (Button)	Click this button to reset LDAP settings on the server after making changes.

Table 6-2

LDAP Server Object
Log File Options

Option	Description
File Name	Specifies the name and location of the LDAP log file. If no name is specified, no log file will be kept.
File Size	Specifies the maximum size of the LDAP log file in bytes. Default is 100,000. Minimum is 2,048. Maximum is 4,294,967,295.
Backup File	When a log file reaches its maximum size, it is renamed using the name specified in the Backup File field. The logging then continues under the original filename.

The Log Options enable you to select the types of events to be recorded in the log file. Table 6-3 describes the various options.

The Screen Options page enables you to configure the types of events that will be displayed on the NLDAP server screen. The same options are available for both screen display and log file. See the preceding discussion for details on each option.

The Catalog pages are used to define catalog usage for LDAP searches (see Figure 6-33). Select the Usage page to select the appropriate catalog object from NDS and to define how it should be used.

The Schedule page automatically will be filled in according to how the catalog is configured (see Figure 6-34). This information can be modified from the catalog object rather than the LDAP Server object. Remember that catalogs are configured through NetWare Administrator, not ConsoleOne.

Given that NDS 8 already maintains specific LDAP search indexes internally, you likely will benefit very little from catalog use. This is mostly a legacy feature from previous versions of NDS. That said, if you have

	Log Option	Description
Table 6-3		
LDAP Server Object Log Options	Trace Function Calls	Records information about internal program code paths. Programmers can use this trace to troubleshoot problems.
	LDAP Request Information	Records information about LDAP request types.
	Connection Information	Records specifics about TCP and SSL connections between LDAP clients and the LDAP server.
	BER Decoding	Logs a decoded version of the LDAP requests and responses.
	Search Filter Processing	Logs information about the LDAP filter used to process a request.
	Configuration Processing	Logs startup parameters for LDAP services.
	Client Request Summary	Logs a summary of LDAP requests that the server has processed.
	Search Response Summary	Logs a summary of the information sent in response to LDAP searches.
	Error Messages from All Options	Logs all error messages generated by the LDAP server, including errors caused by external events, such as user errors.
	Server Console Messages for LDAP	Logs all LDAP Services from the server console.

Figure 6-33
LDAP Catalog
Usage page

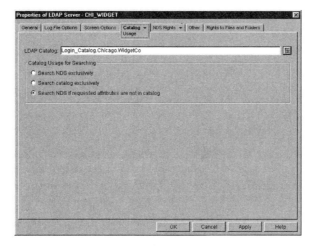

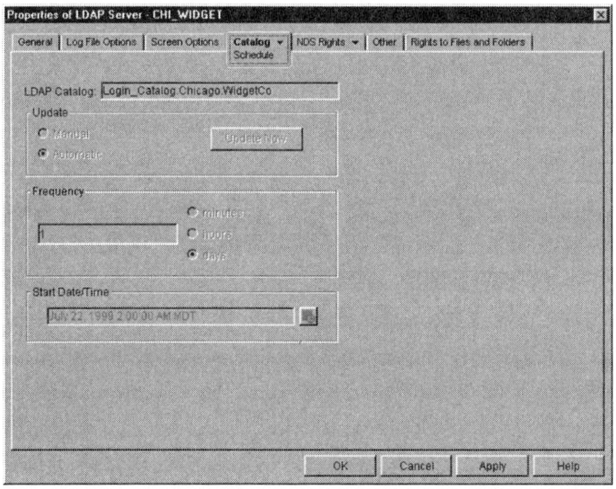

Figure 6-34
LDAP Catalog
Schedule page

unusual search criteria or very specific needs, a catalog still might be useful. Configuring custom NDS indexes will be discussed in Chapter 10, "Other NDS Administration Tools."

The LDAP Group Object enables you to configure user access to the LDAP server (see Figure 6-35). By default, an LDAP Group object will be created for each LDAP Server object, but if multiple servers will be accessed using the same user configuration, they can be combined under a single LDAP Group.

The LDAP Group General page enables you to define how the LDAP server will interact with LDAP clients. These General options are described in Table 6-4. The Referral Option determines how the LDAP server will react if it is unable to process the LDAP request directly.

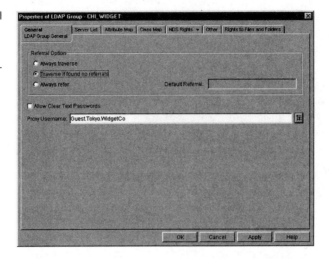

Figure 6-35
LDAP Group General
Properties page

Table 6-4	Field	Description
LDAP Group General Options	Always Traverse	LDAP clients never get back referrals. NDS uses traversal by default instead of referral because it eliminates involving the client in the process. Instead of telling you where to go to get what is needed, NDS goes and gets it for you.
	Traverse if found no referrals	If the LDAP server has a valid referral for the data, it will return it to the LDAP client. If it doesn't have a valid referral, it will traverse the directory tree to get the data.
	Always Refer	The LDAP server will never traverse the directory tree looking for the data. If the server does not have a valid LDAP referral, an error is returned to the client.
	Default Referral	This field specifies the referral that will be sent to the client if no request-specific referral can be located. Similar to a default router in the IP world.
	Allow Clear Text Passwords	Permits the transmission of connection requests that include passwords over unencrypted connections. Due to security risks, this option is not recommended. If the Allows Cleartext Passwords option is not checked, the LDAP service rejects all binds that include passwords on non-SSL connections. This allows only anonymous binds or binds by users without a password (such as the proxy user).
	Proxy Username	Allows administrators to specify a user object for anonymous binds. An anonymous bind is an LDAP connection that does not contain a username. The Proxy User object should not have a password and should not be allowed to create or change the password. The rights assigned to the proxy user are assigned to all anonymous binds.

Field	Description
	If a Proxy Username is not assigned to the LDAP Group object, all anonymous requests are validated to NDS as the [Public] user. Because any NDS rights granted to [Public] for LDAP access are also granted to all NDS users, using a proxy provides better control over the NDS security environment.

Figure 6-36
LDAP Group Server
List page

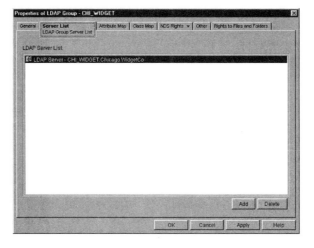

LDAP referrals are mechanisms for transferring clients between LDAP servers. If an LDAP server is unable to locate an object requested by a client the LDAP server will return the client a Referral. The LDAP client must support this option. A referral is a URL that contains information needed to connect to another LDAP server that does have access to the requested object.

The Server List page enables you to specify the LDAP servers that will be accessed through the LDAP Group information contained in this LDAP Group object (see Figure 6-36). Add servers by clicking Add and locating the appropriate LDAP Server object in NDS. To delete a server, highlight it in the list and click Delete.

The Class and Attribute Map pages enable an administrator to associate LDAP schema classes and attributes to corresponding NDS schema classes and attributes (see Figure 6-37). This way, an LDAP client can request NDS data by LDAP specification rather than NDS specification.

A default set of mappings is defined when the LDAP group is created, but this leaves many LDAP classes and attributes unmapped. If administrators have specific needs, they can map LDAP classes and attributes as they see fit.

Figure 6-37
LDAP Group Class
Map page

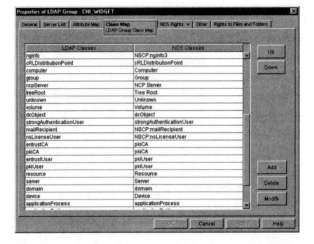

Figure 6-38
LDAP Group Attribute
Map page

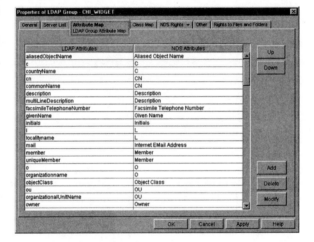

Because certain LDAP attributes, such as CN and common name, map to
the same NDS value, LDAP Services supports multivalue associations (see
Figure 6-38).

NOTE: *When the LDAP server returns LDAP attribute information, it
returns the value of the first matching attribute it locates in the list. If you
map multiple LDAP attributes to a single NDS attribute, make sure that
you order the list with the most important attributes at the top because
they will take precedence.*

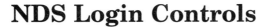

NDS Login Controls

The preceding sections of this chapter have presented information about implementing security measures that can help securely connect your organization to the rest of the world. However, they do not as yet address the need to be able to secure network resources internally as well.

Again, NDS provides a powerful foundation for securing network access as well as controlling the access of those users after they have been authenticated. This section covers the traditional security concepts that have been confronting LAN administrators for many years. NDS enables you to extend the reach of your authentication, to control access policies across platforms, and to manage it all from a common set of administrative utilities.

NDS Authentication

NDS authentication provides the first line of defense in protecting your network resources. NDS is widely recognized as a provider of strong authentication tools. Those tools will soon be augmented even more by the Secure Authentication Services, a relatively new addition to the NDS security arsenal.

At this time, NDS still uses a proprietary authentication mechanism with the NDAP protocol discussed previously. However, Novell's direction is toward a standards-based X.509 authentication process. Only now have the cryptographic standards gained enough maturity to warrant this change. To understand the lengths to which NDS goes to protect password security, it is worthwhile to examine the primary authentication process that is currently used with NDS.

Several variable names are used in describing the primary authentication process. These names are used only to keep track of how the variables are used during authentication and do not correspond to actual variable names used in Novell software code.

The NDS Primary Authentication Process involves the following steps:

1. The user enters a network ID and password through a login utility, such as the Novell Client, running on the workstation. The login utility locates the nearest NDS server for the specified tree and then encapsulates the user's distinguished network ID in an authentication request, which is sent to the NDS server.

━━ ━━ ━━ ━━ ━━ ━━ ━━ ━━ ━━ ━━ ━━ ━━ ━━ ━━ ━━ ━━ ━━ ━━ ━━

NOTE: *If the NDS server does not have a replica with the necessary user object, it will use links it maintains with replicas further up the tree to locate an NDS server that does maintain a copy of the necessary user object. The user connection then is transferred to this new server to process the authentication.*

2. The NDS server that receives the authentication request uses the distinguished name to obtain a reference to the appropriate user object. The user object contains the public and private keys, as well as the hash value calculated from the password that will be used to authenticate the user. Remember that a hash function creates a fixed-length value based upon some variable length input data.

3. Each NDS tree maintains a random number, which we call NDS_Value. NDS_Value exists specifically for use in authentication transactions. The NDS server communicating with the client generates a second random number we call Server_Value. Server_Value will be used during this authentication session only. Both NDS_Value and Server_Value, together with the NDS tree public key, are then sent back to the client login utility.

4. The login utility uses the password entered by the user together with NDS_Value to create a hash value, called ClientHash_1.

5. The login utility then generates another random number, Client_Value, and hashes it together with ClientHash_1 to obtain ClientHash_2.

6. The login utility encrypts ClientHash_2 and Client_Value using the NDS tree public key and sends the resulting message to the NDS server. When the NDS server receives this message, it uses the NDS tree private key to decrypt ClientHash_2 and Client_Value.

7. The NDS server now retrieves the password hash value that is stored in the user object and hashes it with NDS_Value to obtain ServerHash_1.

8. The NDS server performs a second hash using ServerHash_1 and Client_Value to get ServerHash_2.

9. The server then compares ServerHash_2 and ClientHash_2. If these two values are equal, it proves mathematically that the client must have entered the correct password. This is more of the hash algorithm magic.

10. With the password authenticity proven, the NDS server uses the private key stored in the NDS user object together with a session

timeout value to create a temporary key, Temp_Key. Because of the mathematical algorithm used to derive Temp_Key, it is functionally equivalent to the user's private key, but it is timestamped so that it will expire after a specific length of time.

11. The NDS server uses a symmetric encryption algorithm to encrypt Temp_Key. It uses ClientHash_2 as the symmetric key because the login utility client already possesses it. The NDS server then sends the encrypted message to the client and destroys all the temporary values used during the authentication process.

12. The login utility uses ClientHash_2 to decrypt the message from the NDS server to obtain Temp_Key. The workstation is now authenticated to the NDS tree. It can now use Temp_Key to perform background authentication, which does not require user intervention, to other network resources until the Temp_Key expires.

Through the process described here, NDS can authenticate a workstation without ever having to pass secure materials, such as password or private key across the network. By doing this, NDS effectively removes the network as a potential point of failure for the authentication process. Recognize that the workstation was authenticated, not the user. The workstation itself is responsible to implement security measures so that the user of the workstation is verified before they ever attempt to access the network.

NDS Login Controls

NDS provides a variety of login controls designed to help secure the network. Those controls are found in the properties of each user object. To see them, double-click on a user object in ConsoleOne and select the Restrictions tab. These restrictions are not configurable through Group or Container objects, so it is important to create users through templates to automate the configuration of these controls. Templates are discussed in Chapter 5, "Administering NDS Objects." The various types of restrictions offered by NDS include:

- Password restrictions
- Login restrictions
- Time restrictions
- Address restrictions
- Intruder lockout

The Account Balance page provides usage-based billing for network resources. This little-used accounting feature is not be discussed in this chapter.

Password Restrictions The default restriction page is the Password Restrictions page (see Figure 6-39). By default, the only selected option is Allow user to change password. However, this will not provide any significant degree of security, so you will want to enable some of the other options.

- *Require a password* Checking this box forces users to use an account password. It also enables all other password options. Associated with this option is a Minimum password length field that can be used to require passwords of at least a given number of characters. The default is 5, but the value can be set from 1 to 128 characters.

- *Force periodic password changes* This field enables you to require users to change their password regularly. Associated with this option is a Days between forced changes field that defines how often the password must be changed in days. The default is 40, but the value can be set between 1 and 365 days.

  The Date and time password expires field enables you to define the password expiration date and time. It also shows when the password will next expire. When the user resets his or her password, the system

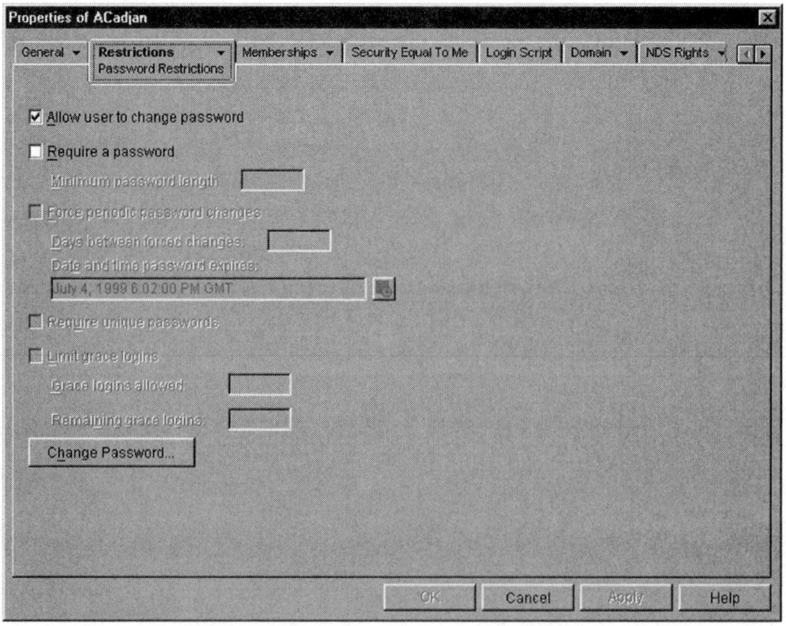

Figure 6-39
Password Restrictions page

Properties of ACadjan	✕

General ▾ | **Restrictions** ▾ | Memberships ▾ | Security Equal To Me | Login Script | Domain ▾ | NDS Rights ▾ | ◀ ▶
Password Restrictions

☑ Allow user to change password

☐ Require a password

   Minimum password length   [   ]

☐ Force periodic password changes

   Days between forced changes: [   ]
   Date and time password expires:
   [July 4, 1999 6:02:00 PM GMT   ▦]

☐ Require unique passwords

☐ Limit grace logins

   Grace logins allowed: [   ]

   Remaining grace logins: [   ]

[Change Password...]

| | OK | Cancel | Apply | Help |

will automatically reset this date forward by the number of days specified in the Days between forced changes field.

NOTE: *The time value in this field is interpreted as UTC time, or Greenwich Mean Time (GMT). If you want the password to expire at a specific time, you need to take into account the time zone offset between your location and GMT. For example, Mountain Standard Time (MST) is –7:00 hours in relation to GMT. Therefore, to set your password to expire at 1:00 A.M. MST, you would have to set the expiration time to 8:00 A.M. GMT (8:00–7:00 = 1:00).*

To force ConsoleOne to use the local time rather than UTC, you need to set an environment variable on the workstation from which ConsoleOne is running. Consult the documentation for your workstation operating system to determine how this is done.

Because ConsoleOne is Java-based and not a Windows program, it does not recognize the Windows-based time zone information. To set system-level time zone information for Windows 95/98 and Windows NT, add the TZ= environment variable to one of the login scripts or AUTOEXEC.BAT file. For example, SET TZ=MST7MDT will instruct the system to use Mountain Standard Time instead of GMT when displaying time information. This information will be used by non-windows applications, such as ConsoleOne.

■ *Require unique passwords* Checking the Require unique passwords option enables NDS to track the last eight passwords used with this account and prevents the user from reusing these old passwords. However, NDS does not implement any pattern-recognition algorithms to force the user to change the password to a significantly different value. Users can change the value by a single character, and NDS will not complain. Users should be taught that this is an unacceptable practice.

Similarly, NDS does not have an option for requiring numeric or special characters as part of the password. Users also should be taught to use numbers and special characters as part of their password to increase its effectiveness.

■ *Limit grace logins* This option limits the number of times users are allowed to log in after their passwords have expired. Associated with this option are two fields. The Grace Logins Allowed field enables the administrator to set how many grace logins will be permitted. The default is 6, but the value can be set between 1 and 200.

The Remaining grace logins field tracks how many grace logins remain before the account is locked out. The administrator can also reset this value to give an expired account more time to reset their password, if necessary.

- *Change password (button)* This button enables an authorized user to reset the password on a user account immediately. Pressing this button spawns a new applet as shown in Figure 6-40.

The first thing you might notice about the Create Authentication Secrets applet is that it is a global applet, meaning that this dialog box can be used to reset any user account password, not just the user account with which you are currently working. Simply change the Context and/or Username fields and then type the new password.

NOTE: *Be very careful when changing the password in this fashion. The Create Authentication Secrets applet does not ask for a password confirmation, so clumsy fingers may reset the password to a value different than that intended.*

- *ConsoleOne Web Edition* You also can change passwords through ConsoleOne Web Edition. More information on installing and using ConsoleOne Web Edition is found in Chapter 5, "Administering NDS Objects."

    1. Open ConsoleOne Web Edition and click the Password Management folder in the left window.

    2. Click Set Password.

    3. Enter the name of the user whose password will be set.

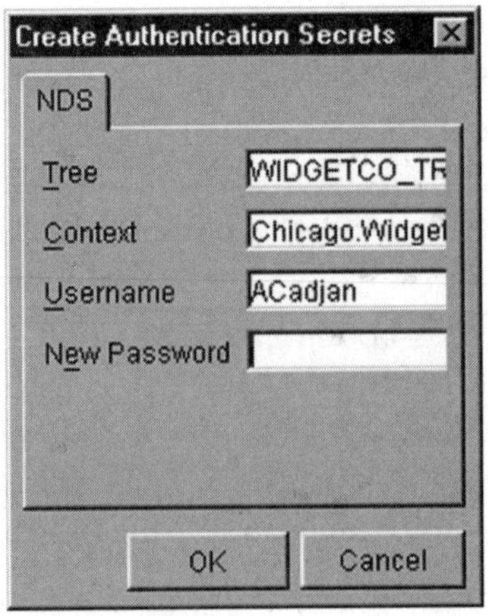

Figure 6-40
Change Password
dialog in
ConsoleOne

Create Authentication Secrets

NDS

Tree   WIDGETCO_TR

Context   Chicago.Widge

Username   ACadjan

New Password

OK   Cancel

NOTE: *If you cannot remember the exact User object name, or you cannot remember the exact context, you can search for that user in the middle pane. You can use an asterisk (*) as a wildcard search term if you are not sure of a spelling.*

   4. Enter the new password.

   5. Re-enter the new password.

   6. Click Set. The password is reset.

   7. Click Continue.

Login Restrictions   The Login Restrictions page enables you to limit how this user account can be used. Three options are available on the Login Restrictions page (see Figure 6-41).

■ *Account disabled*   Checking this box disables the user account and prevents future login attempts. However, this will not affect users that are currently logged in.

■ *Account has expiration date*   Checking this box enables you to set a date when the user account will be automatically disabled. This option might be used for contract employees or consultants who will be working for a predefined period of time.

Figure 6-41
Login Restrictions
page

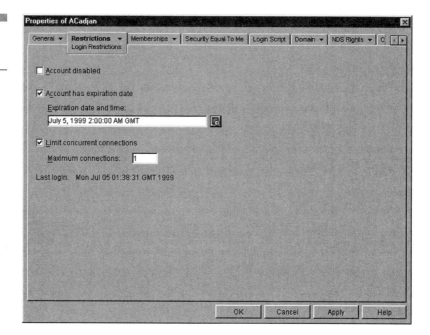

■ *Limit concurrent connections*   This option enables the administrator to define how many times the same account can be used to log in from different workstations simultaneously. If enabled, the default is 1, but any value between 1 and 32,000 can be selected.

NOTE: *Be careful when setting concurrent connections because some users may have multiple system at their desks that they use simultaneously.*

Time Restrictions   The Time Restrictions page is used to limit the time(s) of day when a user can access the network (see Figure 6-42). By default, no restrictions are applied.

Simply click and drag the cursor over the time(s) that you want the user account locked out. Each grid square is 30 minutes. If users are logged in when their lockout periods are reached, they are issued a 5-minute warning, after which they will be logged out.

NOTE: *The only caveat to time restrictions is that they are governed by the users' home time and not their current time. For example, if a user in New York takes a trip to Los Angeles and is going to dial in to the home network, the time in New York, rather than the time in Los Angeles, will determine the time restriction. A 6:00 P.M. EST time restriction would shut the user down at 3:00 P.M. PST. Although that may give your employee time*

Figure 6-42
Time Restrictions
page

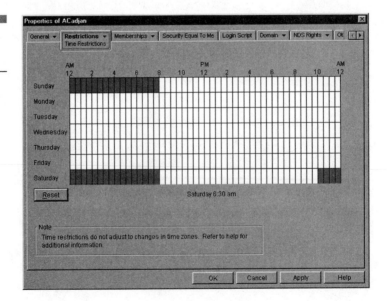

to get in a round of golf, it may not be what you intended when configuring the time restriction in the first place.

Address Restrictions   The Address Restrictions page can be used to tie a user account to a specific workstation, forcing them to log in from that hardware location only (see Figure 6-43).

In today's world of dynamic addressing and roaming users, this option is not as useful as it once might have been, but in very security-conscious environments, it can still be necessary. However, TCP/IP functionality is severely limited by the fact that the utility assumes a Class B subnet mask (255.255.0.0) for all IP addressing. This is not very practical in today's overloaded IP world.

Intruder Lockout   The Intruder Lockout page is useful only after a user account has been locked out (see Figure 6-44). Intruder lockout refers to the disabling of a user account after a certain number of unsuccessful login attempts has been made. To re-enable a locked-out account, the administrator will uncheck the Account locked box on this page. The other three entries simply provide information about the status of the locked account.

You can also re-enable a locked account through ConsoleOne Web Edition.

1. Open ConsoleOne Web Edition and click Clear Lockout in the left pane (see Figure 6-45).

2. Enter the username in the right pane. Remember to use the complete context.

3. Click Clear. You will receive confirmation that the lock has been cleared.

Figure 6-43
Address Restrictions page

Create Network Address   ☒

NetAddress Type

IPX ▼

NetAddress

Network (4 bytes): ▢

Node (6 bytes): ▢

Socket (2 bytes): ▢

OK   Cancel   Help

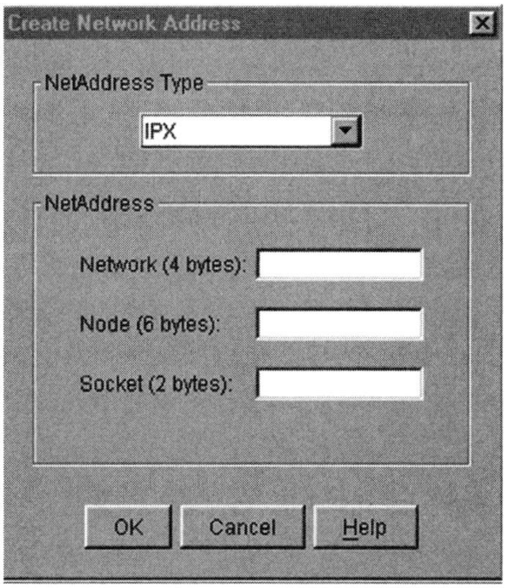

Figure 6-44
Intruder Lockout
page

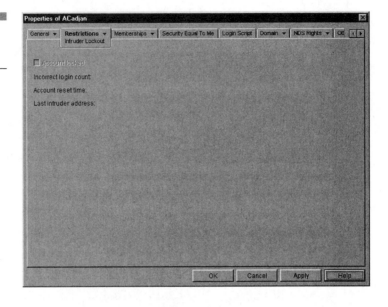

Figure 6-45
Clear Lockout Page in
ConsoleOne Web
Edition

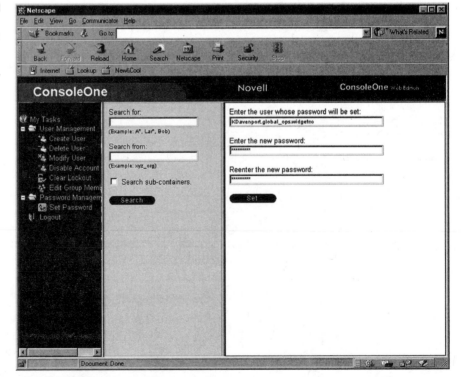

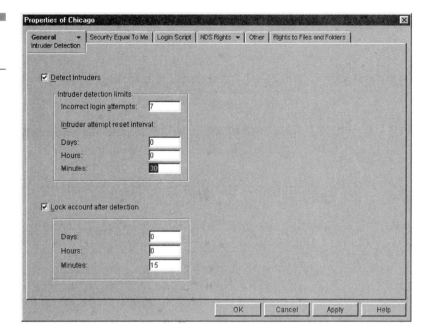

Figure 6-46
Intruder Lockout
configuration page

The actual intruder detection system is configured at the container level rather than at the user level. To configure your intruder detection environment, complete the following steps:

1. Open ConsoleOne, right click on the container object and select Properties.

2. Click on the General tab and select Intruder Detection (see Figure 6-46).

3. Check the Detect Intruders box to enable intruder detection system for this container. Associated with this check box are fields that enable you to set the number of incorrect login attempts before intruder lockout is activated—default is 7—and the interval within which the unsuccessful attempts must occur—default is 30 minutes.

4. Check the Lock account after detection box to enable the account lockout feature. Associated with this check box are fields that enable you to specify the time period for which the account will be locked— default is 15 minutes. At the end of this period, the account will be reactivated automatically.

Integrating NT Security with NDS

NDS enables organizations to implement a single security strategy across the NetWare, NT, and Solaris platforms. This section touches on a few integration topics unique to the NT platform.

Two primary activities need to be covered when integrating NT security with NDS: password synchronization and cross-domain authentication.

Cross-domain authentication is a very simple process using NDS. No trust relationships or administrative difficulties exist to worry about. You can add domain access to either a user object or a template object. To enable cross-domain authentication, complete the following:

1. Double-click on the appropriate object and then click the Domain tab twice. Click Domain Access (see Figure 6-47).

2. Click Add and select the domain for which you want to grant access. You also can specify any group associations and rights you want to give the user. Click OK.

3. After adding the required domain rights, click Apply and OK to commit the changes to NDS.

With the NDS and NT Domain environments integrated, it is very useful to be able to synchronize passwords across the two systems. When users or administrators change passwords, we want them to remain identical across NDS and NT regardless of the utility used to change the password. This can be accomplished through the Force Password Sync option.

Force Password Sync can be enabled at three different times: during the migration of Domain users to NDS, through the creation of an NDS user template, or directly through the NDS user object.

Figure 6-47
ConsoleOne Domain
Access page

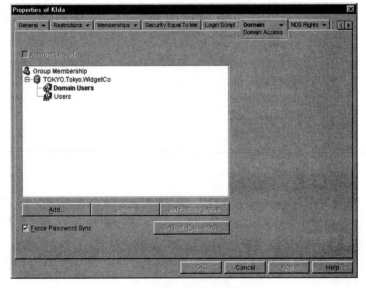

To synchronize NDS and NT passwords for a user, complete the following:

1. In ConsoleOne, double-click the User or template object for the user(s) whose password(s) you want to change.
2. Click the Domain tab twice and select the Domain Access page. If you have not already done so, assign the user(s) group or domain membership by clicking Add and selecting the domain to which the user(s) should have access.
3. Check the Force Password Sync box and then click OK.

At this point, if you were operating on a Template object, you would go ahead and click Apply and OK to commit the changes to NDS.

To create a synchronized password, complete the following:

1. Double-click on a specific user object created with that template.
2. Click the Restrictions tab and then click Change Passwords.
3. Enter a password in the New Password field.
4. Click OK to make the password change effective.

NDS will make sure that this new password is synchronized across all appropriate domains as well as resetting the NDS password itself.

Integrating Solaris Security with NDS

NDS for Solaris provides *Pluggable Authentication Module* (PAM) and *Name Service Switch* (NSS) files that enable Solaris utilities and applications to access NDS user and group information. They are able to do this in exactly the same way that the information was accessed when stored in Solaris /etc/passwd, /etc/group, or Sun's own NIS or NIS+ user account directories. The big difference is that NDS is much more scaleable and centrally manageable than the Sun solutions.

The advantage of this configuration is that Solaris—and all its utilities and applications—automatically use NDS for all authentication tasks. All of these tasks are now configurable and manageable through common NDS administration utilities such as ConsoleOne.

The integration of the PAM and NSS modules with NDS is accomplished as part of the installation process for NDS on Solaris. Refer to Chapter 3, "Installing and Upgrading NDS," for information on installing NDS on Solaris.

NDS Access Controls

Now that users have authenticated to the NDS tree, you must provide them with access to all the resources they need. This process also entails preventing them from accessing resources that they do not need. It wouldn't do to have sensitive documents describing future products open to access by all persons within the organization. Unfortunately, the nature of corporate security these days requires that some resources be maintained as need to know.

While determining exactly who needs to know what is something that each organization is going to have to decide, NDS provides powerful tools for enacting those decisions. This section discusses NDS access control concepts and how they work together to provide proper access to objects in the NDS tree.

Inheritance

Inheritance is one of the most powerful—and sometimes frustrating—concepts in NDS security planning. Inheritance is involved with the determination of effective rights at any given point in the NDS tree. On one hand, inheritance promises to save untold amounts of work by automating the assignment of rights in the NDS tree. On the other hand, because of the way that inheritance works, things sometimes don't happen exactly as you might have planned.

Novell has been using inheritance for a long time. Before NDS even existed, Novell used inherited rights in its NetWare 2 and NetWare 3 products as part of the file system. If a user was granted rights at a specific directory, those rights implicitly applied to everything from that point down in the directory structure—until explicitly removed. The same principle applies to NDS.

If a user is granted rights at a given container object, those rights are implicitly applied to each object in the tree form that point downward—until explicitly removed.

Dynamic Inheritance   NDS implements inheritance through a dynamic model. This means that rights are calculated in real-time whenever an NDS object attempts to perform any directory operation. To do this, NDS starts at [Root] and walks down the implicit security equivalence chain in order to build a set of effective rights for that object. We will see, in upcoming sections, that effective rights are a little more complicated than this.

If the requested operation is allowed under the effective rights for that object, the operation is allowed to continue. If not, an insufficient rights message is returned. For example, user ACadjan might suddenly decide that his NDS tree does not need a Security object. Because ACadjan does not have supervisory rights over the Security object, his effective rights do not allow him to perform this operation. When he then attempts to delete said object, he receives the message shown in Figure 6-48. Not even ACadjan, WidgetCo's CTO, should have the power to do something this foolish.

Some might rightly point out that having to traverse the NDS directory tree from [Root] in order to determine effective rights may not be a good thing. What happens if a user in Munich wants to access an NDS object? A replica of the entire NDS tree, from which to build the user's effective rights, may not be handy. Does that mean that NDS has to trace back across an expensive WAN link in order to build a list of that user's effective rights? Fortunately, Novell has considered this problem and resolves it through the use of External References.

External References exist primarily to protect database integrity. To provide database integrity, they store security equivalence information from partitions that do not reside locally. In other words, the Master replica of the Munich partition will maintain an external reference to [Root]. To determine the effective rights for a Munich user, NDS needs consult only the locally stored external references instead of crossing the WAN link to find the information it needs. This reduces network traffic and increases the speed of NDS tremendously.

Static Inheritance   In contrast to dynamic inheritance, some directory products—most notably Microsoft's Active Directory—use a static inheritance model. This method, although accomplishing the task of providing inheritance, suffers from several shortcomings:

■ *Database Size*   The first problem with static inheritance is that it requires each object to maintain all its rights information. This may sound fine until you recognize the fact that this requires *every* object in a container to duplicate the rights information maintained in the

Figure 6-48
Sample rights error message

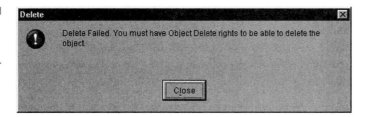

container object. This leads to a tremendous increase in database size when management rights are added to the tree.

For example, assume that WidgetCo decides to assign THarris administrative rights to the Chicago container. If we assume that 5000 objects exist in the Chicago container, a static inheritance model dictates that we must add THarris as an administrative trustee to the ACL of each of the 5000 objects in the Chicago container. Further assuming that each ACL modification adds just 256 bytes to each ACL, our directory database has just grown by 1,280,000 bytes!

In comparison, a dynamic inheritance model makes the ACL addition at the Chicago container object only, for a directory database increase of 256 bytes.

- *Replication Traffic* The second problem with static inheritance revolves around replication traffic. Any decent directory must support replication of the database across multiple servers to provide fault tolerance. Continuing our example, if we assume that the Chicago partition of the WidgetCo directory is replicated across five servers, each ACL change would have to be replicated five times—once for each replica server. Under the static inheritance model, this works out to $5 \times 1{,}280{,}000 = 6{,}400{,}000$ bytes of network traffic.

In comparison, the dynamic inheritance model requires $5 \times 256 = 1{,}280$ bytes to accomplish the same task.

- *Delayed recognition of changes* The third problem with static inheritance revolves around when ACL information is read. Because the information is considered static, ACLs are read upon user login. The problem arises when changes are made to a user's ACL while he or she is logged in. If these new administrative rights for THarris are applied while he is logged in, the changes will not be recognized until he logs out and logs back in again.

Dynamic inheritance calculates effective rights each time an operation is requested. This means that the new administrative rights assigned to THarris will be recognized immediately.

Obviously, the static inheritance model is vastly inferior to dynamic inheritance from the perspective of efficiency, but it is significantly easier to implement. This might explain the decision of some vendors to implement the static inheritance model.

In small networks, this difference in performance might not be noticeable, but in a large enterprise, the extra database size and network overhead could result in a dramatic increase in costs.

Security Equivalence

Security equivalence in NDS is used to assign one object in NDS rights identical to those of another object. NDS offers explicit and implicit security equivalence. Under the rules of inheritance described in the preceding section, security equivalence will continue to flow down from the point it is granted. In other words, if THarris in Chicago.WidgetCo is granted equivalence to the Admin object, those rights will be granted at [Root] just like they are for Admin. Equivalence provides a method to grant users in one branch of the NDS tree access to objects in a different branch of the NDS tree.

NOTE: *Using security equivalence is not as efficient as allowing inheritance to do the access control for you. If you find yourself having to grant lots of security equivalence, it is a strong indication that problems with your fundamental NDS design might exist. NDS design issues are discussed in Chapter 2, "Designing NDS."*

Implicit Security Equivalence Implicit security equivalence occurs automatically when an object is inserted into the NDS tree. Each object has security equivalence with the following objects:

- [Root] object
- [Public] Trustee
- Each container between the object and [Root]

Security equivalence to these objects and trustees provides basic access to NDS so that the new object can navigate properly through the directory. Leveraging these default rights is a good way to avoid serious pitfalls when creating your security environment. Table 6-5 lists the default rights assigned to some basic NDS objects when they are created.

Remember that these implicit rights, through inheritance, flow down from the point they are granted. Because all these rights are granted very

Table 6-5

Default NDS rights

Object Type	Default Entry Rights	All Attributes Rights
[Root]	Browse for all: Users, Groups, Volumes	None
[Public]	Browse for [Root] Browse for all Users Browse for all Servers Browse for all NLS Licenses	Read and Compare for NLS Licenses
Admin	Supervisor for [Root] (implies all object rights)	All All Attributes Rights for [Root]
Container	Browse for itself	None
Server	Supervisor for itself Supervisor for its container	All All Attributes Rights for itself All All AttributesRights for its container
User	Browse for itself	Read and Compare for itself

high in the tree, a user ends up receiving basic rights to every container and object in NDS. With these rights, he or she can browse the entire WidgetCo tree and see all objects. The user can browse his or her own object attributes and the attributes of *Novell Licensing Service* (NLS) objects.

TIP: *Users are also granted rights to a couple of specific attributes. Users have the Write and Add Self rights to their own Login Script and Print Job Configuration attributes. These rights allow users to create personal login scripts, which are discussed in "Managing Login Scripts," later in this chapter, and personalize their printing environment. On a few rare occasions, other objects, like [Public], are granted some specific attribute rights. These are generally needed for the internal workings of NDS and not for specific administrative purposes.*

Furthermore, because the right to browse all servers is granted through [Public], this user can locate those servers in order to authenticate. What they can't do is change *anything*. This is just as it should be. For 98 percent of the NDS users in the world, NDS is there to locate and access network resources—not to be modified.

That said, as an NDS tree grows, it may become desirable to restrict the ability to access some portions of the tree for some users. In an upcoming section, we will discuss methods—and pitfalls—of doing this.

Explicit Security Equivalence   Explicit security equivalence is identical to implicit security equivalence, except the network administrator has to assign the equivalence manually. Use explicit security equivalence whenever one user needs identical rights as another user but cannot get those rights through normal inheritance or implicit security equivalence.

Explicit security equivalence is most often used with Group objects. Each member of an NDS group is assigned as security equal to the Group object. In this way, each user receives the rights associated with that Group. Groups are discussed in more detail later in this chapter.

However, not all potential uses of explicit security equivalence are appropriate. For example, some administrators have used explicit security equivalence to make their user object equivalent to the Admin object. This gives them all rights associated with the Admin object. The danger in this is that when you derive your rights from another object, those rights are never specifically recorded in your object. For example, if we make THarris security equal to the Admin object, whenever THarris attempts to perform some directory operation, NDS will note the security equivalence and go look at the rights assigned to Admin. If Admin has sufficient rights to perform the operation then THarris, as a security equal, is granted permission as well.

Can you see the danger? Two or three years down the road THarris has been happily administering the NDS tree and he thinks to himself, "Why do I keep this Admin object around? I never use it for anything." So THarris deletes the Admin object, and THarris loses all his administrative rights. THarris forgot that all his administrative rights were derived from the Admin object and not explicitly assigned.

Even worse, unless some other object has been explicitly granted supervisory rights to the NDS tree, deleting the Admin object may delete the ability to administer the objects in the NDS tree. Most organizations want to avoid a directory that cannot be managed.

Finally, one important thing to remember about security equivalence is that it is cumulative. In other words, a user's implicit and explicit security equivalence will be added together to determine the effective rights.

NOTE: *Explicit security equivalence is not transferable. For example, if THarris is security equal to Admin, and ACadjan is made security equal to THarris, this does NOT make ACadjan security equal to Admin. ACadjan gets those rights that are explicitly assigned to THarris and nothing more. Just another wrinkle in the NDS rights story.*

The bottom line is that explicit security equivalence can be a powerful tool, but you can end up laying a trap for yourself—or others who might come after you. In most cases, the explicit security equivalence should be restricted to use with Group objects. For assigning specific rights to a single object, it is often best to assign those rights directly rather than rely on another object to supply them.

Groups

Groups are a specific implementation of explicit security equivalence. Groups can be used to provide the following:

- A uniform set of privileges to a collection of users who do not reside in the same NDS container.
- More granular control of rights for subgroups within a given container.

WidgetCo wants to create a group for the *Chief Technology Officer's Office* (CTO Office). This group has a need to access project information maintained on CHI_Widget. To create this group, the WidgetCo admin completes the following:

1. Open ConsoleOne and right-click on the Chicago container.
2. Select New and Group.
3. Type a name for the group and check the Define Additional Properties box (see Figure 6-49).
4. Specify the properties associated with this Group, including members and Group rights (see Figure 6-50).
5. (Optional) Record detailed information in the General Identification tab.
6. Click the Members tab and then click the Add button. Browse the NDS tree and select all users who need to be members of this Group; then click OK. If users are in different containers, you may need to repeat this step multiple times.

Figure 6-49
Create a new group in ConsoleOne.

Figure 6-50
Group Properties
screen

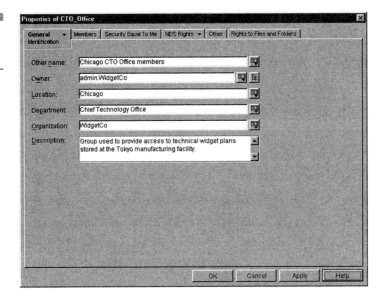

━━━ ━━━ ━━━ ━━━ ━━━ ━━━ ━━━ ━━━ ━━━ ━━━ ━━━ ━━━ ━━━ ━━━ ━━━

TIP: *You can select multiple objects simultaneously by pressing the Ctrl key while clicking on the objects.*

7. Click the Security Equal to Me tab just to note that all members in the Group are being granted security equivalence to the Group object. This is how a Group functions.

8. Click the NDS Rights tab to add a trustee to the Group object (see Figure 6-51). For this example, we are adding ACadjan as a trustee because he is the CTO. That way, he can manage the members of the group without having to involve the Admin.

9. Click the Rights to Files and Folders tab. Click Show and select the volume, or volumes, to which you want the group to have access. By default, this will assign explicit rights to the group from the root of the volume. If you want to restrict rights assignment to a specific directory within the volume, click Add and drill down to the specific directory that you want to make accessible to this group. In our example, we want to make the Confidential folder on CHI_Widget visible to the CTO team so that they can keep up on the latest R&D projects.

Figure 6-51
Adding a trustee to
the Group object

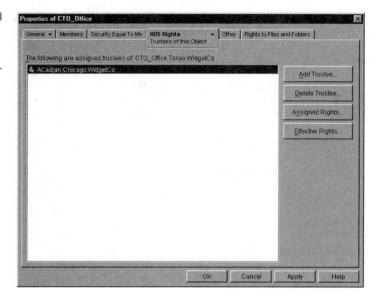

NT and Solaris file systems are not yet integrated with NDS in this
way. File-system rights for the NT and Solaris platforms are managed
through groups created for those platforms. Both Solaris and NT
groups are imported into NDS when it is installed on these platforms.
At that point, NDS users and groups can be assigned as members of
Solaris or NT groups in order to provide specific file-system rights.

Novell is currently looking at a tighter directory/file-system integration
plan for non-NetWare platforms, but no specific plans are yet available.

10. Check the file system rights you want to grant the group. Because the
CTO group needs only to be able to see and add files to this directory,
we have prevented them from modifying or deleting files from this
directory. See Figure 6-52.

NOTE: *The directory and file rights for Group objects are applicable only
to NetWare volumes at this time. NDS is not as tightly integrated with the
file systems of NT and Solaris yet, so file-system rights are still handled
through the native platform utilities for NT and Solaris. For example, the
NDS group can be associated with an NT domain group, and then the
domain group can be assigned the desired file system rights.*

Figure 6-52
Select file system
for use with Group
object.

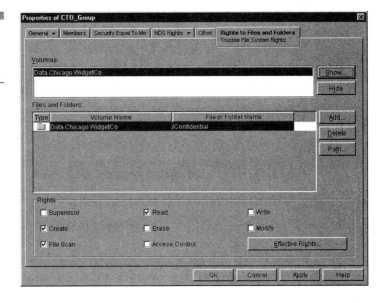

With the `CTO_Office` group in place, group members are able to access resources on `CHI_Widget` for which we would otherwise have to create individual rights. As noted previously, a Group provides rights via security equivalence. This means that Group rights are added onto existing inherited rights for group members. It also means that group member rights will flow down from the `CHI_Widget\Data:Confidential` directory unless specifically prevented from doing so by an Inherited Rights filter. This makes the assignment of the Group rights fairly important. Make group rights assignments as specific as possible to avoid exposing directory or file resources unnecessarily.

The other issue many administrators forget is that the group object will also inherit rights flowing down through the branch of the tree in which it is placed. These implicit rights will be passed on to members of the group because they are security equivalent. After creating a group object, do some testing to make sure that group members are not going to inherit rights to resources in another branch of the tree to which they should not have access.

Organizational Roles

Organizational Roles function like groups of one. They use explicit security equivalence to provide specific rights to a user who needs to be able to perform a specific task. Organizational Roles are generally used to grant some degree of administrative ability for a tree—or branch of the tree. The use of

Organizational Roles is discussed in Chapter 5, "Administering NDS Objects."

Inherited Rights Filters

Inherited Rights Filters (IRF) are used to restrict inheritance in a directory tree. IRF use looks pretty straightforward on the surface, but their use can cause all kinds of interesting situations to arise. So, we issue a warning here: *Don't implement IRFs unless you are absolutely sure you understand the consequences of doing so.* More calls have been logged to Novell's Technical Support groups because administrators got carried away with controlling every single aspect of NDS security instead of just trusting the environment to handle things properly.

That said, it is sometimes desirable to limit the flow of rights through the NDS tree; either to segment administration of the tree or to isolate sensitive sections of the tree. If this becomes necessary, IRFs are the way to go. Just remember that less is usually more in this case. If you find yourself creating a large number of IRFs, it is probably advisable to review Chapter 2, "Designing NDS," and re-examine your NDS tree design.

The first thing to recognize about IRFs is that they can filter supervisory rights, unlike supervisory rights in the NetWare file system. This makes it possible to limit the control of Admin users higher up in the tree, but it also threatens to destroy your ability to administer the directory tree properly.

Let's go back to our scenario in which Admin wants to hand off administrative rights to the Chicago.WidgetCo container to THarris. Tired of the administrative politics that take place at the corporate headquarters, Admin wants to prevent himself from being able to make changes at the Chicago site. This is easy to do with an IRF. To configure this IRF, Admin completes the following steps:

1. Launch ConsoleOne

2. Right-click on the Chicago container and select Trustees of this object.

3. Click on the NDS Rights tab in the upper left and select Inherited Rights Filters.

4. Click the Add Filter button (see Figure 6-53).

   Because Admin doesn't want to be able to do anything, he is going to restrict both Entry and Attribute rights.

5. Highlight [All Attribute Rights] and click OK. By default, all rights are allowed to flow through. To prevent this, uncheck the appropriate

Figure 6-53
ConsoleOne IRF
page

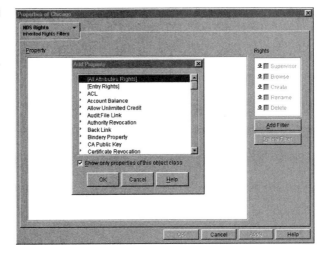

Figure 6-54
IRF error message

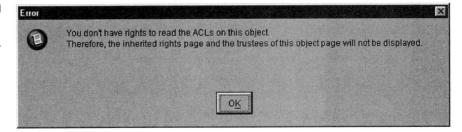

Rights boxes. In this case, Admin wants to be able to see attributes without being able to change them, so he unchecks everything except Read and Compare. Then click Apply.

6. Then repeat this process for Entry rights by clicking Add Filter again and selecting [Entry Rights]. Uncheck all Rights except Browse and click Apply.

With that done, Admin just has to set THarris as the Admin for the Chicago container, and his problems are solved.

7. Right-click on the Chicago container and select Trustees of this Object (see Figure 6-54).

The error in Figure 6-54 occurs because Admin forgot about the dynamic nature of NDS rights. The newly created IRF is recognized immediately, and Admin is locked out of the Chicago container. Admin can still see everything; he just can't do anything! If no users exist who have administrative rights to the Chicago container, Admin has just locked the tree from that point down. The only way around this is to make a call to Novell Technical

Support so they can dial in to your network and break in to the NDS tree using special tools designed for this purpose.

Obviously, the correct way to do this is to assign THarris administrative rights to the Chicago container first and then insert the IRF. However, the preceding example serves to illustrate the dangers of playing with IRFs without understanding exactly how things are going to happen. Before making any IRF changes to your NDS tree, explicitly assign administrative rights both above and below the IRF so that if a problem does arise, you are able to reverse the process.

Explicit Rights

Explicit rights are those rights specifically assigned to an object at some point in the NDS tree. When one object is given specific rights to another, it is called a *trustee*. Our preceding example, when THarris was made the `Chicago.WidgetCo` administrator, entails assigning him specific rights to the `Chicago.WidgetCo` container. THarris becomes a trustee of `Chicago.WidgetCo`. To assign explicit rights, complete the following:

1. Open ConsoleOne and right-click on the Chicago container. Select Trustee of this Object.

2. Click the Add Trustee button and select the object to which you wish to grant rights—in our case THarris.

3. Highlight [Entry Rights] and select the rights that the user needs by checking the appropriate checkbox. Do the same thing for [All Attribute Rights] and then click OK.

4. Click Apply to make the changes active and then click OK. Note that the user—THarris in this example—has been added to the trustee list (see Figure 6-55).

Starting with the NetWare 5 version of NDS, Novell has added an option that enables administrators to control the flow of rights from containers to the subordinate objects contained within. This option is displayed as an Inheritable checkbox on the Assigned Rights page of the container properties. The Inheritable option applies only to explicit rights assignments, not to implicit rights received from higher in the tree—either by inheritance or security equivalence.

Checking the Inheritable box enables those rights to flow down to objects contained within the container. The inheritable option applies to the whole class of rights, such as Entry or All Attributes, and not to specific rights,

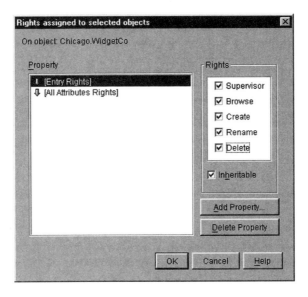

Figure 6-55
Entry rights assigned
to THarris

such as Supervisor, Browse, or Write. By default, Entry and All Attribute rights are allowed to flow down to subordinate objects. In other words, the Inheritable box is checked by default.

However, Specific Attribute rights are not allowed to flow down to subordinate objects by default; the Inheritable checkbox is unchecked.

If Admin wants THarris to be able to administer the `Chicago.WidgetCo` container and all subordinate objects, he will want to make sure that the Inheritable box Is checked. Otherwise, THarris would have control over the `Chicago.WidgetCo` container object itself and nothing else. Normally, as in our example here, the default options will be appropriate, but the Inheritable option gives the NDS administrator more granularity in configuring the directory environment.

Assigning explicit rights is a very straight-forward process, but there are some caveats to making explicit assignments. Unlike security equivalence, explicit assignments are not additive. An explicit assignment pre-empts the implicit rights that users might have had through inheritance.

For example, we know that Admin is granted Supervisor rights at [Root] automatically when NDS is installed. To assign Admin specific rights at the `Chicago.WidgetCo` container, for whatever reason, you would complete the following steps:

1. Open ConsoleOne and right-click on the Chicago container; then select Trustees of this Object.

2. Click Add Trustee and select the Admin user; then click OK. Because Admin has only the Supervisor right granted, we want to explicitly add Browse—just in case.

3. Highlight [Entry Attributes] and check only the box by Browse. Click OK.

4. Click Apply to make the changes active and then click OK.

If we then start browsing objects in the NDS tree, we will note that while we can still see all objects and attributes, we can no longer make any changes. This well-intentioned addition of explicit rights now prevents Admin from administering the Chicago container.

The bottom line is that in making explicit rights assignments, we may end up eliminating rights that existed previously. Make sure that you understand what is being provided through inheritance and security equivalence and how your explicit assignment will affect those existing rights before making any wholesale changes to your NDS rights structure.

Effective Rights

Now that we have seen all the different mechanisms for providing rights to objects in the directory tree, it is time to see just how the rights mechanisms of inheritance and security equivalence work together to provide an object with its effective rights.

Effective rights are the cumulative result of all the different rights tools working together. Eight different ways exist for one object to get rights to another object in NDS:

1. Object 1 is a trustee of Object 2.

2. One of Object 1's parent containers is a trustee of Object 2. This occurs due to implicit security equivalence.

3. Object 1 has explicit security equivalence to Object 3, which is a trustee of Object 2. This is explicit security equivalence.

4. [Public] is a trustee of Object 2. Again, Object 1 receives rights through implicit security equivalence to [Public].

5. [Public] is a trustee of one of Object 2's parent containers.

6. Object 1 is a trustee of one of Object 2's parent containers. Inheritance allows trustee rights to flow down unless specifically prevented with an IRF.

7. One of Object 1's parent containers is a trustee of one of Object 2's parent containers. Again, this is a more convoluted example of inheritance at work.

8. Object 1 is security equivalent to Object 3, which is a trustee of one of Object 2's parents. This is an example of how security equivalence and inheritance can combine to create effective rights.

NOTE: *Inherited Rights Filters (IRFs) will not affect numbers 1–4 because no inheritance is being used. However, IRFs can eliminate the rights provided in numbers 5-8 because these rights are derived from Object 2's parent container(s) through inheritance.*

Eight different ways to derive effective rights between two objects! It is easy to see how rights issues can get complicated very quickly. In a complex enterprise directory, the interaction between inheritance, security equivalence, and explicit assignment can quickly make it difficult to determine exactly how effective rights are derived.

In most cases, the best solution to this problem is to do everything possible to prevent the rights issue from becoming complicated. Novell Technical Support engineers recommend letting inheritance do the work or access control wherever possible. The default set of implicit security equivalence, coupled with NDS' dynamic inheritance, is suitable for 90 percent of the directory installations out there. Assign rights through containers and let them flow downward. As your directory tree grows, situations arise that cannot be satisfied by inheritance alone. Use Groups, explicit assignments, and IRFs sparingly to address these exceptions, but *be careful!* Always test the results of changes to NDS access controls to be sure that it does what is expected. Examine the changes you make against the eight ways in which rights are derived—listed previously.

When using IRFs, never be so restrictive that a single object becomes a point of failure. Consider what might happen if a user object is corrupted, or if that user becomes malicious. Always have a second and even third option for accessing a branch of the tree that is restricted. Just as the military establishes a chain of command so that the mission can continue if one man is lost, NDS administrators have to make sure that proper access can continue—or at least be repaired—if the standard form of access is lost.

The variety of NDS implementations in the world makes it difficult to create a universally meaningful example of a complex access control problem, so it is important that all NDS administrators take a thorough look at their own environments. Take time to understand why things are configured as they are. If something doesn't make sense the way it is, change it! A needlessly complex access control configuration in NDS is one sure way to work lots of overtime!

Relationship between Directory and File System

Another important issue involves the relationship between the directory and the server file system. Because the doorways between the directory and the file system are the Server and Volume objects, assigning certain types of directory rights to these objects opens the door to accessing the file system as well. It is important to recognize this when granting rights to users and groups.

The first thing to recognize is that granting the Write right implicity grants the Add Self right as well. What does this mean? It means that a user with the Write right can modify the ACL of an object and add him or herself as a trustee!

The Write right is even more dangerous when applied to server and volume objects in NDS. As doorways to the file system, any rights granted to these two types of objects imply the same rights to the file system itself—unless explicitly withdrawn through an IRF.

As an example, Fkupens.CTO.Chicago is a user with no special rights to the WidgetCo or Chicago containers. When he logs into the NDS tree, he is only able to see the Login, Mail, and Public directories on CHI_Widget, as it should be. However, by explicitly assigning Fkupens the Write right on the CHI_Widget, he suddenly has rights to see every directory and file on the entire system! Not only that, but he can also move, delete, and modify those files. That's enough to send chills down the spine of most any network administrator!

Now most of us are not silly enough to inadvertently do an explicit trustee assignment, but Fkupens could just as easily have received those rights indirectly through a Group, security equivalence, or inheritance. The point is that you need to be vigilant when making assignments so that no unintended rights are granted.

NDS Login Scripts

One other point of interaction between the Directory and file system is the login script. The NDS login script is a batch file that outlines basic operations that should be performed every time the user logs into the network. Login script operations can include environment variables, drive mappings, program execution, and message display. We will not go into exhaustive detail about the various commands and variables that are usable within a login script, but we have included those commands as an appendix.

Four types of login scripts can be configured for use in NDS:

- Container
- Profile
- User
- Default

A container login script is the most general form of login script. It executes for all users located within a given container. The container login script executes first and should be used to configure all general environment attributes. Obviously, the greater the percentage of environment information that can be provided via a container login script, the easier things will be to manage. All users recognize changes to a container login script the next time they log in.

A profile login scripts executes after the container login script and function like a group login script. Each user associated with a profile login script will execute it automatically when they log in.

User login scripts execute after the container and profile scripts and are meant to provide user-specific environment configuration that cannot be handled on a container or group basis. If at all possible, you should avoid user scripts, because they can quickly become very cumbersome to manage.

The default login script is part of the LOGIN utility itself. It automatically creates basic drive and search mappings that enable the user to access the server in the absence of another login script. The default script will execute automatically if the user login script does not exist. It will execute after the container and profile login scripts just like the user login script does.

NOTE: *Because all three of these scripts can potentially execute during a login, any conflicting commands will be decided by the last script to execute. In other words, the user login script will override the container and profile login scripts.*

All of these login scripts, except the default login script, can be created and/or modified through ConsoleOne.

Profile login scripts are created as separate objects in the NDS tree by completing the following steps:

1. Right-click on the container where you would like to create the profile login script and select New and Object. Select the Profile object type and click OK.

2. Specify the name of the Profile (see Figure 6-56). Click Define Additional Properties and then click OK.

3. Write the desired script in the Login Script window. Click Apply and then OK when finished.

After the objects have been created in the NDS tree, each type of login script can be accessed for creation or modification by doing the following:

1. Right-click on the desired object and select Properties.
2. Click Login Script. Create, edit, or view the login script from this page (see Figure 6-57).
3. Click Apply and OK when finished.

NOTE: *The user login script page contains an additional field where a Profile login script can be specified, if necessary.*

Figure 6-56
Create a profile
login script

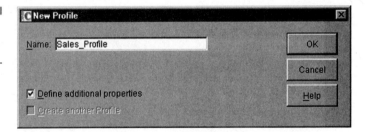

Figure 6-57
User login
script page

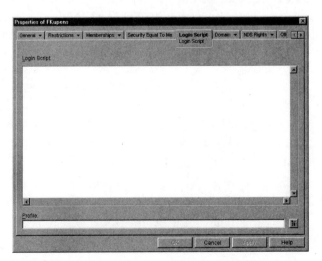

SUMMARY

Security is one of the hottest topics in the computer network industry at this time. The explosion of Internet use and the lure of e-commerce and on-line business transactions make the ability to keep networks secure a matter of extreme importance.

This involves being able to confidently identify the person on the other end of the wire. It also involves making sure that necessary information is available to those who need it. With this in mind, NDS has waded into the security technology arena. NDS has a strong reputation in the area of Authentication and Authorization already, but it was necessary to convert proprietary methods into standards-based options that will be usable in an Internet environment.

To accomplish this, NDS now offers a strong foundation for the creation of an organizational PKI. All of the tools are not yet in place, but over the next 6-9 months, Novell expects to release several enhancements to their security package that will more closely align NDS with industry standards as well as increasing the feature set significantly.

The most important thing to remember is that security topics, such as secure communications with SSL, digital certificates, and PKI, will become more prevalent. Take the time to study and understand the underlying technologies now, and you will be more valuable—and more marketable—as you look to build your career.

For More Information

We have covered a great deal of security-related information in this chapter. Security is a hot topic in the computing world since the Internet hit prime time, so many sources of information exist concerning computing security in general and PKI in specific. Internet searches will reveal loads of sites concerned with security protocols, standards, and strategies. A few areas we have found useful are listed here.

Books

- *Cryptography and Network Security—Principles and Practice*, 2nd Edition, by William Stallings, Prentice Hall, 1999

William Stallings is one of the foremost minds in computer networking and architecture. This book is written in a college text format. It covers almost anything you might need to know about the nuts and bolts of cryptography and its associated algorithms. Stallings also discusses system security from a more general vantage point as well and tries to build an understanding of why network security issues are so critical. This book is definitely not an easy read, but if you have the nerve to ask detailed cryptography questions, this book will supply many of the answers.

■ *Commercial Use of Cryptography*, by Jeremy Hilton and Nick Mansfield. Available through the International Commerce Exchange. Email: info@icx.org to request a copy.

This booklet does a great job of presenting the dilemma that spawned PKI and explains how PKI can be used to solve today's complex network security issues. It presents the technologies and standards that play a role in the PKI solution. Unlike William Stallings' book, this booklet is easy to read and understand. If you want a quick overview of PKI so you can understand the concepts and terminology, this booklet is a great way to go.

Web Sites

NDS Web site: http://www.novell.com/products/nds/index.html

NDS Security Web site: http://www.novell.com/corp/security/index.html

RSA Security Standards Web site: http://www.rsa.com/standards/

Web Articles

"Designing NetWare 4.x Security" http://developer.novell.com/research/appnotes/1993/november/a2frame.htm

"Understanding NetWare Directory Services Rights" http://developer.novell.com/research/appnotes/1993/april/a4frame.htm

Technical Information Documents

Novell Technical Services documents specific solutions to customer problems covering the whole range of Novell products. These TIDs can be very valuable for learning new concepts as well as troubleshooting existing problems that can be located at `http://support.novell.com/servlet/Knowledgebase`.

2946878	DS Design, Replication, and Partition Strategy
2949161	Minimum DS Rights for NDS User Pwd/Login Settings
2934034	Creating a Group Administrator Role in NDS

Administering Workstations

Second only to the time you spend administering network resources, administering workstations and user environments is probably the most time-consuming task that you will do as a network administrator. Most administrators work with users who understand enough about computers to get their workstations and environments out of whack, but who do not understand enough about computers to fix them when they do. This means spending precious time to make sure that the workstations and desktop environments are in top shape and that users have access to all the programs they need.

In addition to maintaining the status quo on the workstations, you might find it necessary to set up custom environments for different users at different times of the day depending on the abilities of your users. Think, for example, about administrators who work in school districts. As different classes use the computer lab, they have different learning needs and abilities. The first-grade students probably need fewer programs and bigger icons. The sixth-grade students probably need more advanced programs and probably can change more workstation environment settings. In a school district, it is probable that both these groups of users will be using the same workstations to access network resources. Managing the differences in needs and the errors and problems caused by these inquisitive minds could be a network administrator's worst nightmare.

This chapter explains how ZENworks 2.0 and NDS work together to reduce the overall administrative burden and reduce the time, cost, and resources it takes to keep desktops running correctly.

How ZENworks Integrates with NDS

NDS has come to the rescue of school district network administrators as well as all other administrators with a set of ingenious snap-ins that add functionality to manage change and restore default settings when the users have either deliberately or inadvertently changed them. These snap-ins ship in a product called ZENworks 2.0. ZENworks means *Zero Effort Networking*.

ZENworks harnesses the power of NDS to do the following:

■ Set up and manage desktop environments

■ Create a digital persona that follows a user to whatever workstation they log in from

- Manage workstations

- Manage and distribute applications

- Launch applications on the workstation automatically for users

- Import Workstation object information into NDS

- Distribute and update print drivers dynamically

- Centralize the location and administration of user profiles

- View and update client configurations without visiting the workstation

- Update workstation software automatically from your office

- Create Scheduled Actions for users

- Remotely control user desktops to provide quick error resolution (using NDS-authenticated remote control)

- Provide end-users with a help request system

- Create workstation inventories from the NDS database automatically for tracking and troubleshooting

ZENworks adds new NDS objects (Workstation, Workstation Group, and Policy Package objects) and uses existing NDS objects (User, Group, Organizations, Organizational Units, and Application objects) to help reduce your administrative burden. Workstation objects are created when you register and import workstations in your NDS tree. They represent physical workstations and serve many functions. With the full product, for example, you can collect workstation inventory and use remote control.

You use NetWare Administrator to create Policy Packages (see Figure 7-1). These packages are then associated with User, Group, Workstation,

Figure 7-1
ZENworks Policy
Package

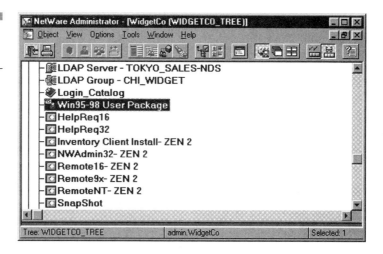

Workstation Group, or container level objects. Within Policy Packages are Policies that you can apply to one or more objects.

These Policies set things, such as the desktop preferences, help desk policy, and login restrictions. After you enable one or more Policies in a User Policy Package, all Users and Users within Groups or containers associated with the Policy Package will be affected by the enabled Policies in the package.

NOTE: *You cannot currently create ZENworks objects with ConsoleOne. This functionality should be added in the next release of ZENworks. However, after the objects are created with NetWare Administrator, you can manage these objects from ConsoleOne.*

Understanding Workstation Objects

Most NDS objects are created manually, but if you have installed the Novell Client with the Workstation Manager components (the default setting), Workstation objects are created automatically when the user logs in to the network. To create these objects, users must have the Write right to the WM:Registered Workstation attribute on the container where the Workstation object will be created. These rights are created automatically for all existing containers during the ZENworks installation. You can set these rights manually by using the Prepare Workstation Registration utility in the Tools menu or by running wsrights.exe explicitly from SYS\PUBLIC. Any containers you add after installing ZENworks will need rights set up manually to the WM:Registered Workstation attribute in the container.

When these rights are set, workstations can register with NDS. The registered workstation is imported into a container object. The import process adds a *Distinguished Name* (DN) to the Workstation entry and then adds a Workstation object to the tree, naming it automatically according to the name format specified in the Workstation Import Policy in the User Policy Package associated with the user (see Figure 7-2).

After a Workstation entry is imported, the Workstation Registration program must run again to find the Workstation object's DN, store the DN locally on the workstation, and then update the Workstation object. Now the workstation is synchronized with its NDS object, and each time the Workstation Registration program runs on this workstation, it will update the Workstation object with the following information: registration time, network address, last server, and last user.

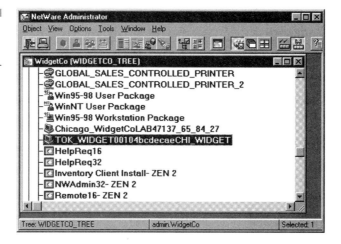

Figure 7-2
A Workstation object
in the NDS tree

To make this process easier to manage, ZENworks adds a Workstation Group object that lets you manage or maintain a group of workstations. By creating Workstation Group objects according to various group needs, you reduce the time it takes to maintain software versions and workstation configurations. For example, if a group of Windows 95 workstations contain the same accounting software, they might all need to be upgraded at the same time to the newest version of the software. You can create a Workstation Group object called Windows 95 and add the workstations to the group. Then, when you need to make a change, apply the change to the Workstation Group object instead of the individual Workstation objects. You can add a Workstation object to a Workstation Group by adding it to the Members page of the Workstation Group object or adding a Workstation Group to the Workstation Groups page of the Workstation object.

ZENworks Requirements

If you are managing a Windows NT-only or Solaris-only network, you will have to wait for the benefits of ZENworks on your network. For the time being, you must have a NetWare 4.x or NetWare 5 server to run ZENworks. There are plans to make ZENworks functionality available on Windows NT and Solaris as well as other platforms, but no definite date or announcement has been made about ZENworks' cross-platform functionality.

ZENworks software is distributed in two different ways. First, a full software product package, called ZENworks, ships with all the features previously mentioned. This software package is available for sale independent of other Novell products such as the Novell Client or NetWare 5. In addition, a subset of these features is available for free from Novell and is included in most product bundles that Novell ships today. If you have recently purchased Novell software, you probably received ZENworks Starter Pack with the Novell Client (the light version). You can also download the Client components of ZENworks with the Novell Client from the Novell corporate download Web site at www.novell.com/download.

Installing ZENworks on the Server

Before you can take advantage of ZENworks, you must install some components on the NetWare server and some on the workstations (installed with the latest Novell Client). The components you install on the server extend the NDS schema and make it possible to create and manage the new objects. The components that are installed with the Novell Client make it possible for the workstations to register with NDS so that Application Launcher and Workstation Manager can distribute applications and manage the workstation.

NOTE: *When you install the latest Novell Client, make sure that you have selected to install the Novell Workstation Manager and Application Launcher files during installation. By default, these are enabled during the typical installation. If these components are not installed, you will not be able to use ZENworks effectively. The latest Novell Client with ZENworks Starter Pack is available from* www.novell.com/download. *More information about installing Novell Clients is available in Chapter 4, "Installing Novell Client."*

Your server must be running NetWare 4.11 or higher, and it must have 40M of available memory and 175M of disk space to install ZENworks. Make sure that you have Admin rights on the server and on the container where you will install ZENworks. You must also have rights to modify the NDS tree schema. To install ZENworks on the server and extend the NDS schema, complete the following steps:

1. Log in as Admin to the NDS tree from a Windows 95 or NT workstation.

2. Insert the ZENworks CD-ROM. If you downloaded the software with the Novell Client, just double-click WINSETUP.EXE.

3. In the ZENworks installation screen, click ZENworks and then click Install (see Figure 7-3).

4. Click the language you want to install.

5. Click ZENworks.

6. Click Install ZENworks and then click Next.

7. Click Next and then click Yes to accept the license agreement.

8. Click Next to accept the typical installation.

9. Select the tree where you want to install ZENworks and then click Next (see Figure 7-4).

10. Select the tree or servers where you want to install ZENworks and then click Next.

11. Select the server on which to install the database and then click Next. This is where all inventory information will be stored.

Figure 7-3
ZENworks installation screen

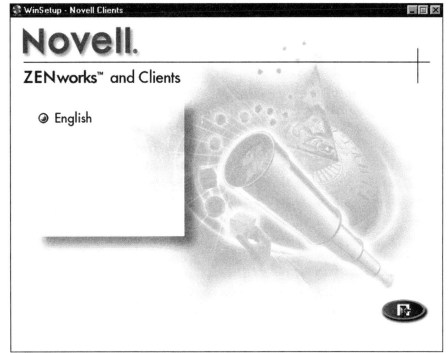

Figure 7-4
ZENworks installation
list of trees

Figure 7-5
ZENworks inventory
database volume
selection screen

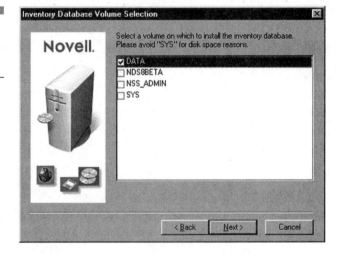

NOTE: *This server should be the same as the preferred server where
users will log in. If it is not the same server, workstations will not register
when users log in to the network.*

12. Select the volume where the inventory database will be installed and then click Next (see Figure 7-5).

13. Click OK.

14. Select the languages you want to install and then click Next.

15. Review the summary window and then click Next to begin the file copy.

16. Select the context where users of workstation objects will have rights and then click Next (see Figure 7-6).

17. Click OK.

18. Click Finish.

When the installation is complete, you will want to make sure that all your Novell Clients are up-to-date (see Chapter 4, "Installing the Novell Client") and that you have updated any shortcuts you have to NetWare Administrator. For now, you cannot use ConsoleOne to create ZENworks application objects.

Now that you have installed ZENworks, you can harness the power of ZENworks and NDS to do the following:

- Manage workstations
- Manage desktop environments
- Manage applications

We will also discuss the features of the full ZENworks product that integrate help desk notification, remote control, and workstation inventory directly into the NDS directory for easier, more centralized management.

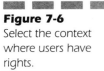

Figure 7-6
Select the context where users have rights.

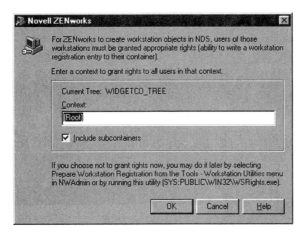

Managing Workstations

One of the best features of ZENworks is the capability to create NDS Workstation objects that can be used to manage the software and hardware on the workstations in your network. Managing workstations is the key to using all the ZENworks functionality, including hardware and software inventory, application distribution, remote control and help requests. In order to manage workstations, you must register them and then import them in to NDS. This process includes the following steps:

1. Prepare the workstations.
2. Create a User Policy Package and set up the Workstation Import Policy for each workstation platform on your network (Windows 3.1, Windows 95/98, Windows NT)
3. Register workstations in the NDS tree.
4. Import the workstations to NDS.
5. Update workstation registration information in NDS.

After you have completed these steps, you have set the groundwork for managing your workstations, your desktops, and your application distribution.

Preparing User Workstations

Before you can import workstations and create workstation objects, you must make sure that the correct ZENworks components are running on the Client workstations. These components can be installed one of three ways:

- During the Novell Client installation
- Using a login script
- Through Application Launcher (described later in this chapter)

By far, the easiest and least messy way is to install the correct ZENworks Workstation Manager components when you install the Novell Client (see Chapter 4 for more information on installing Novell Clients). If you choose the typical installation, these are installed by default. If you customize the Novell Client install, make sure that you select Workstation Manager as one of the components to be installed. This component installs a file called WSREG32.DLL, which automatically sends notification to NDS when users that have the Workstation Registration policy (in the User Policy Package) set up login to the network. After the notification is sent, the workstations can be imported into NDS and managed.

If for some reason, you do not install the Novell Client with the correct components, you can also run Workstation Manager either from a login script, or you can create an Application Object and run it through Application Launcher (explained in the next section). Detailed instructions on modifying your login scripts are available on the Novell Documentation Web site at `www.novell.com\download`. However, the best and easiest way is to install the correct client components. This will save you management headaches and possible login script errors.

Creating a User Policy Package

After you have installed the correct Novell Client components, you must create a User Policy Package that contains a Workstation Registration Policy. Policy Packages are groups of policies that apply to a specific platform or NetWare technology. They are grouped into packages to reduce the number of objects displayed in the Directory tree view. After a Policy Package has been created, you can view and edit any of the Policies associated with that Policy Package. You must create a Policy Package, however, before you can view or edit any of its associated policies. Some Policy Packages that can be applied to users and to workstations. The Workstation Registration Policy is a part of the User Policy Package.

To make the creation of Policy Packages easy, ZENworks provides a Policy Package Wizard. To use this wizard to create a User Policy Package and to set up the Workstation Registration Policy, complete the following steps:

1. Launch NetWare Administrator.

2. Right-click a container object and then click Create.

3. Click Policy Package and then click OK.

4. In the Policy Package Wizard, click the User Policy Package that corresponds to the workstation platform (see Figure 7-7). You will need to create separate User Policy Packages for each workstation platform in your network.

5. Click Next.

6. Provide a name and location for this Policy Package and then click Next. By default, the Policy Package title, along with an appended number, is automatically entered into the Name field. Change the name if you want or keep the default name. The container in which this

Figure 7-7

Policy Package
Wizard

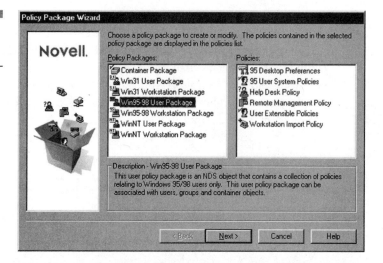

Figure 7-8

Workstation Import
Policy checked in the
Policy Package

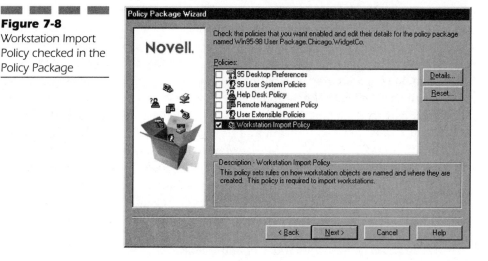

Policy Package will be created is also already included in the Create in
field. You can change its location as well if you want.

7. Check the Workstation Import Policy checkbox and then click Details
(see Figure 7-8).

NOTE: *You can set up several other Policies for Users. These policies are
explained later in this chapter.*

8. Select the container where these workstations will be imported. If you want Workstation objects to be in the same location as User objects, then accept the default User Container. If you want to change the location, click Selected Container and enter the location (see Figure 7-9). You can also choose to create the Workstation objects in the container associated with the Workstation Import Policy.

9. Click Workstation Naming and set up how you want the workstation names to appear (see Figure 7-10). You can add information to the

Figure 7-9
Workstation
Location page

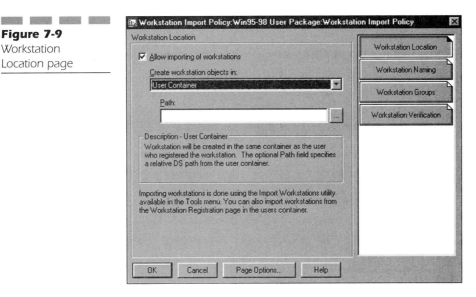

Figure 7-10
Workstation
Naming page

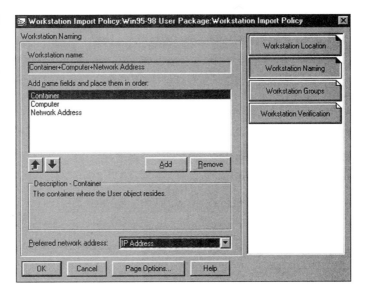

name by clicking Add and choosing other information that will appear in the workstation name. You can also delete name fields.

10. Click OK and then Click Next.

11. Click Add to associate this Policy Package with users, groups, or containers (see Figure 7-11). The most efficient way to associate this package is to associate it with containers or groups so that it is applied to all the members of that container or group.

12. When you have competed associating this package, click Next to view the summary.

13. Click Finish.

Now that you have created a User Policy Package, you can view or modify the configuration of the policies within the Policy Package. To do so, simply double-click the Policy Package object in the Directory tree, select the Policy you want to view or modify the configuration of, and then click Details.

You might also want to check to make sure that the associations you have made in this Policy Package have been applied to the container or group with which you associated it. You can check the Associated Policy Packages page in these NDS objects to make sure that the associations have been made (see Figure 7-12).

NOTE: *You probably noticed while creating the User Policy Package that there is another set of policies called Workstation Policy Package. These policies work on workstations regardless of which users are logged in to the workstation. They configure things such as printer settings, Novell Client*

Figure 7-11
Adding associations

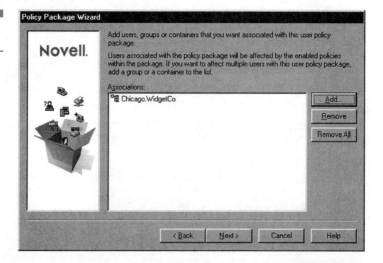

Figure 7-12
Associated Policy
Packages page

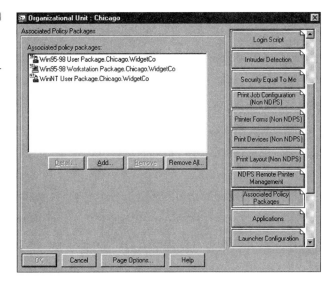

settings, and Workstation Inventory settings. More information about Workstation Policy Packages is included later in this chapter.

Registering Workstations

The workstations must register with NDS so that they appear on a waiting list to be imported. This is kind of like calling ahead for reservations at an exclusive restaurant. If you don't call, when you get there, you probably won't get seated. If you do not register workstations, they will not be imported, and workstation objects will not be created. As previously described, you can get the correct Workstation Manager components on the workstation in several ways.

After you have made sure that the correct components are on the workstations, you must have users log out and log in again to the network. When they log in, WSREG32 is run from the Client, the login script, or from Application Launcher. WSREG32 sends a message to NDS, where a list of registered workstations appears in container's Workstation Registration page. These workstations now need to be imported into NDS so that they become a part of the NDS database.

Importing Workstations to NDS

After workstations have been registered with NDS, you can import them so that NDS can create Workstation objects for them. To import workstations for the first time, complete the following steps:

1. Right-click the container where the User objects whose workstations you want to import reside and then click Details. This is the container that you should have associated with the User Policy package in the preceding steps (directly or indirectly).

2. Click the Workstation Registration page (in the right list of pages).

3. Select the workstations that you want to register and then click Import (see Figure 7-13).

4. Click OK.

You can now view the workstation objects in the NDS tree. You may first need to collapse the container and open it again so that the list is refreshed.

Updating Workstation Data

Because NDS needs to synchronize changes made to its database, you cannot update the workstation until you register the workstation again. This enables NDS to synchronize, and it makes all associations with the workstation effective. To register workstations again, users must log in again. Then, each time the user logs in to the network, the Workstation object is updated.

Figure 7-13
Workstation
Registration page

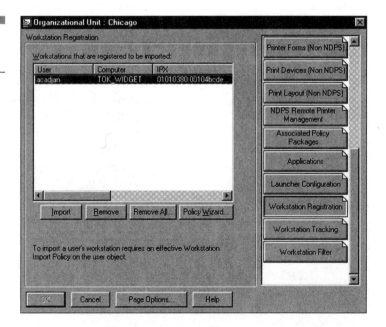

Managing Desktop Environments

You can also set up desktop environment preferences using Policies found in the User Policy Package. You can even set up different environments for different users. For example, if you want all students in Mrs. Smith's class to have the same wallpaper, you can specify the bitmap file to be used on all workstations into which they log. Then, you can specify a different wallpaper and icon size for Mr. Davis' first grade class. When they log in, the desktop and icon size changes automatically, making it easier for small hands to locate and click icons. In this way, ZENworks takes advantage of the possibilities in Windows 95/98 and NT to create specific environments for specific users and adds the ability to distribute these environments throughout the network instead of on just one local workstation.

Managing the user desktop environment means that users get the same desktop experience no matter for where or from which workstation they log in to the network. And it is as easy as making a few additional changes to the User Policy Package you have already created. If you did not create a User Policy Package, see "Creating User Policy Packages" in the preceding section. When creating a User Policy Package, you can set the following desktop preferences:

- Wallpaper display
- Screen save options
- Energy-saving options
- Color scheme
- Visual settings, such as icon size and show contents while dragging
- Cursor blink rate
- Mouse button configuration (left- or right-handed)
- Pointer speed
- Sound scheme

Basically, you can set any of the options that are available to any Windows workstation.

In addition to creating specific user desktop preferences, you can also set up the User profile as a Roaming Profile so that no matter where the user logs in to the network, the user's environment is the same. Normally a profile works on just one workstation. However, a profile stored on the network follows the user regardless of where the user logs in from.

To set up a User Profile's Desktop Preferences, complete the following steps:

1. Right-click the User Policy Package you want to modify and then click Details.

2. Check the Desktop Preferences checkbox and then click Details.

3. Set up the desktop preferences you want to make standard (see Figure 7-14).

4. If you want the desktop preferences to be in effect no matter where a user logs in, click Roaming Profile.

5. Check the Roaming Profile checkbox (see Figure 7-15).

6. Check the Enable Storage of Roaming Profiles checkbox and choose to store the profile in the users home directory or to locate it on the network. If you choose to store it in the user's home directory, you must already have created user home directories on the network. If more than one user will use this profile, locate it on the network and enter the path to this directory.

7. When you have completed making changes to the desktop preferences, click OK.

In addition to setting the user desktop preferences, you can also set other policies in the User Policy Packages. Setting up the Help Desk Policy and Remote Management Policies are discussed later in this chapter.

Figure 7-14
Desktop
Preferences page

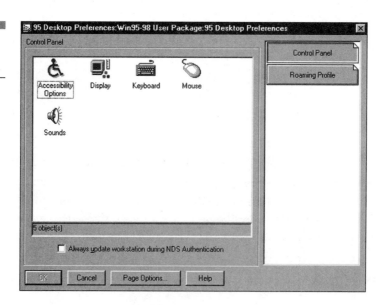

Figure 7-15
Roaming
Profiles page

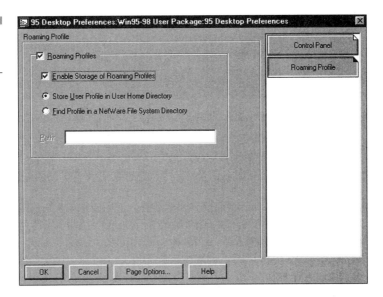

Managing Applications

One of the largest amounts of time that a network administrator spends is making sure that users have the applications that they need. This involves installing applications, updating applications and drivers as things change, and fixing software that has had parts inadvertently deleted by users. Application Launcher enables you to install and update applications running on individual user workstations and from the network. Of course, it is easier to manage network applications because the network is set up to handle these, but with Application Launcher, you can even deliver and manage applications on the user workstations. This is useful for applications that you do not want to be shared. For example, if you have accountants running specific accounting software, you may want to deliver that software directly to the desktop instead of making it a network application to which others might inadvertently gain access.

The great thing about Application Launcher is that you can set up application distribution and manage applications without leaving your desk to visit each workstation in the network. Because ZENworks registers users and workstations in the NDS database, all the information you need to manage applications can also be kept in the database. This allows you to free yourself from expensive trips to the users' workstation and allows you to customize the applications that are received by various users. In our earlier example of a school district, the power of ZENworks and NDS really come through. You can set up various applications and desktop settings for each teacher so that when the class logs in for computer time, the same applications and desktop preferences appear on each computer. Even if some mischievous student in the previous class deleted a program, it is restored when the students from the next class log in.

Push and Pull Application Distribution

Application Launcher has two different modes of application distribution: *push* and *pull* distribution. In the push distribution method, users do not have a choice over which tasks are performed. The tasks are done as a Forced Run. This is the best choice when software must be updated and when there are certain programs that must run when the user logs in. Pull distribution enables the user to initiate the installation or execution of the application. You provide the icon for the application, and the user has the choice of when to start the application. When a user clicks on an Application Launcher application icon, the application is started, and any necessary workstation configuration changes are made. Then the application is run.

Setting Up Application Launcher

Setting up Application Launcher takes several steps. The following is a brief synopsis of the steps you will need to take. Then, each step is explained in detail later in this chapter.

1. Decide which applications you want to distribute.

2. Determine the typical workstation and hardware configuration necessary to run this application. You should then set up a workstation with this typical hardware and software setup.

IMPORTANT: *If you do not have a standard or typical workstation in your office, you should decide what the most common hardware configuration is and use this type of workstation. You may have to create application object templates for different kinds of workstations. For example, if you have both Windows 95 and Windows NT workstations, you will have to create different application object templates for both platforms.*

3. From the typical workstation, take a snAppShot of the typical workstation's configuration. snAppShot creates an AOT file that

defines the associated properties when creating Application objects in the NDS Tree (discussed in "Creating a Workstation snAppShot").

4. Create an Application object (discussed in "Creating an Application Object").

5. Associate other objects with this object in NetWare Administrator (discussed in "Associating an Application Object")

6. Determine whether this application should be distributed by a push or pull method.

7. Distribute the appropriate Application Launcher executable software to the users' workstations so that they can launch and use the applications either from Windows Launcher or Windows Explorer (discussed in "Distributing Applications").

Although the setup may seem extensive, after you have NDS distributing and updating applications, your overall administrative overhead will reduce dramatically. Just the time it takes to distribute one application to all desktops is more than the time invested in this setup process. Ultimately, you will reduce your help desk calls and make the users' experiences more enjoyable.

Creating a Workstation snAppShot

The snAppShot utility helps you create *application object templates* (AOT) that can be used to identify a specific Application object and the workstation configuration associated with the application. When the application is installed on user workstations, the computer's configuration is set up to maximize performance for the application. Because many applications make modification to workstation settings while being installed, it is important to create a different AOT file for each application you intend to install on the workstation.

You capture the changes that an application makes to a workstation by running snAppShot twice to take two different pictures of the baseline workstation—once without the application installed and once with the application installed. First, you take a snAppShot of a clean, well-configured workstation that represents the ideal workstation for your network. Then, you install the application and take another snAppShot of the workstation. snAppShot compares the two images and creates an AOT showing the differences.

snAppShot also captures all the files that the application installs and copies them to the network directory that you specify. It then renames these files numerically and gives them FIL extensions. These are the files that Application Launcher will use. When you create the Application object in NDS, you specify it to use the AOT file, and Application Launcher will know what changes to make to the workstation. Note that Application Launcher works best for applications that do not require specific hardware, because hardware may vary between workstations. If you have applications that require specific hardware, you may have to create Application objects for each type of hardware and then apply these to the corresponding workstations.

It is best to either locate or set up a workstation that will serve as the baseline workstation. Choose a workstation that represents the majority of workstations in your network. To capture the workstation's configuration, complete the following steps:

1. From the baseline workstation, log in to the network.

2. Run SNAPSHOT.EXE from the SYS:PUBLIC\SNAPSHOT directory.

3. Click the type of discovery process you want to take. You will generally want to perform a Standard discovery that uses the default settings (see Figure 7-16).

Figure 7-16
snAppShot
introductory screen

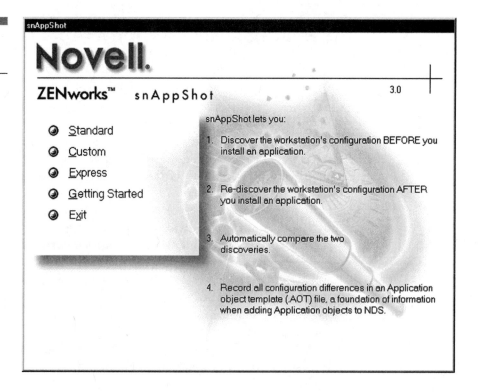

NOTE: *There is a Getting Started Section that provides an overview of snAppShot. Also, after you mouse-over the option, each type of discovery is briefly explained below the list.*

4. Enter the name of the Application object you are going to create and the name of the Application icon. By default, snAppShot provides the same name for the Application object and Application icon (see Figure 7-17). It is probably best to keep them the same so that the object and icon are closely associated.

5. Click Next.

6. Enter the location where snAppShot can store files needed later for creating the NDS Application object (see Figure 7-18). You should locate these files in a network directory that all users have access to. It is also best to use a UNC path. Remember that you will need to create a unique directory for each application.

7. Click Next.

8. Click Next again to accept the default filename and location for the Application object template or enter the filename and the location you want to use for the Application object template and then click Next. It is best to keep the default.

9. Choose the drives you want snAppShot to scan and then click Next.

10. Review the summary of your selections and click Next (see Figure 7-19). If you need to make changes, click Back and make the necessary changes before continuing.

Figure 7-17
snAppShot window
NDS Application
object name screen

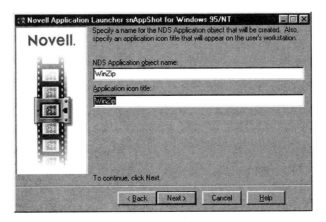

Figure 7-18
snAppShot file
location screen

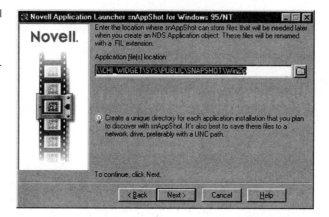

Figure 7-19
snAppShot
Summary window

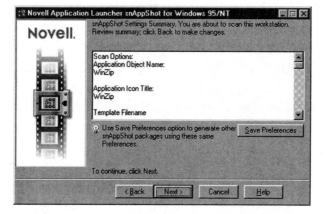

NOTE: *If you will be creating other snAppShot packages, click Save Preferences to create an INI file you can use later to create other Application packages.*

11. When snAppShot finishes scanning the workstation, click Run Application Install to run and set up the application you want to install. You will need to select the executable program for the application you want to run (see Figure 7-20).

12. When the installation is completed, you are automatically returned to the snAppShot utility. Click Next.

Figure 7-20
snAppShot Run
Application window

Figure 7-21
snAppShot generates
an Application Object
template.

13. Enter the path to the executable and then click Next. snAppShot rescans the workstation. Then it compares the two images and generates an AOT file of all the changes made to the workstation (see Figure 7-21).

14. When snAppShot is finished, review the Completion Summary and note where snAppShot put the installation files.

15. Click Finish to exit snAppShot.

You are now ready to create an Application object.

Creating an Application Object

To manage your applications from the NDS directory, you will need to create Application objects for them. Each Application object becomes an integral part of the NDS database. To create an Application object, complete the following steps:

1. In NetWare Administrator, right-click the container that will hold the Application object and then click Create.

2. Click Application and then click OK.

3. Click Create an Application Object with an AOT/AXT file and then click Next (see Figure 7-22).

NOTE: *The basic difference between an AOT and an AXT file is that a text editor cannot read an AOT file, although it can read an AXT file.*

4. Enter the path to the AOT file you just created and then click Next.

5. Click Next to accept the default information about the Application object. If necessary, you can change this information, but make sure that you enter the correct object name, source path, and target path (see Figure 7-23).

6. Review your choices and check the Display Details After Creation checkbox.

7. Click Finish.

You can now continue to associate this object with other NDS objects.

Figure 7-22
Click Create an
Application Object.

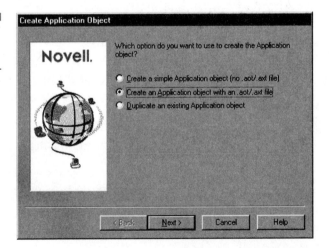

Figure 7-23
Customize
Application Object
window.

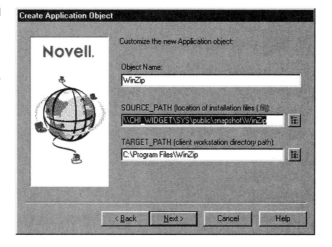

Associating Objects with an Application Object

You can associate the new Application object with the following objects:

- Organization
- Organizational Unit
- Group
- User
- Country

After you have associated the Application object with other objects, users will have the right to the application. To associate the Application object you just created with other objects, complete the following steps:

1. In the Application object property pages, click the Associations page (see Figure 7-24).

NOTE: *If you closed the Application object after creating it in the preceding section, just right-click on the Application object and then click Details.*

2. Click Add and select the objects you want to associate with this object.

Figure 7-24
Application Object
Associations page

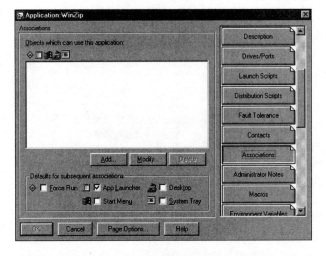

Figure 7-25
Defaults for
subsequent
associations

3. Choose where the application will run from by checking the appropriate checkboxes next to the objects that can use this application. You can choose any or all of the options. You can also set the default for subsequent associations (see Figure 7-25).

4. Set up additional properties as necessary. For example, you can set up the platforms on which the application will run on the System Requirements page.

5. Click OK to save the changes and exit the property pages.

Distributing Application Launcher

When you have created the Application object and associated it with other objects, you must decide how the application will be distributed. Before you continue, you should make sure that users who will be accessing the applications have file system rights to the directory where the application is located and that ZENworks is installed on the file server so that Application Launcher is available.

When you associated the Application object with other objects, you indicated where the application would be launched from (see Step 3 in "Associating Objects with an Application Object"). This also specifies where the application icon will appear and indicates which Application Launcher you will need to distribute to users. Two Application Launcher executables exist. NAL.EXE enables users to execute the application from the Start menu. NALEXPLD.EXE enables users to execute applications from Windows Explorer (available only for Windows 95/98 and Windows NT).

NOTE: *If you are in doubt about which option you chose, you could always open the container or user object's property pages and click Applications to see how the application has been set up.*

You can place the appropriate Application Launcher executable in either a login script or on the Startup menu. If you place it in the login script, Application Launcher is run when the user logs in, and the applications distributed by Application Launcher are available to the user.

To execute Application Launcher from the login script, complete the following steps:

1. In NetWare Administrator, right-click the object (Container, Group, or User) you associated with the Application object and then click Details.

2. Click the Login Script page. For more information about login scripts, see Chapter 6, "Controlling Network Access."

3. Add a command at the bottom of the login script to execute either NAL.EXE or NALEXPLD.EXE.

   ```
   @\\server\sys\public\nal.exe
   ```

   or

   ```
   @\\server\sys\public\nalexpld.exe
   ```

4. Click OK.

When the user logs in, the Application Launcher (or Explorer) program will run, and the applications you set up to be installed will also run.

To have Application Launcher run at the user's workstation, complete the following steps:

1. At the user's workstation, right-click the Start button.

2. Click Explore.

3. Locate SYS:PUBLIC on the file server and expand that directory.

4. Locate either NAL.EXE or NALEXPLD.EXE and drag it to the C:\WINDOWS\START MENU directory on the user's workstation.

5. Double-click the file you just dropped. The Application Launcher icon is displayed on the desktop.

When the user needs an application, he can find it in the Application Launcher icon on the desktop.

Managing Workstation Policies

ZENworks makes the managing of mundane workstation configuration easy and time efficient. For example, with ZENworks you do not have to create printer objects and install printer drivers on each individual Windows NT and Windows 95/98 workstation. You can associate printers and printer drivers with individual users. When a user logs in to the network from any workstation, the appropriate printer objects are created, and printer drivers are installed on that workstation. Users have access to the printers they prefer, no matter which workstation they use. If you need to change a user's printer configuration, you can make the necessary modifications without leaving your office. You can also associate a printer with an individual Windows NT or Windows 95/98 workstation. For example, you could associate a printer with a group of nearby workstations, and any person using one of the workstations could then access that printer.

In addition to configuring printers, you can also configure other things, such as the Novell Client. You can change Novell Client properties, such as Preferred server, Packet Burst, and Name context for any group of selected workstations. After you make modifications, they are implemented on the selected workstations the next time the workstations are used to authenticate to the network. This eliminates the need for you to physically visit every workstation in your organization to change the settings.

Making all this magic happen is just as easy as it was to set up a User Policy Package. You just need to know the types of workstation configuration options you want to set, and you're ready to go. Here are some of the workstation configurations you can set with a Workstation Policy Package:

■ Set first network drive

■ Set default client location profiles

- Set client protocols
- Set up Workstation Manager
- Select default printer for workstation
- Define other available printers
- Assign print drivers for available printers
- Enable Dial-up Networking (Remote Access Services)
- Enable File and Print Sharing
- Enable SNMP
- Set up Remote Access
- Set up Remote Management
- Set up login restrictions
- Set up Workstation Inventory

This is just a short list of what you can do with policies in the Workstation Policy Package. In addition to setting these configurations, you can schedule the appropriate time when these policies will be enforced. This is quite useful for keeping your network running smoothly. Some workstation configuration settings you will want to schedule every day, and other polices you might want to enforce on a weekly or monthly basis.

To create a workstation Policy Package, complete the following steps:

1. Launch NetWare Administrator.
2. Right-click a container object and then click Create.
3. Click Policy Package and then click OK.
4. In the Policy Package Wizard, click the Workstation Policy Package that corresponds to the workstation platform (see Figure 7-26). You will need to create separate Workstation Policy Packages for each workstation platform in your network.
5. Click Next.
6. Provide a name and location for this Policy Package and then click Next. By default, the Policy Package title, along with an appended number, is automatically entered into the Name field (see Figure 7-27). Change the name if you want or keep the default name. The container in which this Policy Package will be created is also included in the Create in field. You can change its location as well if you want.
7. Check the box that corresponds to the workstation configuration policy you want to set up and then click Details.

Figure 7-26
Policy Package
wizard

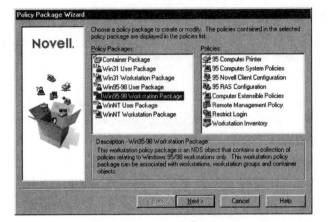

Figure 7-27
Default Names in
the Policy Package
wizard

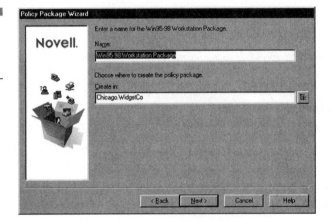

8. Set up the workstation configuration.

9. Click Policy Schedule to set up the schedule for this policy. You can use the default package schedule or change it to another schedule.

NOTE: *Scheduling is an important aspect of ZENworks. You can schedule to run these policies at the times that make most sense. For example, you might want to run certain policies every day and others only once a week. The workstation scheduler lets you determine when and how often the scheduled actions are run.*

10. When you are finished setting up all workstation configurations, click OK.

11. Click Next.

12. Click Add to associate this Policy Package with workstations.

13. Click Next to view the summary.

14. Click Finish.

Now that you have created a Workstation Policy Package, you can view or modify the configuration of the policies within the Policy Package. To do so, simply double-click the Policy Package object in the Directory tree, select the Policy you want to view or modify the configuration of, and then click Details.

Additional Features of ZENworks Full

In addition to the features discussed so far, the Full ZENworks suite contains additional functionality to help you manage your desktops and workstations. These additional features include the following:

- *Workstation Inventory* ZENworks can perform a hardware inventory of all your Windows NT and Windows 95/98 workstations. You can gather information on the amount of RAM a workstation has, the devices and services it is running, and the interrupts and I/O ports in use. Because inventory information is stored in NDS, you can access it anytime from any workstation on the network. The hardware inventory in ZENworks is designed to speed the troubleshooting process and works in conjunction with the Help Requester.

- *Help Requester* With the ZENworks help desk utilities, users can send information about problems to the support person assigned to them

- *Remote Control* After the help desk has been contacted, ZENworks enables the support person to resolve software-related problems from a remote location. There is often no need for someone to visit the workstation to fix the problem, which saves time and resources.

Using the Full ZENworks suite really demonstrates the power of NDS to reduce costs and help you manage you network more wisely. Even though there is never ZERO effort in network administration, ZENworks makes it a whole lot easier.

Setting Up Workstation Inventory

Because NDS is so flexible and extensible, it can hold all types of information. One of the most useful applications of this is the ZENworks Workstation Inventory policy that enables you to create and update an inventory of all workstations on the network which have been imported in to NDS (for more information on importing workstations, see "Managing Workstations" earlier in this chapter). This information can then help you track workstations and troubleshoot problems when they occur. For example, when users contact the help desk through ZENworks Help Requester, the workstation inventory provides information, such as the NIC card and MAC address. To set up the Workstation Inventory policy, complete the following steps:

1. Launch NetWare Administrator.
2. Right-click on the Workstation Policy Package you created earlier (and which corresponds to the correct operating system). If you have not created a Workstation Policy Package, see "Managing Workstation Policies" earlier in this chapter.
3. Check the Workstation Inventory checkbox and then click Details.
4. Click Scanner Configuration and select the server where you want to run the scan (see Figure 7-28).

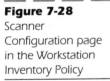

Figure 7-28
Scanner Configuration page in the Workstation Inventory Policy

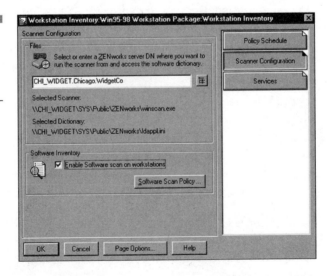

NOTE: *For more information on these features, click Help.*

5. Click Services and then select the inventory and database servers (see Figure 7-29).

6. Click Policy Schedule and make sure that this policy is scheduled to run when the user logs in. In the Schedule drop-down menu, choose Event, and then choose to run this policy when users log in (see Figure 7-30).

7. Click OK.

When the workstations log in the next time, the agent runs, and the information is sent to the Workstation object's Workstation Inventory page.

Setting Up Help Requester

Sometimes, the hardest thing for the help desk is getting enough information from a user to solve the problem. Users do not always know how to describe what has happened in terms that are useful to the technicians. And, some users do not even know how to contact the help desk when they have problems. The help desk component of ZENworks enables you to enter

Figure 7-29
Services page in the Workstation Inventory Policy

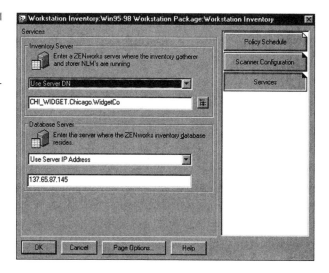

Figure 7-30
Policy Schedule
window

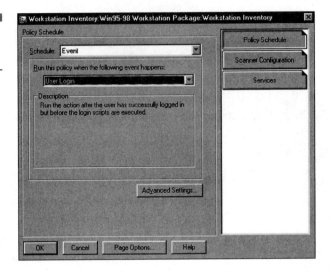

information about your organization's support personnel, such as names, telephone numbers, and email addresses, and associate this contact information with User or Group objects in NDS. Then you deploy the help request application to workstations on your network. When users double-click the application's icon, a window appears that displays the contact information. The user can cut and paste error messages into the help request application interface and send them to the appropriate support person. Because support personnel receive the correct error messages, they can investigate the problem more quickly and accurately.

As with all other NDS snap-ins, Help Requester is highly customizable. You can limit the amount of information that the users see or need to enter depending on your network and your help desk set up. You also decide how you want to receive this information—in email or by phone. Of course, sending email messages is available only to networks that have an email system like GroupWise already set up.

For the users to run Help Requester, it must be loaded on their workstations. You can use Application Launcher to distribute the application to the workstations. You also need to make sure that users have sufficient rights to run Help Requester. Because Help Requester is a part of ZENworks, the applications reside in the part of the Directory tree where you installed ZENworks in the SYS:PUBLIC directory. By default, users automatically have Read and File Scan rights to this directory, and this should be sufficient. If you have modified the SYS:PUBLIC rights, make sure that users at least have Read and File Scan rights. Users also need Read and Compare All Rights rights to the application objects. This should be taken care of automatically. You then need to associate the users with the application objects. For more information, see "Managing Applications" earlier in this chapter.

Creating a Help Desk Policy   The Help Desk policy is a part of the User Policy package. This chapter already discussed creating a User Policy Package (see "Managing Workstations"). To enable and configure the Help Desk policy in the User Policy Package, complete the following steps:

1. Right-click the appropriate User Policy Package and then click Details. If you have not created a User Policy Package previously, see "Managing Workstations" earlier in this chapter.

2. Check the Help Desk policy checkbox and then click Details.

3. Click the Information page and enter the name, email address, and telephone number of the appropriate contact (see Figure 7-31).

4. Click the Help Requester page.

5. If you want users to be able to launch the Help Requester, check the Allow Users to Launch the Help Requester checkbox (see Figure 7-32).

6. If your network has an appropriate email system and you want users to be able to send trouble tickets (email messages) from Help Requester, check the Allow Users to Send Trouble Tickets from Help Requester checkbox. Detailed information about setting up the mail server is provided with the complete ZEN product.

Figure 7-31
Contact Information page in the Help Desk Policy

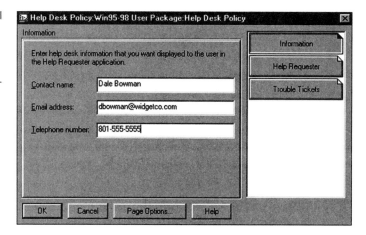

Figure 7-32
Help Requester page
in the Help Desk
Policy

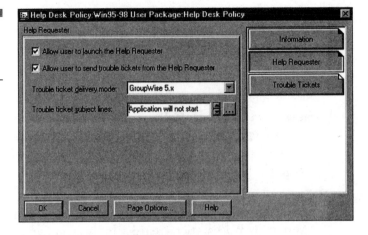

Figure 7-33
Trouble Ticket page in
the Help Desk Policy

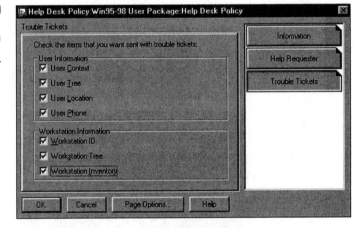

7. Select the trouble ticket delivery mode from the drop-down menu.

8. Double-click the Browse button (three dotted lines) to set up the trouble ticket subject lines from which you want users to be able to select.

9. Click Add to add new ticket subject lines.

10. Type in the subject lines and click OK.

11. Click OK.

12. Click the Trouble Ticket page (see Figure 7-33).

13. Check the checkboxes that correspond to the information about the user and workstation that you want to appear in the trouble ticket.

IMPORTANT: *Some of this information is gathered by the Workstation Inventory component of ZENworks. For this information to be gathered correctly, you must create a Workstation Inventory policy. If you have not set up Workstation Inventory, you will not receive all the requested information. See "Setting Up Workstation Inventory" earlier in this chapter.*

14. Click OK.

Now that you have created the Help Desk policy in the User Policy Package, make sure that you have associated this User Policy Package with one or more User, Group, or Container objects to make it effective. If you have already associated this User Policy Package, you might just want to check these associations at this time to see whether you want to change these associations. If you have not associated the User Policy Package with other objects, click Associations and do so now. Additional instructions on how to associate User Policy Packages are included in "Creating a User Policy Package" earlier in this chapter.

You must also make sure that the Help Requester application is distributed to all workstations. The easiest way to do this is using Application Launcher. You can either make it available through Application Launcher (NAL.EXE) or Application Explorer (NALEXPLD.EXE). In ZENworks 2, these application objects have been created for you.

Using Help Requester   Now that you have created a Help Desk policy, associated the User Policy Package with the appropriate objects, and distributed the Help Requester application, users can use Help Requester to send you information and request help. When they launch Help Requester, they have three options for locating information about their computer and their contact: Mail, Call, and Info (see Figure 7-34).

If you have enabled the Mail features, users can click Mail, select a subject line from those you already preset in the Help Desk policy, and then type a message to the Help Desk explaining their problem. Additional information about the workstation and the users, such as the user's location and phone number and the workstation ID, is included automatically in the mail message without the user needing to add it.

NOTE: *The Mail button is deactivated if you do not have the trouble ticket feature enabled.*

Figure 7-34
Help Requester

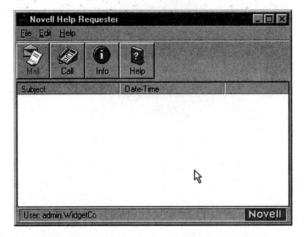

Figure 7-35
Information provided
in Help Requester

A Help button is also available, which provides users with information on how to user the Help Requester utility. Users can now select the best way to contact the Help Desk. These windows provide information on how to contact someone and the workstation configuration (see Figure 7-35).

Help Requester allows both you and the users to get the information necessary to start troubleshooting workstation problems. You will no longer have to explain to users how to locate information such as their IPX address or Video driver type. All this information is sent to you so you have what you need to start tracking the problem down.

Setting Up Remote Control

When a problem has been identified, ZENworks and NDS enable support personnel to take control of the problem PC remotely and fix any software-related problem. Because help request messages generated by Help Requester include the user's context and the context of the user's workstation, you can quickly navigate through the NDS tree to the appropriate workstation object to fix the problem. Only personnel who have been granted rights within NDS can access the workstation remotely.

NOTE: *In order to user Remote Control, you must have registered the workstations in NDS by creating a Workstation object. For more information on creating Workstation objects, see "Managing Workstations" earlier in this chapter.*

Creating a Remote Management Policy   Remote control is a function of the Remote Management policy in the User Policy Package. To set up remote control, complete the following steps:

1. Launch NetWare Administrator.
2. Right-click the appropriate User Policy Package and then click Details. If you have not created a User Policy Package previously, see "Managing Workstations" earlier in this chapter.
3. Check the Remote Management checkbox and then click Details.
4. Set the Remote Control settings you want. Make sure that you check each tab and decide how you want remote sessions to be administered.
5. When you are finished setting up Remote Management, click OK.

You must now distribute the remote control agents to the various workstations on your network.

Setting Up Remote Control Agents   Each workstation that you want to control remotely must have a remote control agent installed on it. This application is installed automatically in Windows NT workstations. However, it must be distributed to Windows 95/98 workstations. To set up the remote control agent, complete the following steps:

1. Right-click the container object containing the workstations and then click Details.
2. Click Applications (see Figure 7-36).

Figure 7-36
Applications page

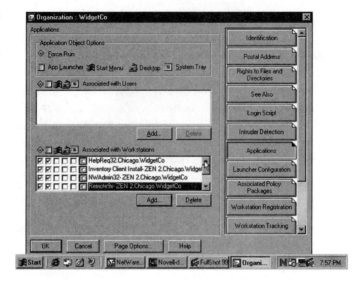

Figure 7-36
Applications page

3. Click Add (below Associated with Workstations, not Associated with Users).

4. Browse to the container where the ZENworks server resides.

5. In the Available Objects list, click Remote 32, and then click OK. In ZENworks 2, these are called Remote NT and Remote 9x.

6. Check the Force Run checkbox and then Click OK.

When users reboot their workstations, the remote control agent will be enabled. The workstations can then be remotely controlled.

Controlling Workstations Remotely   After you have set up the Remote Management policy and have distributed the remote control agents, it is easy to remotely control workstations. This makes it easier for you to troubleshoot and deal with issues. You no longer have to go to the workstation to find out what is wrong. To start a remote control session, complete the following steps:

1. Launch NetWare Administrator.

2. Click the workstation you want to control remotely.

3. Click the Tools menu and then click Workstation Remote Management (see Figure 7-37).

Figure 7-37
Workstation Remote
Management
Options menu

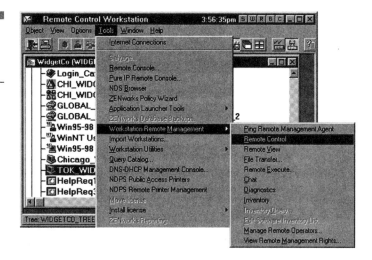

Figure 7-38
The Remote Control
Viewer

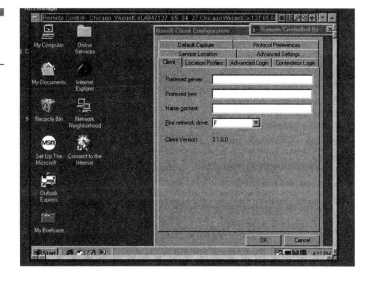

NOTE: *Several different options are possible for remote management. For example, you can view remote management rights to see whether you have rights to control a specific workstation remotely, or you can do an Inventory Query.*

4. Click Remote Control (see Figure 7-38).

A message is sent to the user that someone is trying to start a remote session. The user must click OK in five seconds, or the remote session is canceled. After the remote session is established, you will see a viewer screen that looks like the user's desktop. You can navigate it using special keystrokes and buttons. These are explained in Table 7-1.

To end the remote session, double-click the dash (–) in the upper lefthand corner of the viewer screen.

Table 7-1

Navigating the Remote Control Viewer

Button/Keystroke	Remote Action Performed
Start button	Sends a Ctrl-Esc key sequence to the workstation. It opens the target workstation's Start menu, depending on the workstation's operating system. With the Start menu open, you can use the cursor and the mouse to start various applications.
Application Switcher Button	Enables you to choose an application that is currently running on the remote workstation. Click the Application Switcher button and then press Tab to select the application.
System Key Pass-Through Button	Gives you the ability to use the Ctrl and Alt keys on or off at the remote workstation. If you do not turn them on, you will not be able to use the Ctrl or Alt keys on the remote workstation.
Navigation Button	Minimizes the desktop on the target workstation so that you can frame an area of the target desktop and change the view to that area. This makes it easier for you to navigate the remote workstation desktop.
Ctrl-Alt-A	Increases the Viewing window refresh rate without changing the remote workstation's refresh rate
Ctrl-Alt-H	Enables the Control Options hot key on the remote workstation
Ctrl-Alt-M	Sizes the Viewing window to your monitor's screen size (no borders)
Ctrl-Alt-R	Refreshes the remote workstation's desktop
Ctrl-Alt-S	Passes Windows reserved keystrokes (like Alt-Tab) to the remote workstation so that all keystrokes affect only the remote workstation
Ctrl-Alt-T	Reconnects your workstation to the remote workstation and refreshes the Viewing window

SUMMARY

ZENworks is an excellent way to reduce your administrative costs in time and resources. It uses the power of NDS to manage user desktops and applications in order to reduce the time you spend administrating workstations. ZENworks is powerful enough to handle even complex systems that need to provide different applications and environments to different users no matter where they log in to the network. ZENworks lets you set up location-independent profiles that provide users with the access and applications they need from anywhere on the network. ZENworks enables you to import and manage workstation objects in NDS, which can provide excellent value to your network. You can create User Policy Packages and Workstation Policy Packages to manage desktop environments, application distribution, and workstation settings. You can distribute applications across the network using either a push or a pull method with Application Launcher.

Additional features are available in the full ZENworks product that ships independently of NDS. These include options for setting up workstation hardware and software inventory, help desk policies, and remote control capabilities. These additional features enable you to further reduce the amount of time needed at individual user workstations.

For More Information

Here are some additional resources for information on ZENworks.

Web Sites

ZENworks Homepage `http://www.novell.com/products/nds/zenworks`

Cool Solutions ZENworks Community `http://www.novell.com/coolsolutions/zenworks`

ZENworks Documentation
`http://www.novell.com/documentation/lg/zen2/docui/index.html`

Competitive Info `http://www.novell.com/advantage/zen`

ZENworks FAQ `http://developer.novell.com/dev_resources/faq/zenfaq.htm`

Retrieve ZENworks Literature `http://webapps.novell.com/`
`cgi-bin/custom/corp/collateral/results?source=`
`Novell+Search&division=Z.E.N.works&doc_type=`
`ALL&language=ALL`

Web Articles

"Using ZENworks to Manage Users' Desktops" `http://developer.`
`novell.com/research/appnotes/1998/june/a3frame.htm`

"An Introduction to ZENworks: Zero Effort Networking for Users"
`http://www.developer.novell.com/research/appnotes/`
`1998/may/a2frame.htm`

"A ZENworks-Friendly Location Independence Strategy for NetWare
Networks" `http://www.developer.novell.com/research/`
`appnotes/1998/october/a3frame.htm`

"Using ZENworks to Distribute and Manage Applications on a Network"
`http://www.developer.novell.com/research/appnotes/1998/`
`october/a2frame.htm`

"Using ZENworks to Manage Users' Desktops" `http://www.`
`developer.novell.com/research/appnotes/1998/june/`
`a3frame.htm`

"Using ZENworks to Check Workstation Hardware for Year 2000
Compatibility"
`http://www.developer.novell.com/research/appnotes/`
`1999/january/a1frame.htm`

"A ZENworks-Friendly Location Independence Strategy for NetWare
Networks" `http://www.developer.novell.com/research/`
`appnotes/1998/october/a3frame.htm`

"ZENDS Design for Large Sites: Implementing a Replicated ZEN
Container" `http://www.developer.novell.com/research/`
`appnotes/1998/november/a3frame.htm`

"Distributing Netscape Navigator Using Novell's ZENworks"
`http://www.developer.novell.com/research/appnotes/`
`1999/february/a2frame.htm`

"Using ZENworks to Distribute Windows NT Service Packs"
`http://www.developer.novell.com/research/appnotes/`
`1999/march/a3frame.htm`

"A Practical Guide to Using Novell Application Launcher (NAL) 2.01"
`http://www.developer.novell.com/research/appnotes/`
`1998/january/a3frame.htm`

"Integrating Thin-Client Servers with ZENworks and NDS"
`http://www.developer.novell.com/research/appnotes/`
`1999/july/a2frame.htm`

Technical Information Documents

Novell Technical Support provides further information on Novell products. The following is a list of TIDs that can be located at `www.support.novell.com`.

2940854	Troubleshooting ZEN Policy Packages not Downloading
2939246	Troubleshooting ZEN Workstation Registration
2940069	Microsoft Policies and ZENworks
2945431	Not Able to Register a Workstation
2941526	ZENworks and Remote Control Tips

Administering NDPS Printing

One of the greatest advantages of a network is the ability to share expensive resources like printers. Networked printers enable multiple users to share printers that are connected to the network. Because of the cost savings, you can often buy a more sophisticated printer and still save money, because you don't have to buy each workstation its own printer.

Because the printers are on the network, the users can also send print jobs to the printer and free up their workstations so that they can continue to work without waiting for the print job to clear. Print jobs can also be prioritized so that an important report for a meeting is not kept waiting behind someone printing their child's most recent computer art creation. Also, users can have access to a wider variety of printers, such as color printers or other specialty printers, no matter where they are located on the network. With networked printers, there is no need to copy necessary files to a disk or to locate the workstation hooked up to the printer you want to use.

Despite all its advantages, network printing is not always the easiest thing to set up in a network. For NetWare networks, NDS has a solution—*Novell Distributed Print Services* (NDPS). NDPS takes away much of the headache associated with queue-based printing, because you can manage printing though NDS objects.

TIP: *At this time, NDPS is best used in a NetWare or a mixed operating system environment with NetWare servers. The solutions for native NT and Solaris environments are being developed but have not been released to the public. For now, using the existing print solutions for NT and Solaris are your best bet. Or, if you have NetWare and Solaris, you can use queue-based printing, Novell's older and more complex solution for printing. Because queue-based printing is not an NDS solution, it is not covered in this book.*

This chapter describes NDPS, how to set it up, and how to administer it. If you are running a native Windows NT or Windows Solaris network, NDPS is not for you. It requires a NetWare 5 server. However, you should have no problems using your existing network printing solution in your NDS environment.

Understanding NDPS

Novell Distributed Print Services (NDPS) takes advantage of NDS to simplify the setup, administration, and access to network printing. NDPS was developed in conjunction with three companies—Novell, Hewlett-Packard, and Xerox. The goal of this partnership was to create print services that are independent of network servers and that provide better printing services. Some of the goals of NDSP were as follows:

- Reduce printing problems
- Reduce cost to administer printing
- Reduce time needed to administer printing
- Reduce network traffic caused by network printing
- Improve network performance

NDPS has achieved these goals with a high level of success.

NDPS has many useful features that were included in queue-based printing. However, it has additional features and functions that you probably should consider when implementing a network printing solution in your network:

- Compatibility with non-NDPS printers
- Support for Windows 3.1x, Windows 95/98, and Windows NT workstations
- Plug-and-print capabilities and immediate access to printers after they are on the network
- NDPS-enabled printers available from many printer manufacturers
- Ability to use common print drivers and to download them to the workstation
- Bidirectional feedback on the status of print jobs (available to both administrators and end users)
- Event notification
- Advanced print job scheduling options
- Elimination of SAP traffic on the network

In addition to all these features, the tight integration of NDPS with NDS means reduced administrative burdens. You still have only a single point of network administration. For now, NDPS must be administered through NetWare Administrator. Snap-ins for ConsoleOne are scheduled for the year 2000.

One of the other advantages of NDPS is that you can set printers to be public access printers or controlled access printers. Public access printers are available to everyone on the network with print capabilities. There is no security associated with public access printers. These printers do not have

NDS objects, but they can easily be managed from the Tools menu in Net-Ware Administrator.

Controlled access printers, on the other hand, are printers associated with specific NDS objects. They can be highly restricted and tightly administered through NDS. Because they are represented by NDS objects, you can more tightly administer and customize their configuration and event and status notification. One of the best things about using controlled access printers and creating NDS objects for these printers is that all User objects in the container where the printer object resides automatically have access to the controlled access printer. If others in other containers need rights, you can assign rights to them. If you need to, you can also tightly control access to them through NDS security options. For example, if you have an expensive color printer that only certain people can access, you can set up access rights so that unauthorized users cannot print to that printer.

NDPS is very flexible. If, for example, you create a public access printer that you later decide needs to be a controlled access printer, it is easy to convert the printer without having to undo anything you have already done. You just need to create an NDS object for the printer in the NDS tree. Then, you can manage that printer as a controlled access printer.

NDPS Components

NDPS is set up to take care of multiple printers working at the same time to provide print services for users. To deal with the traffic and potential errors on the network, NDPS has four components that help control network printing:

- NDPS Broker
- NDPS Manager
- Gateway
- NDPS Printer Agents

Each of these is described in the following sections. You need to understand the function of each part of NDPS so that if there are network printing problems, you have an idea of where to start troubleshooting (see Figure 8-1).

NOTE: *If all the printers on your network are NDPS-aware (they have Printer Agents embedded in them), the only component you will need is the NDPS Broker. The Broker handles all NDPS functions for NDPS-aware printers including event notification, service registry for public-access*

Figure 8-1

New NDPS objects you can create in NDS

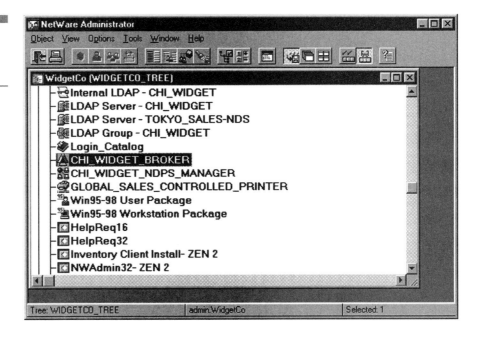

printers, and automatic downloading of printer drivers. If you have at least one printer that is not NDPS-aware, you will need all of the following components.

NDPS Broker The NDPS Broker is a *NetWare Loadable Module* (NLM) that is loaded on the server. When loaded, it adds an NDPS Broker object to the NDS tree. To load the NLM at any time, you first must install some software on the server. Generally, this is done during a server installation. However, NetWare 5 has made it quite easy to load this software at a later date. This is quite useful, for example, if you already have queue-based printing and you slowly want to convert to NDPS. When you are ready to convert a specific server to NDPS, you can load the NDPS software on the server. Then, the NLM will be loaded, and the object will be created in the Directory tree.

The whole goal of the NDPS Broker is to provide three services not available in queue-based printing:

■ *Resource Management Service* (RMS) Enables you to store printing resources such as printer drivers, fonts, banners, and printer definition files, in one centralized network location. Then, these components can be installed or updated to network printers and workstations on demand. When a workstation, for example, needs a new printer driver, the Broker automatically downloads that driver information from this centralized location.

- *Event Notification Service* (ENS)   Enables printers to send notices about the printer status or the status of print jobs to the appropriate network users. Users can be notified of printer events by various methods, such as NetWare pop-up messages on the workstation, in log files, or via GroupWise email.

- *Service Registry Service* (SRS)   Enables public-access printers to advertise themselves on the network so that users can print to them.

An NDPS Broker does not need to exist in every NetWare server, so if you install multiple NetWare 5 servers, the installation program will decide if a Broker needs to be installed and will act accordingly. As long as there is an NDPS Broker within three hops of the server you are installing, the installation program will not install a Broker. And, depending on the size of your site, you may need only one NDPS Broker for all servers. However, you may want to install a second Broker for fault tolerance.

NDPS Printer Agent   A printer agent is a software representation of a physical printer. Each printer agent represents only one printer on the network. If you have NDPS-aware printers, these printers already have printer agents embedded in the printer itself. If you have printers that are not NDPS-aware, you must create a printer agent for each printer. The printer agent can represent a printer connected directly to the network or connected to a workstation on the network. The printer agent completes the following tasks:

- Managing print job
- Receiving notification when something goes wrong with a print job
- Providing network clients with information about the printer status and the status of print jobs
- Providing services for existing queue-based print setups
- Notifying users when print jobs are completed or when problems occur

NDPS Manager   NDPS Manager does just what its name implies—it manages the entire NDPS printing process. Its main focus is to manage NDPS *printer agents*. One NDPS Manager can manage multiple printer agents. As a rule, you should create one NDPS Manger for each server on the network. Then it will manage all printers associated with that server. If you have printers that are NDPS-aware and have embedded printer agents, you will not need an NDPS Manager. However, if you have printers that are not NDPS-aware, you will need to have at least one NDPS Manager. NDPS Manager is configured and set up in NDS where an NDPS Manager object resides in the container that corresponds to the users on that particular server.

NDPS Gateway   If you have printers that are not NDPS-aware and need printer agents, you will also need to have a Gateway on the server. The NDPS Gateway is software that ensures that printers, including some Macintosh and UNIX printers, can process print jobs in an NDPS environment. The Gateway's main function is to translate NDPS commands into language that the printer can understand. Currently, several types of Gateways are available, including the following:

- Hewlett-Packard
- Xerox
- Novell

If either Hewlett-Packard or Xerox does not manufacture your printer, you can use the generic Novell Gateway, or you can check the company's Web site to see whether they have a gateway available. Novell's Gateway was created to allow Novell's earlier non-NDPS aware printing environments (using NPRINTER) and environments that use print queues to take advantage of NDPS-management features. Novell's Gateway has two parts: the print device subsystem and the port handler. The print-device subsystem provides an interface for creating printer agents. The port handler that makes sure that the print device subsystem can communicate with the printer regardless of how the printer is connected to the network (parallel port, serial port, QMS protocol, or remote/network printer protocol).

When you create a new printer agent, you will need to choose a Gateway for that printer agent. The Gateway holds all the make and model information on the printers it supports so that commands from NDPS can be translated to the printers.

Public-Access Versus Controlled-Access Printers

One of the decisions you will need to make is whether to make printers public-access printers or controlled-access printers. A public-access printer is less administrative overhead but has no security options. Because a public-access printer does not have a corresponding NDS object in the

Directory, you cannot set access rights or other properties. The printer is immediately available to everyone on the network. The public-access printer advertises itself through the NDPS Broker. It is easy to create public-access printers through the NDPS Manager object in NetWare Administrator. However, public-access printers have a limited amount of NDPS features that they support because they do not have a corresponding NDS object. For example, public-access printers have only traditional event notification instead of the extended capabilities provided by NDPS.

If you want your printers to support all NDPS features or if you need additional access restrictions on printers, you can create controlled-access printers. When you create a controlled-access printer, you create an NDPS Printer object in the Directory. After this object is created, the printer agent is automatically created for you. You then can control access to this printer and the properties associated with this printer.

If you are not sure what type of printers to set up, take into consideration what your users' needs are and the amount of time you currently spend administering printers. With controlled-access printers, users, who have the correct rights, can go in to NetWare Administrator and clear a print queue or change the order of print jobs. They may also be able to troubleshoot other issues on their own. If you need to restrict rights to a computer, you would also want to set up a controlled-access printer. And, if you want to support addition notification features and automatic download of printer drivers, you will want to use controlled-access printers.

Setting Up NDPS

NDPS is not difficult to install and configure. If you are used to the world of queue-based printing, you might be amazed at how easy it is to install NDPS. You should consider several things before beginning the installation process so that you minimize problems later. You will also need to make sure that you meet the minimum server requirements. Then you are ready to install NDPS.

Things to Consider

Before you begin setting up NDPS printing, the following hints might help you decide how best to configure and set up your system:

■ NDPS is fully compatible with queue-based printing, so you do not have to choose one printing configuration or the other. You can install and test NDPS on a few servers before converting totally to NDPS.

- If you already have a printing environment with print queues set up, you can configure a printer agent so that it accepts jobs from the print queue. Remember to make sure that the printer agent has space on the volume to hold print jobs (job spooling) while they are waiting to be printed.

- NDPS is supported by only Windows 3.1x, Windows 95/98, and Windows NT workstations running the latest Novell client software. If you have Macintosh or OS/2 workstations, you will need to keep print queues operational for these workstations.

- You do not need an NDPS Broker on each server. However, there should be at least one NDPS Broker for each geographical site, and it is better to have two in case one is disabled. Remember that any server should never be more than three hops away from the Broker.

- Users can have different roles in printer administration. Users can be assigned to be a Manager, Operator, or User. Managers have full control over the printers and the accompanying NDS objects. Operators can control the printers they are assigned to, but they cannot modify the NDS object. Users can control their own print jobs only.

Take some time to decide which printers you want to be public access and which ones you want to be controlled-access printers (see "Public-Access versus Controlled-Access Printers" earlier in this chapter). You will also want to decide which printers will be automatically downloaded to each workstation (with the appropriate printer drivers). After you have taken these things into consideration, you are ready to start installing NDPS.

Minimum Requirements

Although you can install NDPS on NetWare 4 servers, if you are using NDPS with NDS Corporate Edition, you must have NetWare 5 servers with at least 80M of additional disk space on the SYS volume and an additional 4M of RAM.

Installing NDPS

The easiest way to install NDPS is to install it when you are installing a NetWare 5 server or when you are upgrading to NetWare 5. However, if you did not install it during the initial installation, NetWare 5 is forgiving and makes it easy to install the software at a later time. If you choose to install NDPS during the original server installation, you just need to choose it in the Other Products part of the installation (along with several other optional NetWare products). If you did not install NDPS during the initial installation, complete the following steps:

1. Type CDROM at the server console. The NetWare 5 CD-ROM should automatically mount as a volume on the server called NETWARE5. If it doesn't mount type MOUNT NETWARE5 at the server console.

2. Toggle (Ctrl-Esc) to the Graphical Console.

3. From the Novell menu, click Install.

4. Click New Product.

5. Type NETWARE5 in the path or browse to the NETWARE5 volume.

6. Click OK. You may have to wait while the files are copied and the install setup is completed.

7. Check the *Novell Distributed Print Services* (NDPS) checkbox and then click Next.

8. Enter your fully distinguished admin username and password and then click OK. Remember that the fully distinguished name starts with a dot (.admin.widgetco).

NOTE: *Because the Broker is installed by default, you might need to disable one or more Brokers if you have multiple Brokers on the network. You can do this during the installation by clicking the Customize Button.*

9. Click Finish.

The installation program—whether run during the initial installation or later—copies the necessary NDPS files to the server and creates an NDPS Broker object in the NDS tree. All Broker services are enabled. The command for loading NDPS (LOAD NDPS) is added to the AUTOEXE.NCF startup file so that NDPS is loaded each time the server is booted. If the Broker does not start for some reason, you can always type BROKER at the server console to start the utility.

NOTE: *If you need to move the Broker to a different container, you can do so in NetWare Administrator. You can drag and drop it in the correct container. If you move the Broker object and want a different server to load* BROKER, *you must manually edit both servers'* AUTOEXE.NCF *files to indicate the changes (add it to the new one and delete it from the old one).*

Customizing the NDPS Broker   You may need to add printer drivers or other resources to the Broker. Although NetWare 5 ships with an extensive list of printer drivers for common printers, it may not have the one you need. If you have the manufacturer's disk, you can add them to the Broker. You can also add other resources, such as banner pages, to the Broker. To add printer drivers or to customize the Broker, complete the following steps:

1. Log in to the network as Admin and launch NetWare Administrator.

NOTE: *Some NDPS procedures can be performed at the server console. However, because using NDS is usually the easiest way to manage NDPS, all procedures are completed using NetWare Administrator.*

2. Double-click the Broker object (see Figure 8-2).

3. Click the Resource Management page.

4. Click Add Resources and then click the icon for the type of resource you want to add (see Figure 8-3).

Figure 8-2
NDPS Broker object

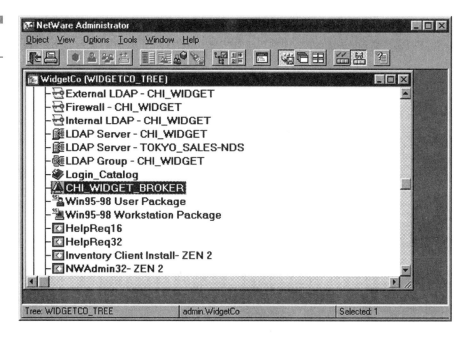

Figure 8-3
Current printer
resources

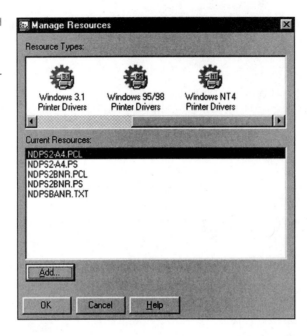

5. If the driver you want does not appear, click Add and browse for the location of the driver.

6. Enter the appropriate information about the printer driver and then click OK.

7. If desired, you also can disable or enable other NDPS Broker services.

IMPORTANT: *Make sure that you do not disable NDPS services that you need on this server. If you disable a service, make sure that there is a server no more than three hops away that provides this service.*

8. Click OK when you are done customizing the NDPS Broker.

After you have installed and customized the NDPS Broker, you will want to create an NDPS Manager object.

Creating NDPS Manager Objects You should create one NDPS Manager for each server on the network so that it can manage all printers associated with that server. You should locate the NDPS Manager in the same container as the server object representing the server where NDPS is installed.

NOTE: *If you have printers that are NDPS-aware and have embedded printer agents, you will not need an NDPS Manager. However, if you have printers that are not NDPS-aware, you will need to have at least one NDPS Manager.*

To create an NDPS Manager object, complete the following steps:

1. In NetWare Administrator, right-click the container object where you want to create the NDPS Manager and then click Create.

2. Select NDPS Manager Object and then click OK.

3. Enter the name of this object.

4. Enter the name of the server where the NDPS software has been loaded.

5. Enter the name of the volume where the NDPS Manager database will be located. This volume should at least have 5MB of space for the database.

6. Check the Define Additional Properties checkbox and then click Create (see Figure 8-4).

7. Specify additional properties for the NDPS Manager object. You must assign the Admin object for each container in the tree to be Managers of the NDPS Manager object. This is done by default, but if you want to add others as managers or modify the list, click Access Control (see Figure 8-5).

8. Click OK.

Figure 8-4
Create NDPS
Manager Object
screen

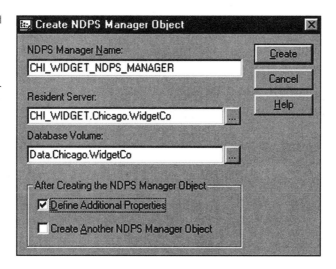

Figure 8-5
NDPS Manager
Access Control list

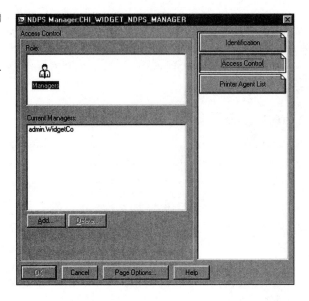

Before you continue, you must load the NDPS Manager at the server. You can either load it manually at the server, or you can add the load command to the AUTOEXEC.NCF file. It is best to load it to the AUTOEXEC.NCF file so that it is loaded each time the server is booted. In either case, the command to load the NDPS Manager is as follows:

```
LOAD NDPSM. ndps_manager_name.context
```

Replace *ndps_manager_name.context* with the name and context of the NDPS Manager you just created. If the NDSP Manager name includes spaces, use underscores instead of the spaces in the name. You are now ready to set up the network printers.

Setting Up Network Printers   After you have created the Broker and the NDPS Manager, you are ready to set up network printers. By this time, you should have decided which printers will be public-access printers and which will be controlled-access printers. In either case, you will need to create printer agents for the printers you want to access through NDPS.

CREATING PUBLIC-ACCESS PRINTERS   Public-access printers are the easiest type of printers to manage. They are immediately available to all users after they are installed. However, they offer few options and cannot be controlled by NDS access rights. To create a public-access printer, complete the following steps:

1. In NetWare Administrator, double-click the NDPS Manager object.

2. Click the Printer Agent List page (see Figure 8-6).

3. Click New to create a Printer Agent.

4. Enter the name for the Printer Agent.

5. Click the Gateway Type to use (see Figure 8-7). If your printer is not manufactured by Hewlett-Packard or Xerox, choose the Novell Printer Gateway.

6. Click OK.

Figure 8-6
NDPS Printer Agent List page

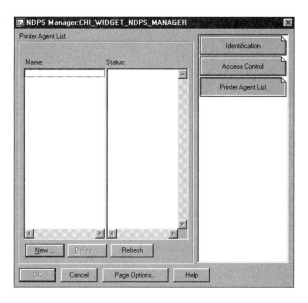

Figure 8-7
Create a printer agent.

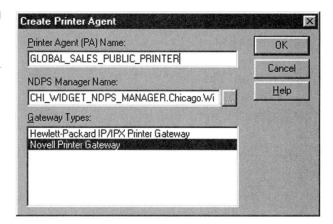

7. Click the printer type and port type for your printer and set up any other additional information requested by the gateway (see Figure 8-8).

8. Select the printer drivers for each workstation operating system that will use this printer. You can select all that apply. If you do not choose a printer driver, the users will have to supply one at their workstation. You can add printer drivers to the Broker (see "Customizing the NDPS Broker" earlier in this chapter).

9. Click Continue.

You can then manage this new public-access printer from the Tools menu in NetWare Administrator. If necessary, you can always convert a public-access printer to a controlled-access printer (see "Converting a Public-Access Printer to a Controlled-Access Printer" later in this section).

CREATING CONTROLLED-ACCESS PRINTERS Controlled-access printers have their own object in NDS and, therefore, can be controlled like other NDS objects. Additional features and access controls are associated with controlled-access printers. To create a controlled-access printer, complete the following steps:

1. Right-click the container where the controlled-access printer will be located and then click Create.

Figure 8-8
NDPS gateway
configuration

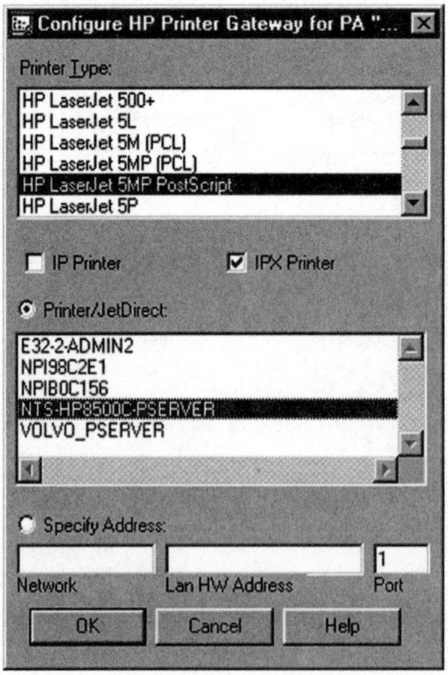

Configure HP Printer Gateway for PA "... ☒

Printer Type:

HP LaserJet 500+
HP LaserJet 5L
HP LaserJet 5M (PCL)
HP LaserJet 5MP (PCL)
HP LaserJet 5MP PostScript
HP LaserJet 5P

☐ IP Printer   ☑ IPX Printer

◉ Printer/JetDirect:

E32-2-ADMIN2
NPI98C2E1
NPIB0C156
NTS-HP8500C-PSERVER
VOLVO_PSERVER

○ Specify Address:

		1
Network	Lan HW Address	Port

| OK | Cancel | Help |

2. Click NDPS Printer and then click OK.

3. Enter the name of the printer object.

4. Make sure that the Create a New NDPS Printer Agent button is active (see Figure 8-9).

5. Check the Define Additional Properties checkbox and then click Create.

6. Assign an NDPS Manager to this printer.

7. Select the gateway you want to use.

8. Click OK.

9. Select the NDPS Manager on the corresponding server and select the gateway type; then click OK (see Figure 8-10).

Figure 8-9
Create NDPS
Printer window

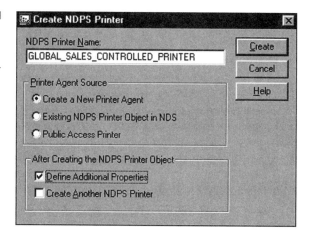

Figure 8-10
NDPS Printer
Agent window

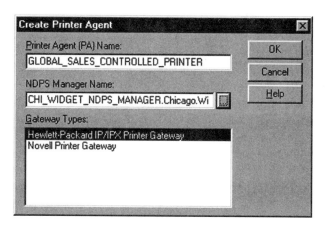

10. Click the printer type and port type for your printer and set up any other additional information requested by the gateway.

11. Select the printer drivers for each workstation operating system that will use this printer. You can select all that apply. If you do not choose a printer driver, the users will have to supply one at their workstation. You can add printer drivers to the Broker (see "Customizing the NDPS Broker" earlier in this chapter).

12. Click Continue (see Figure 8-11).

The new controlled-access printer is set up. You can now set access rights to this printer. You will also need to make sure that the printer's job spooling area on the server volume is set up correctly. Double-click the new NDPS Printer object and then Click Jobs. Click Spooling Configuration and set it up. If you want this printer to service print queues, you can click Add in the Service Jobs from NetWare Queues area and add the print queue to the printer object.

CONVERTING PUBLIC-ACCESS PRINTERS TO CONTROLLED-ACCESS PRINTERS
If you find that you need more control over your public access printers, you can convert them to controlled-access printers. You can do this at any time by creating an NDPS Printer object for the printer in the appropriate container and specifying a public-access printer as the Printer Agent source. To convert a public-access printer to a controlled-access printer, complete the following steps:

Figure 8-11
NDPS printer
information
in NetWare
Administrator

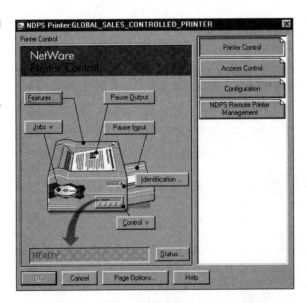

1. Right-click the container where the controlled-access printer will be located and then click Create.

2. Click NDPS Printer and then click OK.

3. Enter the name of the printer object.

4. In the Printer Agent Source field, click Public Access Printer (see Figure 8-12).

5. Check the Define Additional Properties checkbox and click Create.

6. Click OK to accept the warning.

7. From the list of public access printers, select the public access printer you want to convert and then click OK (see Figure 8-13).

8. You have now successfully converted a public-access printer to a controlled-access printer.

Figure 8-12
Create NDPS
Printer screen

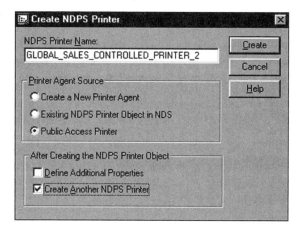

Figure 8-13
NDPS public-access
printers

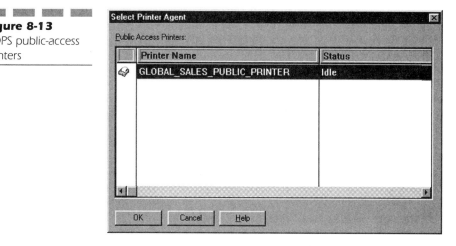

Setting Up Printer Access on Workstations   After you have installed and configured NDPS printers (public and controlled), you will need to make sure that workstations have the correct access to the printers and the printer drivers. You can either make sure that access to these printers is downloaded automatically, or you can leave it up to users to download it manually. Downloading NDPS printer access and setting the default printer automatically enables you to designate which printers should be installed and used as default. This is called *Remote Printer Management*. With Remote Printer Management, you configure printer drivers and other information you want installed. Then, when a user logs in, the Novell Client checks the container object for printer information, and this information is automatically downloaded.

In Remote Printer Management, you can designate the printers you want to automatically download and install on workstations. You can also specify the default printer. You can access Remote Printer Management in three places:

- To manage printers in a single container, right-click the container object, select Details, and then click the NDPS Remote Printer Management page.

- To manage a certain controlled-access printer, double-click the NDPS Printer object and then click the NDPS Remote Printer Management page.

- To manage a certain public-access printer, click the Tools menu and then select NDPS Public Access Printers. Double-click the printer you want to manage and then click the Remote Printer Management page.

When you have located Remote Printer Management, designate the printers you want to automatically download and install on workstations and specify the default printer (see Figure 8-14).

You can also manually install NDPS printers through the Add Printers setting in both Windows 95/98 and Windows NT. To do this, complete the following steps:

1. Click the Start button.
2. Click Settings.
3. Click Printers.
4. Double-click Add Printers.
5. Follow the on-screen prompts to set up the printer.

You can also manually install printer support using the Novell Printer Manager utility (NWPMW32.EXE) located in the SYS/PUBLIC/WIN32 direc-

Figure 8-14
NDPS Remote Printer
Management
window

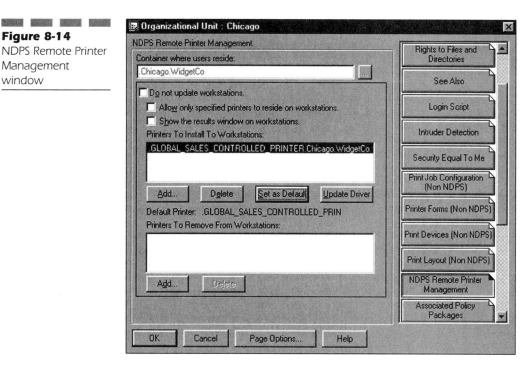

tory on the server. To manually install printers using the Novell Printer Manager utility, complete the following steps:

1. Click the Start menu.
2. Click Run.
3. Enter the name and path to the Novell Printer Manager utility (NWPMW32.EXE) in the SYS/PUBLIC/WIN32 directory on the server.
4. Click the Printer menu and then click New.
5. Click Add to add a new printer.
6. Select the printer from the list of available printers (see Figure 8-15). If the printer does not appear in the list, click Browse to locate the printer object. By default, the public-access printers appear in the list.
7. Click Filter to specify any printer settings and then click OK.
8. Choose the printer you want to install on the workstation.
9. Click Install.
10. Click OK and then click Close.

The printer driver is downloaded, and the user should be able to print to the specified server (see Figure 8-16).

Figure 8-15
List of available
printers

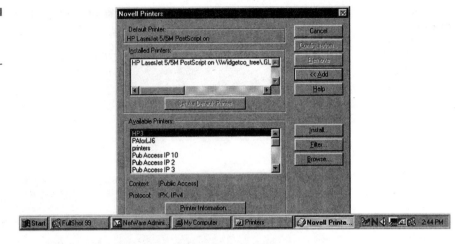

Figure 8-16
Novell Printer
Manager

Managing NDPS

After NDPS is set up, it is relatively easy to manage printing.

Managing Controlled-Access Printers

To manage controlled-access printers, you can double-click the associated
printer object in the NDS tree. In the Details page, you can add or modify

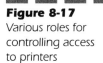

Figure 8-17
Various roles for
controlling access
to printers

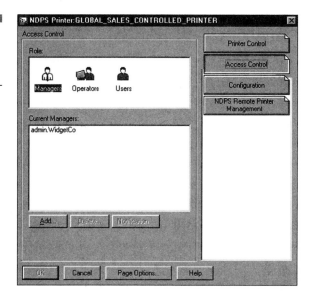

information about the printer. You can also assign users different roles for managing printing. You can assign three roles (see Figure 8-17):

1. *Managers* Can configure the printer, add users, delete users, configure notification profiles, and manage all printer configurations. Managers can manage the order of print jobs. Managers can also troubleshoot the printer and print job problems.

2. *Operators* Can set configuration defaults, maintain the printer's status, and manage print jobs.

3. *Users* Can see information about the printer (but cannot modify the settings) and can manage their own print jobs.

You can also configure the printer notification process. You can, for example, set up Access Control Notification so that Managers and Operators, who can fix problems, are notified when they occur.

In addition to using NetWare Administrator, users can also use Novell Printer Manager to see what printers are loaded and the status of current print jobs.

Managing Public Access Printers

Even though no NDS objects exist for public-access printers, you can still manage them with NetWare Administrator. Just Click the Tools menu and select Public Access Printers (see Figure 8-18).

Figure 8-18
NDPS public-access
printers in NetWare
Administrator

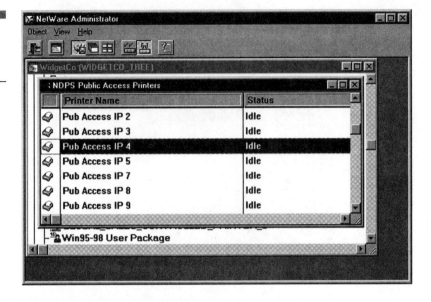

Figure 8-18
NDPS public-access
printers in NetWare
Administrator

Figure 8-19
Locating print jobs
in Novell Printer
Manager

If users want to see information about their print jobs on public-access
printers, they can use the Novell Printer Manager. The Print Manager tells
them the printers currently installed on their workstation and the status of
current print jobs (see Figure 8-19). They can cancel print jobs from the
Novell Print Manager.

Managing Print Jobs

Users can manage their print jobs either from NetWare Administrator (controlled-access printers only) or from the Novell Printer Manager utility. They can see the status of their print jobs and they can do the following:

- View information about a print job
- Modify a print job
- Change job order
- Copy or move a print job
- Cancel a print job
- Place a print job on hold

Operators can perform all these functions on any print jobs at the printer. Because you can use either NetWare Administrator (see Figure 8-11) or the Novell Printer Manager (see Figure 8-19), you will want to decide which option works best for your users. If you routinely allow users to access NetWare Administrator, this is a good option.

However, users may find it overwhelming to use NetWare Administrator to manage print jobs. Instead, you can distribute the Novell Printer Manager right to their desktops using Application Launcher. See Chapter 7, "Administering Workstations," for more details on Application Launcher and ZENworks.

Viewing Information About a Print Job   To view information about a print job in NetWare Administrator, complete the following steps:

1. In NetWare Administrator, double-click the printer object.
2. Click Jobs and then click Job List.
3. Click the specific print job.
4. Click Information.

To view information about a print job in Novell Printer Manager, complete the following steps:

1. In Novell Printer Manager, double-click the printer object.
2. Click the Printer menu and then Click Jobs.
3. Click the specific print job.
4. Click the Job Information button.

Modifying a Print Job   To modify a print job in NetWare Administrator, complete the following steps:

1. In NetWare Administrator, double-click the printer object.
2. Click Jobs and then click Job List.
3. Click the specific print job.
4. Click Job Options and then click Configuration.
5. Change the properties you need to modify on the corresponding tab.
6. Click OK.

To modify a print job in Novell Printer Manager, complete the following steps:

1. In Novell Printer Manager, double-click the printer object.
2. Click the Printer menu and then Click Jobs.
3. Click the specific print job.
4. Click the Printer menu and then click Configuration.
5. Change the properties you need to modify and then click OK.

Changing A Job Order   To change a job order in NetWare Administrator, complete the following steps:

1. In NetWare Administrator, double-click the printer object.
2. Click Jobs and then click Job List.
3. Click the specific print job.
4. Click Job Options and then click Reorder.
5. Move the job to its new position in the print order.
6. Click OK.

To change a job order in Novell Printer Manager, complete the following steps:

1. In Novell Printer Manager, double-click the printer object.
2. Click the Printer menu and then Click Jobs.
3. Click the specific print job.
4. Click the Printer menu and then click Reorder.
5. Move the job to its new position in the print order.
6. Click OK.

Copying a Print Job   To copy a print job to another printer in NetWare Administrator, complete the following steps:

1. In NetWare Administrator, double-click the printer object.
2. Click Jobs and then click Job List.
3. Click the specific print job.
4. Click Job Options and then click Copy.
5. Select the server you want to copy to and then click Copy.

To copy a print job in Novell Printer Manager, complete the following steps:

1. In Novell Printer Manager, double-click the printer object.
2. Click the Printer menu and then Click Jobs.
3. Click the specific print job.
4. Click the Printer menu and then click Copy.
5. Copy the job to its new location.
6. Click OK.

Moving a Print Job   To move a print job to another printer in NetWare Administrator, complete the following steps:

1. In NetWare Administrator, double-click the printer object.
2. Click Jobs and then click Job List.
3. Click the specific print job.
4. Click Job Options and then click Move.
5. Select the server you want to move to and then click Move.

To move a print job in Novell Printer Manager, complete the following steps:

1. In Novell Printer Manager, double-click the printer object.
2. Click the Printer menu and then Click Jobs.
3. Click the specific print job.
4. Click the Printer menu and then click Move.
5. Move the job to its new location.
6. Click OK.

Canceling a Print Job   To cancel a print job in NetWare Administrator, complete the following steps:

1. In NetWare Administrator, double-click the printer object.
2. Click Jobs and then click Job List.
3. Click the specific print job.
4. Click Job Options and then click Delete.
5. Click OK to confirm that you want to delete the job.

To cancel a print job in Novell Printer Manager, complete the following steps:

1. In Novell Printer Manager, double-click the printer object.
2. Click the Printer menu and then Click Jobs.
3. Click the specific print job.
4. Click the Job Cancel button.
5. Click OK to confirm that you want to cancel the job.

Placing a Print Job on Hold   To place a print job on hold in NetWare Administrator, complete the following steps:

1. In NetWare Administrator, double-click the printer object.
2. Click Jobs and then click Job List.
3. Click the specific print job.
4. Click Job Options and then click Hold.
5. Click OK.

To cancel a print job in Novell Printer Manager, complete the following steps:

1. In Novell Printer Manager, double-click the printer object.
2. Click the Printer menu and then Click Jobs.
3. Click the specific print job.
4. Click the Job Pause button.

The Future of NDPS

NDPS is an excellent extension of the power of NDS. Managing printing is much easier in NDS than it was in queue-based printing. The future holds even more features and promises that will make NDPS an even better extension of NDS. If you like NDPS, you will want to look at the future versions that ship independently of NDS. Novell ships a product called Novell Enterprise Print Services. This is a version of NDPS that ships independently of NetWare and has some additional features. Novell Enterprise Print Services version 1 has added functionality for IPP and LPR printing. In future versions, Novell Enterprise Print Services will have additional features to make your print administration easier. Some of these are an NDPS Print Manager that provides extensive information about what is happening with network printing, a Broker services utility that will display what is happening in printing from the Broker's perspective, an SNMP Management utility that will provide information about printing through the SNMP agent, and several other additional features.

SUMMARY

With NDPS, you can harness the power of NDS to simplify the setup, administration, and access to network printing. NDPS was developed in conjunction with Novell, Hewlett-Packard, and Xerox to create print services that are independent of network servers and that provide better printing services. NDPS is compatible with non-NDPS printers. It supports Windows 3.1x, Windows 95/98, and Windows NT workstations. In addition, it has the capability to use common print drivers and to download them to the workstation. It includes bidirectional feedback on the status of print jobs and event notification. The tight integration of NDPS with NDS means reduced administrative burdens. You still have only a single point of network administration. You can set printers to be public-access printers or controlled-access printers. Public-access printers are available to everyone on the network with print capabilities. Controlled-access printers are printers associated with specific NDS objects. They can be highly restricted and tightly administered through NDS.

NDPS has four components that help control network printing. The NDPS Broker is an NLM that is loaded on the server. The NDPS Broker provides *Resource Management Service* (RMS) to store printing resources, such as printer drivers, fonts, banners, and printer definition files, in one location; *Event Notification Service* (ENS) to send notices about the printer or job status; and *Service Registry Service* (SRS) to allow public-access printers to advertise themselves on the network. NDPS Manager manages NDPS printer agents. You should create one NDPS Manger for each server on the network. Then it will manage all printers associated with that server. Printer Gateways translate NDPS commands into language that the printers can understand. Various printer manufacturers provide these Gateways. When you create a new printer agent, you will need to choose a Gateway for that printer agent. The Gateway holds all the make and model information on the printers it supports so that commands from NDPS can be translated to the printers. Finally, NDPS includes NDPS printer agents, or software representations of physical printers. The printer agent manages the print job, receives notification when something goes wrong, provides network clients with information about the printer status and the status of print jobs, provides services for existing queue-based print setups, and notifies users when print jobs are completed or when problems occur.

After NDPS is set up, it is relatively easy to manage printing. You can assign users to one of three roles: Managers, Operators, or Users. You can also manage print jobs from either NetWare Administrator (controlled-access printers only) or from the Novell Printer Manager utility.

For More Information

Here are some additional resources for information on using NDPS and printing.

Web Sites

Novell Distributed Print Services `http://www.novell.com/catalog/qr/sne24105.html`

Novell Enterprise Print Services `http://www.novell.com/products/printing/`

Web Articles

"Determining Your NDPS Strategy" `http://www.novell.com/documentation/lg/nw5/docui/index.html#../usprint/ndps_enu/data/hq37r8rs.html`

"Managing NDPS Manager" `http://www.novell.com/documentation/lg/nw5/docui/index.html#../usprint/ndps_enu/data/hex21b72.html`

"Printing in NetWare 5 with NDPS 2.0" `http://www.developer.novell.com/research/appnotes/1998/septembe/a5frame.htm`

"An Introduction to Novell Distributed Print Services (NDPS)" `http://www.developer.novell.com/research/appnotes/1998/april/a1frame.htm`

Technical Information Documents

Novell Technical Support provides further information on Novell products. The following is a list of TIDs that can be located at `www.support.novell.com`.

2930094	NDPS White Paper
2946479	How to Create a Public Access NDPS Printer
2943863	Print Problems after 3.12 to 5.0 Upgrade
2942680	Installing NDPS 2.0 After NW5 Server Is Up
2946476	Creating a Controlled Access NDPS Printer
2932483	NDPS Gateways not listed
2943419	How to Set NDPS Printer to Service a Queue
2944237	Configuring a Remote Printer in NDPS

Managing the NDS Environment

Up to this point we have discussed the design, installation, and use of NDS. This chapter will look at the activities and tools necessary to maintain the directory itself. Because Novell wants to see NDS as a central focus of an organization's network infrastructure, it is critical that NDS be extremely reliable. It is just as critical that NDS be flexible to the needs of today's complex organizations where mergers, restructuring, and right-sizing have become the norm rather than a rare occurrence.

Fortunately, Novell has been working to address the issues of reliability and flexibility in NDS since its initial release as part of NetWare 4.0 more than six years ago. The result of those efforts is an enterprise directory of unsurpassed stability, reliability, and flexibility.

NDS ships with a set of administrative tools and utilities to help maintain the health of the NDS tree. These tools are designed to provide the administrator with the power to change and repair the NDS environment as required. While NDS has become very stable over the last years, it still hasn't reached the stage where it never has any problems. And, even the best directory designs are going to need to be modified at some point in time. This chapter examines some of the basic administrative tasks associated with NDS and describes the tools available to perform those tasks. When you have finished reading this chapter, you should have a good understanding of the issues and tools related to each of the following tools and concepts:

- NDS Manager
- Time synchronization
- DS Repair
- WAN Traffic Manager
- Backup and restore of the NDS database

NOTE: *Tree merging is not supported in this first release of cross-platform NDS. That functionality is scheduled for the next major release of the product. As such, tree merges will not be covered in this chapter.*

NDS Manager

Partitions and replicas are the foundation for all database organization in NDS. Fortunately, all the basic partition and replica functions can be performed from a simple graphical utility known as NDS Manager. NDS Manager is a client-based utility that will run on any windows-based workstation. It can manage NDS partitions and replicas on any platform. With NDS Manager, you can perform the following operations:

- Partition and replica operations
- Server management
- Selected database repair options
- Partition, replica, and server information

NDS Manager is one of the utilities installed during the initial NDS installation. Chapter 3, "Installing and Upgrading NDS," discusses the NDS install, which includes the installation of management utilities such as NDS Manager. NDS Manager is stored differently depending on the platform on which NDS is running:

- *NetWare*   The NetWare installation places NDS Manager in the following directory by default: SYS:PUBLIC\WIN32\NDSMGR.EXE
- *NT*   The Install Management Utilities option will install NDS Manager during the NDS for NT installation routine. You can choose to install the management utilities locally or to a NetWare server (for mixed environments). The default directory for the local installation is C:\NOVELL\PUBLIC\WIN32. If you install to a NetWare server, the default NetWare installation path is used.
- *Solaris*   NDS Manager is installed as part of the Admin Utilities portion of the NDS for Solaris Windows install. You can choose to install the management utilities locally or to a NetWare server (for mixed environments). The default directory for the local installation is C:\NOVELL\PUBLIC\WIN32. If you install to a NetWare server, the default NetWare installation path is used.

Before starting in on the actual NDS Manager operations, you should note that three directory views are used with NDS Manager:

- Hierarchical Tree view
- Partitions and Servers view
- Partition Continuity view

Each is used for different activities, so we will introduce them when we cover the operations performed from each view.

Partition Operations with NDS Manager

Three primary partition operations can be performed from NDS Manager:

- Create
- Merge
- Prune and Graft

Create Partition

The first operation we want to look at is creating a partition. Remember from Chapter 2, "Designing NDS," that partitioning the tree serves to break the NDS database up into chunks that can be distributed across multiple servers for fault tolerance and increased performance. Partition creation is managed through the Hierarchical Tree view (see Figure 9-1).

NOTE: *NDS partition and replica operations should not be taken lightly. There is a great deal of internal work that goes on to perform these operations. In larger NDS environments, each of the operations described below can take a significant amount of time to process completely. Furthermore, each operation will have to complete before the next can begin. NDS requires that the tree be in a stable and healthy state before it will attempt any partition and replica operations. Bottom line, know why tree changes are being made and make the changes gradually so that the effects can be properly quantified before further modifications are attempted.*

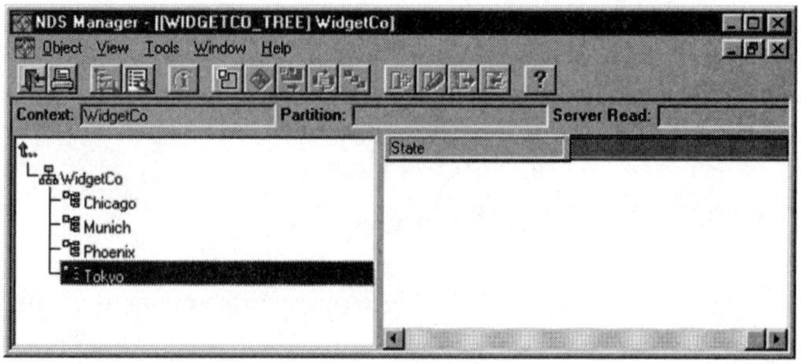

Figure 9-1
NDS Manager
Hierarchical Tree view

NDS Manager - [[WIDGETCO_TREE] WidgetCo]

Object   View   Tools   Window   Help

Context: WidgetCo   Partition: Server Read:

State

WidgetCo
— Chicago
— Munich
— Phoenix
— Tokyo

To create a new partition, complete the following steps:

1. Launch NDS Manager.
2. From the Hierarchical Tree view, right-click on the container you want to create as a new partition and select Create Partition.
3. Confirm that the proper container name is displayed in the Create Partition window and click Yes.
4. If NDS determines that the parent partition is properly synchronized, it will generate a message saying, `Preconditions for this operation have been met. Continue with this operation?` Click Yes. If the operation cannot be completed at this time, an error code will be returned. If this happens, you should make sure that your tree is healthy before continuing. Chapter 10, "Other NDS Administration Tools," and Chapter 11, "Troubleshooting NDS," discuss NDS troubleshooting tools and techniques.
5. You will then see a message that NDS is processing your request. Click Close.

NOTE: *By default, the Master replica of the new partition is created on the server that maintains the Master replica of the parent partition. Read/Write replicas are stored on servers that maintain read/write replicas of the parent partition.*

Partition Merge

Sometimes you want to consolidate partitions. This may be particularly true if you are moving from an existing NDS environment to the new version of NDS. Previously, partition sizes were limited to 1500–3000 objects. This limitation has been shattered in the latest release—it's been tested with millions of objects per partition—so it makes sense to combine all those departmental partitions back into the site partition. This essentially means merging the child partition(s) with its parent partition.

To merge a partition with its parent, complete the following steps:

1. Launch NDS Manager.
2. From the Hierarchical Tree view, right-click the partition that you want to merge with its parent and select Merge.

3. Confirm the operation by clicking Yes. All replicas for the child partition will be removed, and all data from the child partition will be distributed to the replicas maintained for the parent partition.

Prune and Graft a Partition

The last partition operation is commonly known as a *prune and graft*. It involves moving a partition and all its associated containers and objects from one location in the tree to another. Hence, pruning a branch from one area and grafting it in somewhere else. This operation is available only to partitions that do not have any subordinate (child) partitions. If you want to move a partition with subordinates, you have to merge the subordinates into the parent partition first.

WARNING: *If you are going to move a partition, the server that hosts the Master replica of that partition cannot reside within the partition that is being moved. If necessary, create a new replica outside of the partition and designate it as the Master for the duration of the move process. After the move, you can reassign the Master replica back to a server within the partition. Novell has recognized the difficulty this requirement can cause and is working to resolve this issue.*

If you want to prune and graft a partition, complete the following steps:

1. Launch NDS Manager.
2. In the Hierarchical Tree view, right-click on the partition you want to move and select Move.
3. In the Move Partition page, specify the destination context for this partition in the To Context: field. You can browse for the destination context, if necessary.

TIP: *You cannot move a container unless it is a partition root. If you want to move a container that is not a partition, you first need to define it as a partition. Then you can move the container to its new location and merge it with its new parent partition.*

4. (Optional) Check the Create an Alias for this Container Object option. If external applications or entities might be referencing this container, this

option will leave a pointer to the new location so that those external entities can still locate the container in its new location.

5. Click Yes and confirm the operation.

Replica Operations with NDS Manager

Now that you have NDS partitions created and situated within the tree, you may notice that the default placement for the replicas is less than perfect. After all, you probably don't want all the Master replicas on one server, and we certainly don't want to be replicating across our expensive WAN links if it can be helped. Replica operations are best accomplished from the Partitions and Servers view (see Figure 9-2). Four primary replica operations can be performed from NDS Manager:

- Create replica
- Change replica type
- Delete replica
- Check replica sync status

Figure 9-2
NDS Manager
Partitions and
Servers view

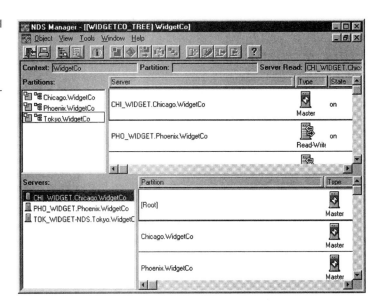

You will see Subordinate Reference replicas listed in this NDS Manager view. This is purely informational because Subordinate References are not manageable through NDS Manager. However, it is useful to see where these internally used replicas are being maintained.

Create Replica

If you want to add a partition replica to a server that does not currently contain a copy of that partition, complete the following steps:

1. Launch NDS Manager. Click View and select Partitions and Servers.
2. In the upper pane of the Partitions and Servers view, right-click on the partition that you would like to replicate and select Add Replica.
3. Browse to the server that should get a replica of this partition.
4. Select the replica type as Read/Write or Read-only.
5. Click OK. Click OK twice more to pass the two messages indicating that Pre-conditions Have Been Met and that NDS Is Processing The Request.

Change Replica Type

Sometimes it is useful to be able change the type of an existing replica. For example, if a Master replica is stored on a server and it is going down for a hardware upgrade, you can change an existing Read/Write replica to be the Master so that NDS partition operations can continue normally.

NOTE: *You cannot change the type of Master replica because a Master replica must exist for every partition. If you want an existing Master replica to be a Read/Write, you must first designate a new Master replica. The existing Master will automatically be converted to a Read/Write.*

If you want to change the type of a replica, complete the following steps:

1. Launch NDS Manager. Click View and select Partitions and Servers.
2. In the lower-left pane of the Partitions and Servers view, select the server on which you would like to change a replica type. This will bring up a list of all replicas maintained on that server in the lower-right pane.

3. Right-click on the replica whose type you want to change and select Change Type.

4. Select the new type for the replica and click OK.

Delete Replica

Sometimes, when partitions have been merged or moved, a given replica is no longer necessary. To delete an existing replica from a server, complete the following steps:

1. Launch NDS Manager. Click View and select Partitions and Servers.

2. In the lower-left pane of the Partitions and Servers view, select the server on which you would like to change the replica type. This will bring up a list of all replicas maintained on that server in the lower-right pane.

3. Right-click on the replica that you want to delete and select Delete.

4. Click OK twice to pass the Pre-condition and Processing messages and complete the operation.

Check Replica Sync Status

Finally, you can also check the synchronization status of a partition's replica ring. A replica ring is the collection of all servers that host replicas for a given partition. Each server in a replica ring must be able to communicate properly with other servers in the ring so that partition updates can be propagated. Because servers can host multiple replicas, they may be members of multiple replica rings.

To check the synchronization status of a partition, complete the following steps:

1. Launch NDS Manager. You will be in the Hierarchical Tree view by default.

2. In the left pane of the Hierarchical Tree view, right-click on the partition whose synchronization status you want to check and select Check Synchronization (see Figure 9-3).

NOTE: *As you work with NDS Manager, you will find there are multiple ways to perform each of these operations using different views, keystrokes, and/or mouse clicks. Feel free to adopt whatever process is most comfortable for you as an administrator.*

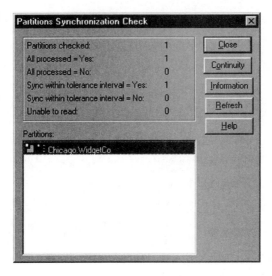

Figure 9-3
NDS Manager
Partitions
Synchronization
Check

Server Management with NDS Manager

There are three main server management functions that can be performed using NDS Manager. Both of these operations are easiest to perform from the Partitions and Servers view in NDS Manager (refer to Figure 9-2).

- Deleting the server from NDS
- Updating the version of DS.NLM running on the server
- Selected Database Repair Tools

Deleting a Server from NDS

As with partition and replica operations, deleting a server from NDS should not be taken lightly. Deleting the server permanently will remove all of its data and resources from directory access as well. Furthermore, if replicas are stored on the servers, deleting it without thinking can cause significant database synchronization and corruption problems. If the server is operational, make sure that you have removed all replicas from the server and have made sure NDS is functioning properly.

NOTE: *Novell recommends removing NDS from the server itself rather than removing the server from NDS. This is accomplished from the server-based DS Repair utility discussed later in this chapter.*

This may not be possible if the server hardware has crashed. In this case, you have few options but to remove the downed server from NDS and then clean up NDS after the fact. We will talk more about NDS repair operations later in this chapter and in Chapter 10, "Other NDS Administration Tools."

To remove a server from NDS, complete the following steps:

1. Bring the server down if this has not already been done.
2. Launch NDS Manager. Click View and select Partitions and Servers.
3. From the Partitions and Servers view, right-click on the server you want to delete.
4. Select Delete. You will get an error if the server is still up when you attempt to delete it.
5. Click OK to confirm the operation.

Updating DS.NLM on a Server

NDS Manager can be used as a crude distribution tool for NDS updates. The version of DS.NLM on one NetWare server can be used to update another. This feature does not support the Solaris and NT platforms, and cross-platform updates are not possible. To update the version of DS.NLM on a NetWare server, complete the following steps:

1. Launch NDS Manager. Click View and select Partitions and Servers.
2. In the Partitions and Servers view, highlight the server that will act as the source for the DS.NLM update.
3. Click the Object drop-down menu. Select NDS Version and Update. This will open the NDS Version Update window (see Figure 9-4).
4. Change context to match that of the server(s) to be updated. All servers in the specified context will be listed in the Servers list.
5. Select the servers that you want to update and click the Arrow button to transfer them to the Target Servers to be Updated list.
6. (Optional) Click Settings if you want to configure the update environment and update log file.
7. Click OK to perform the update.

Figure 9-4
NDS Manager DS
Version Update
window

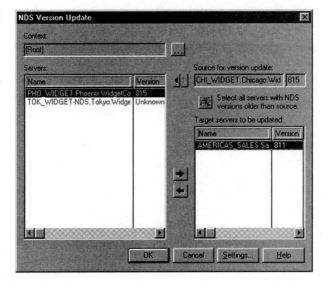

Selected Database Repair Tools

NDS Manager offers the most common tools for NDS database repair, but its toolkit is not comprehensive. DS Repair, discussed later in this chapter, provides the necessary functionality not currently available in NDS Manager. Advanced database repair options are discussed in Chapter 10.

The synchronization and repair options in NDS Manager are accessed from the Partition Continuity view (see Figure 9-5). The Partition Continuity view shows a complete Server/Replica matrix, as discussed in Chapter 2, "Designing NDS." It is very useful in gaining a high level view of how partition information is organized and stored across the network. To enter the Partition Continuity view, you must first select the partition with which you want to work. Then click Object and select Partition Continuity.

Normally, NDS will handle all the necessary replica synchronization tasks automatically. However, if significant changes have been made to a partition or its contents, an administrator can choose to force an immediate synchronization. NDS Manager offers three different ways to do this:

- *Synchronize a partition immediately* This option will initiate an immediate synchronization cycle between all servers that maintain replicas of that partition.

- *Receive updates from Master replica* This option forces a Read/Write or Read-only replica to receive an update from its Master replica.

Figure 9-5
NDS Manager
Partition Continuity
view

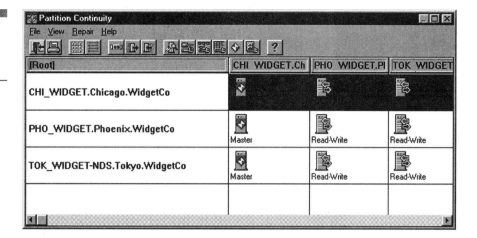

Current replica data will be overwritten by data from the Master replica. This option is used only if a replica has become corrupt and needs to be repopulated with good data from the Master replica.

■ *Send updates from a replica* This option forces a replica to send out an update of its partition data to all other replicas of that partition, including the Master. This will not overwrite existing partition data but will append any new data to that which already exists. Administrators can use this option to more quickly update the replica ring with changes that occurred on a particular replica.

To synchronize a partition immediately, complete the following steps:

1. Launch NDS Manager. Select the partition that you want to synchronize and then click Object and select Partition Continuity.
2. Click Repair and select Synchronize Immediately.
3. Click Yes to confirm the operation and then click OK.

To receive updates from the Master replica, complete the following steps:

1. Launch NDS Manager. Select the partition that you want to synchronize and then click Object and select Partition Continuity.
2. From the Partition Continuity view of the partition with which you are working, select the server that holds the replica you want to update.
3. Click Repair and select Receive Updates.
4. Click Yes to confirm the operation; then click Yes to continue with the operation. Click OK to return to the Partition Continuity view.

To send updates from a local replica, complete the following steps:

1. Launch NDS Manager. Select the partition that you want to synchronize and then click Object and select Partition Continuity.

2. From the Partition Continuity view of the partition with which you are working, select the server that holds the replica that you want to send an update.

3. Click Repair and Send Updates.

4. Click Yes to confirm the operation; then click Yes to continue with the operation. Click OK to return to the Partition Continuity view.

From time to time, the Partition Continuity view may announce a replica error inserting an ! symbol next to a replica icon. To get more information on the error, complete the following steps:

1. Double-click on the replica icon to open the Replica Information screen.

2. Click the ? button next to the Current Sync Error field to see more information about the error code.

Beyond being able to fix database problems by updating replica information from an outside source, NDS Manager offers seven database repair options. Each of these is also available from the server console by using the DS Repair utility, which will be discussed later in this chapter. These database repair options test the consistency of the NDS database and attempt to restore structural and referential integrity to the database files if a problem should occur. The seven database operations are as follows:

- Verify Remote Server IDs
- Repair a Replica
- Repair Network Addresses
- Repair Local Database
- Assign a New Master Replica
- Repair Volume Objects
- Remove a Server from the Replica List

Verify Remote Server IDs A description of this operation has been included so you know what it is. However, it does not apply to the new version of NDS because Server IDs are no longer used. All communications are handled by network address now. This operation verifies the contents of the remote server ID list. This list is maintained by each server in order to communicate with remote servers. Each entry contains the following:

- The remote server name
- The remote server unique NDS ID
- The remote ID, which is the unique ID of the local server as it appears in the remote server's ID list

If errors are detected, Verify Remote Server IDs will attempt to repair the ID list.

Repair a Replica   Repair a Replica communicates with all other servers that host a copy of this replica in order to verify basic replica structure and ID information. Repair a Replica only operates on the specific replica you have selected.

Repair Network Addresses   This operation verifies that NDS maintains valid network address information in its Server and Root Partition objects. It searches local SAP and/or SLP tables and compares the server address information stored there against the information maintained in the Server and Root Partition object properties. If there is a discrepancy, it will repair the server object and root partition object information.

Repair Local Database   This operation attempts to repair local NDS replica corruption by resolving database inconsistencies. Any problem that is found will be logged, and NDS will attempt to repair the problem. If the repair is unsuccessful, the replica should be removed and recreated.

Assign a New Master Replica   Assign a New Master Replica enables a replica ring to recover from a corrupt or lost Master replica. Before assigning a new Master replica, you should try to change an existing Read/Write replica to the Master using the Change Replica Type operation.

Assign a new master replica enables you to arbitrarily convert an existing Read/Write replica into the Master, thereby allowing partition and replica operations to function normally.

Repair Volume Objects   Repair Volume Objects confirms the links between mounted NetWare volumes and Volume objects stored in NDS. If a mounted volume is not associated with a Volume object, this operation will search the context where the host server resides. If the volume is found, then the Volume object is associated with the volume. If a Volume object is not found, it will attempt to create one.

Remove a Server from the Replica List   Remove a Server from the Replica List removes a server from a replica list when it no longer hosts a replica of the partition.

You would use this operation, for example, if you find errors indicating that one replica server still has a record of another server in its replica list, but the second server no longer hosts a replica of the partition in question. Use the Remove Server operation to remove the second server from the first server's replica list. Never use this operation in place of the Delete Server operation, which is slower but much safer.

To access any of these repair options, complete the following steps:

1. Select the partition with which you want to work and then click View and select Partition Continuity.

2. Select the server/replica row with which you want to work.

3. Click Repair and select the appropriate database repair operation.

General NDS Information with NDS Manager

General information about partition, replica, and server status can be accessed from the different NDS Manager views. The Partitions and Servers view is the easiest from which to view information because partitions, replicas, and servers are all accessible in this view.

Each of these information screens gives a thumbnail sketch of the selected resource and its current status. To view the information on a given resource, complete the following steps:

1. Launch NDS Manager. Click View and select Partitions and Servers.

2. Right-click the object in which you are interested and select Information.

Alternatively, you can also double-click the object to access the same information screen. Information about synchronization status and any synchronization errors are listed in these information screens. They can provide valuable clues when problems crop up in your NDS environment.

The Partition information screen, shown in Figure 9-6, contains the following informational fields:

- Partition (name field)
- Server read (for partition info)
- Master replica (server storing Master replica)

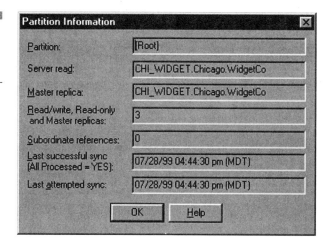

Figure 9-6
NDS Manager
Partition Information
screen

- Read/write, Read-only and Master replicas (total number of replicas)
- Subordinate references (total number)
- Last successful sync {All Processed = YES} (time of last successful synchronization cycle)
- Last attempted sync (time of last attempted synchronization cycle)

The Replica information screen, shown in Figure 9-7, contains the following informational fields:

- Partition (name of partition for which this is a replica)
- Stored on server
- Server read (to gather replica information)
- Replica number (1 = Master, 2 = Subordinate Reference, 3 = Read/Write, 4 = Read Only)
- Replica type (Master, Subordinate Reference, Read/Write, Read Only)
- Replica state (on or off)
- Last successful synch (time of last successful synchronization cycle)
- Referral address
- Current sync error

The Server Information screen, shown in Figure 9-8, contains the following informational fields:

- Server name (distinguished NDS name)
- Full name

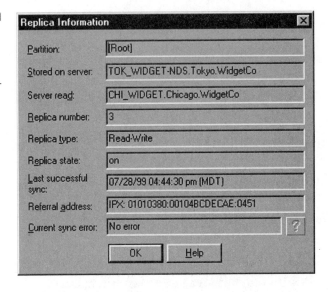

Figure 9-7
NDS Manager
Replica Information
screen

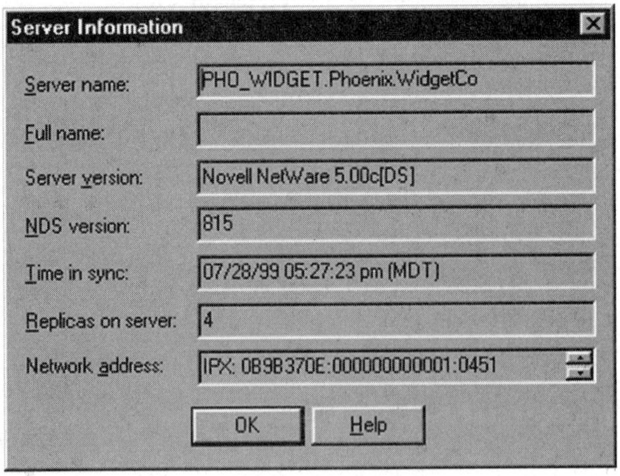

Figure 9-8
NDS Manager Server
Information screen

- Server version
- NDS version (available for NetWare platform only)
- Time in sync
- Replicas on server (total number)
- Network address

Time Synchronization

Time Synchronization is absolutely critical in the NetWare world for proper execution of certain NDS partition operations. Yet, as described in Chapter 2, "Designing NDS," time sync is not an NDS-supplied service. Time sync is provided as a service by the underlying NOS. NDS actually maintains its own internal time stamping service that ensures the proper ordering of NDS packets. However, because NetWare requires servers to be externally time synched in order to process certain NDS operations, it is important to understand time synchronization. Furthermore, because NDS is making a rapid move toward support of multiple NOS platforms, it is important to understand how to integrate NetWare time synchronization with time sync mechanisms for the NT and Solaris platforms. *Network Time Protocol* (NTP) is a standard way for systems hosting distributed services, of which NDS is one, to provide time synchronization.

Novell has only recently added NTP support to its NetWare platform with the release of NetWare 5. This means that NetWare was originally designed with a proprietary time-sync mechanism. Because that mechanism is still used today, we first need to examine how the NetWare time-sync environment is configured and then look at how it integrates with NTP to provide a cross-platform solution. Because we have already discussed the basics of NetWare time sync and NTP in Chapter 2, "Designing NDS," we will dive right in to the configuration of the time-sync environment.

However, because time sync is of only peripheral use by NDS, don't be concerned if you insert an NT or Solaris server into a NetWare environment and find that NetWare servers report it as Synched Up when you haven't done any NTP configuration at all! The NDS software running on NT and Solaris will always report itself as synched with the NetWare environment, regardless of what the system clocks on those servers actually say. Unfortunately, you may still have problems with installations and partition operations if the servers are not truly synched. This is particularly true with Solaris. Time sync is also valuable when attempting to integrate NDS with external services that rely on time sync. The following sections discuss the NetWare and NTP time-sync environments and how they can be tied together.

NetWare Time Synchronization

If you refer to Chapter 2, you will note that there are two ways to implement NetWare time synchronization, the Default and the *Time Provider*

Group (TPG). The default configuration is appropriate for smaller local networks. Time Provider Groups should be used in large or distributed networks. In addition to these synchronization strategies, which were discussed in Chapter 2, you have to decide on an automatic or manual advertisement process for time sync. The underlying network protocol will play a part in this decision.

Time-Sync Advertisement   Time-sync advertisement refers to the process used to propagate information about the time-sync configuration throughout the network. You can distribute time-sync information in two ways:

- Automatic
- Manual

By default, the NetWare time-sync environment will advertise its configuration automatically. If your NetWare environment is running over IPX, time sync will use SAP 26B to advertise timeservers by default. This is true for both the default and TPG configurations. If you are using TCP/IP, which is recommended in this day and age, NetWare does not yet offer automatic advertisement of time-sync services. This should be offered as part of the NetWare 5 Service Pack 3, due out Fall, 1999. After SP3 is installed, NetWare will use SLP over IP to advertise timeservers. In the meantime, IP environments will have to use manual advertisement.

The advantage of automatic advertisement is ease of implementation. Timeservers will communicate without any intervention from the administrator. However, this background communication will also use network bandwidth. In a LAN environment, this is probably not an issue, but on WAN links its best to save bandwidth wherever possible.

Manual advertisement, known as Configured Lists, is the answer to the potential problem of bandwidth utilization for time sync. Configured Lists simply mean that the administrator manually defines the source of network time for each server on the network. This information is specified in the TIMESYNC.CFG file, which is located in the SYS:SYSTEM subdirectory on your NetWare server.

Reference and Single timeservers get their time from their internal clocks or, better yet, from an authoritative time source, such as an Atomic Clock, Radio Clock, or Internet Time Source.

In Figure 9-9 you can see that WidgetCo has chosen to get time from public timeservers located on the Internet. The MIT server WidgetCo references in the TIMESYNC.CFG uses NTP to transmit its time across the Internet. Our NetWare server recognizes this as an NTP server by the use of the :123 in the time source address.

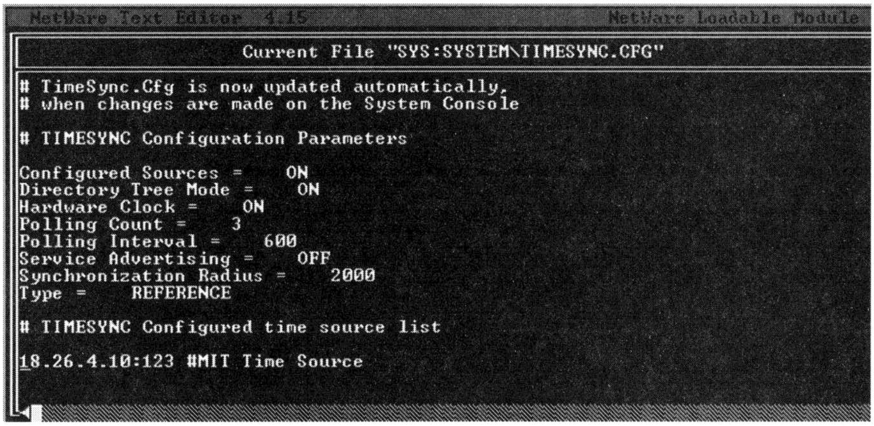

Figure 9-9
Sample
TIMESYNC.CFG

```
NetWare Text Editor 4.15                          NetWare Loadable Module

                    Current File "SYS:SYSTEM\TIMESYNC.CFG"

# TimeSync.Cfg is now updated automatically,
# when changes are made on the System Console

# TIMESYNC Configuration Parameters

Configured Sources =    ON
Directory Tree Mode =   ON
Hardware Clock =    ON
Polling Count =     3
Polling Interval =    600
Service Advertising =    OFF
Synchronization Radius =    2000
Type =    REFERENCE

# TIMESYNC Configured time source list

18.26.4.10:123 #MIT Time Source
```

Primary timeservers will use the Reference or other Primary servers as their time source. Secondary timeservers can be pointed toward either Single, Reference, or Primary servers for their network time, depending on how time sync is configured and what timeserver is easiest to get to. In this way, you build a hierarchy or timeservers that is most appropriate to the size and layout of your physical network.

Configuring Your Time-Sync Environment TIMESYNC.NLM is responsible for all time-sync operations that take place in the NetWare environment. NetWare 5 originally shipped with version 5.07 of TIMESYNC.NLM, but it has since been updated in NetWare 5 support packs. Make sure that you are running the most current version in order to avoid problems. As of this writing, the most current public release of TIMESYNC.NLM is version 5.09. It is included as part of NetWare 5 Support Pack 2 (NW5SP2A.EXE). Check for the latest patches and updates on Novell's technical support Web site at support.novell.com/misc/patlst.htm.

NetWare 5 originally included a separate NTP.NLM to provide integration with NTP time-sync environments. However, that functionality has been rolled into the newer versions of TIMESYNC.NLM so NTP.NLM is no longer needed. Do not load NTP.NLM and the new versions of TIMESYNC.NLM at the same time. They will not play well together.

TIMESYNC.NLM is loaded automatically when NetWare 5 starts. When it loads, it reads the TIMESYNC.CFG file to determine how it should act. As shown in Figure 9-9, several time-sync parameters exist. As mentioned, these parameters can be viewed or modified through EDIT or MONITOR. If you load MONITOR on the server console and select Server Parameters and Time, you will see the whole range of time parameters for NetWare servers.

The first eight parameters are set when the server is installed and will seldom have to be modified.

- TIMESYNC Configuration File
- Time Zone
- Default Time Server Type
- Start of Daylight Savings Time
- End of Daylight Savings Time
- Daylight Savings Time Offset
- Daylight Savings Time Status
- New Time with Daylight Savings Time Status

The 12 parameters used to configure and reset the time-sync environment are described in Table 9-1. Of the 12 parameters listed, nine are used for configuration, and three are used to reset or restart the time-sync service.

Table 9-1

TIMESYNC.CFG parameters

Time Sync Parameter	Possible Values	Description
Configured sources	ON | OFF Default: OFF	Set ON if a list of time sources is used
Directory tree mode	ON | OFF Default: ON	ON means that only time packets from the same directory tree will be recognized when setting time. OFF lets timeservers from other directory trees adjust time for this server. This parameter applies to Secondary time servers only.
Hardware clock	ON | OFF Default: ON	Determines whether or not the Single or Reference server will get network time from its own hardware clock. Set OFF if using an external time source
Polling count	1–1000 Default: 3	Defines how many time packets to exchange during time-polling cycle Increasing this number will add network traffic
Polling interval	10–2678400 seconds Default: 600 2678400 sec = 31 days	Defines the time to wait between time-polling cycles. This value should be the same for every server in the tree
RESET	N/A	Resets internal time-sync variables and clears the configured server list

Time Sync Parameter	Possible Values	Description
Restart Flag	N/A	Restarts the time-sync service. Similar to unloading and reloading TIME SYNC.NLM
Service advertising	ON | OFF	Determines whether or not SAP/SLP advertisement will be used. Turn this off when using Configured Lists
Synchronization radius	0–2147483647 msec Default: 2000	Defines how close a server's time has to be to network time in order to be considered in sync
Time Adjustment	[+ | –]hh:mm:ss [AT date and time]	Used to schedule a time adjustment. This parameter is only configurable on Single, Reference, or Primary timeservers
Type	Single, Reference, Primary, Secondary	Defines what type of timeserver this server is
Time source =	Name of timeserver to query for network time	This is the Configured List of timeservers that this server will query for network time. Multiple Time source = lines can be configured in the TIMESYNC.CFG. If one does not respond, the server will query the next on the list

NTP Time Synchronization

The NetWare time-synchronization methods described in preceding sections are suitable for time sync between NetWare servers. What happens when we throw NT and Solaris servers into the mix? WidgetCo encountered this problem when integrating the Munich and Tokyo offices into a single network. Munich functions on Solaris servers while Tokyo is fond of NT. Both server types had to be able to time sync with the NetWare networks in Chicago and Phoenix. Novell's NTP integration allows this to happen.

First, let's take a look at the NTP configuration for NT and Solaris before discussing their integration with TIMESYNC.

NTP and Windows NT   Windows NT 4.0 does not include an NTP timesync utility by default. However, Microsoft offers an NTP-compatible timeserver as part of the Windows NT 4.0 Resource Kit. The resource kit is available from Microsoft. There is a document that outlines the installation of the TIMESERV files and the configuration of the TIMESERV.INI. It is a lightweight implementation of NTP. Furthermore, the NT time-sync environment is designed around the idea of NT receiving time from other NT servers, except for the top-most time server. Keep that in mind when configuring your time-sync environment.

NOTE: *We found during our testing that the NT platform was ambivalent toward literal time synchronization. We were able to run an NT server in a mixed-platform NDS tree without configuring time sync at all. This is not a recommended option, but it is good to know.*

Three types of time sources are used to configure the Windows NT time service: Top-Level, Primary, and Secondary. These time sources are configured for each NT server and/or workstation in TIMESERV.INI.

The Top-Level time source represents the root of all network time for the NT environment. It should be an accurate time source, such as an Atomic Clock, Radio Clock, or Internet. It could also be a Single or Reference NetWare TIMESYNC server or a low-stratum Solaris NTP server.

The relevant TIMESERV.INI entries for NTP time sync are listed in Table 9-2.

Several third-party NTP utilities are available for Windows NT. These utilities will provide a much more robust NTP implementation and allow for better integration with existing NTP resources, such as UNIX servers. They will also allow you to manage NT servers as part of the overall NTP environment rather than having to establish a special TIMESERV environment just for NT and then having to plug it into the NTP world. Search the Internet for NTP and NT to locate several of these utilities from which you can choose.

NTP and Solaris   Solaris is easier to configure for NTP time synchronization because it includes an NTP time-sync utility by default. At the Solaris terminal, create or modify /etc/inet/ntp.conf file to reference the desired time source. This could be an Internet time source, another UNIX NTP server or a NetWare Single or Reference timeserver. You can specify the source NTP server by DNS name or IP address. For example, server tycho.usno.navy.mil or server 128.118.25.3.

After updating the ntp.conf, run /usr/lib/inet/xntpd start. After xntpd is loaded, it may take 10–15 minutes for time to sync. In order to check time-sync status on Solaris, you can run /usr/sbin/ntptrace.

Variable	Values	Description
Type =	NTP | Primary | Secondary	*NTP*: Select this type when this server will serve as the Root time server for the NT servers in your environment.
		Primary: Select this type when this server will receive time from a Primary timeserver and distribute it to other NT servers in the network.
		Secondary: Select this type for client workstations that will receive time from a Primary time source.
PrimarySource =	Name of timeserver	Used with a Primary timeserver to specify from which server(s) it should receive its time updates
NTPServer =	Name or IP Address of the NTP time server	Specifies the NTP time source to be used as the Root of time for the NT time servers. This could be an Internet timesource, a UNIX NTP server or a NetWare Single or Reference server.
Timesource =	Yes | No	Select yes if this server is a Primary and will be distributing network time
Log =	Yes | No	Good for confirming that time sync is working properly; will log every succesful time set operation

Table 9-2

NTP TIMESERV.INI settings

Integrating TIMESYNC and NTP Environments

The first decision you need to make when integrating TIMESYNC and NTP environments is the direction of the time flow. Do you want NTP to receive time from TIMESYNC or vice versa? Both options are equally valid, but some environments lend themselves more to one method over another. Novell time sync experts have recommended using NTP over WAN links and then letting the NetWare TIMESYNC environments at each site receive their time from NTP. You don't want to be running both NTP and TIMESYNC traffic over a WAN link.

To configure NTP to receive its time from TIMESYNC, set the Reference or Single timeserver as the time source for the NTP environment. For NT, that means editing the TIMESERV.INI file on the NT server and adding the TIMESYNC server as a Primary time source. For Solaris it means editing the /etc/ntp.conf and placing the TIMESYNC server at the top of the timeserver list.

To configure TIMESYNC to receive time from NTP, edit the TIMESYNC.CFG file on the Reference or Single server and change the Time Source = line to point to a stratum 1 or stratum 2 NTP server. We use stratum 1 or stratum 2 servers in order to maintain tight synchronization with UTC.

DS Repair

Every database needs a tool for repairing inconsistencies when they occur. DS Repair has been serving in this capacity as long as NDS has existed. DS Repair offers many features, but they can be grouped into three main categories:

- Unattended Full Repair
- NDS Monitor Operations
- NDS Repair Operations

Unattended Full Repair (UFR) performs the same set of operations regardless of the platform on which DS Repair is running, so an overview of UFR is presented in its own section. The operations available in the other two categories, although similar, will vary from platform to platform. Because of this, descriptions of NDS Monitor and NDS Repair operations will be organized by platform.

Novell has created a DS Repair utility for each platform supported by NDS. Unfortunately, the look, feel, and feature set varies significantly from platform to platform. If you understand what the different DS Repair utilities offer in each of these categories, you will have a pretty good handle on the basic activities necessary to keep your NDS environment healthy.

Unattended Full Repair

The UFR is probably the most-used feature in DS Repair, although the huge database sizes now supported by NDS may change that. It can check for and repair most noncritical NDS errors in the NDS database files of a given server. UFR can be activated in the following ways, depending on the operating system platform being used:

- *NetWare* Select Unattended Full Repair from the main DS Repair menu.
- *NT* Click Repair and select Unattended Full Repair.
- *Solaris* /bin/ndsrepair-U

The UFR performs eight primary operations each time it is run; none of which require any intervention by the administrator. These operations are described in Table 9-3. During some of these operations, the local database is locked. UFR builds a temporary set of local database files and runs the repair operations against those files. That way, if a serious problem develops the original files are still in tact.

NOTE: *Rebuilding the operational indexes used by NDS is only possible when the local database is locked. Given this, it is good to schedule a locked database repair on a regular basis, even in large NDS environments.*

Table 9-3 Operations performed by unattended full repair	**Operation**	**Locked?**	**Description**
	Database Structure and Index Check	Yes	Reviews the structure and format of database records and indexes. This ensures that no structural corruption has been introduced into the NDS environment at the database level.
	Rebuild the Entire Database	Yes	This operation is used to resolve errors found during structure and index checks. It restores proper data structures and recreates the NDS database and index files.
	Perform Tree Structure Check	Yes	Examines the links between database records to make sure that each child record has a valid parent. This helps ensure database consistency. Invalid records are marked so that they can be restored from another partition replica during the NDS replica synchronization process.
	Repair All Local Replicas	Yes	This operation resolves NDS database inconsistencies by checking each object and attribute against schema definitions. It also checks the format of all internal data structures.

continues

Table 9-3

continued

Operation	Locked?	Description
		Repair All Local Replicas can also resolve inconsistencies found during the tree structure check by removing invalid records from the database. As a result, all child records linked through the invalid record will be marked as orphans. These orphan records are not lost, but this process could potentially generate a large number of errors while the database is being rebuilt. Do not be overly alarmed. This is normal, and the orphan objects will be reorganized automatically over the course of replica synchronization.
Check Local References	Yes	Local References are pointers to other objects maintained in the NDS database on this file server. Check Local References will evaluate the internal database pointers to make sure that they are pointing to the correct NDS objects. If invalid references are found, an error will be reported in DSREPAIR.LOG.
Repair Network Addresses	No	This operation checks server network addresses stored in NDS against the values maintained in local SAP or SLP tables to make sure that NDS still has accurate information. If a discrepancy is found, NDS will be updated with the correct information.
Validate Stream Syntax Files	Yes	Stream Syntax Files, such as login scripts, are stored in a special area of the NDS database. Validate Stream Syntax Files checks to make sure that each stream syntax file is associated with a valid NDS object. If not, the stream syntax file is deleted.
Validate Mail Directories (NetWare Only)	Yes	By default, NDS creates mail directories in the SYS:Mail directory of NetWare servers in order to support legacy bindery users. Login scripts for bindery users are stored in their mail directory. Validate Mail Directories checks to make sure that each mail directory is associated with a valid NDS user object. If not, the mail directory is deleted.

Operation	Locked?	Description
Check Volume Objects And Trustees (NetWare Only)	No	Check Volume Objects and Trustees first makes sure that each volume on the NetWare server is associated with a Volume object in NDS. If not, it will search the context in which the server resides to see whether a Volume object exists. If no Volume object exists, one will be created.
		After validating the volume information, the list of trustee IDs will be validated. Each object in NDS has a unique trustee ID. This ID is used to grant rights to other objects, including NetWare volumes, in the NDS tree. This task makes sure that each trustee ID in the volume list is a valid NDS object. If not, the trustee ID is removed from the volume list.

WARNING: *When the local database is locked, no changes will be permitted while the operations execute. Some of these operations, when performed on the very large database files permitted by NDS, will take an extended period of time to complete. When working with a large NDS database, it is best to schedule these types of operations carefully so as not to disrupt network operations.*

DS Repair on NetWare

Those of you with a NetWare background will recognize the blue C-worthy DS Repair interface, shown in Figure 9-10, that has made Novell server utilities famous—or infamous!

DS Repair on NetWare contains several operations that are not available on the NT and Solaris platforms. The primary reason for this is that when DS Repair on NetWare was first developed, it had to do it all. There wasn't

Figure 9-10
NetWare DS Repair
interface

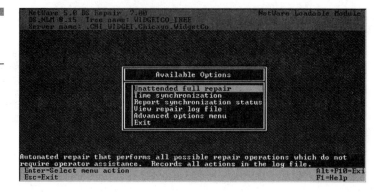

an NDS Manager or ConsoleOne to take some of the management burden. DS Repair still carries all those extra features today.

To load DS Repair on the NetWare platform, load DSREPAIR.NLM at the server console. Throughout this section, when describing steps for performing a DS Repair operation on NetWare, it is assumed that you have already loaded the utility.

All DS Repair operations and results can be logged to file for review. The default log file SYS:SYSTEM\DSREPAIR.LOG. DS Repair on NetWare has a menu for configuring the log file. To access this menu, select the Advanced Options menu and then select Log File And Login Configuration.

This following three sections describe the features available in each of the three main categories of DS Repair operations: NDS Monitor Operations, NDS Repair Operations, and Unattended Full Repair.

NDS Monitor Operations on NetWare   DS Repair offers several partition, replica, and server operations that are available to monitor the health of the NDS environment. These operations can be performed individually or as groups to help keep NDS stable and healthy.

The first category of operations can be loosely grouped into Monitor operations that are designed to report NDS status and health. Table 9-4 describes the monitor operations available with DSREPAIR.NLM.

NDS Repair Operations on NetWare   Although monitoring the condition of the NDS database is important, it does little good if there are no tools for repairing inconsistencies when they occur. DSREPAIR offers several NDS repair operations. These repair operations can be organized into three categories:

- Database Repair Operations
- Partition and Replica Repair Operations
- Other Repair Operations

All Database Repair Operations are accessible from the same menu in DSREPAIR. To access these operations, select the Advanced Options menu and then Repair Local DS Database (see Figure 9-11). Table 9-5 describes the repair operations available from this menu.

	Operation	How to Access	Description
Table 9-4 DS Repair monitor operations on NetWare	Report Sync Status	1. Select Report Synchronization Status	Reports the sync status for every partition that hosts a replica on this server
	Report Sync Status of All Servers	1. Select Advanced Options menu. 2. Select Replica And Partition Operations and then select a partition. 3. Select Report Synchronization Status of All Servers	Queries each server hosting a replica of the selected partition and reports the sync status of each replica
	Report Sync Status on Selected Server	1. Select Advanced Options menu. 2. Select Replica and Partition Operations and then select a partition. 3. Select View Replica Ring and choose a server. 4. Select Report Synchronization Status on Selected Server.	Reports the sync status of the replica hosted by this server for the selected partition
	Time Sync	1. Select Time Synchronization	Reports status of Time Synchronization
	Perform Database Structure and Index Check	1. Select Advanced Options menu and then Repair Local DS Database.	Reviews the structure and format of database records and indexes. This ensures that no structural corruption has been introduced into the NDS environment at the database level.

continues

Table 9-4

continued

Operation	How to Access	Description
Perform Tree Structure Check	1. Select Advanced Options menu and then Repair local DS database.	Examines the links between database records to make sure that each child record has a valid parent. This helps ensure database consistency. Invalid records are marked so that they can be restored from another partition replica during the NDS replica synchronization process.
Servers Known to This Database	1. Select Advanced Options menu and then select Servers Known To This Database.	Queries the local database and compiles a list of servers known to this partition
View Entire Server Name	1. Select Advanced Options menu and then select Servers Known To This Database. 2. Select a server and then select View Entire Server's Name.	Displays the distinguished NDS name for this server
View Replica Ring	1. Select Advanced Options and then select Replica And Partition Operations. 2. Select a partition and then select View Replica Ring.	Displays a list of all servers that host a replica of the selected partition
View Entire Partition Name	1. Select Advanced options menu and then select Replica and Partition Operations. 2. Select a partition and then select View Entire Partition Name.	Displays the distinguished NDS name for this partition root object

Figure 9-11
DSREPAIR database operations on NetWare

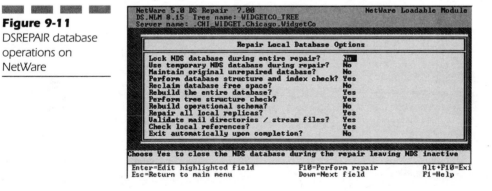

Operation	Description
Table 9-5 DSREPAIR database operations on NetWare	**Operation**	**Description**

Operation	Description
Rebuild Entire Database	This operation is used to resolve errors found during structure and index checks. It restores proper data structures and recreates the NDS database and index files.
Repair All Local Replicas	This operation resolves NDS database inconsistencies by checking each object and attribute against schema definitions. It also checks the format of all internal data structures. Repair All Local Replicas can also resolve inconsistencies found during the tree structure check by removing invalid records from the database. As a result, all child records linked through the invalid record will be marked as orphans. These orphan records are not lost, but this process could potentially generate a large number of errors while the database is being rebuilt. Do not be overly alarmed. This is normal, and the orphan objects will be reorganized automatically over the course of replica synchronization.
Validate Mail Directories and Stream Syntax Files	Both of these operations are used only with NetWare. By default, NDS creates mail directories in the SYS:Mail directory of NetWare servers in order to support legacy bindery users. Login scripts for bindery users are stored in users' mail directories. Validate Mail Directories checks to make sure that each mail directory is associated with a valid NDS user object. If not, the mail directory is deleted. Stream Syntax Files, such as login scripts, are stored in a special area of the NDS database. Validate Stream Syntax Files checks to make sure that each stream syntax file is associated with a valid NDS object. If not, the stream syntax file is deleted.
Check Local References	Local References are pointers to other objects maintained in the NDS database on this file server. Check Local References will evaluate the internal database pointers to make sure that they are pointing to the correct NDS objects. If invalid references are found, an error will be reported in DSREPAIR.LOG.
Reclaim Database Free Space	This operation searches for unused database records and deletes them to free up disk space.
Rebuild Operational Schema	This operation rebuilds the base schema classes and attributes needed by NDS for basic functionality.

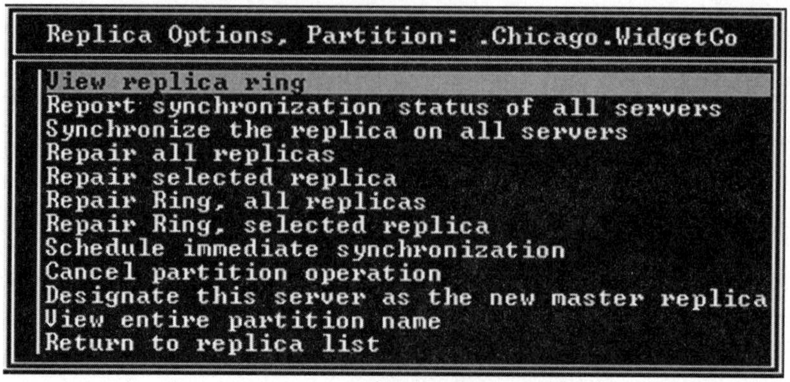

Figure 9-12
DSREPAIR partition
and replica
operations on
NetWare

```
Replica Options, Partition: .Chicago.WidgetCo
View replica ring
Report synchronization status of all servers
Synchronize the replica on all servers
Repair all replicas
Repair selected replica
Repair Ring, all replicas
Repair Ring, selected replica
Schedule immediate synchronization
Cancel partition operation
Designate this server as the new master replica
View entire partition name
Return to replica list
```

In addition to these database repair options, DSREPAIR offers a menu of partition and replica operations designed to keep the distributed NDS environment functioning properly (see Figure 9-12). This changes our focus from the local database to the partition—and all the replicas of that partition stored on servers across the network.

Table 9-6 describes the various partition and replica operations that are available. To access these operations, select the Advanced Options menu and then select Replica And Partition Operations.

Three other replica operations are available by doing the following:

1. Select the Advanced Options menu and then select Replica And Partition Operations.

2. Select a replica and then choose View Replica Ring.

3. Select a server from the list.

These three operations are described in Table 9-7. You will also recognize these operations as being available from NDS Manager.

Finally, four miscellaneous repair operations are accessible from other areas of the DSREPAIR utility. Table 9-8 describes these operations.

By using the operations described in this section, you can manage most noncatastrophic problems in your NDS environment. More information on DSREPAIR and other advanced troubleshooting tools is found in Chapter 10.

DSREPAIR Command Line Switches on NetWare Novell recommends that some DSREPAIR operations be performed on a regular basis in order to keep the NDS tree healthy. To facilitate this, Novell has also made DSREPAIR functionality available through command line switches. These switches make it possible to use batch schedulers to perform regular NDS

Table 9-6

DSREPAIR partition
and replica opera-
tions on NetWare

Operation	Description
Sync Replica On All Servers	Each server holding a replica of the selected partition is contacted, and then a synchronization cycle is initiated.
Repair All Replicas	This operation resolves NDS database inconsistencies by checking each object and attribute against schema definitions. It also checks the format of all internal data structures.
Repair Selected Replica	Performs a replica repair on the selected replica only
Repair Ring—Selected Replicas	Performs a replica repair operation on each server that hosts a replica of the selected partition
Repair Ring—All Replicas	Performs the replica ring repair operation for each replica ring in which this server participates
Schedule Immediate Sync	Initiates a replica synchronization cycle for each partition with a replica hosted on this server. This is useful for forcing the recognition of recent database changes.
Designate This Server As New Master Replica	If the Master replica of a given partition is lost due to hardware failure, this operation can be used to designate a new Master in order for partition operations to function normally.

Table 9-7

DSREPAIR Replica
Ring operations on
NetWare

Operation	Description
Synchronize the Replica on the Selected Server	Reports the synchronization status of the selected partition's replica that is hosted on this server
Send All Objects To Every Replica in the Ring	The operation will rebuild every replica in the ring according to the objects found in this server's replica. Warning: Any changes made to other replicas that have not yet updated to this server will be lost.
Receive All Objects from Master to This Replica	This operation will rebuild the local replica from object information received from the Master replica. Warning: Any changes made to this replica that have not yet updated to the Master replica will be lost.

tree maintenance automatically without any input from the administrator. Table 9-9 describes the various command line switches that are provided for automating basic DSREPAIR tasks on these two platforms.

Table 9-8

DSREPAIR other
operations on
NetWare

Operation	How to Access	Description
Repair All Network Addresses	1. Select the Advanced Options menu and then Servers Known To This Database. 2. Select a server from the list.	This operation checks server network addresses stored in all Root Partition objects in the tree against the values maintained in local SAP or SLP tables. If a discrepancy is found, NDS will be updated with the correct information. If no corresponding SAP or SLP entry is found, DSREPAIR will report an error.
Repair Selected Server's Network Addresses.	1. Select the Advanced Options menu and then select Servers Known To This Database. 2. Select a server and then select Repair Selected Server's Network Addresses.	Same as preceding, but only the Root Partition objects on the local server are checked
Check Volume Objects and Trustees	1. Select the Advanced Options menu and then Check Volume Objects And Trustees.	Check Volume Objects and Trustees first makes sure that each volume on the NetWare server is associated with a Volume object in NDS. If not, it will search the context in which the server resides to see whether a Volume object exists. If no Volume object exists, one will be created. After validating the volume information, the list of trustee IDs will be validated. Each object in NDS has a unique trustee ID. This ID is used to grant rights to other objects, including NetWare volumes, in the NDS tree. This task makes sure that each trustee ID in the volume list is a valid NDS object. If not, the trustee ID is removed from the volume list.
Check External References	1. Select the Advanced Options menu and then Check External References.	External References are pointers to NDS objects not stored in partition replicas on this server. Check External References evaluates each reference to an external object to make sure that it is pointing to a valid NDS object.

Operation	How to Access	Description
		The external reference check also verifies the need for all obituaries maintained in the local database. An obituary is used to maintain database consistency while NDS is replicating changes such as object moves, deletes, or name changes. If a replica attempts to reference the changed object using old information because it has not received the replica sync yet, the obituary entry permits it to do so without generating an error. After all replicas have synchronized the new information, the Janitor process eliminates the obituary.

Table 9-9

Command line
DSREPAIR switches
for NetWare
and NT

Switch	Parameter	Description
-D	None	Performs a database repair on the DIB with the filename extension specified as an argument. Default extension is NDS.
-L	Filename (with path)	Specifies the location for the DSREPAIR log file. Appends to existing log file if it exists. Default is SYS:SYSTEM\DSREPAIR.LOG.
-U	None	Performs Unattended Full Repair and automatically unloads when complete
-RC	None	Creates an NDS Dump File. This file is a snapshot of the local NDS database that can be used for troubleshooting. The dump file is stored as SYS:SYSTEM\DSR_DIB.
-RD	None	Repair Local Database. Executes using default database repair options, which include: Structure and Index check, Rebuild database, Tree Structure check, Repair all local replicas, Validate Mail/Stream files, and Check local references
-RN	None	Repair Network Addresses
-RV	None	Perform Volume Object Repair
-RVT	Volume Name	Perform Volume Object Repair and Trustee Check

DS Repair on NT

The DS Repair utility for NT enjoys the benefits of a modern graphical interface, and the underlying functionality is very similar to that offered by DS Repair on NetWare (see Figure 9-13). Nearly everything you can do from a NetWare console, you can now accomplish from the NT server. The only operations that have been excluded are those specific to the NetWare platform.

DS Repair on NT is started through NDSCONSOLE (NDSCONS.EXE), as are all other NDS services on NT. NDSCONSOLE is located in the directory where you installed NDS. It functions like the NT Service Manager. To load DS Repair on NT, do the following:

1. Start NDSCONSOLE by executing NDSCONS.EXE.

2. Locate DS Repair in the NDS service list and highlight it.

3. Click Start.

Throughout this section, when describing steps for performing a DS Repair operation on NT, it is assumed that you have already loaded the utility.

All DS Repair operations and results can be logged to file for review. The default log file is C:\NOVELL\NDS\DSREPAIR.LOG. DS Repair on NT has

Figure 9-13

NT DS Repair interface

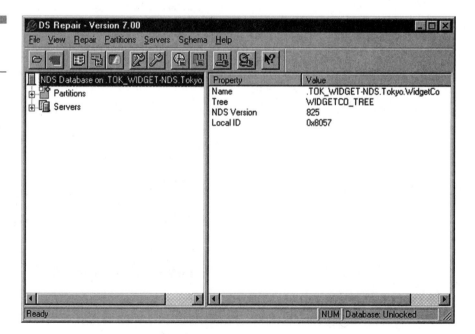

a menu for configuring the log file. To access this menu, click File and select Log File Options.

This section will describe the features available in each of the three main categories of DS Repair operations: NDS Monitor Operations, NDS Repair Operations, and Unattended Full Repair.

NDS Monitor Operations on NT   DS Repair offers several partition, replica, and server operations that are available to monitor the health of the NDS environment. These operations can be performed individually or as groups to help keep NDS stable and healthy.

The first category of operations can be loosely grouped into monitor operations that are designed to report NDS status and health. Table 9-10 describes the monitor operations available with DS Repair.

	Operation	How to Access	Description
Table 9-10 DS Repair monitor operations on NT	Report Sync Status	1. Click Repair and select Report Synchronization Status	Reports the sync status for every partition that hosts a replica on this server
	Report Sync Status of All Servers	1. Select a partition. 2. Click Partitions and select Report Synchronization Status of All Servers.	Queries each server hosting a replica of the selected partition and reports the sync status of each replica
	Time Sync	1. Click Repair and select Time Synchronization	Reports status of Time Synchronization
	Perform database structure and index check	1. Select a server. 2. Click Repair and select Local Database Repair.	Reviews the structure and format of database records and indexes. This ensures that no structural corruption has been introduced into the NDS environment at the database level
	Perform Tree Structure Check	1. Select a server. 2. Click Repair and select Local Database Repair.	Examines the links between database records to make sure that each child record has a valid parent. This helps ensure database consistency. Invalid records are marked so that they can be restored from another partition replica during the NDS replica synchronization process.

continues

Table 9-10

continued

Operation	How to Access	Description
Servers Known to This Database	1. All servers are displayed in the left pane of DS Repair.	Queries the local database and compiles a list of servers known to this partition
View Entire Server Name	1. The distinguished names of all servers are displayed in the left pane of DS Repair.	Displays the distinguished NDS name for this server
View Replica Ring	1. Click on a Partition object in the left pane of DS Repair. Servers hosting a replica of this partition are listed below the partition name.	Displays a list of all servers that host a replica of the selected partition
View Entire Partition Name	1. The distinguished name of each partition is listed in the left pane of DS Repair.	Displays the distinguished NDS name for this partition root object

NDS Repair Operations on NT   Although monitoring the condition of the NDS database is important, it does little good if there are no tools for repairing inconsistencies when they occur. DS Repair offers several NDS repair operations. These repair operations can be organized into three categories:

■ Database Repair Operations

■ Partition and Replica Repair Operations

■ Other Repair Operations

All Database Repair Operations are accessible from the same menu in DS Repair. To access these operations, do the following:

1. Select a server in the left pane of DS Repair

2. Click Repair and select Local Database Repair (see Figure 9-14).

The repair operations available from this menu are described in Table 9-11.
In addition to these database repair options, DS Repair offers a menu of partition and replica operations designed to keep the distributed NDS environment functioning properly (see Figure 9-15). This changes our focus from the local database to the partition—and all the replicas of that partition stored on servers across the network.

Figure 9-14
DS Repair Database
Operations menu
on NT

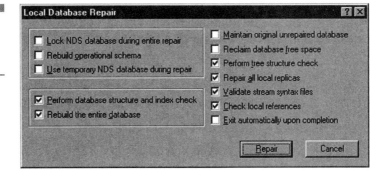

Operation	Description
Table 9-11 DS Repair database operations on NT	
Rebuild Entire Database	This operation is used to resolve errors found during structure and index checks. It restores proper data structures and recreates the NDS database and index files.
Repair All Local Replicas	This operation resolves NDS database inconsistencies by checking each object and attribute against schema definitions. It also checks the format of all internal data structures.
	Repair All Local Replicas can also resolve inconsistencies found during the tree structure check by removing invalid records from the database. As a result, all child records linked through the invalid record will be marked as orphans. These orphan records are not lost, but this process could potentially generate a large number of errors while the database is being rebuilt. Do not be overly alarmed. This is normal, and the orphan objects will be reorganized automatically over the course of replica synchronization.
Validate Stream Syntax Files	Stream Syntax Files, such as login scripts, are stored in a special area of the NDS database. Validate Stream Syntax Files checks to make sure that each stream syntax file is associated with a valid NDS object. If not, the stream syntax file is deleted.
Check Local References	Local References are pointers to other objects maintained in the NDS database on this file server. Check Local References will evaluate the internal database pointers to make sure that they are pointing to the correct NDS objects. If invalid references are found, an error will be reported in DSREPAIR.LOG.
Reclaim Database Free Space	This operation searches for unused database records and deletes them to free up disk space.
Rebuild Operational Schema	This operation rebuilds the base schema classes and attributes needed by NDS for basic functionality.

Figure 9-15

DS Repair partition
and replica
operations on NT

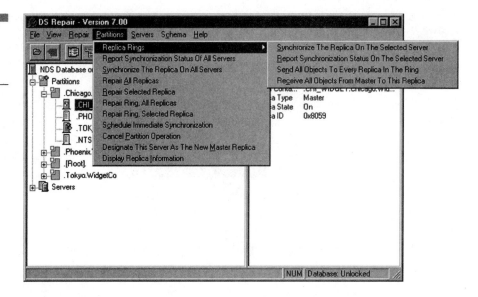

Figure 9-15

DS Repair partition
and replica
operations on NT

Table 9-12

DS Repair partition
and replica
operations on NT

Operation	Description
Sync Replica On All Servers	Each server holding a replica of the selected partition is contacted, and then a synchronization cycle is initiated.
Repair All Replicas	This operation resolves NDS database inconsistencies by checking each object and attribute against schema definitions. It also checks the format of all internal data structures.
Repair Selected Replica	Performs a replica repair on the selected replica only
Repair Ring, All Replicas	Performs the replica ring repair operation for each replica ring in which this server participates
Repair Ring, Selected Replica	Performs a replica repair operation on each server that hosts a replica of the selected partition
Schedule Immediate Sync	Initiates a replica synchronization cycle for each partition with a replica hosted on this server. This is useful for forcing the recognition of recent database changes.
Designate This Server As New Master Replica	If the Master replica of a given partition is lost due to hardware failure, this operation can be used to designate a new Master in order for partition operations to function normally.

Table 9-12 describes the various partition and replica operations that are available. To access these operations, do the following:

1. Select a partition in the left pane of DS Repair.

2. Click Partitions.

Three other replica operations are available by doing the following:

1. Select a partition in the left pane of DSREPAIR.
2. Click Partitions and select Replica Rings.

These operations are described in Table 9-13. You will also recognize these operations as being available from NDS Manager.

Finally, two miscellaneous repair operations are accessible from other areas of the DS Repair utility. Table 9-14 describes these operations.

Table 9-13	**Operation**	**Description**
DS Repair Replica Ring operations on NT	Synchronize The Replica On The Selected Server	Reports the synchronization status of the selected partition's replica that is hosted on this server
	Send All Objects To Every Replica In The Ring	The operation will rebuild every replica in the ring according to the objects found in this server's replica.
		Warning: Any changes made to other replicas that have not yet updated to this server will be lost.
	Receive All Objects From Master To This Replica	This operation will rebuild the local replica from object information received from the Master replica.
		Warning: Any changes made to this replica that have not yet updated to the Master replica will be lost.

Table 9-14	**Operation**	**How to Access**	**Description**
DS Repair other operations on NT	Repair All Network Addresses	1. Click Servers and select Repair All Network Addresses.	This operation checks server network addresses stored in all Root Partition objects in the tree against the values maintained in local SAP or SLP tables. If a discrepancy is found, NDS will be updated with the correct information.
			If no corresponding SAP or SLP entry is found, DS Repair will report an error.
	Repair Selected Server's Network Addresses	1. Select a server in the left pane of NDS Repair. 2. Click Servers and select Repair Selected Server's Network Addresses.	Same as preceding, but only the Root Partition objects on the local server are checked

By using the operations described in this section, you will be able to manage most noncatastrophic problems in your NDS environment. Information on advanced troubleshooting tools is found in Chapter 11, "Troubleshooting NDS."

DS Repair on Solaris

Solaris doesn't really offer a user interface *per se*, unless you count a command line as a user interface. In today's graphical world, that is not usually the case. Although radically different from the NetWare and NT platforms, this command-line philosophy is consistent with how things are done in the UNIX world. DS Repair on Solaris is not as robust as it is on either NetWare or NT. Because this utility was developed after the advent of tools like NDS Manager and ConsoleOne, many of the minor operations are left to these new client-based tools rather than duplicate the effort in DS Repair on Solaris. DS Repair on Solaris has the bare number of operations necessary to get by and nothing else.

Two conventions in this section are different from other sections of this chapter:

1. Because Solaris commands are case sensitive, filenames and command line parameters must be typed *exactly* as they appear in this text. "ndsrepair -f" does NOT equal "ndsrepair -F".

2. When describing how to perform a specific ndsrepair operation, the command is listed rather than describing the process of using a File Manager window.

To load DS Repair on the Solaris platform, type the following: /bin/ ndsrepair—together with all desired command-line switches—in a Solaris terminal window. The ndsrepair utility can also be executed from a File Manager window by double-clicking on the ndsrepair icon in the /bin directory. If you start ndsrepair using a File Manager, Solaris will open a dialog box in which you can enter the desired command-line switches.

All DS Repair operations and results can be logged to file for review. The default log file /var/nds/ndsrepair.log. DS Repair on Solaris offers the following command-line switches related to the log file:

- ndsrepair -F [filename]   Specify the log file name.
- ndsrepair -O   Turns file logging on. This option is set by default.
- ndsrepair -A   Appends log information to the existing log file. This option is set by default.

The remainder of this section describes the features available in each of the three main categories of ndsrepair operations: NDS Monitor Operations, NDS Repair Operations, and Unattended Full Repair.

NDS Monitor Operations on Solaris DS Repair offers several partition, replica, and server operations that are available to monitor the health of the NDS environment. These operations can be performed individually or as groups to help keep NDS stable and healthy.

The first category of operations can be loosely grouped into Monitor operations that are designed to report NDS status and health. Table 9-15 described the monitor operations available with ndsrepair. Note that Solaris implements a much smaller list of operations because it relies on NDS Manager to view the basic partition, replica, and server information.

Table 9-15

ndsrepair monitor operations on Solaris

Operation	How to Access	Description
Report Sync Status	/bin/ndsrepair -E	Reports the sync status for every partition that hosts a replica on this server
Time Sync	Use /usr/sbin/ ntptrace to check time sync status.	Reports status of Time Synchronization
Perform Database Structure And Index Check	/bin/ndsrepair -Ri	Reviews the structure and format of database records and indexes. This ensures that no structural corruption has been introduced into the NDS environment at the database level.
Perform Tree Structure Check	/bin/ndsrepair -Rt	Examines the links between database records to make sure that each child record has a valid parent. This helps ensure database consistency. Invalid records are marked so that they can be restored from another partition replica during the NDS replica synchronization process.
Servers Known To This Database	Use NDS Manager	Queries the local databases and compiles a list of servers known to this partition

continues

Table 9-15

continued

Operation	How to Access	Description
View Entire Server Name	Use NDS Manager	Displays the distinguished NDS name for this server
View Replica Ring	Use NDS Manager	Displays a list of all servers that host a replica of the selected partition
View Entire Partition Name	Use NDS Manager	Displays the distinguished NDS name for this partition root object

NDS Repair Operations on Solaris Although monitoring the condition of the NDS database is important, it does little good if there are no tools for repairing inconsistencies when they occur. Solaris offers several NDS repair operations through ndsrepair. These repair operations can be organized into three categories:

- Database repair operations
- Partition and replica repair operations
- Other repair operations

The database repair operations available in ndsrepair are described in Table 9-16.

Table 9-16

ndsrepair database repair operations on Solaris

Operation	How to Access	Description
Rebuild Entire Database	/bin/ndsrepair -Rd	This operation is used to resolve errors found during structure and index checks. It restores proper data structures and recreates the NDS database and index files.
Repair All Local Replicas	/bin/ndsrepair -Rr	This operation resolves NDS database inconsistencies by checking each object and attribute against schema definitions. It also checks the format of all internal data structures.
		Repair All Local Replicas can also resolve inconsistencies found during the tree structure check by removing invalid records from the database. As a result, all child records linked through the invalid record will be marked as orphans. These orphan records are not lost, but this

Operation	How to Access	Description
		process could potentially generate a large number of errors while the database is being rebuilt. Do not be overly alarmed. This is normal, and the orphan objects will be reorganized automatically over the course of replica synchronization.
Check Local References	/bin/ndsrepair -Rc	Local References are pointers to other objects maintained in the NDS database on this file server. Check Local References will evaluate the internal database pointers to make sure that they are pointing to the correct NDS objects. If invalid references are found, an error will be reported in DSRE-PAIR.LOG.
Reclaim Database Free Space	/bin/ndsrepair -Rf	This operation searches for unused database records and deletes them to free up disk space.
Rebuild Operational Schema	/bin/ndsrepair -Ro	This operation rebuilds the base schema classes and attributes needed by NDS for basic functionality.
Validate Stream Syntax Files	/bin/ndsrepair -Rv	Stream Syntax Files, such as login scripts, are stored in a special area of the NDS database. Validate Stream Syntax Files checks to make sure that each stream syntax file is associated with a valid NDS object. If not, the stream syntax file is deleted.

In addition to these database repair options, ndsrepair offers a menu of partition and replica operations designed to keep the distributed NDS environment functioning properly. This changes your focus from the local database to the partition—and all the replicas of that partition stored on servers across the network. The partition repair operations are described in Table 9-17.

WAN Traffic Manager

NDS offers a standard utility for managing the NDS-related traffic between servers. *WAN Traffic Manager* (WANMAN) is a policy-based solution that

Table 9-17

NDS partition
repair operations in
ndsrepair

Operation	How to Access	Description
Repair all Replicas	1. /bin/ndsrepair -P 2. Select a Replica. 3. Select Repair All Replicas.	This operation resolves NDS database inconsistencies by checking each object and attribute against schema definitions. It also checks the format of all internal data structures. Repair All Replicas can also resolve found during the tree structure check by removing invalid records from the database. As a result, all child records linked through the invalid record will be marked as orphans. These orphan records are not lost, but this process could potentially generate a large number of errors while the database is being rebuilt. Do not be overly alarmed. This is normal, and the orphan objects will be reorganized automatically over the course of replica synchronization.
Repair Selected Replica	1. /bin/ndsrepair -P 2. Select a Replica. 3. Select Repair Selected Replica.	Same operation as preceding, but only performed on the selected replica
Schedule Immediate Sync	1. /bin/nDSREPAIR -P 2. Select a Replica. 3. Select Schedule Immediate Sync	Initiates a replica synchronization cycle for each partition with a replica hosted on this server. This is useful for forcing the recognition of recent database changes.
Designate This Server As The New Master Replica	1. /bin/nDSREPAIR -P 2. Select a Replica. 3. Select Designate This Server As The New Master Replica.	If the Master replica of a given partition is lost due to hardware failure, this operation can be used to designate a new Master in order for partition operations to function normally

enables you to control the flow of NDS background traffic based on the time of day, the type of traffic, and/or other configurable settings. As its name implies, it was originally designed to control the flow of NDS background traffic over expensive WAN connections. However, WANMAN can be used to manage NDS background traffic over any type of network connection.

WANMAN does not manage client-to-server traffic or non-NDS traffic between servers, such as time sync or service advertisement—SAP or SLP. These communications can also affect WAN links if not properly configured or filtered.

The three pieces to the WANMAN solution are as follows:

1. *WTM*   This executable enables the server to read the WAN Traffic Policies that determine how NDS background traffic is to be managed. The appropriate file needs to be loaded on each server for which NDS traffic needs to be controlled. There is a WTM executable available for the NetWare (WTM.NLM) and NT (WTM.DLL) platforms. A WTM module for Solaris may be developed for a future release, but no specifics are available at this time.

2. *WAN Traffic Manager Policies*   The administrator configures WANMAN policies to define how different types of NDS traffic will be managed. Each policy is capable of managing only one type of traffic. For example, one WANMAN policy can be created to manage Janitor traffic, another policy for Replica Sync traffic, and so on. WANMAN policies can be assigned on a server-by-server basis or through a LAN Area object that enables groups of servers to be managed together through the same policy definitions.

3. *ConsoleOne Snap-In*   This snap-in to the ConsoleOne administrative utility enables administrators to create the necessary WANMAN objects and to manage the creation and assignment of WAN Traffic Policies to the servers under their control. The WANMAN snap-in will be installed automatically when ConsoleOne is first installed from the NDS CD.

WAN Traffic Manager Policy Structure

A WANMAN policy consists of three pieces:

1. *Declarations*   The declaration section of a WANMAN policy defines all the variables to be used in the policy including local variables and external values passed in by WANMAN clients. The variables defined in the Declaration section are used by the Selector and Provider to determine whether or not the NDS traffic should be permitted.

2. *Selector*   The Selector section is used to determine whether or not a policy should be executed for any given request received by WANMAN.

When a WANMAN request is received, the Selector section of every loaded policy will be evaluated. The Selector will return an integer value between 0 and 100. The higher the number, the more applicable the policy is to the specific request that was received. The policy returning the highest value will be chosen to handle the request.

3. *Provider* The Provider section contains the actual logic that will determine whether or not to allow the NDS traffic to be generated. The Provider section executes only if its policy is selected to manage the NDS process request. The result of the Provider section calculations will be a Return value of SEND or DONT_SEND.

WANMAN Policy Syntax

As with any policy system, WANMAN defines certain format and syntax requirements that must be followed when creating NDS traffic policies. Anyone who is familiar with programming or script languages will recognize that the WANMAN format and syntax rules are fairly standard. If you have never written programs or scripts in a structured language before, it would be wise to do some research first before tackling a WANMAN policy. In any case, apply new policies slowly and methodically and test their operation before installing them on a large number of NDS servers.

Four types of syntax and format rules must be applied when creating or editing a WANMAN policy. Each will be discussed in a following section.

- Naming conventions
- Broadcast versus addressed traffic
- Variable types
- Variable scope

Naming Conventions In order to be able to interpret the variable names used in creating policy definitions, WANMAN imposes a few rules when naming and initializing policy variables:

- Any length variable name is allowed, but only the first 31 characters are actually used by the system. This means that the first 31 characters of each variable name must be unique.
- WANMAN variable names are case sensitive.

- WANMAN variable names can contain alphanumeric characters, but the name must begin with a letter.

- Variables are initialized with values using the : = operator, similar to the C programming language.

Broadcast versus Addressed Traffic When an NDS background process needs to send—or request—information, there are two ways of doing so:

1. The information—or request—is general in nature and needs to be delivered to all NDS servers on the network. This communication is done through a broadcast message. No destination address is specified.

2. The information—or request—is specific in nature and should be delivered only to the server(s) that needs it. This communication is done through an addressed message. A specific destination address is specified.

The identifier, NO_ADDRESSES, is required for policies that will manage NDS traffic types that utilize broadcast messages. This includes the following NDS traffic types:

- NDS_BACKLINKS

- NDS_JANITOR

- NDS_LIMBER

- NDS_SCHEMA_SYNC

- NDS_CHECK_LOGIN_RESTRICTION

Policies written to manage these traffic types must include the NO_ADDRESSES identifier as the first statement in the Declarations section.

Unfortunately, the same background processes that generate broadcast traffic can also send addressed communications. To accommodate this, a second traffic type has been defined for each of these background processes. This second traffic type is identified by appending "_OPEN" to the end of its name. Thus, we also have the following NDS traffic types:

- NDS_BACKLINKS_OPEN

- NDS_JANITOR_OPEN

- NDS_LIMBER_OPEN

- NDS_SCHEMA_SYNC_OPEN

- NDS_CHECK_LOGIN_RESTRICTION_OPEN

Addressed traffic types such as these do not use the NO_ADDRESSES identifier, so each of these traffic types must be managed through a different policy. For example, in order to manage NDS Backlink traffic, you would have to define a policy for both the NDS_BACKLINKS traffic type and the NDS_BACKLINKS_OPEN traffic type.

Variable Type   Variable type refers to the values that can be contained within a defined variable. For example, a variable might be of type Integer and contain values such as 1, 3, and 98. That same Integer variable could not store the value 3.14159 or the text string 'Joshua Gary Harris'. The reason for specifying variables like this is that it defines the set of valid operations that can be performed on that variable. WANMAN defined only four valid variable types for use in policy definitions.

Variables of type INT hold signed integer values. The high-order bit determines whether or not the value is positive (1) or negative (0).

Variables of type BOOLEAN are capable of holding only two values: TRUE (Binary 1) or FALSE (Binary 0). BOOLEAN variables must be initialized to a default value, either TRUE or FALSE, when they are created in the Declaration section of the WANMAN policy.

Variables of type TIME are used to pass in network time values for use in policy calculations. TIME variables are never initialized in the Declarations section because it does not make any sense to define a default time. TIME is always passed in as part of the WANMAN client request.

TIME variables are structures containing five fields. Each field enables you to access a specific portion of the time/date as needed. Use dot (.) notation to access a specific field, as shown in Table 9-18.

TIME variables use a 24-hour time format (hour : minute), numeric day of month, text string month, and four-digit year. For example, the network time 5:23 P.M., 22 May 1994, when passed into the TIME variable AUSTIN, will occupy the fields of AUSTIN as shown in Table 9-18.

Variables of type NETADDRESS are used to pass in network addresses for use in policy calculations. The NETADDRESS variable is never initialized in the Declarations section because it does not make sense to define a default network destination address. NETADDRESS is always be passed in as part of the WANMAN client request.

Table 9-18

TIME variable structure

AUSTIN.min	AUSTIN.hour	AUSTIN.mday	AUSTIN.mon	AUSTIN.year
23	17	22	5 or MAY	1994

NETADDRESS variables are structures containing 13 fields. Field 1 holds the network type (IPX or IP). The other 12 fields hold values from 0-255 decimal (0-FF Hex), corresponding to a portion of the actual network address. Each field enables you to access a specific portion of the network address as needed. Use the dot (.) notation to access a specific field, as shown in Table 9-19.

Variable Scope   Variable Scope defines how important a variable is to the proper operation of the policy calculator. Scope also defines where a variable must be initialized and how it must be used. Four different levels of scope exist within WANMAN policies.

Variables of scope REQUIRED are critical for proper policy function. The WANMAN client provides these values, which will allow WANMAN to determine whether or not the specified NDS traffic should be allowed. The policy will not execute if a REQUIRED variable is not initialized.

Variables of scope OPTIONAL may or may not be passed in by the WANMAN client. Because it is unknown whether or not a value will be provided, the OPTIONAL variable must be initialized with a default value when it is declared. If the WANMAN client does not pass in a value, the default will be used when performing policy calculations.

Variables of scope LOCAL are used during the course of the policy calculation only. LOCAL variables might be used to hold some intermediate value during the policy calculation. This value is used only during the policy calculation and is never passed in or out of the policy definition itself.

Variables of scope SYSTEM are predefined variables of various types that can be used to receive system-supplied parameters. SYSTEM variables include are outlined in Table 9-20.

Table 9-19

NETADDRESS
variable structure

IPX addresses take the form NETWORK : NODE : SOCKET. IPX addresses are hex values.

The IPX address 11023889:9A236DC119E5:220C, when passed into the NETADDRESS variable X, will occupy the fields of X as shown here.

X.type	X.a	X.b	X.c	X.d	X.e	X.f	X.g	X.h	X.i	X.j	X.k	X.l
IPX	11	02	38	89	9A	23	6D	C1	19	E5	22	0C

IP addresses use a 4-byte value that is divided between NETWORK and NODE by the IP network mask. IP addresses can be specified in either decimal or hex values. The IP address 137.65.87.145, when passed into the NETADDRESS variable Y, will occupy the fields of Y as shown here:

Y.type	Y.a	Y.b	Y.c	Y.d	Y.e	Y.f	Y.g	Y.h	Y.i	Y.j	Y.k	Y.l
IP	137	65	87	145	N/A	N/A	N/A	N/A	N/A	N/A	N/A	N/A

Table 9-20

WANMAN SYSTEM
variables

Variable Name	Variable Type	Description
DestAddress	NETADDRESS	Destination address of the server to which traffic is to be sent
SrcAddress	NETADDRESS	Source address of the server attempting to send traffic
Now	TIME	Local time when the WANMAN policy began processing
UTCNow	TIME	UTC time when the WANMAN policy began processing
DayOfWeek	INT	The day of the week associated with the Now time variable. It is maintained in the DayOfWeek system symbol in both string (Sunday, Monday,..., etc.) and numeric (0–6) formats
DayOfWeekUTC	INT	The day of the week associated with the NowUTC time variable. It is maintained in the DayOfWeek system symbol in both string (Sunday, Monday,..., etc.) and numeric (0–6) formats.
TrafficType	INT	Specifies the NDS traffic type for which this policy should be run. See the INT NDS_ <Traffic Type> entry for more information.
DestCost	INT	This is an administrator-supplied value identifying the cost of communicating with the given server or LAN Area. More information on setting traffic costs will be given.
NDS_<Traffic Type>	INT	These are system-defined constants for each NDS traffic type. The <Traffic Type> argument in the variable name at left can be replaced with any of the following in order to identify a specific type of NDS traffic: SYNC JANITOR JANITOR_OPEN LIMBER LIMBER_OPEN BACKLINKS BACKLINKS_OPEN SCHEMA_SYNC SCHEMA_SYNC_OPEN CHECK_LOGIN_RESTRICTIONS CHECK_LOGIN_RESTRICTIONS_OPEN

Configuring WAN Traffic Manager

Four main steps are involved in configuring WANMAN for use:

1. Extend schema for WANMAN.
2. Load WANMAN on the NDS server.
3. Identify and/or create WANMAN policies.
4. Assign the necessary WANMAN policies.
5. (Optional) Create a LAN Area Object.

Extend Schema for WANMAN The schema of your NDS tree will be extended automatically during the installation of NDS as long as you have selected WAN Traffic Manager as a component to install. If you haven't done this, rerun the NDS installation utility and install WAN Traffic Manager. See Chapter 3, "Installing and Upgrading NDS," for more information on installing NDS and its components.

Load WANMAN on the NDS Server Load the appropriate WANMAN executable on each server that needs to follow WANMAN policies.

■ *NetWare* Load WTM.NLM at the server console.

You can automate the loading of WTM.NLM by inserting it into the AUTOEXEC.NCF. This will open a new WTM.NLM monitor screen on the NetWare console. It also opens the SYS:SYSTEM\WANMAN.LOG, which will record everything that goes on in the WANMAN environment.

■ *NT* Load NDSCONSOLE by loading NDSCONS.EXE.

■ Highlight WTM the NDSCONSOLE service list and click Start.

You can also configure this service to start automatically by clicking Startup and selecting Automatic.

Identify or Create WANMAN Policies WANMAN policies are script files that define rules for determining whether or not NDS traffic will be allowed. WANMAN ships with several predefined policy groups that can be used as templates for managing background NDS traffic. These policy groups are stored with the ConsoleOne program files. The default paths for these policy group files are as follows:

■ *NetWare* SYS:SYSTEM\PUBLIC\CONSOLEONE\1.2\LIB\WANMAN

■ *NT* C:\NOVELL\CONSOLEONE\1.2\LIB\WANMAN

In a few cases these templates may serve just fine. However, in most cases, you will need to make some modifications in order to get the policies to fit the dynamics of your network and organization. That said, it is almost always much easier to edit these predefined policies to fit your needs rather than creating a completely new set of policies for your specific situation. Table 9-21 outlines the predefined WANMAN policy groups and the policies each contains.

	Policy Group	Included Policies
Table 9-21	1_3AM..WMG	Prevent all NDS traffic between 1:00 A.M. and 3:00 A.M.
Predefined WANMAN policy groups		Allow all NDS traffic only between 1:00 A.M. and 3:00 A.M.
	7A.M._6PM..WMG	Prevent all NDS traffic between 7:00 A.M. and 6:00 P.M.
		Allow all NDS traffic only between 7:00 A.M. and 6:00 P.M.
		These policies are mutually exclusive, so choose one of them and delete the other.
	COSTLT20.WMG	Only allow NDS traffic of Cost < 20
		Allow address-based policies to execute when necessary for nontime-based traffic management
	IPX.WMG	Only allows NDS traffic over IPX
		Allow address-based policies to execute when necessary for nontime-based traffic management
	NDSTTYPS.WMG	Default policy that will execute when no other qualifies
		Allow only NDS Replica Sync traffic
		Allow NDS to open Backlink connections and send Backlink traffic
		Allow NDS to open Janitor connections and send Janitor traffic
		Allow NDS to open Limber connections and send Limber traffic
		Allow NDS to open Schema Sync connections and send Schema Sync traffic
	ONOSPOOF.WMG	Only allow traffic over currently open connections to be sent
		Allow address-based policies to execute when necessary for nontime-based traffic management
	OPNSPOOF.WMG	Examine open connections to see whether updates have been sent recently. If not, allow NDS Traffic to be sent.

Policy Group	Included Policies
	Allow address-based policies to execute when necessary for nontime-based traffic management
SAMEAREA.WMG	Allow NDS traffic over IPX in the same network only
	Allow address-based policies to execute when necessary for nontime-based traffic management
	Allow NDS traffic over TCPIP in the same network only
TCPIP.WMG	Only allow NDS traffic over TCP/IP
	Allow address-based policies to execute when necessary for nontime-based traffic management
TIMECOST.WMG	Allow NDS traffic if cost <20
	Prevent any low priority NDS traffic
	Allow only NDS sync traffic between 1:00 A.M. and 1:30 A.M. as long as cost < 20
	Allow all NDS traffic to run four times a day (1:00 A.M., 7:00 A.M., 1:00 P.M., 7:00 P.M.)
	Allow all NDS traffic to run between 1:00 A.M. and 1:30 A.M.

The policies in the predefined WANMAN policy groups may be mixed and matched in order to accomplish an overall NDS traffic management strategy. In fact, you will note that several of the policy groups contain policies that are mutually exclusive. Choose the one you want to work with and delete the other. You will also note that some of the policies are supplemental. These policies warn you against running them alone because they can prevent any NDS traffic from occurring.

To use one or more of these preconfigured policy groups to create your WANMAN policy definitions, complete the following steps:

1. Launch ConsoleOne.

2. Right-click on a Server or LAN Area object and select Properties.

3. Click the WAN Traffic Manager tab twice and select Policies.

4. Click Load and select a policy group. This will populate the Policies field with a list of policies (see Figure 9-16).

5. Highlight the policy you would like to modify and click Edit.

▬▬ ▬▬ ▬▬ ▬▬
Figure 9-16
ConsoleOne
WANMAN
Policies page

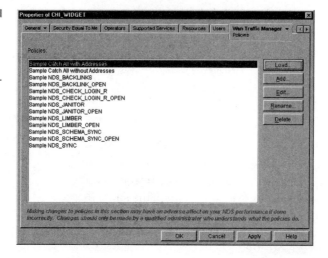

▬▬ ▬▬ ▬▬ ▬▬
Figure 9-17
Modify WANMAN
policies

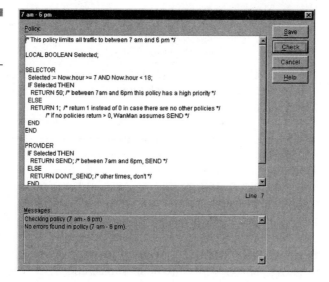

6. Make the appropriate changes to the policy, making sure to observe all structure and syntax rules. When finished, verify the policy by clicking Check (see Figure 9-17).

7. If no errors are found click Save to return to the Policies page.

If you want to create a brand new policy, complete the following steps:

1. Launch ConsoleOne.

2. Right-click on the Server or LAN Area object for which you want to create a WANMAN policy and select Properties.

3. Click the WAN Traffic Manager tab twice and select Policies from the

drop-own menu.

4. Click Advanced and enter a name for the policy. Click New.

5. Write the policy using the text editor provided.

6. After you have the policy written, verify its format by clicking Check.

7. If no errors are found, click Save.

Assign the Necessary WANMAN Policies   Now that you have your policies defined, you have done the hard work. Now you just need to define those servers or LAN Area objects that will use your newly defined WANMAN policy definitions. This same process can be used for assigning policies to either server objects or LAN Area objects as needed. The creation of LAN Area objects is described in the next step.

1. Launch ConsoleOne.

2. Right-click on a Server or LAN Area object and select Properties.

3. Click the WAN Traffic Manager tab twice and select Policies.

4. Click Load and browse to the policy, or policies, that you want to use. Highlight the Policy and click Open. The selected policies will now appear in the Policies box.

If you have loaded policies from a predefined group, you can delete those individual policies that you do not want to apply to you by highlighting the policy and clicking Delete.

After you have only the policies you want applied showing in the Policies: box, click OK.

(Optional) Create a LAN Area Object   If several servers—perhaps all those at a given site—need to be managed using the same set of WANMAN policies, you can create a LAN Area object. The LAN Area object functions like a group for WANMAN servers. You assign policies to the LAN Area object and then associate the appropriate servers to the LAN Area object. Those servers are then governed by the WANMAN policies assigned to the LAN Area object.

To create a LAN Area object, complete the following steps:

1. Launch ConsoleOne.

2. Right-click on the container in which you want to create the LAN Area object, select New, and then click Object.

3. Browse to the WANMAN: LAN AREA object class and click OK.

4. Specify the name of the LAN Area object in the Name: field and check the Define additional properties box; then click OK.

5. Click Policies to assign policies to the LAN Area object. Use the steps outlined previously.

6. Click Members to assign servers as members of the LAN Area.

7. Click Add and browse to each server you want to add to the LAN Area. Select it and click OK.

8. Click Apply and then OK to commit any changes.

NDS Traffic Costs

Costs are a way of defining the difficulty of communicating from one server or group of servers to another. Through costs, we can define traffic restrictions on something other than time. WANMAN enables you to define destination-based cost and/or default cost that can be used when no specific cost is defined. WANMAN costs must be defined as nonnegative integers. No units are assigned to the Cost values, so you have to be sure that WAN-MAN costs across the network are defined using common criteria such as Dollars, Packets per Second, etc. This way, all WANMAN costs will be relative and useful when comparing one against another.

When a policy is being evaluated, policy variables can be compared to assigned cost values through the INT DestCost SYSTEM variable. The DestCost variable will be initialized to the cost assigned to the network address for which NDS traffic is being requested. In this way, a policy can determine whether or not to allow the traffic based on the administrator-defined costs for that communication. To assign costs to a Server or LAN Area object, complete the following steps:

1. Launch ConsoleOne.

2. Right-click on a Server or LAN Area object and select Properties.

3. If you are assigning costs to a LAN Area object, click the Cost tab. If you are assigning costs to a Server object, click the WAN Traffic Manager tab twice, and select Cost (see Figure 9-18).

4. Define costs for either TCP/IP or IPX addresses by clicking the appropriate button (see Figures 9-19 and 9-20). Enter the address range for which you want to assign a cost and specify the cost value for communicating with this range of addresses. Then click OK.

Figure 9-18
WANMAN Cost
Definition page

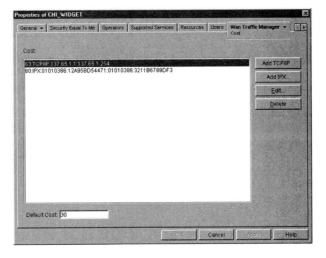

Figure 9-19
Defining WANMAN
costs for TCP/IP

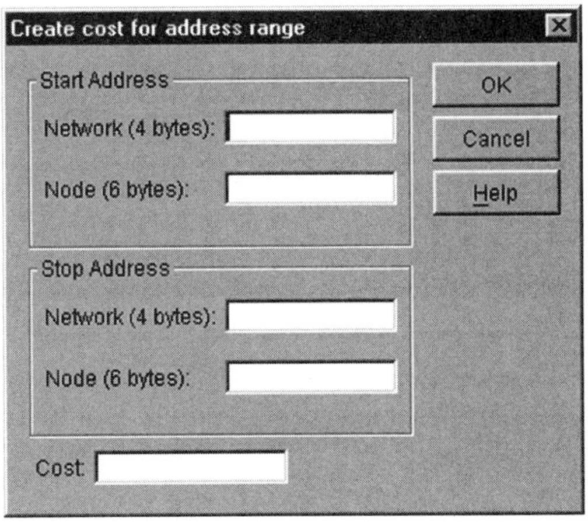

Figure 9-20
Defining WANMAN
costs for IPX

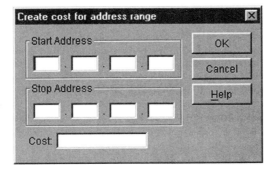

5. (Optional) Enter a cost in the Default Cost field. This value will be used when no specific cost has been defined for a given network address.

6. Click Apply and then OK to save changes.

Backup and Restore of the NDS Database

The first thing to recognize is that by properly designing and replicating, your NDS tree archives become much less critical. That said, directory archives must still be kept to stand as the last line of defense against catastrophic losses. Most likely, you will want to integrate your NDS backup tasks into the overall network archive strategy that you have implemented to protect server files. It is likely that your existing archive solution will be able to support NDS if it is running on NetWare or NT. The only platform for which NDS provides a database backup/restore solution is Solaris. NDS relies on the use of existing backup solutions for the NetWare and NT platforms.

NDS Backup on NetWare and NT

NDS ships with an SMS-compliant *Target Service Agent* (TSA) for both Net-Ware and NT. TSANDS allows NDS to properly format and pass critical directory data, structures, and relationships to an SMS-compliant backup solution. SMS solutions include Novell's own SBackup for NetWare and Computer Associates ArcServIT, which is available on both the NetWare and NT platforms. Several other solutions may also be available. Check with your reseller or current backup provider to see whether other archive solutions will work.

WARNING: *The NDS tree should never be archived by simply making copies of the NDS databases on each server. Although data will be preserved, all the relationships between NDS objects and partitions will be lost. Only use SMS-compliant backup solutions to archive NDS.*

TSANDS allows the entire NDS tree to be backed up through a single server, if desired, although in a large network environment you may want to have at least one backup server per site to avoid archiving data across WAN links. The important thing is that you don't have to implement a backup solution on every server in the network.

To provide this flexibility, TSANDS enables you to specify what objects and/or containers you want to backup through each server. This way, large trees can be divided up into distinct archive processes for backup and restore operations. Everything from a single object to the entire tree can be specified during the backup and restore operations. For more information on SMS-compliant backup, see your NetWare or NT documentation.

NDS Backup on Solaris

NDS for Solaris provides /bin/ndsbackup as an NDS archive solution for the Solaris platform. If you are operating in a mixed platform environment, ndsbackup may not be necessary, but in a Solaris-only shop, you won't have any other choice for protecting the NDS tree data. The ndsbackup utility does have the advantage of being able to take advantage of existing Solaris Tape Drive support. Simply direct the output to the desired storage device, and Solaris handles the rest.

The ndsbackup utility executes using the familiar UNIX command-line switches to define functionality. Table 9-22 lists the various switches available when running ndsbackup. Remember that all UNIX filenames and switches are case sensitive.

Table 9-22

ndsbackup
command-line
switches

Function Name	Switch	Description
Create	c	Creates a new NDS backup file using the name specified on the command line. If the file already exists, it will be overwritten.
Replace	r	Effectively updates an existing ndsbackup file by replacing previously backed up objects with new copies of those objects. New objects are appended to the file
Scan	s	Scans the objects in the NDS tree
Table of Contents	t	Generates a list of the names of the specified object types that exist in the NDS backup file. If no object types are specified, this will generate a list of all objects in the NDS backup file.
Restore	x	The specified NDS objects are extracted from the NDS backup file and restored to the NDS tree. If a container object is specified, all subordinate objects are recursively restored to the NDS tree as well.

continues

Table 9-22

continued

Modifier Name	Switch	Description
File name	f	Specifies that the backup file name will be specified as an argument on the ndsbackup command line. If the f modifier is not specified, ndsbackup will write to standard outpur or read from standard input, as appropriate.
Replica location	R	Allows you to archive or restore NDS objects using an external server. The server's DNS name or IP address is specified as an argument on the ndsbackup command line.
Verbose output	v	Specifies that more complete object information should be reported. Used primarily with the t function
What	w	Forces the administrator to confirm the specified backup/restore operation before it will be executed. Not applicable to the t function
Include specific objects	I	Allows the administrator to create an include-file, which is specified as an argument on the ndsbackup command line. The include-file identifies the type(s) of objects that will be included in the backup/restore operation.
eXclude specific objects	X	Allows the administrator to create an exclude-file, which is specified as an argument on the ndsbackup command line. The exclude-file identifies the type(s) of objects that will be excluded from the backup/restore operation. The include-file takes precedence if an object is listed in both include- and exclude-files.

Ndsbackup uses the following command line syntax:

```
ndsbackup <Function><Modifier(s)> < argument(s) >
```

Note that there are no spaces between Function and Modifier switches, but there is a space between switches and subsequent arguments. Each argument is likewise separated by a space.

Following are some sample ndsbackup commands:

■ To backup the OU=Chicago.O=WidgetCo container:

```
ndsbackup cf  chi_backup .OU=Chicago.O=WidgetCo
```

■ To backup the NDS tree schema:

```
ndsbackup cf widgetco_schema Schema
```

ndsbackup Tips

- When using include- and/or exclude-files, be very careful that no extra white spaces exist at the end of lines. Any syntax errors on include- or exclude- files will cause them not to run.

- If you want to back up the entire tree, every replica must be healthy and accessible. Use ndsrepair to make sure that the tree is healthy before attempting a full backup.

- Novell recommends a weekly NDS tree backup routine as a general rule. Very dynamic trees may need to be backed up more often.

- If corruption occurs, a partial restoration of a partition is not generally recommended due to subtle problems that can result. Object IDs can change. External references can be improperly assigned. Some objects rely on others and will not work properly until their dependent objects are also restored. Bottom line, if a partition restoration needs to occur, it is usually best to restore the whole partition. Remember that most of the objects in an NDS tree will be fairly static after they are created.

SUMMARY

Besides just maintaining and managing all of the resources stored in an NDS tree, it is critical that the underlying NDS database be kept healthy and error free. An NDS administrator must be concerned with these things on a daily basis. By creating a stable, efficient NDS infrastructure, all the subsequent object and security management becomes much easier.

Novell provides a comprehensive set of tools for performing the tasks necessary to keep an NDS tree in top shape. These tools enable you to manage replicas and partitions, control the flow of NDS traffic over the network, and monitor and repair NDS database files as necessary. Beyond this, Novell is making it as easy as possible to archive and protect critical NDS files by integrating NDS with standards-based backup standards.

More than anything else, the tools that allow you to accomplish these tasks will become the world through which you will view NDS. It is critical that every administrator takes the time to get to know and understand the operation of each of these tools. This chapter has set you on that road.

For More Information

Since NDS has been around since 1993, Novell has had time to develop a lot of good information about it. However, because NDS has only now been separated from the underlying NetWare operating system, a lot of this information is tied up in NetWare discussions. If you have a NetWare environment that is OK but are running a native NT or Solaris environment, you have to be able to pick out the NDS-specific information and not worry about the rest.

Some of the links we have found most valuable are as follows.

Books

- *Novell's Guide to NetWare 5 Networks*, by Jeffrey F. Hughes and Blair W. Thomas, IDG Books, 1999.

  This book is focused on NetWare 5, but it discusses a lot of NDS-related topics as a matter of course. Hughes and Thomas are well known and respected for their work in NDS design, configuration, and troubleshooting. Their book does not cover the latest version of NDS because it is written from the perspective of NetWare 5. However, many of the design and theoretical issues they discuss are still applicable.

- *NDS for NT*, Jeffrey F. Hughes and Blair W. Thomas, IDG Books, 1998.

  Another Hughes and Thomas effort, NDS for NT is written from the perspective of earlier versions of NDS for NT, which were limited to operating within an existing NetWare environment. Because of this, there is no discussion of the new NT-based administrative tools for NDS. However, the information provided with regards to the interaction between NDS and NT domains is valuable from the perspective of understanding how to get them to work more efficiently together.

Web Sites

NDS Web site `http://www.novell.com/products/nds/index.html`

NDS Cool Solutions Web site `http://www.novell.com/coolsolutions/nds/`

Web Articles

Maintaining a Healthy NDS Environment (Part 1) `http://developer.novell.com/research/appnotes/1997/august/a3frame.htm`

Using Network Time Protocol (NTP) with NetWare 5 `http://developer.novell.com/research/appnotes/1999/july/a3frame.htm`

Troubleshooting Synchronization with NDS Manager. `http://developer.novell.com/research/appnotes/1998/august/a2frame.htm`

Troubleshooting NDS in NetWare 5 with DSREPAIR and DSTRACE: `http://developer.novell.com/research/appnotes/1999/january/a2frame.htm`

Technical Information Documents

Novell Technical Services documents specific solutions to customer problems covering the whole range of Novell products. These TIDs can be very valuable for learning new concepts as well as troubleshooting existing problems that can be located at `http://support.novell.com/servlet/Knowledgebase`.

Many TIDs concern the utilities that have been discussed in this chapter. You can find them by performing a keyword search in Novell's Knowledgebase using some—or all—of the following words: DSREPAIR, NDS Manager, WANMAN, WAN Traffic Manager, and time sync. A few recommended TIDs include:

2951627	Common DSREPAIR Switches—with Explanations
2921231	Correcting Synthetic Time Errors
2942837	Resolving Obituaries without Calling Novell
2946536	Timesync Lost after XXX Polling Loops (-698)

NDS
Administration
Tools

Now that Chapter 9, "Administering NDS," has given us a feel for the day-to-day operations necessary to maintain an NDS environment, this chapter will delve a little deeper into the more advanced NDS concepts. NDS is a complex environment and in order to properly administer and troubleshoot an NDS environment, it is important to have an understanding of what is happening "beneath the hood." What types of operations does NDS take care of automatically? How can those automated operations be monitored and repaired, if necessary?

This chapter looks at the various integrity features offered by NDS for protecting directory data and structure. It also examines tools offered by Novell and third parties for more advanced types of directory monitoring and repair. By the end of this chapter you should have an understanding of the following tools and concepts:

- Database integrity
- Referential integrity
- NDS background processes
- Advanced DSRepair switches
- DS Trace
- IXEdit

Before we start talking about the more advanced administrative tools that are available, you should know where NDS stores its database files on each platform. You normally will not do anything with the NDS database files, but it is sometimes useful to be able to check file timestamps to be sure that updates are occurring properly.

- *NetWare* NetWare stores NDS database files in a hidden directory, SYS:_NETWARE. The contents of SYS:_NETWARE can be viewed by doing the following:

  1. Load NETBASIC at the NetWare server console.
  2. Type SHELL to enter the NetWare DOS shell. From this shell, you can use many DOS commands from the server console.
  3. Type DIR SYS:_NETWARE /P to get a listing of the contents of SYS:_NETWARE.

NDS database files are identified with the following extensions: NDS, DB, and 01. Note that this directory will also contain old database files from previous versions of NDS, such as the version that ships with NetWare 5. These files do not affect the operation of the current version of NDS in any way.

- *NT*   NDS files are stored, unhidden, in the directory that you specified for the installation of NDS for NT. By default, this is C:\NOVELL\NDS. NDS database files are identified with the following extensions: DB, DSD, and NDS
- *Solaris*   NDS files are stored, unhidden, in the /var/nds/dib directory when NDS for Solaris is installed. NDS database files are identified by the following extensions: nds and db

NDS Integrity Features

One of the most important aspects of a database—and at its core that is all a directory is—is the ability to ensure that whatever is stored there is safe from loss or corruption. The introduction of the FLAIM database with NDS 8 strengthens the database integrity features that have been available in NDS previously.

However, beyond just the safety of the actual data, a distributed database like NDS must provide what is known as *referential integrity*. Referential integrity refers to the capability of objects in NDS to refer, or point, to one another in order to define some relationship. The dynamic nature of Directory data makes this a critical issue. For example, if a user is a member of a group and the user object is moved or deleted; how does the group object know the fate of that user object to which it has a relationship? This section also discusses the powerful referential integrity features implemented within NDS to automatically maintain these relationships.

Database Integrity

A mnemonic is used to help remember the four principles of database integrity: *Atomicity, Consistency, Isolation and Durability* (ACID). Every piece of software that claims to be a database must be able to pass the ACID test. It is useful to discuss the various database integrity features in FLAIM from the perspective of how they help NDS achieve the goals outlined by ACID.

Atomicity   *Atomicity* refers to the fact that some database operations need to be "all or nothing." For example, you wouldn't want your bank to withdraw money from your checking account and then have the system crash before the payment was posted to the proper creditor. If the money gets taken out of your account, it should make it to the proper destination.

To achieve atomicity, databases have developed the idea of transactions. Transactions are indivisible sets of database operations. In order to support transactions, FLAIM implements checkpoints and a rollback log. A checkpoint is simply a point in time in which the database is know to be completely current—no outstanding transactions need to be committed to disk. The rollback log takes a snap shot of the state of the database at each checkpoint. If, for whatever reason, the transaction does not process in its entirety, the database will be rolled back to the state in which it existed prior to beginning the transaction. This prevents partially completed transactions from being committed to the database.

Consistency   *Consistency* builds on the concept of atomicity. It refers to the need to maintain synchronization between all the interdependent data in the database. For its part, FLAIM maintains a checksum on each data block to make sure that any abnormal changes can be recognized.

However, a lot of the consistency in a database is the responsibility of the system creating the transactions. The software that interacts with the directory must be sure that its transactions consider the relationships that exist between different database records and attributes. If transactions are not truly atomic, the database will not be able to maintain consistency between the various data blocks involved in that transaction.

To continue with the banking example of the previous paragraphs, suppose that you have queried the bank database to calculate the combined balance of your checking and savings accounts. The system reads the checking balance, but before it reads the savings balance, interest is credited to both accounts. The system now reads the savings balance and adds it to the checking balance to determine a total. Unfortunately, the balance you receive is not accurate when you receive it, because the transaction did not properly maintain database consistency. This transaction should have either included or excluded the interest on both accounts in order to be consistent.

NOTE: *The consistency principle deals with internal database operations and not the synchronization needs of a distributed directory like NDS. The loose consistency between NDS replicas is a completely different topic.*

Isolation   *Isolation* builds on the idea of consistency. It refers to the requirement that concurrent database operations do not interfere with each other. When a transaction in a FLAIM database accesses a record for the purpose of changing it, the record will be locked. Other transactions can view, or read, the record, but they will not be permitted to perform any change operations until the previous transaction has completed its operation(s). This FLAIM strategy is known as "Many readers–Single writer."

Note that a single database query, say for a list of checks written against your account in the last month, will be made up of many read transactions. Each read transaction might return a single check listing. When the read transaction occurs, it views the database at a specific moment in time. Between read transactions, other transactions may occur, like the entry of a new check written against your account. In this way, an ongoing query can pick up database changes dynamically.

Durability   Finally, database durability refers to the need to guarantee that information committed to the database is actually written to disk. To support this requirement, FLAIM uses Direct File System access rather than relying on the underlying operating system to handle the database writes.

However, due to the overhead associated with immediately writing each transaction to disk, FLAIM implements a database cache in memory together with a roll-forward log of each transaction. When a transaction starts, all of the modifications it will make to the database are logged, and then the transaction can operate against the cached database file. If a database transaction were to run and the system were to crash prior to committing the transaction to disk, when FLAIM restarts, it would exist in the state defined at the last checkpoint. FLAIM then automatically reruns each transaction stored in the roll-forward log to recreate all database activity since the checkpoint. In this way, durability can be guaranteed while still taking advantage of database caching techniques to increase performance.

FLAIM also offers a robust set of database utilities that can be used to monitor the health of the database and repair any problems that arise. These utilities are exposed primarily by the DS Repair utility that we discussed in Chapter 9. As part of its standard operation, DS Repair checks more than 100 different conditions on each block of data maintained in the database to make sure that it is healthy.

Referential Integrity

Referential integrity moves up a layer in the NDS model. It refers to the capability to maintain the distributed structure of NDS and all the references that exist between different NDS objects. The technologies that help provide referential integrity include subordinate references, external references, and *Distributed Reference Links* (DRL).

Subordinate References   Subordinate references were previously discussed in Chapter 2, "Designing NDS," (see Figure 10-1). They provide the

Figure 10-1
Subordinate
references between
partitions

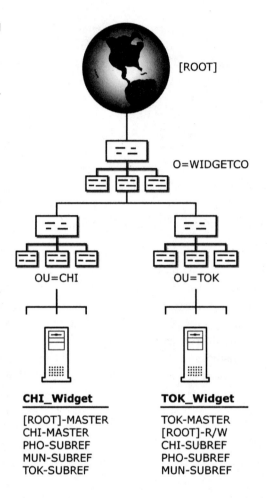

CHI_Widget	TOK_Widget
[ROOT]-MASTER	TOK-MASTER
CHI-MASTER	[ROOT]-R/W
PHO-SUBREF	CHI-SUBREF
MUN-SUBREF	PHO-SUBREF
TOK-SUBREF	MUN-SUBREF

capability to "walk" the tree when doing NDS object searches. Subordinate references can be seen with the NDS Manager utility described in Chapter 9.

Distributed Reference Links (DRL)   One of the core features of a directory service is the capability to maintain relationships between objects within a distributed directory. NDS includes two key features that ensure database integrity: an external reference, known as an X-ref, and a DRL.

Sometimes NDS needs to refer to other objects within the directory. An X-ref is a pointer to another NDS object. Any object that is referenced by an X-ref has a DRL, which indicates all objects that currently point to it. For example, a group object will maintain X-refs to each of the users associated with that group. Each user object, in turn, will maintain a DRL pointing to the group that is referencing it.

X-refs and DRLs are important because they maintain the consistency of the NDS database during, and after, certain events, such as the following:

- Moving an NDS object
- Deleting an NDS object
- Renaming an NDS object
- Moving a container from one location in the NDS tree to another

When any of these events take place, NDS can automatically update the involved objects through the use of the X-Ref/DRL pair. All directory-enabled services track users through their fully distinguished names, such as `THARRIS.CTO.Chicago.WidgetCo`. These services don't store any direct information about the user. They use an X-ref that points to the user's actual object in the directory, where they can retrieve user object information as needed.

If a user object is deleted, the group that user is assigned to automatically "knows" it is gone and will no longer display that user in the group members' list. If a user object is moved or renamed, the new context and/or name are automatically recognized by the group object. The updated context and/or name information is immediately available to the group object.

Imagine what would happen if X-refs and DRLs did not exist. As user objects associated with a group were moved or deleted, the group information would not be updated to recognize the changes. An administrator would have to search for all other objects with which that user was associated and make the necessary changes manually. Over time, the directory could grow to contain a whole host of outdated and incorrect references that were never cleaned up properly.

Interestingly, significant competitors to NDS, such as Microsoft Active Directory and Netscape Directory, do not implement the equivalent of X-refs and DRLs. Netscape ignores the issue completely—you can add invalid objects into Netscape lists—while Microsoft implements a one-way reference mechanism that doesn't allow the directory to transparently clean up after delete/move/rename operations.

NDS Background Processes

As you probably know by now, NDS is an extremely complex environment. Fortunately, it is largely self-contained. Most of the day-to-day tasks of maintaining and protecting directory data are handled automatically and transparently. Not only does NDS have many built-in integrity features, but it also employs several background processes that keep the directory environment stable and healthy. In this section, we will take a brief look at the nine primary background processes that handle all NDS synchronization, modification, and update operations:

- Database initialization
- Flat cleaner
- Janitor
- Replica sync
- Replica purger
- Limber
- Backlinker
- Schema sync
- Time sync

Database Initialization The *Database Initialization* (DB Init) background process is automatically initiated whenever the file system is mounted on the NDS server. It also executes anytime the NDS database is opened or if NDS is reloaded. DB Init is responsible for the following:

1. Verifying the usability of the NDS database files on this server
2. Scheduling the running of other NDS background processes
3. Initializing the various global variables and data structures used by NDS
4. Opening the NDS database files for use by the version of NDS running on this server

DS Trace provides the ability to monitor the DB Init process directly. DS Trace will be discussed later in this chapter.

Flat Cleaner The Flat Cleaner backgound process is used to eliminate NDS variables and attributes that are no longer needed by the database. Flat Cleaner is responsible for the following:

1. Eliminating unused Bindery and External Reference (X-ref) objects and/or attributes
2. Making sure that the objects in a partition replica maintained on this server each have a valid Public Key attribute
3. Eliminating X-ref obituaries that have been set as purgeable

4. Making sure that the server objects in partition replicas hosted on this server have maintained accurate Status and Version attributes. The server object maintains an attribute that specifies server status—up, down, initializing, etc. It also keeps a record of the version of NDS running on that server.

Flat Cleaner can be indirectly monitored through the use of Check External References in DS Repair. DS Trace also provides the ability to monitor the Janitor process directly. DS Trace will be discussed later in this chapter.

Janitor   As its name implies, the Janitor process is responsible for routine cleanup of the NDS environment. Janitor is responsible for the following:

1. Monitoring the value of the NCP status attribute maintained in the NDS Server object for this server

2. Keeping track of the [Root]-most partition replica on the server and the overall replica depth of the server. The [Root]-most partition is the Partition Root object highest in the tree (closest to [Root]). Replica depth describes how many levels down from [Root] the highest partition replica hosted by that server is.

3. Executing the Flat Cleaner process at regular intervals

4. Optimizing the NDS database at regular intervals

5. Reporting synthetic time use by a partition replica on the server. Synthetic time is caused by a server clock that is reset to a future time and then set back to the correct time again—for whatever reason. Any NDS changes made while the clock was set at the future time will bear incorrect time stamps. This problem will self-correct as long as the gap between current and synthetic time is not too large.

6. Making sure that the inherited rights for each partition root object on this server are properly maintained.

Like Flat Cleaner, Janitor can be monitored indirectly by examining the Replica Ring repair options, Time Synchronization status, and Replica Synchronization status operations. DS Trace also provides the ability to monitor the Janitor process directly. DS Trace will be discussed later in this chapter.

Replica Sync   The Replica Synchronization background process is responsible for two primary tasks:

1. Distributing modifications to NDS objects contained within partition replicas maintained by the NDS server

2. Receiving and processing partition operations involving partition replicas hosted by the NDS server

DS Repair can report the status of the replica synchronization process from a number of different perspectives:

- Report synchronization status
- Report synchronization status of all servers
- Report synchronization status on the selected server

DS Trace also provides the ability to monitor the Replica Synchronization process directly. DS Trace will be discussed later in this chapter.

Replica Purger   Replica Sync schedules the execution of the Replica Purger background process. It is responsible for the following:

1. Purging any unused objects and/or attributes that exist in NDS partition replicas hosted on this server

2. Processing obituaries for objects maintained within partition replicas hosted on this server

DS Trace also provides the ability to monitor the Replica Purger process directly. DS Trace will be discussed later in this chapter.

Limber   After questioning several different sources, it is still unclear about why this process is named Limber, so that will remain a mystery for now. However, naming issues aside, Limber is responsible for the following:

1. Making sure that the NDS referral information for this server is properly maintained in each partition hosted on this server

2. Making sure that the server hosting the Master replica of the partition in which the Server object for this server resides has the correct *Relative Distinguished Name* (RDN) for this server. The RDN identifies a target NDS object's context in relation to the context of the source NDS object. For example, the admin object in O=WidgetCo would receive the following RDN for CN=Tharris.OU=CTO. OU=Chicago.O=WidgetCo: Tharris.CTO.Chicago. The O=WidgetCo is assumed from the location of the admin object itself.

3. Making sure that the server object in NDS correctly reflects the operating system version and network address in use on this server

4. Making sure the name of the NDS tree in which this server resides is correctly reported

5. Monitoring the external reference/DRL links between this server and the partition replica that holds this server's NDS Server object. This is done to make sure that the NDS server can be properly accessed via its NDS object.

6. Making sure that this server's identification information is correct.

Limber can be monitored indirectly through Check External Reference, Report Synchronization Status, and Replica Ring repair options. DS Trace also provides the ability to monitor Limber directly. DS Trace will be discussed later in this chapter.

Backlinker   The Backlinker background process helps maintain referential integrity within the NDS environment. Backlinker is responsible for the following:

1. Making sure that all external references (X-Ref) maintained by this server are still required

2. Making sure that each X-Ref is properly backlinked to a server that hosts a partition replica which holds the NDS object specified in the X-ref

3. Eliminating X-refs that are no longer necessary. As part of doing this, the server hosting the partition replica that holds the referenced NDS object is notified of the elimination of the X-ref.

Backlinker can be monitored indirectly through Check External References in DS Repair. DS Trace also provides the ability to monitor Backlinker directly. DS Trace will be discussed later in this chapter.

Schema Sync   The Schema Sync background process is responsible for synchronizing the schema updates received by this server with other NDS servers.

DS Trace also provides the ability to monitor Schema Synchronization directly. DS Trace will be discussed later in this chapter.

Time Sync   Although time sync is not an NDS process, it is necessary in order to perform some partition operations, such as moves or merges, especially on the NetWare and Solaris platforms. The underlying time sync mechanism is not as important as making sure that the servers are in fact synched. NDS can report servers as being time synched when in fact they are not. Although this does not appear to be a significant problem with NT, it can cause significant problems with partitions and replicas hosted on the Solaris platform.

Time Sync can be monitored directly through the Time Synchronization option in DS Repair. NTP environments also provide tools, such as *ntptrace* on the Solaris platform, with which you can monitor time sync from an NTP perspective as well.

Advanced DSRepair Switches

In addition to the numerous functions described in Chapter 9, DS Repair also has some advanced features that are hidden from normal use. These features are currently available on the NetWare platform. However, because all three platforms access DS Repair functionality through a common code base, functionality across the three platforms should converge over time.

WARNING: *The features described in this section can—and will—cause irreversible damage to your NDS tree if used improperly. We recommend that these features only be used under the guidance of Novell's Technical Services team in order to resolve serious database issues. Always make a full backup of the NDS tree before using any of these features on a production tree. If you are going to use these features be sure you understand all the consequences before proceeding.*

These advanced features are enabled through switches when loading the DS Repair utility. Table 10-1 provide an overview of the advanced functionality available on each platform.

These advanced options are seldom used because they are needed only for the most serious of cases. However, it is nice to know they exist when you get into a jam. *Novell Technical Services* (NTS) offers Advanced Technical Training courses that cover the use of these options in the repair of serious NDS problems. For information on NTS Advanced Technical Training courses, visit the NTS Web site at

    http://support.novell.com/additional/advtt/.

It is highly recommended that you work with these switches in a test environment and study carefully the ramifications of these radical operations. Sometimes the cure may be worse than the problem.

Table 10-1	**Switch**	**Description**
Advanced DS repair features for NetWare	-M	Reports "move inhibit" obituaries. This will tell you if a partition Move operation has completed. If it hasn't, move inhibit obituaries may still be processing or be broken.
	-MR	Removes all "move inhibit" obituaries
	-N	Limits the number of days a user object can be connected to a given server to the number specified as a command line argument. When this number is reached, a user connection will be terminated. The default value is 60 days.
	-OR	Deletes all obituaries.
	-P	Marks all NDS objects of type "Unknown" as referenced. Referenced objects do not participate in the NDS replica synchronization process.
	-RS	Removes the server identified by the Partition Root ID provided as a command line argument from the replica ring for that partition. This might be necessary if a Read/Write replica becomes corrupt and needs to be eliminated.
	-A	Load DS Repair with advanced options available. This uncovers additional menu options that are not normally visible. Select the Advanced Options menu, then select Replica And Partition Operations, and choose the partition with which you want to work. You will see the following additional menu items:

■ Repair time stamps and declare a new epoch

■ Destroy the selected replica on this server

■ Delete unknown leaf objects

This switch also allows the Designate this server option as the new master replica option to assign a subordinate reference as the new Master replica. Be Careful!!

If you select the View Replica Ring option and select a replica, you will see an additional option on that menu as well:

■ Remove this server from the replica ring

| | -XK2 | Kill all NDS objects in this server's NDS database. This operation is used only to destroy a corrupt replica that cannot be removed in any other way. |
| | -XK3 | Kill all external references in this server's NDS database. This operation is used to destroy all external references in a nonfunctioning replica. If the references are the source of the problem, NDS can then recreate the references in order to get the replica functioning again. |

DS Repair provides many repair features for NDS but provides only basic monitoring tools for identifying problems and troubleshooting errors. The primary utility for monitoring NDS operations and identifying and tracking NDS errors is DS Trace.

DS Trace

DS Trace is a monitor tool that enables you to view the real time flow of NDS communications between partition replicas. It also allows you to perform certain operations that are very useful in understanding what is happening within the NDS environment. DS Trace is available on NetWare, NT, and Solaris, and functionality is fairly equivalent across all three platforms. When DS Trace is loaded, it provides the ability to open a configurable monitor window and/or a log file that displays messages from the various NDS processes that are running on the network. You can monitor the execution of background processes, note any errors, and use DS Trace to isolate the cause of any problems.

DS Trace was originally designed to help engineering and support staff locate problems in the NDS environment on the NetWare platform. It is not a highly refined tool, but it provides invaluable information about the state of the NDS environment. Regardless of the platform on which DS Trace is run, two main tasks are performed by the DS Trace utility:

- Monitor NDS background processes
- Activate and tune NDS background processes

The following sections look at these tasks on each platform currently supported by NDS.

DS Trace on NetWare

DS Trace (see Figure 10-2) functionality is actually available in two different ways on the NetWare platform. The traditional method is through a

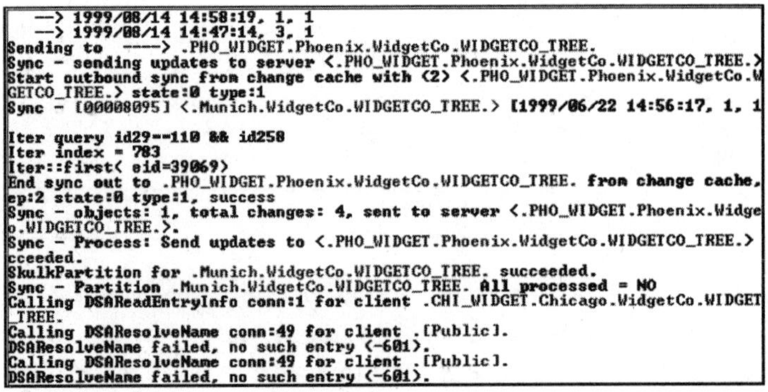

Figure 10-2

Sample DS Trace monitor screen

```
   ─> 1999/08/14 14:58:19, 1, 1
   ─> 1999/08/14 14:47:14, 3, 1
Sending to   ──> .PHO_WIDGET.Phoenix.WidgetCo.WIDGETCO_TREE.
Sync - sending updates to server <.PHO_WIDGET.Phoenix.WidgetCo.WIDGETCO_TREE.>
Start outbound sync from change cache with (2) <.PHO_WIDGET.Phoenix.WidgetCo.W
GETCO_TREE.> state:0 type:1
Sync - [00008095] <.Munich.WidgetCo.WIDGETCO_TREE.> [1999/06/22 14:56:17, 1, 1

Iter query id29--110 && id258
Iter index = 783
Iter::first( eid=39069)
End sync out to .PHO_WIDGET.Phoenix.WidgetCo.WIDGETCO_TREE. from change cache,
ep:2 state:0 type:1, success
Sync - objects: 1, total changes: 4, sent to server <.PHO_WIDGET.Phoenix.Widge
o.WIDGETCO_TREE.>.
Sync - Process: Send updates to <.PHO_WIDGET.Phoenix.WidgetCo.WIDGETCO_TREE.>
cceeded.
SkulkPartition for .Munich.WidgetCo.WIDGETCO_TREE. succeeded.
Sync - Partition .Munich.WidgetCo.WIDGETCO_TREE. All processed = NO
Calling DSAReadEntryInfo conn:1 for client .CHI_WIDGET.Chicago.WidgetCo.WIDGET
_TREE.
Calling DSAResolveName conn:49 for client .[Public].
DSAResolveName failed, no such entry (-601).
Calling DSAResolveName conn:49 for client .[Public].
DSAResolveName failed, no such entry (-601).
```

Directory Services Trace screen that is built into DS.NLM. The second method, new with NetWare 5 and later versions of NDS, is DSTRACE.NLM. Both methods provide similar information and both make use of the same tools for activating and tuning NDS background processes. The difference lies in the monitor interface for NDS background processes.

Both *Directory Services Trace* (DST) and DS Trace are started, configured, and used through an extensive set of command line parameters. The command line parameters are not case sensitive in either utility. Some differences exist between the actual parameters used with either utility, but the operators are similar. The operators available for both utilities are described in Table 10-2. Besides sharing most operators, both DST and DS Trace also share all commands related to the activation and tuning of NDS background processes. These commands make use of the * and ! operators and take the following form:

```
SET DSTRACE= <operator> <parameter> [optional argument]
```

Arguments are not required in every case. Table 10-3 describes the valid star and bang commands available for DST and DS Trace.

Table 10-2	**Operator**	**Description**
Valid operators for DS Trace flags	+	Enables a DS Trace flag. If a flag is specified with no operator, the + is assumed. For example, either of the following commands enables the replica synchronization flag: SET DSTRACE= +SYNC or SET DSTRACE= SYNC.
	−	Disables a DS Trace filter. For example, the following command disables the replica synchronization flag: SET DSTRACE= -SYNC.
	( )	This operator is valid with DST only.
		Enclosing a flag within parenthesis enables that flag while simultaneously disabling all other flags that are currently enabled. For example, the following command enables the replica synchronization flag while disabling all other flags: SET DSTRACE= (SYNC).
	*	The star operator is used to activate NDS background processes. For example, the following command executes the Janitor process immediately: SET DSTRACE= *J.
	!	The bang operator is used to configure the tunable parameters for NDS background processes. For example, the following command configures the Backlink process to occur every eight minutes: SET DSTRACE= !B8

Table 10-3

DS Trace star and
bang commands

Command	Argument(s)	Description
*.	None	Unloads and reloads NDS executable. Enables you to update the version of NDS without having to restart the server
*B	None	Forces the backlink process to run. This can be a traffic-intensive operation. Schedule during times of off-peak network usage
!B	Interval in minutes Min: 2 Max: 10080 Default:1500	Sets the interval for the Backlink process
*C	None	Checks all *Dynamic Reference Links* (DRL)
*CD	None	Displays the source server's connection table (comma delimited)
*CT	None	Displays the source server's connection table (space delimited)
*D	None	Aborts the Send All Updates process (*I). This process can loop endlessly if one of the servers in the replica ring is unreachable.
*F	None	Forces the Flat Cleaner process to run
!F	Interval in minutes Min: 2 Max: N/A Default: 240	Sets the interval for the Flat Cleaner process
*G	None	Sets the server status to Down in NDS. Used when a server has become overloaded with pending NDS requests
*H	None	Forces the NDS replica synchronization and schema synchronization processes to run. This is also known as the NDS *Heartbeat.*
!H	Interval in minutes Min: 1 Max: 1440 Default: 30	Sets the interval for the NDS Replica Synchronization process
*I	Partition Root ID	Forces the replica specified to send a copy of all its objects to all other servers hosting replicas of the same partition. Same as Send All Objects operation in DS Repair
!I	Interval in minutes Min: 2 Max: 1440 Default: 30	Sets the interval for schema synchronization

Command	Argument(s)	Description
*J	None	Forces the Janitor process to run
!J	Interval in minutes Min: 1 Max: 10080 Default:2	Sets the interval for the Janitor process
*L	None	Forces the Limber process to run
*M	File Size in Bytes Min: 10,000 Max: 100 MB Default: 500,000	Used with DST only. Sets the maximize size of the DST debug file. If the maximum file size is reached, the debug file will *wrap around* and start writing at the beginning again.
*P	None	Displays the DS Trace tunable parameters and their default settings
*R	Filename	Resets the DST debug file. All previously saved information will be lost. If no filename is specified, this command will specify the default `SYS:SYSTEM\DSTRACE.DBG`.
*S	None	Forces the replica synchronization process to run. Any replicas scheduled for synchronization will be synchronized. Will not synchronize replicas not already scheduled for synchronization
*SS	None	Forces schema synchronization process to run. This targets only servers with which the background schema sync process has not synchronized in the last 24 hours.
*SSA	None	Forces schema synchronization process to run. All servers should be synchronized.
*SSD	None	Resets the server's target schema sync list. This list identifies the servers to which this server should sync during a schema synchronization cycle.
*SSL	None	Displays the schema sync list. Also identifies other servers that are holding this server open for a schema operation
*ST	None	Display server's background process status. Includes information on External Reference, Schema, Obituary, and Limber
*STL	None	Displays the server's Backlink background process status

continues

Command	Argument(s)	Description
Table 10-3

continued !T | Interval in minutes
Min: 1
Max: 720
Default: 30 | Sets the interval for checking the server state (UP, DOWN, etc.) |
*U	Server ID (optional)	Forces the server state of all servers in a replica list to UP. This may allow certain partition operations to complete successfully.
*UD	Server ID (optional)	Forces the server state of all servers in a replica list to DOWN
!V	List of NDS versions	Defines those versions of NDS with which this server should not interact. This is useful in case older versions of NDS are inadvertently running in the same replica ring with newer versions of NDS.
!W	Interval in ticks Min: 1 Max: 2000 Default: 15	Changes the length of time to wait after getting a transport protocol time-out before resending the packet
!X	Number of retries Min: 1 Max: 50 Default: 3	Changes the number of transport protocol retries for the DS (server-to-server) client. Exceeding this retry count causes an NDS error - 625 to be displayed.
!Y	Integer Min: 0 Max: 530 Default: 2	The integer input is used to calculate the estimated trip delay using the equation: Time-out = $(T * Y) + Z$. This is where T is equal to the ticks required to get to the destination server.
!Z	Integer Min: 0 Max: 500 Default: 4	Specifies the additional delay for the transport protocol time-out. When increasing the time-out, it is best to change this parameter first. It is used in the equation IPX Time-out = $(T * Y) + Z$, where T is equal to the ticks required to get to the destination server.

So, what you do and how you do it is similar across both utilities. However, what you see and how you see it is significantly different. The following two sections describe how to monitor NDS background processes using these two distinct utilities.

DST Monitor NDS administrators and Novell Support personnel have used the DST Monitor for years. DST functions most consistently when a single parameter is specified per command line. For this reason, it is useful to create NCF files for the DST configuration you use most. That way, you just have to execute the NCF file to execute all the commands you want. Every DST command takes the following form:

```
SET DSTRACE=<operator><parameter>[optional argument]
```

The following are some sample DST commands:

- SET DSTRACE=ON
- SET DSTRACE= +SYNC
- SET DSTRACE= *H
- SET DSTRACE= !J20

DST is started and configured using the parameters described in Table 10-4.

	Parameter	Description
Table 10-4 Directory Service Trace configuration parameters	ON	Starts the NDS trace screen. If this is the first time that DST has been used since DS.NLM was last loaded, the Minimum flag is activated. Otherwise, DST will start using the same configuration used previously.
	OFF	Disables the DST monitor. The current configuration will be retained as long as DS.NLM itself is not unloaded.
	ALL	Starts the DST monitor with all flags enabled. When a flag is enabled, information of that type will be displayed on screen and/or in the log file.
	AGENT	Starts the NDS trace screen with the following flags enabled: BACKLINK, DSAGENT, JANITOR, RESNAME, and VCLIENT.

This parameter also activates a global variable used by the Flat Cleaner background process. This variable causes the local entry IDs of the records being examined by Flat Cleaner to be displayed. |
| | DEBUG | Turns on DST with the following flags enabled: BACKLINK, ERRORS, EMU, FRAGGER, INIT, INSPECTOR, JANITOR, LIMBER, MISC, PART, RECMAN, REPAIR, SCHEMA, SKULKER, STREAMS, and VCLIENT.

Warning: This action instructs the server to automatically open the NetWare debugger in the event of certain error conditions. This option should be used only for brief periods of time when tracking a specific issue. |
| | NODEBUG | This parameter leaves the Directory Service Trace screen ON but disables all previously enabled flags. This is useful when you want to reconfigure DST. |

After DST is initially configured, it can be fine-tuned to monitor only the information necessary to support your current needs. This is done through the enabling and/or disabling of trace flags. Flags are enabled or disabled from the command line by using the + and - operators from Table 10-2.

The actual flags supported by DST are enumerated in Table 10-5. Some flags can be enabled using multiple names. These alternative names have been listed as well.

Unfortunately, this DST monitor information does little good when it is whizzing by faster than it can be read. In a large network environment, this is often the case.

Table 10-5

Flags supported by DST

Flag	Description
AUDIT	Trace messages related to NDS audit
AUTHEN	Trace messages related to NDS authentication events
BACKLINK (BLINK)	Trace messages related to the Backlink process
BUFFERS	Trace messages related to the allocation of inbound and outbound packet buffers related to NDS requests
COLLISION (COLL)	Trace messages related to the receipt of duplicate update packets; these duplicate packets usually occur on very busy networks.
DSAGENT	Trace messages related to incoming NDS requests
EMU	Trace messages related to Bindery Emulation
ERRET	Displays debug errors; this option is of use only to NDS engineers.
ERRORS (ERR, E)	Displays error messages in DST. What is the error, and where did it came from?
FRAGGER (FRAG)	Trace messages related to the packet fragmenter that breaks up NDS messages for transmission in multiple packets
IN	Trace messages related to incoming NDS requests and processes
INIT	Trace messages related to the opening of the local NDS database

Flag	Description
INSPECTOR I	Messages related to the Inspector process; Inspector is part of the Janitor that verifies the structural integrity of the NDS database.
JANITOR J	Trace Janitor messages; the Janitor cleans up NDS by removing objects that are no longer needed.
LIMBER	Trace Limber messages; the Limber monitors connectivity between all replicas.
LOCKING	Text TK
LOCKS	Trace messages related to manipulation of the local NDS database locks
MIN	Minimum functionality. Trace generic messages and error reports rom various sources in NDS. By default, SET DSTRACE=ON enables this flag only.
MISC	Trace all miscellaneous messages
PART	Trace partition operations and messages
RECMAN	Trace messages related to low-level database operations.
RESNAME (RN)	Trace messages related to NDS name resolution
SAP	Trace messages related to the SAP protocol
SCHEMA	Trace schema modification and synchronization messages
SKULKER (SYNC, S)	Trace messages related to the Skulker process, which manages replica and schema synchronization
STREAMS	Trace messages related to Stream attributes in NDS
TIMEVECTOR (TV)	Trace messages related to transitive vectors, which describe how caught up the replica is in the synchronization process
VCLIENT (VC)	Trace messages related to server-to-server Virtual Client connections
WANMAN	Trace messages related to WAN Traffic Manager

WARNING: *The DST log file does not impose any maximum size, so it will continue to grow in size as long as logging is enabled. For this reason, it is not recommended to use the DST log file option continuously. Enable the log file as needed to capture information and then shut it down.*

To resolve this problem, DST monitor information can be logged to a file. This file holds any messages displayed on the DST monitor. It also includes event-timing information that can be used to identify which messages should be grouped together. The DST debug file is stored in the SYS:SYS-TEM subdirectory by default. The default file name is DSTRACE.DBG. To enable the DST debug file, you must execute the following console command: SET TTF=ON.

The *M and *R DSTRACE commands can be used to configure the DST debug file. These two commands are described in Table 10-3.

The information in the DST debug file includes timing information that enables you to identify event sequence; group related messages together; and determine how long ago a problem occurred. This can be critical when analyzing DST data off-line.

Figure 10-3 shows the additional timing information appended to DST messages in the DST log file.

The DST debug message appends four sets of numbers, separated by colons, to the front of the message. From left to right, each of these numbers corresponds to the following:

Figure 10-3

Sample DST log file

```
37C33F45:305091429:d249e700:046 1999/08/24 18:56:37 * SchemaPurger processing deleted class
37C33F45:305091431:d0441b80:041 all replicas of .WIDGETCO_TREE. have seen this ring state
37C33F45:305091431:d0441b80:041 Finish state transitions for .WIDGETCO_TREE.
37C33F45:305091431:d0441b80:041 Start state transitions for .WIDGETCO_TREE., current state
37C33F45:305091431:d0441b80:041 all replicas of .WIDGETCO_TREE. have seen this ring state
37C33F45:305091431:d0441b80:041 Finish state transitions for .WIDGETCO_TREE.
37C33F45:305091441:d0441b80:047 Sync - Start outbound sync with (#=3, state=0, type=1 parti
37C33F45:305091443:d0441b80:040 LocalSetServerVersion succeeded, for server .TOK_WIDGET-NDS
37C33F45:305091451:d0441b80:047 Sync - using version 6 on server <.TOK_WIDGET-NDS.Tokyo.Wid
37C33F45:305091451:d0441b80:047 Sending to  ----> .TOK_WIDGET-NDS.Tokyo.WidgetCo.WIDGETCO_1
37C33F45:305091451:d0441b80:047 Sync - sending updates to server <.TOK_WIDGET-NDS.Tokyo.Wid
37C33F45:305091451:d0441b80:047 Start outbound sync from change cache with (3) <.TOK_WIDGET
37C33F45:305091452:d0441b80:047 Sync - [0000805d] <.WIDGETCO_TREE.> [1999/06/20 20:07:32, 
37C33F45:305091467:d0441b80:047 End sync out to .TOK_WIDGET-NDS.Tokyo.WidgetCo.WIDGETCO_TRE
37C33F45:305091467:d0441b80:047 Sync - objects: 1, total changes: 2, sent to server <.TOK_
37C33F45:305091467:d0441b80:047 Sync - Process: Send updates to <.TOK_WIDGET-NDS.Tokyo.Widg
37C33F45:305091474:d249e700:046 1999/08/24 18:56:37 * SchemaPurger processing deleted attri
37C33F45:305091481:d0441b80:047 Sync - Start outbound sync with (#=2, state=0, type=1 parti
37C33F45:305091482:d0441b80:040 LocalSetServerVersion succeeded, for server .PHO_WIDGET.Pho
37C33F45:305091486:d0441b80:047 Sync - using version 6 on server <.PHO_WIDGET.Phoenix.Widge
37C33F45:305091486:d0441b80:047 Sending to  ----> .PHO_WIDGET.Phoenix.WidgetCo.WIDGETCO_TRE
37C33F45:305091486:d0441b80:047 Sync - sending updates to server <.PHO_WIDGET.Phoenix.Widge
```

- Date and time in seconds
- Number of events this second
- Operating system thread generating this message
- The Connection ID associated with this operation

Table 10-6 describes each of these timing elements in more detail.

The rest of the message is identical to what is found on the DST monitor screen itself. See Figures 10-10 and 10-11 for a look at the type of information available from DST messages.

DSTRACE.NLM DSTRACE.NLM is a new way of accessing DS Trace information. It first shipped with NetWare 5 and looks to be the preferred way to monitor NDS events today. To load DS Trace load DSTRACE.NLM at the server console. After DS Trace is loaded, it can be configured through the use of the configuration options outlined in Table 10-7.

Table 10-6	**Timing Element**	**Description**
DST Debug timing information	Date and time	The date and time when this DST message was displayed. This hex value is the number of seconds that have elapsed since 00:00:00, January 1, 1970.
	Number of events	The number of events that have occurred during this second. The sample DST debug message is the 317th event to occur that second. This is a decimal value. A 0 is returned if more than 999 events occur during any given second.
	Operating system thread	This hex value identifies the operating system thread assigned to the NDS background process or function that generated this DST message. Because DST messages can become intermixed, this value can be used to identify those messages generated by the same NDS background process or operation.

Note: Thread numbers are reusable values, so it is not a good idea to rely solely on this value when identifying messages generated by a given process. If a great deal of time has passed—as noted by the date and time value—then it is likely that these messages are from two different processes using the same thread number. |
| | Connection ID | This is the numeric identifier assigned to the process when it began to execute. |

Configuration Option	Description
DSTRACE ON	Enables DS Trace. Default options are Journal, Print to Screen, Print to File DSTRACE.LOG. The following flags are set for capture: BASE, MISC, PART, VCLN, AREQ, BEMU, FRAG, JNTR, MOVE, SAPM, SKLK, BLNK, INIT, LMBR, SCMA, STRM, and TVEC. DSTRACE flags are described in the next section of this chapter.
DSTRACE OFF	Disables DS Trace
DSTRACE FILE	Specifies that DS Trace should write its data to a log file
DSTRACE FMAX=	Specifies maximum log file size in bytes
DSTRACE FNAME=	Specifies name of log file; default is DSTRACE.LOG.
DSTRACE SCREEN	Specifies that DS Trace should write to the server console
DSTRACE INLINE	Have NDS handle the actual display to screen function that sends DS Trace data to the console screen. This is a faster method of displaying the data but places increased overhead on the NDS processing thread.
DSTRACE JOURNAL	Pass DS Trace data to the standard display queue processing thread for the print to screen function. This relieves NDS of some overhead but can also delay the display of DS Trace messages because they will have to wait their turn in the queue.

Selecting DSTrace Flags

DSTRACE, shown in Figure 10-4, enables administrators to specify the type(s) of information that will be displayed and logged in DSTRACE.log.

In large NDS tree environments, a great number of things can be happening. In order to use DSTRACE effectively, you need to know what you are looking for and how to best view that information. DSTRACE flag commands take the following form:

```
DSTRACE <operator><flag>
```

The + and – operators are used with DSTRACE flag commands. Some possible DSTRACE flag commands include the following:

- DSTRACE +SYNC
- DSTRACE -JNTR

Table 10-8 lists the available flags for use with DSTRACE.

Figure 10-4

NetWare DSTrace
configuration screen

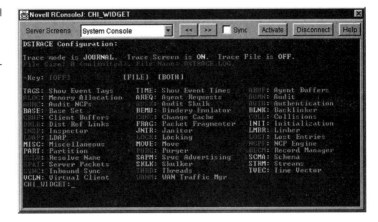

DSTRACE Flag	Description
Table 10-8 DSTRACE flags	
ABUF	Trace messages related to allocation of inbound and outbound packet buffers related to NDS requests
ALOC	Trace messages related to allocation of memory for NDS processes
AREQ	Trace messages related to incoming NDS requests
AUMN	Trace messages related to the NDS audit process
AUNC	Trace Audit NCP (NetWare Core Protocol) events
AUSK	Trace audit messages related to the replica sync process
AUTH	Trace messages related to NDS authentication events
BASE	Trace a base set of NDS messages
BEMU	Trace messages related to Bindery Emulation
BLNK	Trace messages related to the Backlink process
CBUF	Events related to memory buffers maintained for client connections
CHNG	Trace messages related to the changing of the NDS memory cache
COLL	Trace messages related to the receipt of duplicate update packets; these duplicate packets usually occur on very busy networks.
DRLK	Trace messages related to Distributed Reference Link operations
FRAG	Trace messages related to the packet fragmenter that breaks up NDS messages for transmission in multiple packets

continues

Table 10-8

continued

DSTRACE Flag	Description
INIT	Trace messages related to the opening of the local NDS database
INSP	Messages related to the Inspector process. Inspector is part of the Janitor that verifies the structural integrity of the NDS database.
JNTR	Trace Janitor messages. The Janitor cleans up NDS by removing objects that are no longer needed.
LMBR	Trace Limber messages. The Limber monitors connectivity between all replicas.
LDAP	Trace messages related to LDAP communications
LOCK	Trace messages related to manipulation of the local NDS database locks
LOST	Trace messages related to obituaries, NDS attributes, and stream files
MISC	Trace all miscellaneous messages
MOVE	Trace messages related to NDS Object move operations
NCPE	Trace messages related to the NCP engine
PART	Trace partition operations and messages
PURG	Trace replica purger messages
RECM	Trace messages related to low-level database operations.
RSLV	Trace messages related to NDS name resolution when traversing the NDS tree
SAPM	Trace messages related to the SAP protocol
SCMA	Trace schema modification and synchronization messages
SPKT	Trace messages related to server packets
SKLK	Trace messages related to the Skulker process, which manages replica and schema synchronization
STRM	Trace messages related to Stream attributes in NDS
SYNC	Trace messages related to background replica sync
TAGS	Show event tags as part of the DSTRACE messages
THRD	Trace messages related to the management of processor threads used with NDS
TIME	Show event times as part of DSTRACE output

DSTRACE Flag	Description
TVEC	Trace messages related to transitive vectors, which describe how caught up the replica is in the synchronization process
VCLN	Trace messages related to server-to-server Virtual Client connections
WANM	Trace messages related to WAN Traffic Manager

DSTRACE uses the exact same SET commands to configure and activate NDS background processes as are used with DST. Those commands are outlined in Table 10-3.

Unfortunately, this DSTRACE monitor information does little good when it is whizzing by faster than it can be read. In a large network environment, this is often the case. To resolve this problem, DSTRACE enables you to log trace information to a file for review off-line. The default filename is SYS: SYSTEM\DSTRACE.LOG. However, DSTRACE enables you to configure the log file using the DSTRACE commands described in Table 10-7. The log file contains information identical to the DSTRACE monitor screen. However, it is organized slightly differently, as shown in Figure 10-5.

The first column identifies the NDS process that generated this message. The second column, enclosed in angle brackets [ ], provides timestamp information so that the timing of the message can be determined. Thankfully, it is much less cryptic than the DST timing information.

The rest of the message is identical in format to the message as it appears on the DSTRACE monitor screen.

Figure 10-5
Sample
DSTRACE.LOG

DS Trace on NT

DS Trace is available through the NDS Console on NT Server (see Figure 10-6). To enable it, simply highlight Dstrace in NDS Console and click Start.

DS Trace on NT provides similar functionality to the versions of DS Trace available on NetWare. However, it benefits from a nice graphical interface that makes it easier to configure. Three drop-down menus are associated with the DS Trace screen.

The File menu enables you to configure the log file for DS Trace. Three options are under the File menu:

- *New*   Creates a new log file of the name and location you specify in the Create Log File dialog

- *Open*   Opens an existing log file and appends new data to that file

- *Close*   Turns off DS Trace file logging (see Figure 10-7)

The Edit menu is where you will spend most of your time. It has two options:

- *Copy*   It is possible to highlight text in the DS Trace monitor. The Copy command enables you to copy selected text to the clipboard so that it can be pasted in another file. This might be valuable when describing an error condition in an email or some other document.

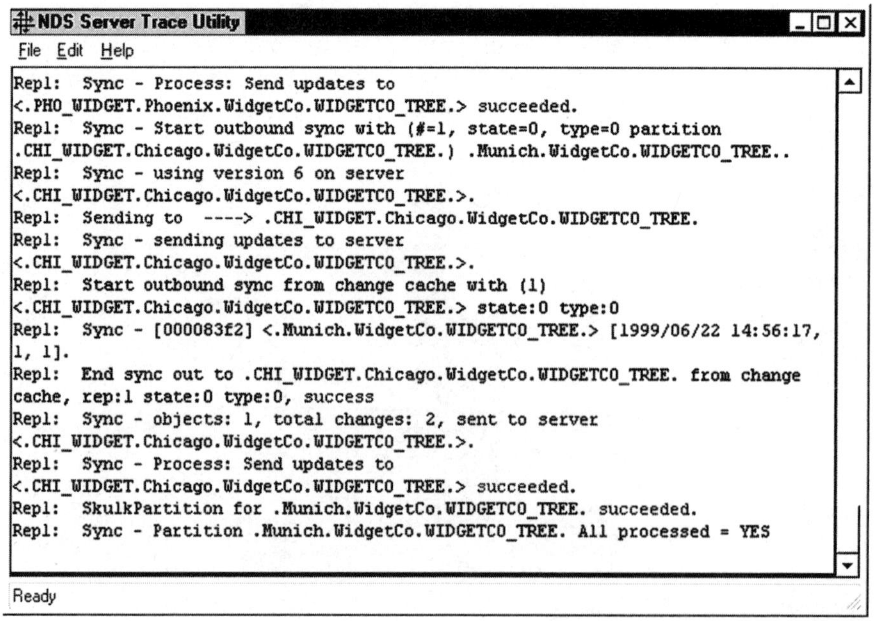

Figure 10-6

DSTrace monitor on NT

```
NDS Server Trace Utility                                          _ □ ×
File  Edit  Help
Repl:  Sync - Process: Send updates to
<.PHO_WIDGET.Phoenix.WidgetCo.WIDGETCO_TREE.> succeeded.
Repl:  Sync - Start outbound sync with (#=1, state=0, type=0 partition
.CHI_WIDGET.Chicago.WidgetCo.WIDGETCO_TREE.) .Munich.WidgetCo.WIDGETCO_TREE..
Repl:  Sync - using version 6 on server
<.CHI_WIDGET.Chicago.WidgetCo.WIDGETCO_TREE.>.
Repl:  Sending to  ----> .CHI_WIDGET.Chicago.WidgetCo.WIDGETCO_TREE.
Repl:  Sync - sending updates to server
<.CHI_WIDGET.Chicago.WidgetCo.WIDGETCO_TREE.>.
Repl:  Start outbound sync from change cache with (1)
<.CHI_WIDGET.Chicago.WidgetCo.WIDGETCO_TREE.> state:0 type:0
Repl:  Sync - [000083f2] <.Munich.WidgetCo.WIDGETCO_TREE.> [1999/06/22 14:56:17,
1, 1].
Repl:  End sync out to .CHI_WIDGET.Chicago.WidgetCo.WIDGETCO_TREE. from change
cache, rep:1 state:0 type:0, success
Repl:  Sync - objects: 1, total changes: 2, sent to server
<.CHI_WIDGET.Chicago.WidgetCo.WIDGETCO_TREE.>.
Repl:  Sync - Process: Send updates to
<.CHI_WIDGET.Chicago.WidgetCo.WIDGETCO_TREE.> succeeded.
Repl:  SkulkPartition for .Munich.WidgetCo.WIDGETCO_TREE. succeeded.
Repl:  Sync - Partition .Munich.WidgetCo.WIDGETCO_TREE. All processed = YES
Ready
```

■ *Options*   This selection opens the Configuration window for DS Trace. From this menu, you can configure DS Trace flags and start NDS processes. These options are described in detail later in this section.

The Help menu provides access to the DS Trace help file.

As previously mentioned, you can configure DS Trace by selecting the Edit drop-down menu and then selecting Options (see Figure 10-8).

The default tab is the Events tab. From this page, you can configure the flags that determine what information is displayed on the DS Trace monitor. All the same flag options offered for NetWare are also available for NT,

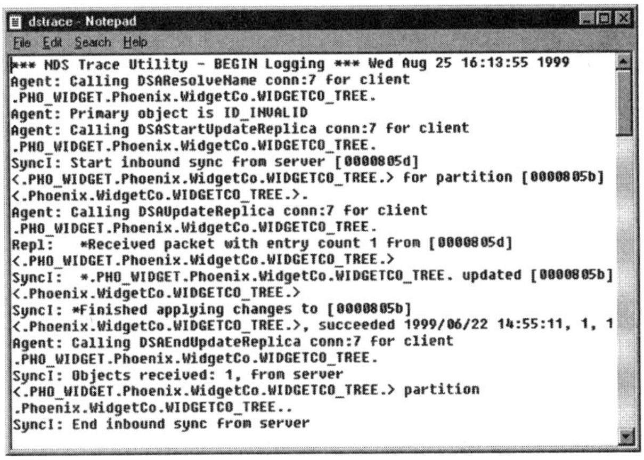

Figure 10-7

Sample DSTrace log file on NT

Figure 10-8

DSTrace flag options on NT

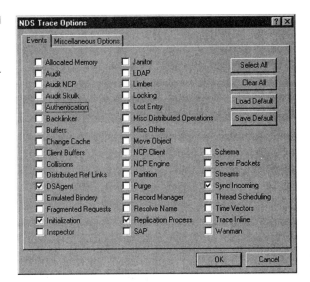

under slightly different names. Simply check the box next to the flag(s) you want to enable. Table 10-9 describes the various DS Trace options.

Table 10-9

DSTrace flag
options on NT

DS Trace Flag	Description
Allocated Memory	Trace messages related to allocation of memory for NDS processes
Audit	Trace messages related to the NDS audit process
Audit NCP	Trace Audit *NetWare Core Protocol* (NCP) events
Audit Skulk	Trace audit messages related to the replica sync process
Authentication	Trace messages related to NDS authentication events
Backlinker	Trace messages related to the Backlink process
Buffers	Trace messages related to allocation of inbound and outbound packet buffers related to NDS requests
Change Cache	Trace messages related to the changing of the NDS memory cache
Client Buffers	Events related to memory buffers maintained for client connections
Collisions	Trace messages related to the receipt of duplicate update packets; these duplicate packets usually occur on very busy networks.
Distributed Ref Links	Trace messages related to Distributed Reference Link operations
DSAgent	Trace messages related to incoming NDS requests
Emulated Bindery	Trace messages related to Bindery Emulation
Fragmented Requests	Trace messages related to the packet fragmenter that breaks up NDS messages for transmission in multiple packets
Initialization	Trace messages related to the opening of the local NDS database
Inspector	Messages related to the Inspector process. Inspector is part of the Janitor that verifies the structural integrity of the NDS database.
Janitor	Trace Janitor messages. The Janitor cleans up NDS by removing objects that are no longer needed.
LDAP	Trace messages related to LDAP communications

DS Trace Flag	Description
Limber	Trace Limber messages. The Limber monitors connectivity between all replicas.
Locking	Trace messages related to manipulation of the local NDS database locks
Lost Entry	Trace messages related to obituaries, NDS attributes, and stream files
Misc Distributed	Trace all nonspecific NDS messages involving Operations communication with external NDS entities such as other servers. Nonspecific messages are those not directly attributable to a specific NDS process.
Misc Other	Trace all other nonspecific NDS messages
Move Object	Trace messages related to NDS Object move operations
NCP Client	Trace messages related to NCP Client requests
NCP Engine	Trace messages related to the NCP engine operations
Partition	Trace partition operations and messages
Purge	Trace replica purger messages
Record Manager	Trace messages related to low-level database operations.
Resolve Name	Trace messages related to NDS name resolution when traversing the NDS tree
SAP	Trace messages related to the SAP protocol
Schema	Trace schema modification and synchronization messages
Server Packets	Trace messages related to server packets
Streams	Trace messages related to Stream attributes in NDS
Sync Incoming	Trace messages related to incoming synchronization events
Thread Scheduling	Trace messages related to the management of processor threads used with NDS
Time Vectors	Trace messages related to transitive vectors, which describe how caught up the replica is in the synchronization process
Trace Inline	Have NDS handle the actual display to screen function that sends DS Trace data to the console screen. This is a more direct method of displaying the data but places increased overhead on the NDS processing thread.
Wanman	Trace messages related to WAN Traffic Manager

By default, the following flags are enabled:

- DSAgent
- Initialization
- Replication process
- Sync incoming

You can change this default configuration by selecting the flags you wanted enabled automatically and clicking Save Default. You can also revert to your default configuration quickly by clicking Load Default. The Select All and Clear All buttons will enable all flags or disable all flags, respectively.

DS Trace on NT does not offer * and ! switches—described in the DS Trace on NetWare section of this chapter—to activate and tune NDS background processes. A fully functional DS Trace utility will be offered in a future release.

Clicking on the Miscellaneous Options tab will open a page from which you can activate certain processes (see Figure 10-9). Simply check the box next to the process you want activated and then click OK. Processes that can be activated from this page include:

- Start Janitor
- Start Replication
- Check Partition Connectivity (Limber)

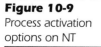

Figure 10-9
Process activation
options on NT

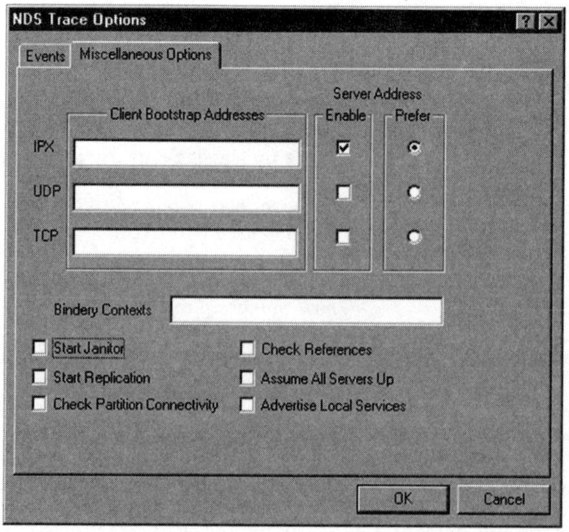

- Check References (corresponds to Check External References in DS Repair)
- Assume All Servers Up (same as to *U on NetWare and Solaris platforms)
- Advertise Local Services (activates the SAP or SLP service advertisement protocol)

Two other configurable parameters are available from the Miscellaneous Options page. The Client Bootstrap Addresses section is a troubleshooting tool. You can specify the address of a default server to which clients can attempt to connect if their primary server does not respond properly. Addresses can be specified for IPX, UDP, and/or TCP connections. The Enabled check box activates the default server capability for that protocol. The Prefer check box indicates which protocol connection should be attempted first.

The Bindery Contexts field enables you to define a Bindery Context for legacy services or clients that do not understand NDS naming. One example of this is the Microsoft Client for NetWare Networks that, in default configuration, does not include NDS support. Defining a Bindery context in this field will allow those legacy clients to attach to login to NDS properly. Up to 16 Bindery contexts can be specified. Separate each entry with a semicolon (;).

DSTrace on Solaris

DSTrace on Solaris is a command-line utility, unlike the version for NT. Fortunately, DSTrace on Solaris supports identical command-line syntax, operators, and parameters as those used with DSTRACE.NLM on the NetWare platform. For those of you operating NDS in mixed environments, this makes it a lot easier to move from platform to platform.

Load DSTrace for Solaris by executing /bin/ndstrace from a terminal window. This will open the ndstrace monitor screen. From this point, ndstrace functions exactly the same as DSTRACE.NLM. It makes use of the same operators, flags, and parameters. Remember that Solaris commands are case sensitive. All ndstrace flags and parameters MUST be entered in the lowercase.

The bottom line of the ndstrace monitor screen is reserved as the ndstrace command line. Syntax for the various ndstrace commands is as follows:

Start and configure ndstrace   The same environment configuration options used with DSTRACE.NLM on NetWare are available for ndstrace on Solaris. A complete list of these options is available in

Table 10-7. These commands are also used to configure the log file usage. The default log file is `/var/nds/ndstrace.log`. Following are three sample ndstrace configuration commands:

- `ndstrace on`
- `ndstrace fmax=500000`
- `ndstrace file off`

Enable and disable ndstrace flags   See Table 10-8 for a complete list of ndstrace flags. Enable flags with the + operator and disable flags with the – operator. Following are three sample flag commands:

- `ndstrace +sync`
- `Ndstrace -jntr`
- `Ndstrace +coll`

Activating and tuning background processes   See Table 10-3 for a complete list of activation and tuning parameters for ndsrepair. Activation parameters use the * operator, and tuning parameters use the ! operator. Syntax for these parameters is very precise. There must be a <space> before and after the = sign in order for the command to be recognized. Following are three sample ndstrace activation and tuning commands:

- `set ndstrace = *h`
- `set ndstrace = *s`
- `set ndstrace = !j20`

Similarities across All Platforms

Unfortunately, this section is not as large as you might have hoped. Each version of DS Trace has its own personality, so you will have to play with each a little to understand how each works. Fortunately, there are a few similarities that make the transition from one platform to another less painful.

Data Organization   Fortunately, the organization of the data on the DSTrace monitor screen is identical across all platforms and utilities. DSTrace will report messages based upon the flags you have enabled. All messages use a similar organization. When interpreting the data on the DSTrace monitor, it is best to look for those few primary message pieces that provide the most information. Figure 10-10 identifies some of these important message components.

Unfortunately, all messages are not so benign as those shown in Figure 10-10. The main purpose of DSTrace is to monitor NDS processes in order to identify any problems that occur. A sample NDS error is shown in Figure 10-11.

The best way to familiarize yourself with DSTrace is to use it regularly to monitor what is happening. Take the time to decipher messages regularly to get used to the syntax and format of the information. There is a tremendous amount of information that can be gleaned from DSTrace if you take the time to get to know the utility.

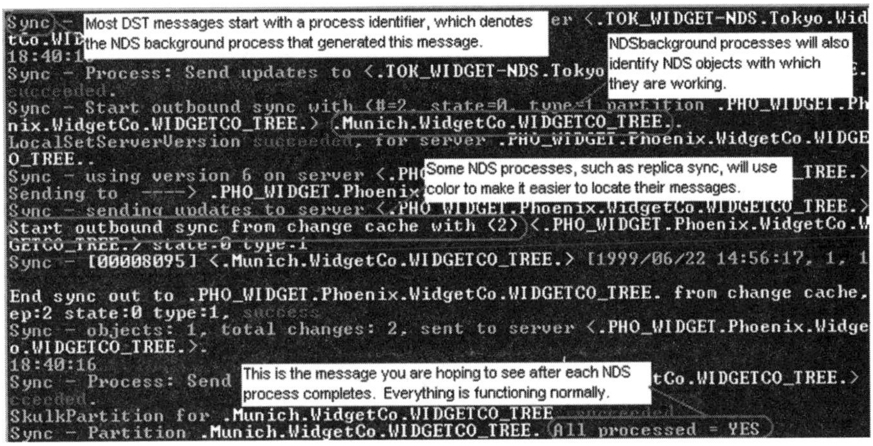

Figure 10-10
DS Trace message
components

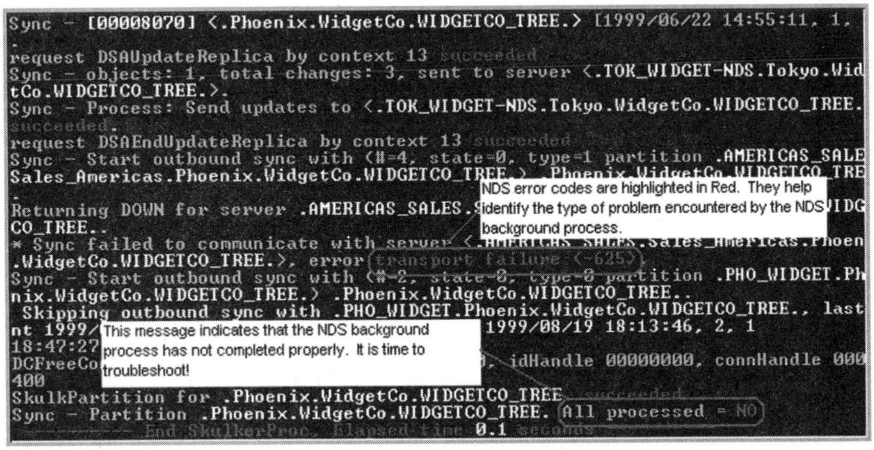

Figure 10-11
DS Trace error
message

NOTE: *This common look does not extend to the various DSTrace log files that can be enabled on each platform. Refer to the section describing DSTrace on each platform in order to get a look at the log file format.*

Color   DSTrace monitor messages are color coded on every platform to make it easier to pick out process messages. Do not get hung up on assigning a specific meaning to each color you see. The only two colors that consistently mean the same thing are

- *Red*   This is the universal WARNING color. Red is usually bad and indicates an NDS error code or the unsuccessful completion of a background process.
- *Green*   Green is the universal GOOD color. Green indicates the successful completion of a background process or operation.

Beyond those two, you may also see colors like White, Pink, Dark Blue, Light Blue, Yellow, and Purple. The usage of these secondary colors varies across the different NDS platforms and DSTrace utilities. They are generally used to highlight important information, such as NDS object names and background process status messages.

IXEdit

NDS now brings the advantage of full indexing capabilities to NDS networks. Indexes are mini databases that are sorted on a specific value or attribute. When a directory search is performed, it can search the index instead of having to walk the entire directory tree looking for pertinent information. This greatly increased search times and reduces network overhead.

Indexing is a tremendous improvement over catalogs, which are basically external indexes. The problem with catalogs is that they need to rebuild periodically by *dredging* the directory and updating the index if any information has changed. This requires significant overhead. The result is a constant tradeoff between catalog currency and network overhead.

Now, NDS has pulled the indexing process into the directory software itself. This greatly reduces the overhead necessary to maintain indexes while at the same time making the index much more current. NDS includes a variety of preconfigured indexes designed to increase the performance of common directory searches, such as LDAP queries, user name searches, etc. More information on NDS indexes is available in Chapter 6, "Controlling Network Access."

However, it is entirely possible that these preconfigured NDS indexes will not be adequate for addressing very specific types of queries that might be needed by an organization. To address this need, it is possible to create custom indexes. This first release of the custom index tool, known as IXEdit, is not a highly refined tool (see Figure 10-12). It was initially designed to help some of Novell's largest customers create indexes to heir large, distributed networks. IXEdit lets you create custom indexes, but it does so with a minimum of bells and whistles. IXEdit does not ship with NDS. It is available through Novell's NDS Product Management team. Furthermore, IXEdit is only available as a NetWare NLM at this time. Novell is currently studying the value of releasing a more refined version of this utility for public use. To get a copy of IXEdit, contact Novell Technical Services (NTS) at 1-800-858-4000. Table 10-10 describes the IXEDIT options.

WARNING: *Creating custom indexes for NDS should be done only by someone very familiar with the NDS environment and with a clear understanding of what the index is to accomplish. Improperly designed indexes can end up slowing down the very searches they are intended to help. Make sure that you understand how the index will affect your network environment before implementing any custom indexes.*

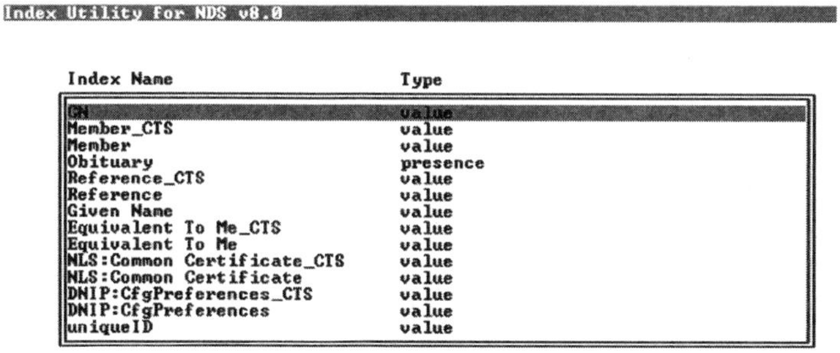

Figure 10-12

IXEdit main screen

```
Index Utility for NDS v8.0

    Index Name                    Type

   CN                             value
   Member_CTS                     value
   Member                         value
   Obituary                       presence
   Reference_CTS                  value
   Reference                      value
   Given Name                     value
   Equivalent To Me_CTS           value
   Equivalent To Me               value
   NLS:Common Certificate_CTS     value
   NLS:Common Certificate         value
   DNIP:CfgPreferences_CTS        value
   DNIP:CfgPreferences            value
   uniqueID                       value
```

Table 10-10

IXEdit options

Option	Description
A	Create a new NDS index
D	Delete an existing NDS index
U	Recreate all predefined NDS indexes
?	Show the available IXEdit options

To create a new NDS index, do the following:

1. Unload DS.NLM. If NLDAP.NLM is loaded, it will be unloaded automatically before DS.NLM unloads.

2. Load DSIXEDIT.NLM.

3. Press A. Enter a name for the NDS index you want to create and press Enter.

4. Select the NDS attribute that you want to act as the Key for this index and press Enter. NDS only supports single key indexes at this time. Novell strongly discourages the use of attributes that contain large values, such as *Description*, as index keys because of the overhead involved in creating and maintaining such an index.

5. Select the type of index you want to create and press Enter. Table 10-11 describes the types of indexes that NDS supports.

6. Press <Esc> to exit IXEdit.

7. Reload DS.NLM. You will have to reload NLDAP.NLM manually as well to permit LDAP communications.

To delete an existing NDS index, do the following:

1. Unload DS.NLM. If NLDAP.NLM is loaded, it will be unloaded automatically before DS.NLM unloads.

2. Load DSIXEDIT.NLM.

3. Highlight the index you want to remove and press D.

Table 10-11	**Type**	**Description**
Index types supported by NDS	Value	A *Value* index will maintain a list of all objects that contain the attribute selected as the index key. The index entries are sorted based on the key attribute value.
	Presence	A *Presence* index simply examines each object to see whether the selected key attribute has been assigned a value. Each object that contains the specified attribute is maintained in the index. This index can answer the question, "Does this object have attribute X?," but cannot answer, "What is the value in stored in attribute X for object Y?"
	Substring	A *Substring* index is useful with attributes of type TEXT on which you may want to perform wildcard searches. Each text value is broken down into all possible substring values, and each is stored as a separate index entry for that object.

NOTE: There are some pre-configured indexes that cannot be deleted. They are identified by a 'CTS' on the end of the name. CTS stands for Creation Time Stamp. *These indexes are used for internal NDS operations.*

4. Confirm the operation and press Enter.

5. Press Esc to exit IXEdit.

6. Reload DS.NLM. You will have to reload NLDAP.NLM manually as well to permit LDAP communications.

To recreate all predefined NDS indexes, do the following:

1. Unload DS.NLM. If NLDAP.NLM is loaded, it will be unloaded automatically before DS.NLM unloads.

2. Load DSIXEDIT.NLM.

3. Press U. IXEdit will check all the preconfigured indexes and rebuild those that have been deleted.

4. Press Esc to exit IXEdit.

5. Reload DS.NLM. You will have to reload NLDAP.NLM manually as well to permit LDAP communications.

IXEdit is not a utility that will be used very frequently, but it is nice to know that it exists if your organization is looking for a way to customize your NDS indexes.

SUMMARY

This chapter has covered some of the less known and less glamorous utilities available for use with NDS. These utilities may not be used day in and day out for basic NDS upkeep and health checks, but if something special is needed, or a problem arises, these tools will be worth their weight in gold.

However, these tools also give you enough rope with which to hang yourself. Advanced DS Repair options, for example, provide tremendously powerful—and dangerous—functionality. Be very careful when using these advanced options.

DSTrace doesn't expose any functionality that will destroy your tree, but it can wreak havoc if background processes are activated without thinking through the consequences first. Some of them can generate significant traffic. Get to know DSTrace; it is not a pretty utility, but it provides more information regarding the condition of NDS than any other source. Getting to understand the DSTrace monitor screen is one of the most important skills you can develop.

Bottom line, take it easy and make sure that you know what you are doing. Make sure that regular archives of NDS files are being taken, just in case. If you aren't completely sure what options to use for the problem you are experiencing, contact *Novell Technical Services* (NTS) or a Novell authorized reseller for guidance. Blindly performing these advanced partition and replica operations is a quick way to destroy an NDS tree—and lose a job in the process.

For More Information

Since NDS has been around since 1993, Novell has had time to develop a lot of good information about it. However, because NDS has only now been separated from the underlying NetWare operating system, a lot of this information is tied up in NetWare discussions. If you have a NetWare environment that is OK, but if you are running a native NT or Solaris environment, you have to be able to pick out the NDS-specific information and not worry about the rest.

Some of the links we have found most valuable are listed below.

Books

- *Novell's Guide to NetWare 5 Networks*, by Jeffrey F. Hughes and Blair W. Thomas, IDG Books, 1999

  This book is focused on NetWare 5, but it discusses a lot of NDS-related topics as a matter of course. Hughes and Thomas are well known and respected for their work in NDS design, configuration, and troubleshooting. Their book does not cover the latest version of NDS because it is written from the perspective of NetWare 5. However, many of the design and theoretical issues they discuss as still applicable.

Web Sites

NDS Web site `http://www.novell.com/products/nds/index.html`

NDS Cool Solutions Web site `http://www.novell.com/coolsolutions/nds/`

Web Articles

NDS v8: the Future of Novell Directory Services `http://developer.novell.com/research/appnotes/1999/march/a1frame.htm`

Maintaining a Healthy NDS Environment (Part 1) `http://developer.novell.com/research/appnotes/1997/august/a3frame.htm`

Troubleshooting NDS in NetWare 5 with DSREPAIR and DSTRACE: `http://developer.novell.com/research/appnotes/1999/january/a2frame.htm`

Technical Information Documents (TID)

Novell Technical Services documents specific solutions to customer problems covering the whole range of Novell products. These TIDs, which can be very valuable for learning new concepts as well as troubleshooting existing problems, can be located at `http://support.novell.com/servlet/Knowledgebase`.

There are many TIDs concerning the utilities that have been discussed in this chapter. You can find them by performing a keyword search in Novell's Knowledgebase using some—or all—of the following words: DSREPAIR or DSTRACE. Some of the best TIDs are

2949423	NDS v8 Public Beta FAQ
10011027	Using DSTRACE Commands, Filters, and Processes
2950826	NW5 Dstrace Switches *A and *U
2951626	Common Dstrace Flags— with Explanations

Troubleshooting
NDS

Troubleshooting in general is one of those mystical exercises that causes more gray—or lost—hair than nearly anything else. Troubleshooting a complex environment like NDS makes this problem even worse. Fortunately, there are some common rules for troubleshooting that apply to NDS as well as almost any other computing environment. This chapter will look at the art of troubleshooting and some common approaches that will make life easier.

After we have defined an intelligent troubleshooting philosophy, we will drill down into the NDS world to see how that philosophy applies to NDS specifically. We will also examine some common troubleshooting techniques for NDS. As with most problems, after you understand the steps necessary to isolate it, solving the problem becomes much easier.

Another aspect of troubleshooting is defining a good proactive plan for preventing problems in the first place. There are some recommended schedules for performing proactive maintenance that can prevent your NDS tree from becoming another network casualty.

Even with all this information, nobody will have every answer for every situation. To help out in those cases, Novell has supplied several resources that can be lifesavers for those of you who need to keep NDS on an even keel. Those resources include Web-based troubleshooting documents, NDS LogicSource, and *Novell Technical Services* (NTS). This chapter will discuss when and how to use these resources.

The Art of Troubleshooting

Troubleshooting skills are what make a good network administrator great. The problem is that there is no simple way to acquire good troubleshooting skills. However, there are some techniques—or perhaps personality traits—common to are good troubleshooters. Those techniques include

- Being level-headed
- Talking through the problem
- Not focusing too soon
- Keeping meticulous notes
- Attempting to isolate the problem
- Possessing superior product knowledge

Each of these may seem fairly obvious on the surface, but the person who can exhibit these qualities in the face of a critical system failure or widespread problem will distinguish himself as having what it takes to manage today's complex network environments.

The following suggestions are not meant to be a comprehensive, or exclusive, list of steps to solving a problem, but they are habits that should be cultivated in order to become a more proficient troubleshooter.

Being Level-Headed

A good troubleshooter cannot afford to fly off the handle. Panic is probably the number one enemy of a good troubleshooter. Troubleshooting is an art requiring a certain state of mind. Although we won't go so far as to advocate meditation or Tai Chi as a way to find the necessary inner peace, a calm, methodical, logical approach is needed in order to solve complex problems.

If you find yourself getting tense, take a break! Step back and give yourself a moment to "catch your breath" and let your mind wander a bit. Strangely, this down time is often what the mind needs in order to make that next breakthrough. Don't fight the need to step back and relax a bit. You will be more effective in the long run.

The ability to step back must not be confused with giving up. A troubleshooter must possess a "bulldog" mentality that force them to continue worrying at the problem until it is solved. Bulldogs don't have to constantly fight. They attach themselves and then just wear the problem down until a solution presents itself.

Talk through the Problem

Similar to the "break time" already mentioned, talking through a tough problem with a peer or mentor can help clear away mental roadblocks and expose the solution. You will find others often provide unique perspectives that you might not have stumbled upon on your own.

Don't Focus Too Soon

One of the biggest problems—and one with which I personally struggle—is the need to resist jumping to conclusions. Many symptoms have multiple potential causes. Sometimes we rush ahead thinking we know the problem only to find the problem remains unresolved—or has changed into something new! The goal of any troubleshooting process is not only to solve the problem, but to learn enough to help prevent the same problem from occurring in the future. In rushing ahead, we eliminate the chance to learn from this mistake.

Look at the whole environment. What has changed? Make a complete list down to the most inconsequential event. Often we will find those "inconsequential" changes are the ones that cause the most difficult problems. Why? Because we ignore them as potential factors in the problem. Obviously, you can rank potential causes based on the probability that they actually might have caused the problem. But failing to consider a potential cause, no matter how small the probability, can drag out the troubleshooting process tremendously.

Keep Meticulous Notes

Whenever you start working on a problem, open a notebook and start documenting what is happening. List the symptoms. List the potential causes —all of them! Document a plan of attack in which you propose a solution and then keep track of what happens at each step of the process. The documentation process often introduces potential solutions that might not have been otherwise considered.

Formalize this step. Don't make notes on napkins or scraps of paper that are lying around. Don't keep the checklist in your head—regardless of how good your memory is. Remember, the primary goal of a troubleshooting exercise should be not only to solve the problem, but to learn enough to prevent it from happening again. This means making the information portable. You must be able to pass the lessons learned from one person to another. It should also be available for review at a later date.

Attempt to Isolate the Problem

Perhaps one of the most effective concepts when trying to identify a problem is to isolate the portion of the network environment in which that problem occurs. If we remove a resource from the network, can the problem be reproduced in isolation? By listing the factors that might affect the problem and then removing them one at a time, we greatly reduce the scope of our search.

Similarly, it is often useful to get back to a "known good" state. This might be a default configuration or standard set of options that you know functions in your environment. If the standard configuration eliminates the problem, you can work forward, applying changes one at a time, until the change that causes the breakdown is located.

When the problem is located, don't stop there! In order to prevent this type of problem from occurring in the future, you need to understand how the cause and effect are linked. This is often where the "bulldog" trait is most critical. The temptation is to forget the problem once it is solved. Don't give in! Find the cause / effect relationship to understand how to prevent the same problem from occurring in the future.

Superior Product Knowledge

There is no magic bullet for this piece of the troubleshooting problem. It takes a lot of work to develop a real understanding of complex topics like network directories. This knowledge is what will set you apart from others. It will make you more marketable and more valuable. That should translate into increased responsibility, increased opportunity, and increased compensation. If it doesn't, find someplace where it will!

Product courses, such as those offered by Novell for its *Certified Novell Engineer* (CNE) certification, can be an excellent starting point, but they are not the end of the road, merely the beginning. Most of us have known "paper CNEs" who couldn't troubleshoot themselves out of a paper bag. They did enough to pass the test but did not pursue a real understanding of the material presented as part of the CNE courses.

To get past this, you need to work with the products regularly. You must be confronted with problems in order to develop the skills to solve them. In addition, find a mentor from whom you can learn the obscure facts that will make you better at solving tough problems. This might not necessarily be someone in your company. It could even be someone from a Web site or product chat room that enjoys giving advice.

Mentors are great for talking through difficult problems and providing advice and direction. However, they won't be too interested in helping solve every little problem that comes your way. Use them sparingly as a precious resource.

General NDS Troubleshooting

Prior to troubleshooting NDS, you should familiarize yourself with a few concepts. There are several ways in which NDS errors can be categorized as a first step to isolating the problem. The first two of these error categories are

- Temporary
- Persistent

Properly categorizing the error can help you focus your troubleshooting as you attempt to isolate the problem. It is important to note that the same NDS error code can be caused by both temporary and persistent conditions. When first looking at a problem, don't focus solely on the error code and what it means. Look at how and when the error occurs for clues as to the source of the error.

Temporary Errors

Temporary errors occur intermittently in response to some condition that affects the operation of NDS. Temporary errors are generally caused by environmental conditions external to the NDS server that reports the error. One example of a temporary error is a network communications problem that prevents servers hosting replicas of the same NDS partition from synchronizing. The error will continue until the communications problem is resolved. After the external communications problem is resolved, the NDS error will correct itself.

Persistent Errors

Persistent errors are generated by some inconsistency that cannot be resolved without specific intervention. These errors are generally associated with some problem of the directory structure or database, although this is not always the case. One condition that will cause a persistent error is network resources removed without properly deleting the NDS object.

One step below temporary and persistent, there are three error categories that can help us further isolate the problem. Again, this categorization process will provide important information as to the source of the error:

- Informational
- Communications
- Database

Informational Errors

Informational errors can be either temporary or persistent in nature, depending on the specific problem. Informational errors are used to notify an NDS client of one or more of the conditions listed below. A few of the possible informational error codes reported by NDS are listed after the conditions which they are related.

- A resource needed to process the request is in use.
  - –654 Partition Busy
  - –657 Schema Sync in Progress
  - –658 Skulk in Progress
- The client does not have sufficient rights to perform the requested operation.
  - –672 No Access
  - –602 No Such Value
  - –603 No Such Attribute
- Invalid request, invalid object, or improper request syntax
  - –604 No Such Class
  - –608 Illegal Attribute
  - –613 Syntax Violation
- Unable to process the request—unexpected error
  - –635 Remote Failure
  - –636 Unreachable Server
  - –641 Invalid Request

Communications Errors

Communications errors are the result of failures in the LAN or WAN environment. Communications errors are usually temporary. The error will stop when the communications problem is resolved.

In order to function properly, NDS must be able to communicate with resources managed through a given NDS tree. If this is not possible, NDS will generate errors indicating the nature of the problem. When attempting to resolve a communications error, it is most valuable to start from the perspective of the server attempting to do the communicating. DS Trace and DS Repair utilities executed from the server that is attempting to communicate will usually yield more valuable information than the same utilities executed from a server not initiating the communications.

Some causes of communications problems include

- Faulty communications hardware or hardware drivers, including NICs, hubs, switches, etc.
- Overloaded or unreliable communications links that result in packet corruption or loss
- Invalid network address information maintained in NDS (reparable through DS Repair)

Some common NDS error codes associated with communications problems include

- –622 Invalid Transport
- –625 Transport Failure
- –636 Unreachable Server
- –715 Checksum Failure

Database Errors

Database errors are caused by NDS servers hosting partition replicas that contain information inconsistent with similar information maintained in other NDS replicas. Database errors are usually persistent in nature. They require administrator intervention to resolve the inconsistency in the database and make sure all replica servers have to correct data. Some common NDS error codes that indicate a database error include

- –601 No Such Object
- –602 No Such Value
- –603 No Such Attribute
- –608 Illegal Attribute
- –618 Inconsistent Database

NOTE: *Not all database errors, particularly −601 errors, indicate that something needs to be fixed. If a client requests an object that does not exist or fails to supply the proper NDS name for the object, NDS can report an error. This problem must be resolved from the client side and not the database side.*

Isolating the NDS Error

The previous sections have discussed some techniques for troubleshooting in general and troubleshooting NDS in particular. This section continues with the NDS troubleshooting theme by looking at techniques to start isolating the NDS error so it can be resolved.

There are a large number of functions that can encounter an error and respond by generating an NDS error code. However, each of these error conditions can be divided into two categories:

- Operational Errors
- Process Errors

After the type of error is identified, there are steps that can be followed to isolate the cause of the error and develop a solution.

Operational errors occur while processing a request from an external source such as an NDS client or another NDS server. This may include requests from background processes running on other servers.

Process errors occur during the execution of a background process such as Janitor, Limber, or Skulk. Because background processes involve communicating with external servers, a process error can be caused by an operational error on another server. For example, if Server 1 is executing its Replica Synchronization process with Server 2, and Server 2 reports an operational error the replica synchronization process will terminate and Server 1 will report a process error.

Identifying the error as either operational or process tells you where the source of the problem lies. Usually, it is best to move to the source of the problem in order to isolate it because the errors received at the source will provide more complete information.

As previously discussed, DSTrace is the best tool for isolating NDS errors. See Chapter 10, "Advanced NDS Tools," for information on using DSTrace to monitor NDS processes.

Resolving Common Issues

While it is impossible to present information that will cover every potential error or problem, it is possible to examine some of the more common NDS problems in order to learn how the various tools and concepts can be used to resolve problems. Resolving NDS errors first requires that the nature, type, and source of the error be identified. After this is done, it is possible to develop a proper resolution strategy.

When formulating this resolution strategy, it is important to consider not only the problem but the impact of the solution on the NDS environment. The best solution will not only address the problem but also create the fewest number of peripheral consequences. Identifying these peripheral consequences is probably the most difficult part of NDS troubleshooting. The only way to gain this understanding is through study and experience.

The following general rules are meant to demonstrate the types of solutions that can be applied to different NDS problems. This list is not comprehensive and should not be followed to the exclusion of other solutions. This information is intended to help you get a feel for the type of thinking that is necessary in order to resolve NDS issues. As you read through the following scenarios, think about how these operations might affect your network. How might this affect your decision and timing when troubleshooting this type of problem?

Replica Rings

Inconsistencies in replica rings can be the source of numerous NDS errors. General steps in resolving these errors include the following:

1. Using DSTrace or DS Repair, identify the partition affected by the replica ring inconsistencies.

2. With DS Repair, identify all servers that host replicas of this partition and note the replica type on each server.

3. Examine the server hosting the Master replica because it functions as the authoritative source for partition information. If the Master replica is the source of the problem, designate one of the Read/Write replicas as a new Master using NDS Manager or DS Repair.

4. After a healthy Master replica exists, you can perform a Send All Objects operation in DS Repair to eliminate any inconsistencies.

5. Monitor the replica ring after making repairs to make sure that it is successfully send updates between all replica-hosting servers.

Network Address Referrals

Problems with network address referrals will prevent NDS from properly traversing the tree from partition to partition in order to find an object that is not locally maintained. To resolve this type of referral problem, do the following:

1. Identify the actual assigned IP or IPX addresses for each server involved. Each platform—such as NetWare, NT, or Solaris—will have a mechanism for reporting the network address that is being used by that server.

2. Repair Network Addresses on the servers for which other NDS servers are reporting errors. This can be done from the NDS Manager Partition Continuity view. This operation will make sure that the server is properly transmitting its own network address information.

3. More severe problems may require a rebuilding of replicas that have received invalid network address information. This can be resolved by using the Receive All Objects operation in DS Repair on the server hosting the replica. Use Send All Objects if the replica is a Master.

Schema

It is possible that an NDS server, due to communications problems or corruption of synchronization time stamps, will fail to receive schema updates as they are applied to the NDS environment. The resulting schema inconsistencies can be resolved by doing the following:

1. Using DSTrace, identify the server that is reporting schema errors. This will be the server that has not received the schema updates properly.

2. After the server has been identified, there are three ways to resolve this problem:

   a. Declare a new epoch for the NDS tree. This will reset all time stamps and resolve any invalid entries or corruption.

   b. Remove and reinstall NDS on the server that has failed. Make sure that any Master replicas hosted on this server are reassigned if this option is used. This option can cause significant user impact because external references pointing to this server will have to be reset.

   c. Contact Novell Technical Services. They have special tools with which they can resolve time stamp inconsistencies so the affected server can begin to receive schema updates again.

NDS Objects and Attributes

NDS object and attribute inconsistencies involve replicas of the same partition that, for whatever reason, have different information stored about the same NDS object or object attribute. In order to isolate the server(s) that have the faulty information, it is necessary to unload NDS on other servers. This type of troubleshooting can be done only in off hours.

In order to troubleshoot this type of problem, do the following:

1. Identify each server that hosts a replica of the partition having problems.

2. Unload NDS on every server in the replica except one. That way you know you are getting partition information from that server.

3. Use ConsoleOne to query the tree for the faulty objects or attributes. If they are correct, you know this server's replica is not faulty.

4. Repeat Step 3 until the faulty server(s) is/are found.

5. To repair the problem, first attempt a Receive All Objects from the faulty server.

6. If Step 5 fails, attempt to Send All Objects from one of the known good servers. If possible, use the Master for this operation.

7. If Step 6 fails, the replica will have to be destroyed. At this point, you may want to involve Novell Technical Support unless you are very comfortable with the use of advanced DS Repair switches. The replica can be eliminated by loading DS Repair with the -A option. You will then be able to remove the faulty server from the replica ring and then destroy the faulty replica.

8. If the database itself is too corrupt to repair, it may also be necessary to use the DS Repair -XK2 and -XK3 switches options. These switches will destroy all database objects and eliminate all external references in preparation for restoring a new copy of the database on this server.

Because the options discussed in steps 7 and 8 are not available on NT or Solaris yet, you will need to involve Novell Technical Services for help in resolving this type of serious problem on those platforms.

NDS Timestamps

The best-known NDS timestamp issue is synthetic time. Synthetic time is when an NDS object or objects has a modification timestamp ahead of current network time. If the period between current time and the synthetic time is small, this problem will correct itself. However, if the period is large, it is possible to resolve the problem manually. To fix the problems manually, do the following:

1. Review the NDS communications processes to be sure that all replicas are communicating properly.

2. Perform a check on the Master replica using DS Repair to be sure that it does not contain any errors and that it is receiving current updates properly.

3. Timestamps can be repaired in two ways:

   a. Use DS Repair to repair time stamps and declare a New Epoch.

   b. Identify the replica(s) with the synthetic timestamps and rebuild those replicas using Receive All Objects in NDS Manager.

   Consider the following when repairing timestamps with DS Repair:

   - All nonmaster replicas will be restarted in a New status when this operation is performed. No partition operations or replica updates will be possible—except through the Master replica—until the replica(s) pass into the On status.

   - This operation generates a large amount of NDS-related traffic as timestamps for all replicas are reset.

Proactive NDS Repairs

This previously presented information is only a small sampling of the types of issues that can be encountered when dealing with NDS. The goal of this chapter is to present the thinking behind resolving NDS problems rather than present every possible problem itself. That would require a book bigger than you could carry!

However, more impressive than actually resolving an NDS issue is preventing it from occurring in the first place. While this is not always possible, a good program of preventative maintenance will go a long way toward getting you home on time at night. Some of the recommended procedures can be performed in multiple ways using NDS Manager, DS Repair, or DSTrace. Use the method with which you are most comfortable. Some common preventative maintenance procedures include the following:

1. Verify that installed versions of NDS are current. (Quarterly)

   Review Novell's support Web site regularly for updates to NDS-related files. You may not want to apply all updates immediately, but know that the updates exist and what issues they are intended to resolve.

2. Verify that time is synchronized. (Biweekly)

   Use DS Repair to check the time sync status for each partition in the tree. Watch for synthetic time that might prevent background processes from completing normally.

3. Verify that replica synchronization is occurring normally. (Biweekly)

Use NDS Manager, DS Repair, or DSTrace to monitor the replica synchronization process. Any of these utilities can also be used to activate the replica sync process manually so it can be monitored through DSTrace.

4. Check Replica Ring continuity. (Biweekly)

Check Replica Ring information using NDS Manager or DS Repair to be sure that each server holds identical information concerning the members of its replica ring(s).

5. Check backlinks and external references. (Weekly)

Use DS Repair to check external references. This is accomplished through DSTrace on NT. This procedure will make sure that queries are able to traverse the NDS tree properly.

6. Check NDS obituaries. (Bimonthly)

Obituaries are references to deleted objects that are maintained until word of the deletion has been propagated to all servers hosting replicas of the affected partition. DS Repair will note undeleted obituaries during its External Reference check. When no longer needed, obituaries should be deleted by the Janitor process, which can be monitored though DSTrace.

7. Check the NDS schema. (Monthly or after extending schema)

Use DSTrace for force a schema sync (*SS command) to make sure that schema updates are being received by all NDS servers.

8. Review tree for Unknown objects. (Monthly)

Use ConsoleOne to search for Unknown objects. Click the Edit drop-down menu and select Find. Start your search from the Tree level and select Unknown as the object type.

Unknown objects can indicate resources that have not been properly removed from the NDS tree.

9. Backup server NDS database files. (Weekly)

Use your preferred method for backing up NDS database files. NDS backup options are discussed in Chapter 9.

Although performing these maintenance tasks regularly will not guarantee that problems will never surface, it will certainly help prevent catastrophic problems by allowing you to catch problems before they become too serious to resolve easily.

NDS Troubleshooting Resources

Novell has provided four tremendous resources when you hit a wall during your troubleshooting efforts.

- Novell Technical Services
- Knowledgebase
- Novell Product Forums
- LogicSource

Novell Technical Services

NTS is the source of the voice on the other end of the phone if you have ever contacted Novell to get some information or resolve a problem. Novell employs some 350 support engineers, organized by product and customer type, to provide the support necessary to keep Novell products up and running.

These engineers are the source of most of the available information concerning NDS and its quirks and idiosyncrasies. It is useful to know how NTS operates and how they assemble all the information available from Novell's support Web site. By the way, if you haven't book marked this Web site, `http://support.novell.com`, do so NOW. It is an invaluable resource that will keep you up-to-date on service packs, top support issues, and solutions/work-arounds for most problems.

NTS is organized into three main types of support engineers:

- Front Line engineer
- Resolution engineer
- Worldwide Support engineer

Front Line Engineer   Front Line engineers are the folks you will communicate with when you first call NTS. They specialize in a single product or family of products. Each Front Line engineer is required to obtain his or her CNE certification for the product or products they will support.

Each support call is tracked through a huge support database. The specifics of who you are and what your problem is are entered in the database, and then the support engineer takes over. The engineer starts by gathering information about your network environment and identifying the symptoms of the problem. As you talk with the engineer, you will see that she is often following the troubleshooting techniques outlined at the beginning of this chapter. Start at the general problem and work toward the specific one. Don't rush to judgment and never panic. Doing this type of work day in and day out forces you to develop these skills or go crazy.

In order to properly document the problem and resolution, a Front Line engineer is required to make an entry in the support database every time they talk with you. Their comments should outline the topic of discussion, information that was requested, and suggestions that were made.

After a problem is identified and resolved, the Front Line engineer will search Novell's public knowledgebase, which will be discussed shortly, to see whether the solution to this problem has already been documented. If it has been documented, you just wasted money and time on a support call because you didn't do your homework! The Front Line engineer will link your support incident to its documented solution and close the incident.

If the problem has not been previously documented, the Front Line engineer will create a document describing the problem, troubleshooting steps, and ultimate resolution of the problem. In this way your problems can be publicized so that another does not have to call Novell to resolve the same issue.

Resolution Engineer   Sometimes the solution to a problem does not present itself quite so quickly or easily. A Front Line engineer is expected to handle a significant call volume daily in order to keep customer service levels as high as possible. If standard troubleshooting techniques are not sufficient to isolate or resolve the problem, a Front Line engineer may request assistance from a Resolution engineer.

Resolution engineers are the best of Novell's support staff. They are required to achieve MCNE certification in the product area they will support. Resolution engineers serve two roles within NTS. First, Resolution engineers function as product mentors to field questions from Front Line support engineers who have run into a problem with which they are not familiar. These mentors may also organize specialized training or information in order to help the Front Line engineers improve their product skills.

Second, a Resolution engineer may take control of a call if the necessary troubleshooting will require more time and effort than the Front Line engineer can afford to provide. Resolution engineers have intimate knowledge of the products they support and expertise on tools that allow them to dig a little deeper into more complex issues.

A Resolution engineer will maintain control of the support call until it is resolved, hence the name. When a call is resolved, the Resolution engineer is also required to link the call to a document describing the symptoms, troubleshooting steps, and ultimate resolution of the problem.

Worldwide Support Engineer   Resolution engineers will always maintain control of an existing support call and make sure that the customer is regularly updated as to the problem status. However, if troubleshooting isolates a defect in the software itself, a Resolution engineer will involve a Worldwide Support engineer in order to drive the creation of an appropriate patch file.

Worldwide Support (WWS) engineers seldom work directly with customers —except for Novell's very largest. They are responsible for identifying and duplicating software defects and then working with Novell engineering teams to develop a fix for the defect.

WWS engineers often have an understanding down to the code level of the Novell product they support. This is necessary in order to properly identify defects and present them to engineering. WWS engineers are also responsible for the distribution of patches and service packs for their products to the rest of NTS and Novell's customers.

Last but not least, WWS engineers will often develop and teach group courses on the latest products and troubleshooting techniques. In fact, if you have ever attended Novell's Brainshare developer conference, you have probably heard from WWS engineers in many of the "hands on" and application courses.

Knowledgebase

The main reason for presenting the information about NTS and its organization is to provide some insight on how the information gathering and distribution process works. The primary method for distributing information collected by Novell's support staff is through Novell's support Web site, `http://support.novell.com`.

On this Web site, you will find many resources to help you in your efforts to prevent potential problems or solve existing ones. There are links to the most current patch lists, lists of common problem solutions, and beta releases of upcoming product releases. However, the most important link on this Web site is the support Knowledgebase.

The NTS Knowledgebase is a database containing the sum total of all Novell's support wisdom gathered over the years. The documents that each Front Line, Resolution, and WWS engineer is required to create detailing their efforts to solve problems are formatted and released as *Technical Information Documents* (TIDs).

The TID database can be searched by key word or topic to locate information that may be useful to you in your efforts to resolve a problem. Just like any database, the searches are not always useful. The more specific you can be when looking for information the better off you will be. However, the miscellaneous tidbits I can pick up while looking for other information have often amazed me. While I don't recommend reading the Knowledgebase from start to finish, I do suggest you take time regularly to search for updates on your own topics of interest. It's always best to learn before the problem occurs rather than after.

Product Forums

Also available from the Novell support Web site, Novell's product forums are sites where public discussion of Novell products, technologies, and problems can be discussed. Forums are organized around Novell product groups and are moderated by volunteer SysOps.

You can post questions and tap into the collective expertise of Novell customers from around the world. Forum SysOps have a tremendous background in the product for which they are moderating. They can often provide you with insights or solutions that would otherwise require direct contact with NTS. Furthermore, if you succeed in stumping the SysOp, he has direct access to Novell Resolution engineers who will respond to his or her queries.

Another useful approach to the product forums is to review past conversation threads to glean information that can prove very useful to you in your own environment. Remember that Novell does not directly monitor this information, so test the solutions offered before trying them in a production environment.

LogicSource

If you feel you have reached a point where scratching at the surface of NDS issues is no longer enough, LogicSource for NDS may be the next logical step in your directory education. LogicSource is the definitive reference for all things NDS. It is not free, but can be purchased directly from Novell. Information about ordering LogicSource for NDS is available on the Novell support Web site at `http://support.novell.com/logicsource/nds/`.

LogicSource for NDS includes extensive information—more than 1,500 pages worth—on the following topics:

Section I—Understanding Novell Directory Services

1. Directory Services

   Historical Background on Directory Services

2. Novell Directory Services

   NDS Name Space

3. NDS Schema

   Attribute Constraints

   Attribute Syntaxes

   Attribute Comparison Rules

4. Schema Class Definitions

   Object Class Flags

   Super Class List

   Base and Expanded Classes

   Containment List

   Naming Attribute

   Default Access Control List

   Mandatory and Optional Attribute Lists

5. NDS Objects

6. NDS Attributes

7. Object Naming Conventions

   Naming Types

   Naming Syntax

   Naming Formats

8. Partitions

   Partition Boundaries

   [Root] Partition

   Understanding NDS Partitions

   NDS Partition Types

9. Replicas

   Replica Type

Obituary Types

Obituary States

Section II—Novell Directory Services Background Processes

1. Replica Synchronization

2. Janitor

3. Flat Cleaner

4. Limber

5. Backlinker

6. Schema Synchronization

7. Database Initialization

8. Replica Purger

Section III—Novell Directory Services Background Process Requests

1. NDS Ping

2. NDS Start Update Replica

3. NDS End Update Replica

4. NDS Update Replica

5. NDS Start Update Schema

6. NDS End Update Schema

7. NDS Update Schema

8. NDS Sync External Reference

Section IV—Novell Directory Services Partition & Object Operations

1. Add Replica

2. Delete Replica

3. Split Partition

4. Merge Partition

5. Start Merge

6. Move Partition

7. Finish Move Partition

8. Start Move Partition

Section IX—Appendixes

1. Appendix A - NDS Schema Comparison Rules
2. Appendix B - NDS Schema Attribute Syntaxes
3. Appendix C - NDS Schema Attribute Constraints
4. Appendix D - NDS Operational Schema Attribute Definitions
5. Appendix E - NDS "Extended" Schema Attribute Definitions
6. Appendix F - NDS "Expanded" Operational Schema Class Definitions
7. Appendix G - NDS "Expanded" Extended Schema Class Definitions

As you can see from this extensive topic list, LogicSource for NDS includes just about everything you would need to know in order to eat, sleep, and speak NDS fluently. By the way, NTS Worldwide Support engineers did the work necessary to assemble the information in this reference.

At this time, the only drawback for those implementing NDS 8 is the fact the current LogicSource for NDS is based on the NetWare 4 version of NDS. This means that the changes to NDS that were introduced in NetWare 5 and beyond are not reflected in this information. Keep an eye out for updates. The NetWare 5 information should be available soon. No word yet on when a version for NDS eDirectory is planned.

SUMMARY

This is one of the more difficult chapters to assemble. On one hand, it is important to provide practical information that is useful to NDS administrators now. On the other hand, if administrators do not understand the thought processes and flow necessary to troubleshoot effectively, they will be stuck trying to find a written set of steps to solve every problem.

As previously mentioned, troubleshooting is a mystical effort. Some people seem very good at making the leap from sketchy information to the root cause of the problem. Others will struggle with this process and have to work for every victory they achieve. Regardless of which group you fall into, understanding on a conscious level the mindset and logic behind troubleshooting will make it easier to resolve those problems you encounter that have never been seen before. Remember, that the more intimate your product knowledge, the better chance you will have to achieve that ZEN-like ability to move quickly from symptoms to solutions.

For More Information

Troubleshooting in general is one of those topics that doesn't make for very good writing. It's too difficult to quantify and package. However, because NDS has been around since 1993, *Novell Technical Services* (NTS) has had lots of time to develop effective troubleshooting techniques. Unfortunately, documents describing the troubleshooting process are rare because the focus is the solution and not necessarily the winding journey that took you there.

For this reason, the most effective way to discover new troubleshooting techniques is through the more dynamic information sources such as NTS TIDs and the Novell Product Forums. These resources are light on NDS 8 information right now, but they will be the first areas to receive new information as it develops.

Some of the links we have found most valuable are listed below.

Web Sites

NDS Web site: `http://www.novell.com/products/nds/index.html`

NDS Cool Solutions Web site: `http://www.novell.com/coolsolutions/nds/`

Novell Product Forums: `http://support.novell.com/forums/`

Web Articles

NDS v8: the Future of Novell Directory Services: `http://developer.novell.com/research/appnotes/1999/march/a1frame.htm`

Introduction to NDS v8 `http://developer.novell.com/research/devnotes/1999/march/a1frame.htm`

Technical Information Documents

Novell Technical Services documents specific solutions to customer problems covering the whole range of Novell products. These TIDs can be very valuable for learning new concepts as well as troubleshooting existing problems that can be located at `http://support.novell.com/servlet/Knowledgebase`.

Nearly every TID concerning NDS deals with troubleshooting in one way or another. If you need info on a specific error or condition, perform a keyword search in Novell's Knowledgebase specifying the exact error code or message. Some TIDs popular with Novell Support Engineers include

2938838	Before Calling Support for DS Issues
2939526	Before Calling Support for Client Issues
2934901	NDS4NT Troubleshooting Summary (not completely current, but good info)
2909017	Troubleshooting 625 Errors Summary

Customizing NDS

As was discussed briefly in Chapter 2, "Designing NDS," the rules defining valid object types, where they can be stored, and what can be done with them are contained within the NDS schema. Schema provides the logical structure of the NDS tree. Because of this, Novell ships a base set of schema definitions that allow the directory to function. However, because it is impossible for Novell to anticipate every need you or your organization might have with regards to your enterprise directory, NDS has a fully extensible schema. This means that when you want to do something new with your directory, you should think first about what the schema needs to support your wants.

NDS doesn't care what kinds of data you store in it as long as you obey the proper rules for describing and organizing the data. This chapter looks at the structure and components of the NDS schema. How does it organize and define everything that goes on in the directory?

After you have an understanding of what the NDS schema is and how it works, you can begin to look at changing the schema to fit your needs. Because this is an Administrator's guide, it will not focus on using programming tools to develop NDS applications that extend the schema. Rather, it will examine the tools that you can use to customize the directory to store the information you consider most important.

There are two primary tools that make this possible. The first is ConsoleOne. ConsoleOne contains schema management tools that allow you to make modifications to NDS without having to develop an application to do so. The second is an even more exciting tool developed by a small software firm called Netoria. Called ScheMax, this tools allows you to create, organize, and populate new data types in NDS through a simple graphical interface. In fact, Novell found the Netoria technology so exciting that it recently acquired the company. As such, expect ScheMax functionality to find its way into ConsoleOne.

When you are done reading this chapter, you should understand the following:

- NDS Schema Components and Structure
- Extending the NDS Schema
- ConsoleOne Schema Tools
- Netoria ScheMax

NDS Schema Components and Structure

The first thing to understand about NDS schema is that it has three basic components. Each of the components provides increasingly detailed and specific information about the object class that is being described. The three components are

- Object Class
- Attribute Type
- Attribute Syntax

The most general component of the NDS schema is the object class (see Figure 12-1). It is the set of rules that governs the creation of an NDS object. Each time you decide to add an object to your NDS tree, you are selecting an object class. At a lower level, an object class describes a type of record that can be stored in the NDS database. Each instance of an object corresponds to a record stored in the NDS database.

The number of object classes you have in your tree depends on what you have done with your tree. Each new application that uses NDS adds new classes to support the specific functionality and data needs of that application.

Each object class is characterized by a set of attributes. In ConsoleOne, attributes are referred to as properties. Each attribute corresponds to a piece of data the object can maintain. For example, there are more than 80 attributes defined for the object class User.

As seen in Figure 12-2, these attributes include such information as Email Address, Employee ID, Full Name and Group Membership. The attributes are what make the object useful. They contain the data that is added, deleted, searched and manipulated every day in your organization.

Figure 12-1
View of object classes

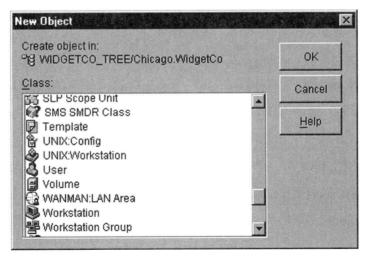

NDS attributes can be defined as either mandatory or optional. Mandatory attributes must be assigned a value in order to create an object of this class. An example of this is the Name attribute in the User object class. You cannot create a User object without supplying a name.

Optional attributes make it possible to store more data in an object than what is absolutely required, but optional attributes do not have to be assigned values in order to create an object of a given class. One example is the Description attribute associated with many different object classes. It can be used to provide more information but is not required.

Attribute Syntax is the most specific component of the NDS schema. The attribute syntax defines the specific data types (Integer, String, Boolean, etc.) that are allowed for each attribute. Attribute syntax also defines the specific rules governing each attribute, such as the range of acceptable values or minimum and maximum value length.

Attribute Syntax also includes a set of optional attribute flags that can be used to further specify how the attribute should function within the NDS schema. Table 12-1 identifies valid NDS attribute flags.

So, attribute syntax defines the attribute, and groups of attributes define an object class. Each of the objects you see in your NDS tree through ConsoleOne is implemented according to the rules set down by its object class, attributes, and attribute syntaxes.

Table 12-1	Flag	Description
NDS schema attribute flags	Single Valued	Allows only one value in the field. If not selected, NDS assumes the attribute will support multiple values per field, as in a membership list
	String	Specifies a text string data type
	Synchronize Immediately	Any changes to this attribute should be propagated to other partition replicas immediately (Fast Sync)
	Public Read	Allows any object in the tree to see the value of this attribute, regardless of rights
	Write Managed	Attribute can be set from only a Read/Write or Master partition replica.
	Per Replica	Attribute is replica specific. It will not be synchronized.
	Sized	Specify that the range of attribute values is bounded by a maximum or minimum limit

Now that you understand the components of the NDS schema, it is time to discuss the way those components work together to define the structure of NDS. There are two aspects to the structure of NDS and the schema is involved with both.

- Class Structure
- NDS Structure

Class Structure

The class structure of NDS is described by the relationship between the various object classes that exist. Just as objects in an NDS tree are organized hierarchically to benefit from inheritance rules, so too are the object classes that make up the NDS schema. In fact, some of the object classes in the NDS schema are there simply to provide functionality and organization for other object classes that will be created further down the schema hierarchy. Object classes that provide inherited functionality to subordinate object classes are called *super classes*.

Just as an NDS object inherits capabilities from all parent objects above it in the tree, class objects can also inherit attributes and functionality from the object classes to which it is subordinate. Novell provides some basic super classes that provide features that most any object class will need, but theoretically any object class can become a super class if another class can be defined that builds upon its effective attribute set.

Every object class in NDS inherits from the root schema class in NDS. This root schema class is properly named Top. Because all other object classes in NDS will inherit characteristics of Top, it defines certain attributes that all objects will need. Those include

- Access Control List
- Backlink
- Last Referenced Time
- Obituary
- Used By

This means that each object class doesn't have to re-invent the wheel by redefining these characteristics as part of its own class definition.

Every object class in NDS has at least one super class—Top. However, just as NDS trees can grow to contain multiple layers of objects, the NDS schema has grown to contain multiple levels of object classes. Each class inherits the attributes of all its super classes. Therefore, the attributes defined by each class in a schema hierarchy start general and become more specific as you move down the hierarchy. For example, the object class User has three super classes: Organizational Person, Person, and Top. As such, User inherits all the attributes of these three classes.

Object classes can be either effective or ineffective. Effective classes can be used to create actual NDS objects. Ineffective classes are used only to define attributes that are inherited by classes below them. The Person and Organizational Person classes previously mentioned are examples of ineffective classes. They exist only to define attributes that will be used by User and any other classes defined below them in the schema hierarchy. Classes such as User that are used to define actual NDS objects are also known as Base Classes.

Just as inherited rights can be filtered in NDS, inherited attributes can be blocked as well, when necessary. There are four rules that govern the inheritance of object class attributes:

1. In order to inherit attributes, an object class must declare another class as its super class. Every object class—except Top—must declare at least one super class. NDS does allow multiple inheritance, in which a class declares two or more super classes.

2. An object class always inherits all attributes from its super class(es). It may also choose to define additional attributes as necessary.

3. An object class always inherits the ACL templates defined by its super classes. An ACL template defines the default rights associated with an object when it is created. An object class may choose to define its own ACL template as necessary.

4. An object class can choose to redefine any attributes inherited from super classes. The attributes defined lower in the class hierarchy always take precedence when determining attribute syntax.

NDS Structure

Now that you understand a little about how object classes are organized internally, it is useful to see how that internal organization translates into the NDS structure that you use every day. There are four main concepts that relate object class structure with NDS tree structure:

- Object Naming
- Containment Classes
- Leaf Classes
- Class Flags

Object Naming NDS object names are identified by their own object name coupled with the names of their parent objects (see Figure 12-3).

An object name is stored in its Naming Attribute. The naming attribute may be inherited from a super class as long as there are no naming conflicts between the super classes. If any conflicts exist, the object class must define its own naming attribute.

This Name attribute is also referred to as the *Relative Distinguished Name* (RDN). It is so called because an object's name must be unique relative to its location in the NDS tree. This corresponds to a *Common Name* (CN) in X.500 parlance. For example, within the container `Americas_Sales.Phoenix.WidgetCo`, only one object can exist with the name AHarris.

The combination of an object's RDN and the names of all parent objects results in a *Distinguished Name* (DN). The DN is an object identifier unique throughout the NDS tree. So, even though there may be an object AHarris (Austin Harris) in `Americas_Sales.Phoenix.WidgetCo` and another object AHarris (Allison Harris) in `Finance.Operations.Chicago.WidgetCo`, there is no ambiguity because the Distinguished Name of each object is distinct:

- Austin Harris: `AHarris.Americas_Sales.Phoenix.WidgetCo`
- Allison Harris: `AHarris.Finance.Operations.Chicago.WidgetCo`

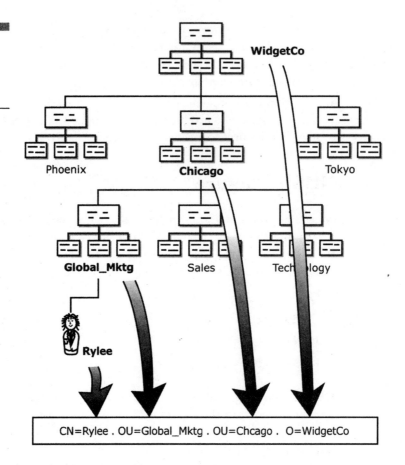

Figure 12-3
NDS names
determined by
Object and Object
parents

Every NDS object class defines one or more naming attributes as part of its definition. At least one naming attribute must be assigned a value when an object of this class is created. The attribute syntax for these naming attributes will define naming restrictions such as maximum length or invalid characters.

You will regularly see or hear the term Fully Distinguished Name in relation to NDS. This is simply a DN that includes the naming attribute identifier for each object class in the DN. These naming attribute identifiers are defined by X.500 naming conventions. Common naming attribute identifiers include

- *CN*   Common Name.
- *OU*   Organizational Unit.
- *L*   Locality

- *O* Organization
- *C* Country

For example, Austin Harris' Fully Distinguished Name is as follows:

```
CN=AHarris.OU=Americas_Sales.OU=Phoenix.O=WidgetCo
```

NOTE: *The naming attribute identifier does not necessarily identify the object class with which it is associated. The CN identifier is used for multiple object classes such as User, Server and Computer. Other identifiers are used only with a single type of object, such as L: Locality.*

NDS also permits multivalued naming attributes. This means that multiple name values can be specified, but only one is flagged as the official naming value. The flagged naming value is used for all NDS indexes and searches.

Containment Classes   Whereas naming defines the rules that permit us to locate an object in the directory, Containment classes exist to provide structure to the NDS tree itself. Containment classes, or Containers, are special object classes that can contain other objects subordinate to themselves. These objects are the only kind that can become parent objects. In NDS, the containment classes defined in the base schema include

- *Tree Root*   Defines the generic root for the NDS Tree
- *Country*   Used to create X.500-compatible geographical directory organizations
- *Locality*   Another X.500-defined container used for geographical directory organization
- *Organization*   Used to define a directory structure based on organizational structure
- *Organizational Unit*   Subordinate containment class used to further define directory structure

Each object class in NDS must define a containment list. This list determines where in the directory tree an object of that class can exist. As with naming, an object class can inherit its containment list from super classes as long as no conflicting containment information exists. If there are conflicts, the object class will have to specifically define its own containment list. Table 12-2 outlines the basic containment rules that exist in base NDS object classes.

Table 12-2

NDS base
containment rules

Object Class	Containment List
Leaf Object	Organizational Unit Organization
Organizational Unit	Organizational Unit Organization Locality
Organization	Locality Country Tree Root
Locality	Organization Locality Country
Country	Tree Root
Tree Root	None

Not every containment class can legally hold every other type of object class. These rules force some semblance of order when creating the NDS tree. It does not make sense to create User objects (Leaf) under the Tree Root, so containment rules prevent this from happening.

Another interesting containment issue is the relationship between the Locality class and the Organization class. Each specifies the other in its containment list. This is because these two object classes represent different philosophies in directory tree design. NDS allows you to choose the implementation that makes the most sense for you.

It is also possible to extend the schema and define new object classes that define containment lists differently from any in Table 12-2. NDS does not restrict your options in this sense. One example is the Security object created when NDS is installed. It is a special type of containment class that can hold only a very specific set of subordinate objects. The Security object is always created off the Tree Root, at a level equivalent with a Country or Organization object.

As with the containment classes themselves, leaf classes can define their own containment lists to restrict how they can be placed within the directory. Table 12-3 highlights a few leaf objects and the type of containment they require. Leaf classes can also inherit their containment from super classes. Table 12-3 also lists the source of the leaf class's containment list.

Table 12-3	Leaf Class	Containment List	Containment Defined By:
Leaf class containment	Alias	Determined by Referenced Object	Alias
	Bindery object	Organization Organizational Unit	Bindery object
	Group	Organization Organizational Unit	Group
	Print Server	Organization Organizational Unit	Server
	User	Organization Organizational Unit	Organizational person
	Unknown	Any (Special Case)	Any

Leaf Classes   Object classes that cannot contain any subordinate objects are referred to as Leaf classes. Leaf classes represent the actual network resources that you access through NDS every day. At this point, you have moved from describing the directory itself to describing the stuff in the directory that is important to you and your organization.

Leaf classes benefit from all the same schema components, inheritance, and containment definitions that have been discussed previously. The biggest difference is that when you create a leaf object, the information you provide is describing something external to the directory rather than some component of the directory itself.

Class Flags   There are five object class flags that can be turned ON or turned OFF as part of a class definition:

- *Container Flag*   The Container flag indicates whether the object can contain other objects. The flag is turned ON for containment classes and turned OFF for leaf classes.

- *Effective Flag*   The Effective flag indicates whether an object class is effective or ineffective. The Effective flag is turned ON for those classes that can be used both to provide definition and to create objects.

- *Nonremovable Flag*   The Nonremovable flag indicates whether or not the class can be deleted from the schema. All NDS base classes have the Nonremovable flag set ON. Schema classes that have been added to extend functionality can have this attribute set OFF.

■ *Ambiguous Naming*   The Ambiguous Naming flag is set OFF in most cases. It indicates whether or not an object class needs to clearly define its naming. This is normally required, but some objects such as Alias and Partition derive their names from the objects they reference. Because of this, Alias objects can be created with ambiguous naming that is defined later.

■ *Ambiguous Container*   The Ambiguous Container flag is set OFF in most cases. It indicates whether or not an object class needs to clearly define its containment classes. This is normally required, but some objects like Alias and Partition derive their containment rules from the objects they reference. Because of this, Alias objects can be created with ambiguous containment rules that are defined later.

The Container and Effective flags can be set by the application or administrator that is extending the schema. The Nonremovable, Ambiguous Naming, and Ambiguous Container flags are set automatically by NDS.

Extending the NDS Schema

The thousands of potential leaf object classes in the world are the primary reasons for Novell's decision to make the NDS schema extensible. While it is just as possible to create new containment classes for NDS, there are only so many ways to organize objects that makes sense and has value.

However, as organizations look to solve increasingly difficult problems with the help of directories, they must be able to define an increasingly wide variety of objects within the logical directory structure. Until recently, the addition of new object classes—or the addition of new attributes to existing object classes—has been a task for a developer skilled in the use of NDS programming interfaces. Extending the schema to support new functionality was not a trivial task.

Fortunately, that is beginning to change with the introduction of two new tools that allow administrators to create new object classes and attributes without having to do any programming at all. The first of these tools is included as part of Novell's ConsoleOne administrative utility. The other is a third-party application that offers a completely graphical interface for interacting with the NDS schema. ScheMax, by Netoria, has really caught the eye of NDS administrators because of the possibilities it creates for administrators to take control of one portion of the NDS environment. Each of these utilities is described here.

NOTE: *Register any new class prefixes that you create for NDS with Novell to ensure that they are unique. You can do this in any of the following ways:*

- *Call Novell Developer Support at 1-800-REDWORD or 801-861-5588.*
- *FAX Novell Developer Support at 801-861-2990*
- *Register through the Developer Support Web site at* `developer.` `novell.com/engsup/schreg2c.`

When registered, you receive a unique prefix for your new attribute and object class definitions. You also receive two *Abstract Syntax Notation One* (ASN.1) IDs, one for object classes and one for attribute definitions. ASN.1 serves as a common syntax for transferring information between two end systems.

ConsoleOne Schema Tools

Schema Manager is Novell's first step down the road toward graphical administration and modification of the NDS schema. It is not a complete solution, but it does offer some indication of where Novell is going in this area. Perhaps an even more telling sign is Novell's recent acquisition of Netoria. Netoria's schema management tool, ScheMax, will be discussed later in this chapter. This application delivers truly comprehensive schema modification and management functionality.

Whenever you are going to work with the NDS schema, you must have full administrative rights to the [Root] of the tree. This is necessary because NDS utilizes a global schema definition. When you make a change to an object class or attribute, that change is applied universally to all areas of the tree. To access the Schema Manager, do the following:

1. Launch ConsoleOne.
2. Click Tools and select Schema Manager (see Figure 12-4).

Everything in Schema Manager is accessible through either the Classes or the Attributes tab. There are four main tasks you can perform from ConsoleOne's Schema Manager:

- View information on a class or attribute.
- Create a new class or attribute.

Figure 12-4
Schema Manager
interface in
ConsoleOne

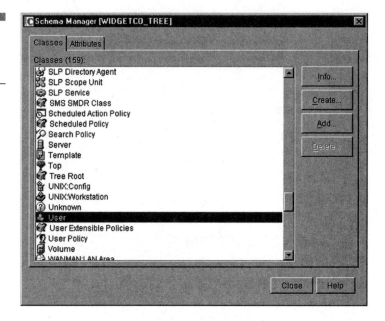

Add an attribute to an existing class.

Delete classes you have previously added.

View Information on a Class or Attribute

To view details on a class or attribute, complete the following steps:

1. Select the Classes or Attributes tab.

2. Select the class or attribute for which you want information and click Info (see Figure 12-5).

The Class and Attribute information screens will display all the vital statistics for the selected class or attribute. Class Info includes the following information:

Mandatory Attributes Identifies those object properties that must be assigned values when the object is first created. For example, the User class requires that the *Common Name* (CN) and Surname attributes be assigned values before the object will be created.

Optional Attributes Lists all other properties that can be populated in objects of this class. This can be an extensive list.

Figure 12-5

Schema Manager
class information

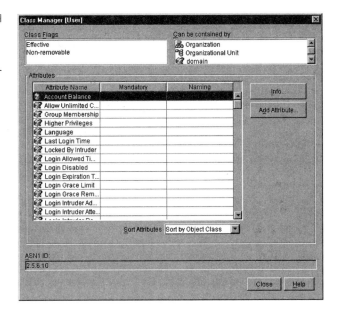

- *Super Classes*   Lists all parent classes associated with the selected class

- *Sub Classes*   Lists all subordinate classes associated with the selected class

- *Containment Classes*   Lists all container objects in which an object of the selected class can reside

- *Naming Attributes*   Identifies the attribute that functions as the naming attribute for objects of the selected class

- *Class Flags*   Lists the class flags associated with this class. Class flags were discussed previously.

- *ASN.1 ID*   ASN.1 serves as a common syntax for transferring information between two end systems.

Similarly, you can use the Info button on the Attributes tab to view the following information (see Figure 12-6):

- *Attribute Syntax*   Specifies that data type used by this attribute

- *ASN.1 ID*   ASN.1 serves as a common syntax for transferring information between two end systems.

- *Attribute Flags*   Spells out the specifics of the Attribute syntax

- *List of classes using the attribute*   Lists all classes that identify this as a valid attribute in their class definitions

Figure 12-6
Schema Manager
attribute information

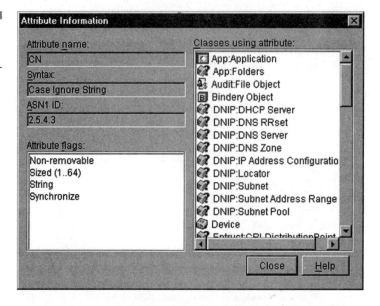

Figure 12-7
The Define Class
dialog box

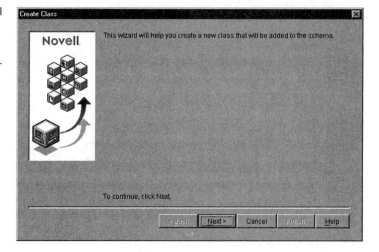

Create a New Class or Attribute

You can also use Schema Manager to create new class or attribute definitions. To create a new schema class, complete the following steps:

1. Select the Classes page and click Create. Click Next to enter the Class
   Creation Wizard (see Figure 12-7).

2. Specify a name for the new class and, optionally, an ASN.1 ID for this
   class. Click Next. Enter an ASN.1 ID only if you have registered your

class prefix with Novell. See instructions on how to do this in a note earlier in this chapter.

3. Select the type of class you are creating and click Next. Effective classes are used to define NDS objects. Non-Effective classes are used provide class definition but are not used to create objects. Auxiliary classes are used with LDAP. You can also specify that your class is a container class.

4. Select the super classes that your new class inherits from and click Next.

5. Select the mandatory attributes for your new class and click Next.

6. Select the optional attributes for your new class and click Next.

7. Select the naming attributes for your new class.

8. Select the Containment List for your new class.

9. Review the summary of your new class for accuracy and click Finish.

You may often find that you need to add new attributes to existing classes. This may include classes of your own creation or existing NDS base classes. To add a new attribute, complete the following steps:

1. Select the Attributes page and click Create. Click Next to start the Attribute Creation Wizard (see Figure 12-8).

2. Specify a name for the new attribute and, optionally, an ASN.1 ID for this attribute. Click Next. Enter an ASN.1 ID only if you have registered your attribute prefix with Novell. See instructions on how to do this in a note earlier in this chapter.

Figure 12-8
Schema Manager
Attribute Creation
Wizard

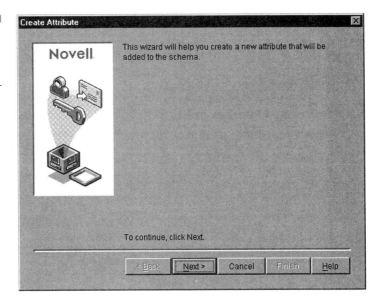

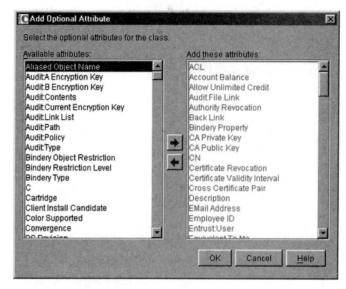

Figure 12-9
Schema Manager
Add Existing Attribute

3. Specify the attribute syntax appropriate for this attribute and click Next.

4. Select the appropriate attribute flags and click Next. Attribute flags were discussed previously.

5. Review the attribute summary for accuracy and click Finish.

Add an Existing Attribute to a Class

You may also need to extend an object class's capabilities by adding an existing attribute to its definition. To add an existing attribute to a class, complete the following steps:

1. Select the Classes tab and highlight the class to which you want to add attributes and then click Info.

2. Click Add Attribute.

3. Select the attribute(s) you want to add in the left pane and click the Right Arrow button.

4. Click OK (see Figure 12-9).

Delete Classes You Have Previously Added

The Delete Class option is not available for NDS base classes, but any other classes that have been used to extend the NDS schema can be removed. To delete an object class, complete the following steps:

1. Use ConsoleOne to search for all objects of this class. Delete any objects of this class before deleting the class itself.

2. From Schema Manager, select the Classes tab and highlight the class that you want to delete.

3. Click Delete and then click Yes.

Netoria ScheMax

ScheMax is truly the Cadillac of schema management tools. It installs and integrates with Novell's NetWare Administrator to make its use as easy as possible. Then, ScheMax allows you to graphically define new object classes and class attributes. After this new schema data has been created, there must be a way to take advantage of it. Previously, this would require the development of a snap-in for NetWare Administrator in order to make the utility capable of understanding the new schema definitions.

ScheMax provides an answer to this problem as well by making ScheMax capable of creating the snap-in automatically. In this way, new classes and attributes are available immediately for use by NDS users. In order to better explain what ScheMax does, this section will look at the following aspects of the ScheMax application:

- Installation
- View and Modify the Schema
- Creating a NetWare Administrator Snap-In

The only real drawback to ScheMax at this time is that it uses NetWare Administrator rather than ConsoleOne. However, a version for ConsoleOne is currently under development and should be available in the near future.

Installation

The easiest way to get ScheMax is to download it from Netoria's Web site. At this time, version 1.01 is in full release. Version 1.10 is in beta. Full-function evaluation copies of either version are available by completing the following steps:

1. Go to www.netoria.com.

2. Select Products and Services.

3. Select ScheMax. Click Download Software at the bottom of the page.

4. Fill out the required customer information and click SUBMIT FORM.

5. Note the download password for future use and click Download Software.

6. Select the version of ScheMax you want and save it to your local drive.

After you have downloaded the software, the installation process includes two steps. First, use the self-extracting installation program to install the ScheMax program files to your workstation. To do this, execute the file you downloaded from Netoria's Web site and follow the onscreen instructions. After installing the program files, you must load NetWare Administrator in order for ScheMax to apply the schema extensions it uses to your NDS tree (see Figure 12-10).

To set up ScheMax in your NDS environment, complete the following steps:

1. Launch NetWare Administrator.

2. Select ScheMax from the Products list.

3. Select the NDS tree in the NDS Trees list that you want to extend.

4. Click Install Schema Modifications and then click Close.

All necessary components of ScheMax are now installed. The following sections describe the capabilities of ScheMax and how it can be used to manage schema in your NDS environment.

Figure 12-10
ScheMax Schema
Extensions dialog box

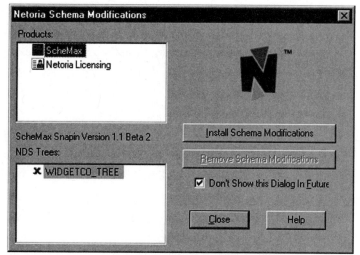

View the NDS Schema

ScheMax provides a snap-in for NetWare Administrator that allows you to view the complete schema of any NDS tree to which you are connected—assuming that the schema of that tree has been extended with the necessary ScheMax object classes. In order to access the ScheMax Schema View in NetWare Administrator, complete the following steps:

1. Launch NetWare Administrator.
2. Click Tools.
3. Select Netoria ScheMax and then Netoria Schema Administrator.
4. Select an NDS Tree the tree list.

ScheMax provides a complete graphical view of the organization of your NDS schema (see Figure 12-11). From this screen, you can see first-hand all the schema components and how they are organized in your NDS tree. There are two panes in the Schema View screen. The left pane is a hierarchical class view that lets you see how all the different classes in the NDS schema interrelate. The right pane is a class details view. When you select a class in the left pane you can see details specific to that object class in the right pane.

Figure 12-11
ScheMax
Schema view

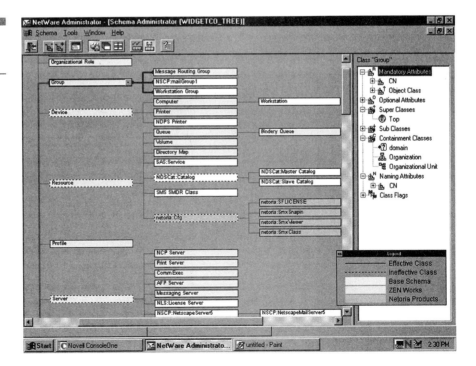

The Legend window simply tells you how the different components of the schema hierarchy are organized. You can close this menu at any time without affecting ScheMax functionality. To restart the Legend, click Schema and then select Show Legend. Some of the characteristics of the hierarchical class view include

- *Effective Classes*   Effective classes are those that you can use to create NDS objects. A solid border identifies them.
- *Ineffective Classes*   Ineffective classes are those that provide inherited functionality to other classes but are not created as objects directly. A dashed border identifies them.
- *Super Class Links*   When you select a class in the left pane, any links to super classes are highlighted in red.
- *Sub Class Links*   When you select a class in the left pane, any links to sub classes are highlighted in blue.
- *Object Class Types*   ScheMax can use color to identify classes associated with different NDS-enabled products. For example, Base NDS classes are colored green, ScheMax classes are colored pink, and ZENworks classes are colored blue.

The class details view shows you the vital statistics for a selected class. From this view, you can see the following:

- *Mandatory Attributes*   Identifies those object properties that must be assigned values when the object is first created. For example, the User class requires that the *Common Name* (CN) and Surname attributes be assigned values before the object will be created.
- *Optional Attributes*   Lists all other properties that can be populated in objects of this class. This can be an extensive list.
- *Super Classes*   Lists all parent classes associated with the selected class
- *Sub Classes*   Lists all subordinate classes associated with the selected class
- *Containment Classes*   Lists all container objects in which an object of the selected class can reside
- *Naming Attributes*   Identifies the attribute that functions as the naming attribute for objects of the selected class
- *Class Flags*   Lists the class flags associated with this class. Class flags were discussed previously.

Using these two panes in the Schema View, you can gain a thorough understanding of how NDS is organized. It makes NDS a lot less cryptic to be able to see the organization and contents of the schema as they are presented by ScheMax.

Modify the NDS Schema

Beyond understanding the organization, ScheMax also allows you to make modifications to the schema as well. There are four main tasks that you can perform from the Schema View:

- Define New Subclass
- Add New Attribute
- Add Existing Attribute
- Delete Class

Define New Subclass   ScheMax allows you to create new object class definitions that will extend the capabilities of NDS into new types of data. To create a new class definition, complete the following steps:

1. Click Schema and select Define New Class. Click Next to open the Class Creation Wizard (see Figure 12-12).
2. Specify the Class Prefix and Class Name and click Next.
3. Select the super class(es) from which your new class should inherit and click Next.

Figure 12-12
ScheMax Class
Creation Wizard

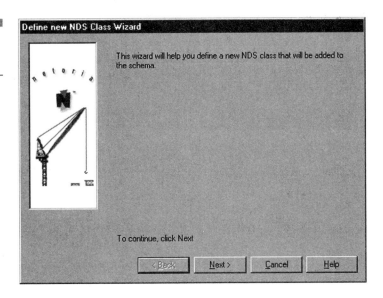

4. Check the appropriate boxes indicating whether your new class is an Effective class and/or a Container class and then click Next.

5. Select the mandatory attributes for your new class and click Next.

6. Select the optional attributes for your new class and click Next.

7. Select the naming attributes for your new class.

8. Select the Containment List for your new class.

9. Review the summary of your new class for accuracy and click Finish.

10. You will see the message in Figure 12-13. Click Define Now to create the new object class and then click OK.

Add New Attribute   You may often find that you need to add new attributes to existing classes. This may include classes of your own creation or existing NDS base classes. To add a new attribute, complete the following steps:

1. Click Schema and select Define New Attribute. Click Next to open the Attribute Creation Wizard (see Figure 12-14).

2. Select whether you want to create an entirely new attribute or copy from an existing attribute. If you choose Copying An Existing Attribute, select the attribute to copy. Click Next. Copying An Existing Attribute allows you to use an existing attribute as a template.

3. Specify the Attribute Prefix and Attribute Name and click Next.

4. Specify the type of data to be stored in the new attribute (see Figure 12-15) and click Next. If you click Advanced, you will see a complete list of all possible NDS attribute syntaxes.

Figure 12-13
ScheMax Class
Creation message

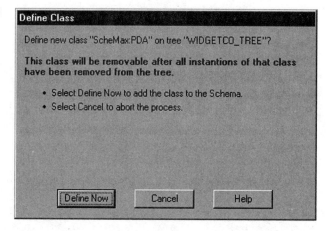

Figure 12-14
ScheMax Attribute
Creation Wizard

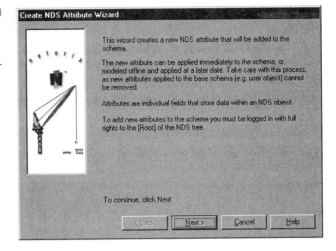

Figure 12-15
ScheMax Attribute
Syntax options

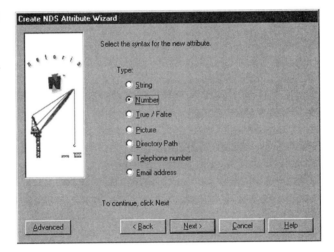

5. Review the attribute summary for accuracy and click Next.

6. Choose to Add The Attribute Now or Add The Attribute Later and click Finish. If you Add The Attribute Later, it will be saved so you can use it to develop a snap-in before committing the new attribute to the schema.

7. If you Add The Attribute Now, click Define Now (Figure 12-16) to commit the attribute to your NDS schema and then click OK.

Add Existing Attribute You may also need to extend an object class's capabilities by adding an existing attribute to its definition (see Figure 12-17). To add an existing attribute to a class, complete the following steps:

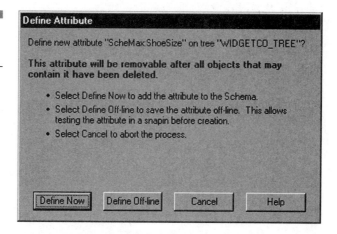

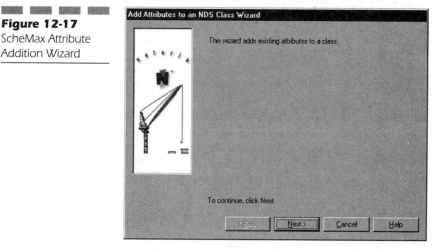

1. Click Schema and select Add Attribute To Class. Click Next.

2. Select the class you want to modify and click Next.

3. Select the attribute you want to add to this class and click Next.

4. Review your attribute choices in the summary and click Finish.

5. Click Add Now (Figure 12-18) to add the attribute to the selected class and then click OK.

Delete Class   The Delete Class option is not available for NDS base classes, but any other classes that have been used to extend the NDS schema can be removed. To delete an object class, complete the following steps:

Figure 12-18
Adding an Attribute
to a Class

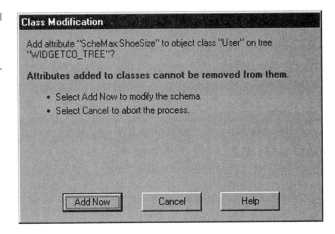

1. Use ConsoleOne to search for all objects of this class. Delete any objects before deleting the class itself.
2. Select the object class in the ScheMax hierarchical class view. Click the dropdown menu button and select Delete Class.
3. Click Yes to delete the object class definition and then click OK.

Creating a NetWare Administrator Snap-In

After a new class or attribute has been created, you need some facility to make that class or attribute visible to the people in your organization who need it. NetWare Administrator will not automatically recognize any schema value other than the base NDS schema classes. In order to get NetWare Administrator to recognize a new class or attribute, you must create a snap-in to tell NetWare Administrator how to deal with this new piece of schema information.

ScheMax provides an automated tool for programming the necessary NetWare Administrator snap-in. ScheMax snap-ins are created as NDS objects. Access to these objects can then be fully controlled by assigning the appropriate NDS rights. See Chapter 6, "Controlling Network Access," for more information on NDS rights and security. To create a ScheMax snap-in, complete the following steps:

1. Launch NetWare Administrator. Locate the container where you want to create the snap-in object.
2. Right-click the container object and select Create.

Figure 12-19
ScheMax Snap-in
Creation dialog box

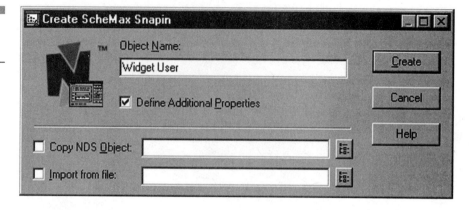

3. Select the Netoria ScheMax Snap-In object class and click OK (see Figure 12-19).

4. Specify a name for the snap-in object and select Define Additional Properties. Select Copy NDS Object or Import From File if you have an existing snap-in that you want to use as a template. Click Create.

5. Select the object classes that will use this snap-in and then click the Snap-In Builder tab (see Figure 12-20).

6. Select the required attribute from the attribute list and then select the type of control you want to use with that attribute. The possible attribute controls such as radio buttons, text boxes, selector boxes, etc., are determined by the attribute syntax selected when the attribute was created.

7. Click Create A New Control and position the control where you want it on the Snap-In grid.

8. Double-click on the control to configure it. What you do next will depend on the control type you have selected. If you are not sure how to configure the control, use the online help. When you have configured the control to your liking, click Apply and then OK (see Figure 12-21).

9. (Optional) Add Static Elements or Pseudo Attributes to your snap-in if desired. Static elements allow you to include other useful information in the snap-in beyond the attribute information. Pseudo attributes allow you to request common information that can be used by the snap-in to perform actions or identify the user. Table 12-4 lists the valid static elements and pseudo attributes.

10. Click the Associations tab. Click Add/Remove to build a list of containers from which this snap-in should be visible and then click OK.

Figure 12-20
ScheMax Snap-In
tools

Figure 12-21
ScheMax Snap-In
builder

After the ScheMax snap-in has been created and associated with the proper containers, your new snap-in will appear as a tab in the object details of an object that utilizes that attribute.

Table 12-4

ScheMax Snap-In static elements and pseudo attributes

Static Elements	
File Store	Allows any file type to be stored, extracted, or launched from NDS
Frame	Draws an outlined or filled frame with no caption
Group Box	Draws a Windows-style groupbox that includes a caption
Horizontal Line	Draws a horizontal line
Icon	Inserts an Icon graphic
Internet Link	Inserts an Internet URL
Static Text	Inserts a static text string
Vertical Line	Draws a vertical line

Pseudo Attributes	
Creation Stamp	Inserts the timestamp for when the object was created
DN	Inserts the Full Distinguished Name of the object
Modification Stamp	Inserts the timestamp for when the object was last modified
Partition Root	Inserts the name of the partition that holds the object
Subordinates	Specifies the number of subordinate objects (for container objects only
Tree Name	Inserts the NDS Tree name

SUMMARY

Schema is that portion of a directory that describes it. Schema describes how the directory can look, what it can do, and how it can do it. Novell has provided NDS with an extremely flexible and extensible schema. This flexibility makes it possible for NDS to be applied to a wide range of applications beyond those envisioned as core directory functionality.

The key to making NDS more accessible and usable is the ability to easily extend the schema to support new types of data and functionality. This is now possible through graphical tools such as ConsoleOne and Netoria ScheMax. These tools give the organization the power to customize NDS to fit their specific needs and ways of doing business. Instead of fitting business processes to the capabilities of the directory, NDS can be customized to best support the most efficient business processes in the organization. The result is increased access to the information and tools necessary to be successful.

For More Information

There is not a lot of information on directory schema in general. However, Novell has some good information on the NDS schema. Some of the best information sources we have found are listed next.

Web Sites

NDS Web site `http://www.novell.com/products/nds/index.html`

NDS Cool Solutions Web site `http://www.novell.com/coolsolutions/nds`

Novell Product Forums `http://support.novell.com/forums/`

Web Articles

NDS Schema Overview `http://developer.novell.com/research/devnotes/1998/october/a6frame.htm`

NDS v8: the Future of Novell Directory Services `http://developer.novell.com/research/appnotes/1999/march/a1frame.htm`

Introduction to NDS v8 `http://developer.novell.com/research/devnotes/1999/march/a1frame.htm`

Technical Information Documents

Novell Technical Services documents specific solutions to customer problems covering the whole range of Novell products. These TIDs, which can be located at `http://support.novell.com/servlet/Knowledgebase`, can be very valuable for learning new concepts as well as troubleshooting existing problems.

Nearly every TID concerning NDS deals with troubleshooting in one way or another. If you need info on a specific error or condition, perform a keyword search in Novell's Knowledgebase specifying the exact error code or message. Some popular schema TIDs include

2942119	Schema Extensions for NDS4NT
2946878	DS Design, Replication, and Partition Strategy
2928015	654 Error in Schema Synchronization

NDS and Directory-Enabled ISP Solutions

One of the areas where NDS has great potential is in products and services that assist *Internet Service Providers* (ISPs) and companies that have remote users. Novell currently offers several products that are well suited for enterprise business remote connectivity. They have recently added features to many of these products that make them extremely well suited for the ISP as well. For example, in addition to NDS Corporate Edition, Novell has created a subset suite called NDS eDirectory, which provides NDS eDirectory functioning for businesses interested in leveraging the power of NDS performance. This is good timing because the Internet service market is growing at a phenomenal rate in both business and consumer markets, with sales estimated at $40 billion by 2002. There is also fierce competition between the ISPs for customers. To be successful, ISPs must provide superior connection service and unique value-added services such as *calendaring*, on-demand software leasing, virtual private networks, profiling, and service level agreements.

NDS eDirectory is the only cross-platform e-directory. With NDS eDirectory, you can integrate existing network infrastructure and accelerate the deployment of e-business solutions. With support for policies and digital communities, NDS enables you to build secure relationships with customers and business partners in order to grant them access to private and highly customized data. NDS also allows Web services and e-business applications to store and execute policies that personalize and customize the e-business experience.

NDS and the power of the Directory are perfectly poised to help both ISPs and enterprise businesses connect to users securely, efficiently, and profitably. Whether you are the administrator of a company that needs to connect to its remote users and set up web sites for your company, or you administer an ISP that has thousands of subscribers who want on-demand software leasing and advanced email capabilities, it is possible with NDS. NDS can provide all these services with only one database to manage—the NDS Directory—instead of one directory for each of the following: remote connectivity, sales, on-demand software ordering, and intranet connectivity. This chapter describes several NDS-enabled products and how they work to gain the best from the Internet age.

NDS Benefits for the Internet and Access

Users want solutions that are powerful and flexible. They are looking for intelligent application and network services that extend the functionality of their Internet service right to their desktop. Also, they want easy access to the resources and services they have contracted for. ISPs must provide highly integrated services with superior security and performance. However, these services must be at a cost that ISPs can afford. Through NDS eDirectory Suite and NDS Corporate Edition, Novell is providing solutions that help ISPs compete in today's markets and in markets of tomorrow. These solutions allow you to build a common platform for management infrastructure for all advanced services, while providing additional value-added services not offered by the competition. Here's just a short explanation of the benefits provided by NDS.

Best-of-Breed

One of the biggest problems all companies face is the choice of which operating system to use. Different operating systems have different strengths and limiting a company to one is a difficult choice—especially when it comes to providing Internet access and remote connectivity. In order to be competitive, you must be able choose the best products, independent of the platforms on which they operate. If you want the best products for each service, this often has means you must implement several different databases for email, security and authentication (RADIUS), public LDAP directories for portal services, e-commerce, DNS, and many other applications. NDS provides you with the ability to use what works for you—there is no need to choose one platform for all services. NDS enables the consolidation of this information into a single LDAP database, regardless of the platform the databases reside on. Instead of managing multiple directories in order to provide the best services to customers, you manage one NDS directory.

Directory-Enabled Management of Servers and Routers

In addition to supporting multiple server operation systems, NDS provides the ability to use policy-based management of routers and switch technology from vendors such as CISCO, Nortel, and Lucent Technologies. This gives you the ability to control access to the Internet. Because people and businesses depend on you for access to the Internet, they want to know that they are getting what they need. This has led to the rise in service agreements or bandwidth agreements where businesses pay more to make sure that they have a specific level of coverage. There are even companies that businesses can pay to verify that you are providing the level of access they are paying for even when the next big news story happens. These businesses want to be able to access CNN events, such as when John Glenn went into space or the verdict in the O.J. Simpson trial was released.

With NDS, you can track and ensure that customers are receiving the dedicated bandwidth they pay for. You can also use the directory to limit the bandwidth for possible SPAM messages to keep them from clogging your e-mail system.

Multimaster, Hierarchical Database

With the emphasis these days on networking and access to the Internet, servers have been taxed with extra workloads. It is important to ensure that users' data and access are always available to them and do not suffer because of the additional workload. NDS uses a multimaster replication model instead of a master-slave model. If a server on the network goes down, another server becomes the new master and handles directory requests dynamically-and seamlessly, to users. This replication model increases the network's reliability and enables construction of a system where server failure, server maintenance, or a temporary loss of a communications link will not affect users. Because NDS has such powerful replication, the network has unlimited scalability.

Dynamic User Profiles

The key to Novell's strategy for delivering the highest level of integration is the management of system-wide profiles through NDS. Profiles are a powerful tool for centralizing and utilizing all the information about users. For instance, user profiles can contain all of the user's customer record data, all of the access rights to any service or resource in the network, any network restrictions, address information, and even data used by the specific resources or services in support of the user. Likewise, NDS can support profiles for resources and services as well.

Leveraging these identity profiles results in dramatic service improvements. You can implement capabilities like customer self-management or service elements that interact with each other to perform a task on behalf of the user. As you do so, you will have a working knowledge of the para-

Figure 13-1
What digitalme
might look like
for end users.

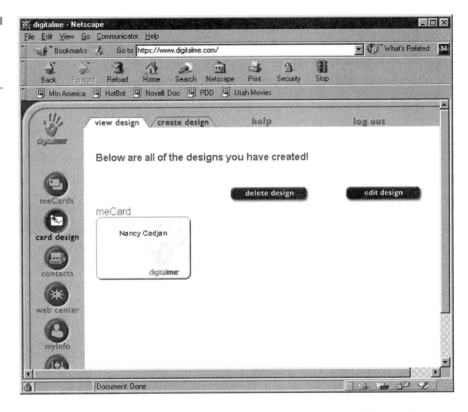

meters that define the service that the user has contracted for. In the near future, profiles will allow users to take advantage of expanded features such as digitalme, an electronic Web profiling tool that allows organizations to customize the information they provide to Web sites (see Figure 13-1).

Through NDS, Novell has embarked upon creating a profile-based solution that helps your customers not only determine and preserve their identity on the Internet, but also control and manage who gets to see the elements that make up their identity. With digitalme, users can fill in their personal information at one time and in one place and manage that information in a secure way. Users can share personal information with family members or online loan officers, and in the next moment, surf the Web anonymously. Customers can control who sees their information and when.

Digitalme leverages the power of NDS to simplify Web shopping. It not only works at sites that are digitalme-enabled; if a site is not enabled, digitalme will take its best guess at filling out the registration forms. According to Novell, online users must remember an average of four passwords, and almost no Web users remember to notify Web sites when their personal information such as e-mail addresses changes. That leaves a lot of unusable information in company databases.

Several software vendors are supporting the digitalme effort, including Compaq, Intel, AOL, ClickMarks, EZ Login, Facetime Communications, Just On, Knowledge Navigators, Privaseek, Verisign, and White Pine. In addition, AOL has introduced instantme, a new communications tool that allows digitalme users to send instant messages to people listed on their digitalme dynamic address book and to AOL Instant Messenger users. Verisign provides security for digitalme with its digital certificate, which authenticates digitalme members cards and helps integrate the databases of different companies. With digitalme, transactions among different companies can be carried out in the consumer's name without any of the companies involved needing all the consumer's information and without transferring sensitive data over the Internet. This means that true integration can happen securely.

Now that we have explored some of the benefits of using NDS in an ISP context, let's look at some specific products, what features they bring to the ISP, and how they leverage the technologies of NDS.

Single Point of Administration

Although this point has been made before in this book, you cannot stress enough that with one point to administer all servers and databases, NDS provides significant savings in training and administrative costs. With NDS, it's no longer necessary to manage multiple databases at different servers with different interfaces. Even if services and applications reside on different databases, all LDAP-compliant databases can be managed from a single source. To administer the entire network, you can use either NetWare Administrator or ConsoleOne. Even if user information needs to reside in multiple databases for messaging and application use, NDS can manage and synchronize all user and resource information.

Novell Internet Caching System

With the increasing popularity of the Internet and Intranets, the demand for Web access continues to grow. Successful e-business requires high performance, content-rich storefronts to attract new customers. It also requires increased buyer satisfaction and new revenue opportunities. However, many users are experiencing the "World Wide Wait" instead because of the traffic demand. In addition, companies are contending with network bandwidth issues, reliability, and performance degradations due in part to the increased use of the Internet within their organizations.

To address these two issues, Novell has created caching solutions that optimize the performance of intranet and Internet systems and services. *Novell Internet Caching System* (Novell ICS) provides a scalable, plug-and-accelerate solution that is deployed as an Internet appliance and is available in partnership with several Intel architecture-based OEMs. It reduces overall bandwidth consumption while leveraging your existing infrastructure. Novel ICS is managed through NDS, which provides great flexibility and security to your network.

According to Novell, the new Internet caching architecture effectively increases the capacity of any common Web server ten-fold, which allows content publishers, ISPs, and enterprises to deploy high-performance, content-rich Web storefronts. Novell ICS also dramatically improves the speed and efficiency of delivering Internet content to employees, business partners, and customers within corporate intranets, as well as across the Internet. The interface for managing Novell ICS is located in a Web browser so that you can access and manage Novell ICS from anywhere (see Figure 13-2).

Figure 13-2
Novell ICS

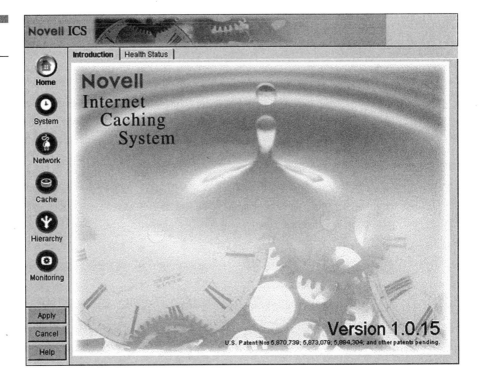

A Web cache stores recently accessed information. This cache is a dedicated computer system within the Internet that monitors Web requests, retrieves them, and then stores them. Subsequent users requesting the same Web sites are served by the local cache instead of the Web site's origin server. The cache eliminates the need to go through multiple hoops on the Internet. By keeping retrieved Web objects closer to the users requesting them, Web caches significantly enhance the speed at which those objects can be accessed and viewed.

Web caching off-loads the demand placed on network. Because the Internet is a series of links, the speed is limited to the speed of the slowest link in that path. If points in the path reach capacity, objects can actually be dropped and need to be retransmitted. This means a lot of extra wait time. A Web site requested in Los Angeles but stored on a Chicago-based server can go through as many as 20 routers. But if there is a cache in Los Angeles, that data need only be transmitted once. Each time that data is subsequently requested, it will be serviced from the cache in Los Angeles. For companies with branch offices or offices overseas, Web caching minimizes the number of requests that must be served via long distance, reducing long-distance transmission charges and the need for larger bandwidth connections. An increase in speed and reliability reflects improved quality of service because there is now a potential for increased employee productivity due to the time saved working on and waiting for the Web.

Novell ICS is an appliance-based solution. Unlike proprietary software caching systems based on various operating systems, caching appliances are simply attached to the network like any other hardware resource such as printers or router boxes. Even though initial cost is higher, these appliances provide better performance because they do not have the inherent OS problems. You can also locate caching appliances at multiple points on the network to increase speed exponentially.

Each appliance serves a specified set of users, groups, or geographies. You can set the type of Web cache configuration depending on what kind of caching is needed. There are three broad categories of caching configurations:

- *Forward Proxy*   Accelerates browser request response times. It require that all users configure their browsers to use the Novell ICS appliance as a proxy server unless Transparent Proxy is also activated. When data is requested and forwarded to a user, all static elements of this accessed Web site are be stored locally on the Novell ICS appliance. When this data is requested again, the request is filled with the data that has been cached locally. Forward Proxy caches can also serve as firewall buffer between the Internet and the network, serving as the contact point between the two systems. This means that only the proxy server need be open to the Internet, thereby securing the network by isolating the network beyond the firewall.

■ *Transparent Cache* Intercepts browser requests transparently and checks to see if the requested file is in the cache. Unlike the Forward Proxy cache, the Transparent Proxy does not require network administrators to explicitly configure each browser to the cache or coordinate the Transparent Cache with other caches on the network. However, Transparent Proxies must operate at the point in the network at which all Internet traffic is guaranteed to pass through. Though it is not difficult to implement, you need a basic knowledge of network routing to effectively place a Transparent Cache.

■ *Reverse Proxy* Accelerates Web server requests. It is placed as the front end to one or more Web servers. The appliance then pretends to be the Web server, and browsers connect to it instead of directly to the Web server. The bulk of the Web service workload is thus offloaded to the cache. The Novell ICS appliance stores the most frequently requested Web objects in RAM, enabling it to respond quickly. Non-cacheable requests are passed through to the Web server, most of the time as fast or faster than if the browser was directly connected.

Novell ICS can be implemented in about 10 minutes within NetWare, UNIX, Cisco, or NT-based Enterprise or ISP networks. They also can be administered from any location via standard management interfaces (Browser, Telnet, FTP, and Serial Connection). Novell ICS also supports SNMP for integration into management consoles. Additionally, Novell ICS includes support for URL filtering and blocking, browser-based monitoring, and logging of usage data and statistics.

Novell Internet Messaging Services

Novell Internet Messaging System (NIMS) lets you provide customized services and unprecedented availability. Because NIMS is backed by NDS, it's possible to give users more freedom to manage their own mail accounts. They will be able to

■ Change passwords

■ Set up proxy mail accounts

■ Specify their own forwarding rules and auto-reply notices

■ Choose language settings

■ Route all messages from multiple email accounts and multiple ISPs to a single NIMS mailbox

NIMS gives customers control over their accounts and freedom from the constraints of ISPs that don't have the technology or support staff to offer customers what they want (see Figure 13-3). You also can provide more third-party directory-enabled services such as calendaring, scheduling, faxing, and paging. NIMS and NDS can help you retain and build your customer base, while billing for new services that the competition can't offer.

Although it is not the most beautiful messaging service on the market, Novell Internet Messaging Services has one thing going for it—NDS. Because it is integrated with NDS, it offers a high degree of security, including

■ *SSL* Server-to-client communications (such as IMAP4) can be encrypted using SSL technology. This lets you maximize the encryption technology by using 56-bit or 128-bit keys to encrypt your communication packets between server and client.

■ *Authenticated SMTP* Users wishing to send email must first receive authentication from NDS or an LDAP directory service.

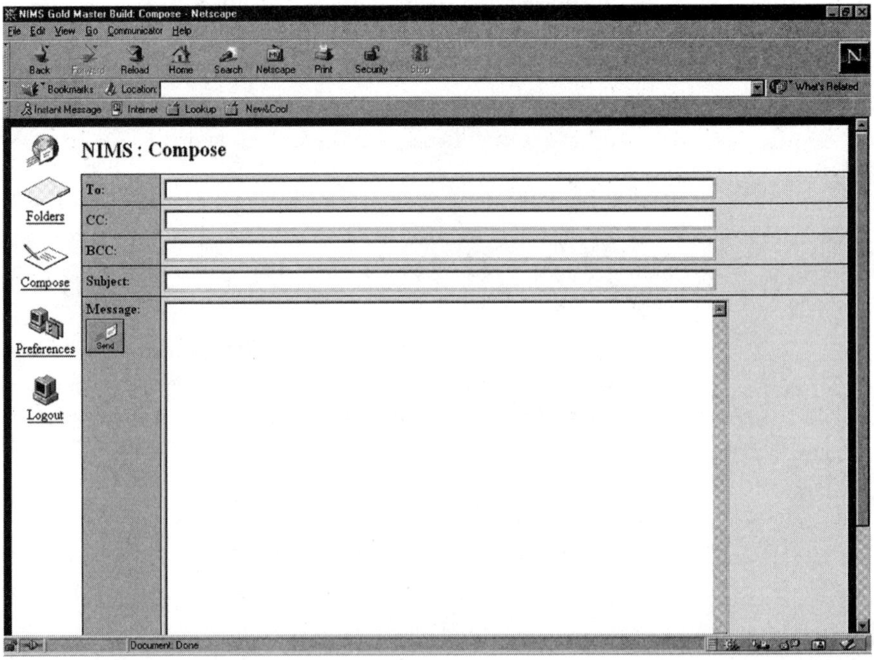

Figure 13-3
Novell Internet
Messaging Systems

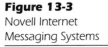

- *S/MIME*   You can send and receive encrypted mail via S/MIME, which uses the same certificates (security keys) used in encrypting client-to-server communications to encrypt electronic messages.

- *Digital signatures*   Messages may contain digital signatures, which allow you to validate the author's identity.

- *S/KEY*   NIMS supports S/KEY (RFC1760) for simple challenge-response authentication between client and server. Although this is not as robust as the SSL technology, it provides a less expensive way to prevent passwords from being detected because it does not require a user certificate.

- *Client certificates*   User certificates (X.509 v3) are supported for user authentication and server login.

- *Encrypted administration*   Includes SSL support for administration, so that user and system forms are fully encrypted at all times.

In addition to these features, NIMS supports a broad range of industry standard protocols and features including SNMP, IMAP4 over SSL, IMAP4 rev 1, message quotas for IMAP4 and POP3, NMAP, delivery status notification, and anti-spam black-out lists. Also, its tight integration with NDS makes management simple and efficient because you don't have to keep a separate directory for email user account information.

Novell On-Demand Software Solution

With the emergence and affordability of broadband technologies such as *Digital Subscriber Line* (xDSL), wireless, and cable, one of the hottest new opportunities for ISPs is software leasing. By 2003, it is estimated that software leasing will be a $6 billion industry (that's almost 1/3 of the application outsourcing market). But how do you get into this lucrative market? NDS makes it easy to deliver software to your customers on demand while making it easy to track and bill for these services (see Figure 13-4).

Through NDS and Novell On-Demand, you can distribute, manage, and bill subscribers for their use of electronic content. Business and home users can gain access to the latest applications and emerging technologies for specific needs and limited-term use. For example, you can provide tax software to customers during tax time, ensuring that they have the latest up-to-date

Figure 13-4
An on-demand Web
site where users can
access software

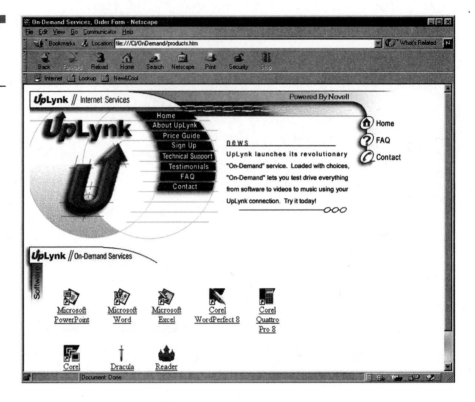

software without the high cost of purchasing the software for a one-time use. Developers and resellers can provide a trial period before customers purchase services.

By leveraging NDS, On-Demand provides secure and easy management of applications, content, and users, without adding additional administrative overhead. Novell On-Demand allows you to provide

- Web-based authentication through Novell's strong security and authentication (discussed in Chapter 6, "Controlling Network Access")

- Application usage tracking through NDS and NetWare Administrator

- Secure electronic billing in conjunction with credit card clearing houses such as Authorize.Net and CyberSource

- Multiuser management within a business or household various users can be differentiated

- User access and budget management

- CD-ROM emulator for applications that require a CD

On-Demand requires high-bandwidth access (such as ADSL, wireless, or cable modem) to the ISP, so it is not for most homeowners yet. But as the telecommunications and cable companies provide access through cable lines, many households will be able to access these services. The use of high-bandwidth connections allows clients to access resources from a service provider at speeds similar to those of a workstation that accesses network resources in a local or wide area network. For wireless providers, the server is typically placed on an Ethernet or ATM backbone in leased collocation space with an ILEC, CLEC, or IXC where DS-1, DS-3, or OC-x connectivity can be terminated. In the cable environment, an On-Demand server is connected to the network where signals from various sources (including broadcast transmissions, satellite-delivered programming, and local television) are received, processed, and then retransmitted through coaxial cable to customers' homes.

Novell On-Demand is a suite of network applications that runs on one or more Novell NetWare 5 servers and the client workstations that access them. On-Demand uses the power of NDS to store information about the hardware and software resources available on the network. User accounts are tracked through NDS. The On-Demand Suite also uses ZENworks (discussed in Chapter 7) to distribute and meter these applications (see Figure 13-6).

Figure 13-5

Making an Application object leasable

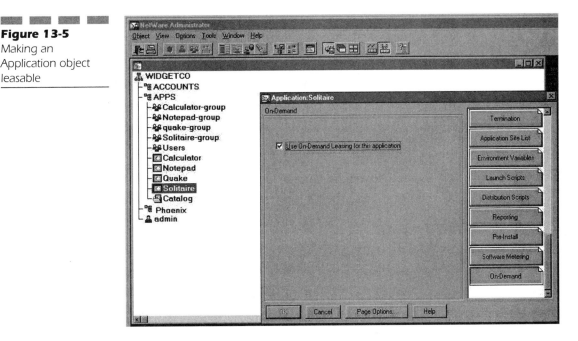

Figure 13-6
Installing Software
Metering as a part
of the ZENworks
installation

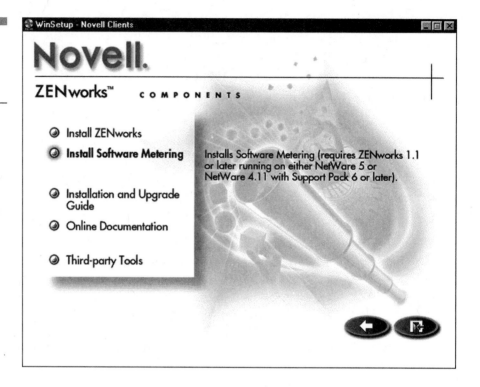

Novell Application Launcher (NAL), a component of ZENworks, lets you associate or assign Application objects to users or groups of users. After users are authenticated through NDS, NAL launches the application(s) on the client.

On-Demand also includes the Oracle8 database that maintains application and client usage information, such as applications available to users, rates and terms for each application, which users have leased each application, lease status of each application, and the lease status of each user. On-Demand provides standard e-commerce functions such as support for payment through credit card. Billing information stored in the Oracle 8 database can be migrated to your existing financial system using an open architecture gateway.

If you already have set up an ISP, you can extend this service to your current customers and attract new customers who are looking for more than just traditional Internet services. If you are setting up a new ISP, this is a service that would set you apart from others. By providing this service, you allow businesses to manage software costs while ensuring that the required number of application licenses are available to maximize productivity.

Netscape Enterprise Server

Many customers are looking for Web hosting and design services. They want to deal with one company that provides access, applications, and Web page services. Netscape Enterprise Server for NetWare is a high-performance Web and application server software. It provides advanced Web publishing capabilities through Web Publisher and offers full indexing and search functions. Intelligent agents in Enterprise Server automatically deliver information to you or others according to rules you specify. Agents then notify users when documents are modified. This allows users with multiple Web sites to receive important information without having to search for it.

Netscape Enterprise Server for NetWare is tightly integrated with NDS, enabling you to manage your system from a single location through one NDS-based directory interface. You can also manage multiple servers simultaneously (cluster management) and delegate certain administrative tasks to others without giving them the authority to administer all aspects of the servers.

BorderManager, Enterprise Edition

BorderManager, Enterprise Edition provides Internet security management by leveraging the power of NDS to provide single sign-on across network services and security policy enforcement transparent. This security works both within the enterprise and between the enterprise and the Internet. It also includes features that provide security protection for companies extending their business as well as secure access to the Internet and Web for an increasingly mobile workforce. For example, with the help of NDS, it allows the use of smart cards and tokens to manage secure passwords and identify users who access the network regardless of their sign-on location. If you have employees who travel often, this makes it easy for these users to access the network while still ensuring that corporate information cannot be accessed or altered by unauthorized parties. These options are open to you if you have a NetWare server in your network. With NDS-based policy management, security administration can be lowered by up to 70 percent.

BorderManager Firewall Services

At the heart of BorderManager is BorderManager Firewall Services, which provides ISPs with NDS-based security policy management for protecting confidential data and managing user access to Internet and Intranet content. BorderManager firewalls can be used to partition the corporate intranet into secure segments to protect sensitive information from internal break-in while allowing you to control incoming and outgoing access from and to the Internet. It implements access control components at all layers of the *Open Standards Interconnection* (OSI) model including

- *Application Proxies*   HTTP, FTP, Gopher, Mail, News, Real Audio / Video, DNS, and a generic TCP and UDP proxy to allow administrators to configure additional application proxies such as LDAP (see Figure 13-7).

- *Circuit Gateways*   A SOCKS gateway and the Novell IP Gateway

- *Network Address Translation*   Dynamic and static IP and IPX network address translation tables you configure with public sets of IP addresses. This address translation hides the addresses of the internal network from the outside world and relieves you from the time-consuming task of managing IP addresses.

- *Packet Filter*   Checks source and destination host IP address to restrict access to and from certain IP hosts; source and destination

Figure 13-7
The Application Proxy Setup in NetWare Administrator

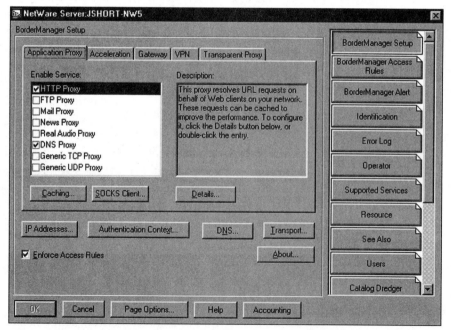

Figure 13-8
BorderManager
Access Rules Setup
in NetWare
Administrator

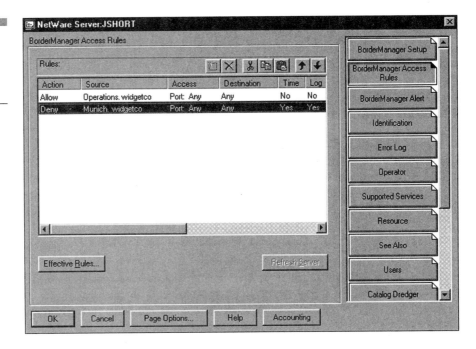

IPX addresses to restrict access to and from certain IPX hosts; IP protocol/port to restrict access to certain Internet protocols and ports, such as HTTP, FTP, Telnet, and Gopher; and IPX Protocol to restrict access to certain types of *NetWare Core Protocol* (NCP) requests.

The real power of NDS and BorderManager is that you no longer have to manage a separate database of users for access to the Internet or to other company locations (see Figure 13-8). You can manage access easily through NetWare Administrator and set up rules allowing you to restrict access to certain hours, addresses, and so forth for specific groups or organizational units. With other systems, you would have to keep this information in a separate database that would have to be managed outside of the normal user object information.

BorderManager Virtual Private Networking Services

In addition to the firewall, BorderManager *Virtual Private Networking* (VPN) Services delivers a cost-effective method for ISPs to offer virtual private network services to their customers in need of access to confidential data over the Internet and increased internal security. Because of the growth in business's reliance on networking, many companies are contracting with ISPs for networking services between their local area networks. This way, they can achieve closer interaction with employees through internal Web servers, with customers through the Internet, and with business partners through extranets at a lower cost.

However, no company is willing to surrender their data to unsecured connections—no matter how low the cost. The Internet is notoriously unsecure. As a result, integrating a corporate network with the Internet exposes it to intrusion from the outside. To provide protection, a number of vendors provide firewalls, which form a protective barrier between the Internet and the corporate network. There is a more severe and more subtle security problem, however, that is more difficult to deal with than Internet hackers. Deploying Internet technologies such as internal Web servers on a corporate network exposes the information stored on them to intruders from within the company. In this case, an Internet firewall provides no protection. VPN Services eliminate a company's need for expensive leased lines or privately owned communication channels without giving up security. Authorized users can enjoy the security of a variety of standard tunneling, encryption, and key exchange mechanisms, including IP SEC, SKIP, RC2, RC5, DES, and 3DES.

Because BorderManager is integrated with NDS, network administrators can control security and access globally from a single, centralized point. As discussed earlier in Chapter 6, security management through NDS allows you to delegate certain access management responsibilities in a controlled and secure manner. Because all authentication is performed through NDS, you do not have to maintain multiple databases for access control and security. In addition, with a single sign-on through NDS, users can access all network resources to which they are authorized, regardless of their network entry point or the location of the resources. They can sign-on from a workstation directly connected to the LAN, from a dial-up LAN workstation, or from a remote VPN client over the Internet (see Figure 13-9).

BorderManager VPN supports *symmetric multiprocessing* (SMP), allowing it to take advantage of multiprocessing hardware to increase speed. It also performs selective encryption, which encrypts only the information sent to and from protected networks as specified by the administrator. It supports a variety of standard tunneling, encryption, and key exchange mechanisms to provide a strong, flexible security framework. It supports tunneling based on the field-proven IP relay mechanism using the IP SEC standard (RFC # 1825-1828). It supports the RC2, RC5, DES, and 3DES encryption algorithms. And it supports the *simple key exchange Internet protocol* (SKIP) standard to allow secure distribution of authentication

Figure 13-9
BorderManager VPN
Setup in NetWare
Administrator

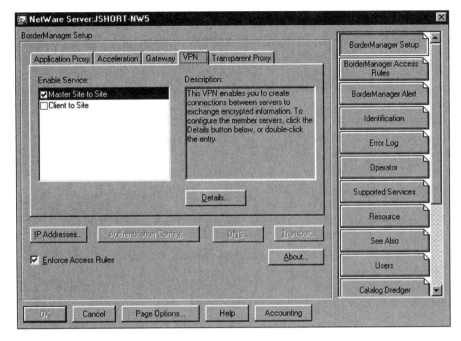

keys. Because it is managed through NDS, you can manage one or more VPNs from a single, centralized point.

BorderManager Authentication Services (BMAS)

BorderManager Authentication Services (BMAS) combines the remote access security allowed by the *Remote Authentication Dial-In User Service* (RADIUS) protocol with the ease and convenience of NDS. BMAS enables remote users to log in to the network over the Internet using only a single password and have access to all their network resources, including applications, files, printers, services, and other network resources. Users can access the network through Novell IP Gateway, a Web browser, a VPN client, or BMAS and RADIUS—all with the same levels of security because all users are authenticated through NDS. This means users have to remember only a single user ID and password—increasing security because users don't need to write passwords down.

Because authentication takes place through NDS, you can manage all access from a single, centralized point. So, you can immediately remove a terminated employee from the network by simply removing that employee's user object from NDS. You don't need to remove the user separately from each server or domain, a time-intensive and error-prone task that could result in the employee retaining access rights to sensitive information long after he is terminated. BorderManager also makes use of all recording and security tracking features of NDS to make sure that the space between your network and the world is guarded. Having the power of NDS security at the border is very important. Chapter 6 provides greater detail in the types of security and recording NDS provides.

SUMMARY

In many ways, NDS has come to the aid of the emerging or existing ISP. NDS provides a solid directory solution to the confusion in the ISP territory while offering value-added advantages that other directories don't. Even though there are other directories in the ISP space, NDS is the one with the longest track record and the largest, most reliable database. With the additional products Novell is developing and with their continued commitment to the ISP market, Novell will continue to innovate in this market space and provide additional services and options that will help you manage the ISP.

For More Information

Here are some additional resources for information on products and solutions that Novell offers for ISPs. Novell has more plans in the future, so you should keep looking for their directions and new product mixes.

Web Sites

Novell ISP Solutions Web site `http://www.novell.com/solutions/isp/`

Case Studies on companies using Novell's ISP solutions `http://www.novell.com/solutions/isp/case_studies.html`

Novell Internet Caching System Web site `http://www.novell.com/products/nics/`

BorderManager Enterprise Edition Web site `http://www.novell.com/bordermanager/`

Novell Internet Messaging Services Web site `http://www.novell.com/catalog/qr/sne34430.html`

Novell On-Demand Web site `http://consulting.novell.com`

digitalme Website `http://www.digitalme.com`

APPENDIX A

The following list contains a set of login script conventions and identifier variables you can use to create login scripts for Novell Clients. It also contains a list of login script commands by the type of tasks the commands perform.

Login Script Conventions

When creating login scripts, you must follow certain conventions. These conventions are listed here.

- *Minimum Login Script*   There is no minimum. You may not have login scripts, and all types of login scripts are optional. Login scripts can vary in length from one line to many lines and can be quite complex. There are no required commands.

- *Case*   You can use either uppercase or lowercase when writing login scripts, although there is one exception to this rule. Identifier variables enclosed in guotation marks and preceded by a percent sign (%) must be uppercase.

- *Characters per line*   You can have a maximum of 512 characters per line, including any variables after they are replaced by their values. However, 78 characters per line is recommended for readability.

- *Punctuation and symbols*   You must type all symbols (#, %, ", _) and punctuation exactly as shown in examples and syntax.

- *Commands per line*   You should start each command on a new line, using one line per command. Note that lines which wrap automatically are considered one command.

- *Sequence of commands*   You should enter commands in the order you want them to execute. If you use # (or @) to execute an external program, the command must follow any necessary MAP commands. If sequence is not important, group similar commands, such as the MAP and WRITE commands, together to make the login script easier to read.

- *Blank lines*   Blank lines don't affect login script execution. You can use them to visually separate groups of commands.

- *Remarks (REMARK, REM, asterisks, and semicolons)*   As with all scripts, lines beginning with REMARK, REM, an asterisk, or a semicolon are comments, and are not displayed when the login script executes. You can use remarks to record the purpose of each command or group of commands or to temporarily keep certain lines from executing.

■ *Identifier Variables*   Identifier variables enable you to replace the variable with specific information, such as a user's last name or the workstation's operating system. This makes the login script more flexible. When the login script executes, it substitutes real values for the identifier variables. By using the variable, you can make the same login script command applicable to multiple users. More information on identifier variables appears later in this appendix.

■ *NDS Attributes*   Any NDS attribute value can be read from a login script. This includes extended names. The login utility does not store the Novell names, but it takes the attribute name and tries to read it. The syntax for acessing NDS attributes is identical to common script variables with a few exceptions.

1. If the name contains a space, you can replace it with an underscore (_).
2. The NDS attribute must be at the end of the string.
3. If multiple variables are required as in a WRITE statement, they must be in separate strings.
4. You must use the actual NDS attribute value names. You cannot use localized names or nicknames.
5. You must have Read rights to read the value of objects other than values associated with your own.

■ *NDS Attribute Values*   Any NDS attribute value can be read from a login script, including extended names. The syntax for accessing NDS attributes is identical to common script variables with a few exceptions. The NDS attribute must be at the end of the string. If multiple variables are required, they must be in separate strings. And, you must use the actual NDS attribute value names. You cannot use localized names or nicknames. Make sure that you have Read rights to read the value of objects other than values associated with your own User object. Finally, if the name contains a space, you can replace it with an underscore (_), but it is not required.

■ *NDS Object Mappings*   NDS objects, such as cluster-enabled volumes, can be mapped in the login script using the object's fully distinguised name and context preceeded by a leading dot (.). To map to a cluster-enabled volume, you would use the following syntax: `MAP N:= .<NDS object's fully distinguished name including context>` such as `MAP N:=_.clust2_vol1.tokyo.widgetco`.

Login Script Commands for Network Connection and Access to Resources

ATTACH

ATTACH establishes a connection between a workstation and a NetWare server. If the server is not in the current tree, a bindery connection is made. This is required mostly for NetWare 3 servers. NetWare 4 and 5 servers no longer need to attach separately to multiple servers and do not need to use the ATTACH command. If users want to connect to multiple trees, they use the TREE command. If users are trying to create persistent drive mappings, they use the MAPcommand.

CONTEXT

CONTEXT sets a user's current context in the NDS tree. Type

```
CONTEXT context
```

To change the current NDS context, replace *context* with the context you want the user to see after login. To change the context to the Organizational Unit CHICAGO, under the Organization Unit WIDGET_CO, add the following line to the login script:

```
CONTEXT .CHICAGO.WIDGET_CO.
```

You can also type a single period instead of a container name to indicate that you want to move up one level. For example, if you are in the context CHICAGO.WIDGET_CO and you want to move up one level to the context WIDGET_CO, type

```
CONTEXT .
```

to the login script. To move up two levels, enter two periods.

DRIVE

DRIVE changes the default drive while the login script is executing. If this command is not included in the login script, the default drive will be set to the first network drive, which is often assigned to the user's home directory. If you don't want the default drive to be the first network drive, map a drive in the login script to the directory you want to be the default; then use the DRIVE command to change the default drive.

Instead of specifying a drive letter, such as F: or G:, you can use an asterisk followed by a number *n* to represent the *n*th network drive (for example, *3). This allows drive letters to reorder themselves automatically if previous drive mappings are deleted or added.

```
DRIVE [drive |*n]
```

Replace the drive with a local or network drive letter, or replace *n* with a drive number. The use of either is dependent on their previously assigned value within the login script.

MAP

MAP maps drives and search drives to network directories. If you use MAP to create drive map assignments, users don't have to map drives every time they log in. If you do not want the result of each mapping to be displayed as it is executed, add the MAP DISPLAY OFF command at the beginning of the login script. When all drive map assignments have been completed, add the line MAP DISPLAY ON and MAP to your login script. This sequence provides a cleaner display for users as they log in.

Instead of specifying drive letters such as F: or G:, you could use an asterisk followed by a number *n* to represent the *n*th network drive. For example, if the first network drive is F:, then using MAP *3 : = would assign H: {1 2 3 = F G H}. Or, if the first network drive is D:, then using MAP *4 : = would assign G: {1 2 3 4 = D E F G}.

This action enables drive letters to reorder themselves automatically when local drives are removed or added or when the first network drive is changed. It also enables users to log in from workstations with a different number of local drives than their regular workstation. Do not map a drive, such as a CD-ROM drive, to a network drive. Use the following syntax:

```
MAP [[options] | [parameters] [drive:=path]
```

Replace drive with any valid network drive letter, local drive letter, or search drive number.

Replace *path* with either a drive letter, a full directory path, or a Directory Map object. When mapping a drive to a directory on an NDS server, begin the path with either the Volume object name or server\volume. More than one command can be on the map line if the commands are separated by a semicolon (;):

```
MAP *1:=SYS:PUBLIC;*2:=SYS:PUBLIC\DOS
```

Replace *options* with either DISPLAY ON|OFF or ERRORS ON|OF. DISPLAY ON|OFF determines whether drive mappings are displayed on the screen when the user logs in. The default setting is ON. ERRORS ON|OFF determines whether MAP error messages are displayed when the user logs in. MAP ERROR OFF must be placed before MAP commands in the login script. The default setting is ON.

Replace *parameter* with one of the following:

- *INS*   Inserts a drive mapping between existing search mappings
- *DEL*   Deletes a drive mapping, making that drive letter available for other mapping assignments
- *ROOT or R*   Maps a fake root. Windows NT is always mapped to the root. Some applications require their executable files to be located in a root directory. Because you might not want users to have rights at the root directory, you can map a fake root to a subdirectory instead. The Windows NT native environment forces a map root on all drives. To prevent a forced map root in a Windows NT environment, set the `MAP ROOT OFF = 1` environment variable. All drives are then mapped as specified, and only explicit map root drives are rooted.
- *C (CHANGE)*   Changes a search drive mapping to a regular mapping, or a regular mapping to a search drive mapping
- *P (PHYSICAL)*   Maps a drive to the physical volume of a server, rather than to the Volume object's name because a Volume object name might conflict with a physical volume name. (For example, object ACCT is an Accounting volume, but there is also an ACCT which is a physical volume.) Therefore, if you prefer to map a drive to the physical volume name, use MAP P.
- *N (NEXT)*   When used without specifying a drive number or letter, maps the next available drive

TREE

The TREE command is used to attach to another NDS tree within the network and to access its resources. The TREE command changes the *focus* of the login script so that all NDS object references in subsequent script commands (for drive mappings, print captures, etc.) apply to the

NDS tree specified in the TREE command. You can include multiple TREE commands within a login script, either to attach to additional trees or to switch the login script's *focus* back to a tree that the user is already attached to. Use the following syntax:

```
TREE tree_name[/complete_name]
```

Replace *tree_name* with the name of the NDS tree that you want the user to attach to.

Replace *complete_name* with the user's complete name (Distinguished Name) for the NDS tree that the user is attaching to. The complete name establishes the user's context in the tree. If you do not include the complete name, the user is prompted for a complete name when the TREE command is executed from the login script.

When the TREE command is executed, the user is prompted for the password.

Login Script Commands for Login Script Execution

BREAK

BREAK ON allows the user to terminate a login script. The default is BREAK OFF. If BREAK ON is included in a login script, the user can press Ctrl+C or Ctrl+Break to abort the normal execution of the login script.

FIRE or FIRE PHASERS

FIRE or FIRE PHASERS emits a phaser sound by playing the phasers.wav sound file. Use FIRE or FIRE PHASERS with the IF...THEN command to make the sound execute a different number of times depending on the circumstances of the login. Use the following syntax:

```
FIRE n soundfile
```

Replace *n* with the number of times you want this sound to occur.

Replace *soundfile* with the name of the sound file you want to play when this command is executed. (The sound file variable cannot be used on DOS workstations.) You can use any .WAV or platform-compatible sound file. For example

```
FIRE 3 RIFLE.WAV
```

To use a variable as the number of times to fire, use % before the variable, as follows:

```
FIRE %variable
```

For more information about using variables, see Identifier Variables.

IF . . . THEN

IF . . . THEN performs an action only under certain conditions. An example of a conditional statement is

```
IF MEMBER OF "OPERATIONS" THEN
```

In this statement, some action is performed if the user who logged in belongs to the Group object named OPERATIONS. Or, you might use the next example:

```
IF DAY_OF_WEEK="MONDAY"
```

In this statement, the equal sign (=) indicates the relationship between the variable (DAY_OF_WEEK) and its value (Monday). Note that the value (Monday) is inside quotation marks.

When using IF . . . THEN statements, you can use AND or OR to include two or more conditionals in an IF . . . THEN statement. Also, values of conditional statements must be enclosed in quotation marks. Finally, values of conditional statements are compared with the assumption that the values are characters, not numeric values. The value of 21, therefore, would be considered greater than the value of 100 when comparing these two characters. To ensure that the system properly calculates numeric values instead of character values, use the VALUE modifier in the IF . . . THEN statement.

The ELSE statement is optional. IF, ELSE, and END must be on separate lines. THEN does not need to be on a separate line. If you include a WRITE command as part of the IF . . . THEN command, the WRITE command must be on a separate line.

In addition, IF . . . THEN statements can be nested (up to 10 levels). If your IF . . . THEN statement consists of only one line, you do not need to include END even if that line wraps. If your IF . . . THEN statement must be on more than one line (for example, if you used ELSE or WRITE, which must be on separate lines), you must include END.

Six relationships are possible between the elements of an IF . . . THEN statement. Represent these relationships with the following symbols:

=	Equals
< >	Does not equal
>	Is greater than
>=	Is greater than or equal to
<	Is less than
<=	Is less than or equal to

When using IF . . . THEN statements, use the following syntax:

```
IF conditional [AND|OR [conditional]] THEN
commands
[ELSE
command]
[END]
```

Replace *conditional* with identifier variables. Replace *commands* with any login script commands that you want to be executed if the specified condition is true. For example, if you place the following command in a login script, the message Status report is due today appears when the user logs in on Friday, and Have a nice day! appears on other days:

```
IF DAY_OF_WEEK="FRIDAY" THEN
   WRITE "Status report is due today."
ELSE
   WRITE "Have a nice day!"
END
```

You can also nest IF . . . THEN statements. Notice that there are two IF statements, so each one must have its own END statement:

```
IF DAY_OF_WEEK="FRIDAY" THEN
   WRITE "Status report is due today."
   IF MEMBER OF OPERATIONS THEN
      WRITE "Your report is due immediately!"
   END
END
```

Conditionals can be joined with commas, the word AND, or the word OR to form compound conditionals. The first line of the following IF . . . THEN statement is a compound conditional that means *If it is the evening of the first day of the month*:

```
IF GREETING_TIME="EVENING" AND DAY="01" THEN
   WRITE "The system will be backed up tonight."
END
```

An IF . . . THEN statement can include several commands that must be executed if the conditional is true.

The following example shows two commands that are executed on Tuesdays: a WRITE command that displays a message about a staff meeting and an INCLUDE command that tells the login script to process any commands or messages contained in the file SYS:PUBLIC\UPDATE.TXT.

```
IF DAY_OF_WEEK="TUESDAY" THEN
   WRITE "Staff meeting today at 10 a.m."
   INCLUDE SYS:PUBLIC\UPDATE.TXT
END
```

INCLUDE

INCLUDE executes independent files or another object's login script as a part of the login script currently being processed. These items can be text files that contain valid login script commands (any of the commands explained in this section) or login scripts that belong to a different object to which you have rights. Text files that contain login script commands and other objects' login scripts can be used as subscripts. Subscripts do not have to have any particular filenames or extensions.

The INCLUDE command executes the login script commands contained in the subscript. It does not display the text of the subscripts. If the subscript is a text file, users must have at least File Scan and Read rights to the directory containing the subscript. If you are using another object's login script as a subscript, users must have the Browse right to the object whose script you are including and the Read right to the object's Login Script property.

```
INCLUDE [path] filename
```

or

```
INCLUDE object_name
```

Replace *path* with either a drive letter or a full directory path beginning with the NetWare volume nameor use a text file as a subscript. Replace *filename* with the complete name (including the extension) of the text file. See the example in the IF . . . THEN section.

You can also replace *object_name* with the name of the object whose login script you want to use.

NO_DEFAULT

NO_DEFAULT in a container or profile login script indicates that you do not want to create any user login scripts, nor do you want the default user login script to run, when this command is added to either the container or the profile login script. If you have created a user login script for someone, that login script executes whether or not the NO_DEFAULT command is in the container or profile login script.

PAUSE

PAUSE creates a pause in the execution of the login script. You can add PAUSE to the login script following a message so that the user has time to read the message before it scrolls off the screen. If you include PAUSE, the message `Strike any key when ready . . .` appears on the workstation screen. NetWare Login then waits for a key to be pressed before it executes the rest of the login script.

PROFILE

PROFILE in a container script overrides a user's assigned or command line-specified profile script. It is useful when defining a group profile. Use the following syntax:

```
PROFILE profile_object_name
```

Replace *profile object name* with the name of the profile you want to override the profile script that was assigned to a user.

Login Script Commands for Workstation Environment

SET

SET sets an environment variable to a specified value. When you use SET in a login script, you must enter quotation marks (" ") around the values. SET commands do not have to be included in login scripts. For example, you might decide to place some SET commands in the workstation's `autoexec.bat` file. Where you use SET commands depends upon your individual needs.

NOTE: *If a variable is set to a path that ends in a \ ", these two characters are interpreted as an embedded quote preceded by an escape character. To avoid this problem, use two backslashes before the ending double quotes (\ \ ").*

After you use the SET command to set a value for an environment variable, you can use that variable in other login script commands. To include an environment variable as an identifier variable in a command, enclose the name of the variable in angle brackets (for example, <emailuser>). Use the following syntax:

```
[TEMP] SET name="value"
```

Replace *name* with an environment parameter that identifies the environment you want to change. Replace *value* with the identifier variable substitutions. Values must be enclosed in quotation marks.

To change the environment for the login script, but not for the workstation itself after the login script has finished executing, use the optional keyword TEMP.

SET_TIME

SET_TIME sets the workstation time equal to the time on the NetWare server to which the workstation first connects. If you include SET_TIME OFF in the login script, the workstation time does not update to the server's time.

Login Script Commands for Text File Usage

#

The # symbol executes a program that is external to the login script and waits until it is finished running before continuing with other login script commands. Use the @ command instead of the # command to run an external program from a login script if that external program will remain open for any length of time. Otherwise, the login script will remain open until that external program is closed. (Login scripts cannot be edited when they are held open.) Use the following syntax:

```
# [path] filename [parameter]
```

Replace *path* with a drive letter. Replace *filename* with an executable file (files that end in EXE, COM, or BAT, for example). It isn't necessary to include the extension, but doing so can speed up the execution of the external program. Replace *parameter* with any parameters that must accompany the executable file.

@

The @ command executes a program that is external to the login script and continues with the script (similar to the Startup group). Use the @ command instead of the # command to run an external program from a login script if that external program remains open for any length of time. Otherwise, the login script will remain open until that external program is closed. (Login scripts cannot be edited when they are held open.) Use the following syntax:

```
@ [path] filename [parameter]
```

Replace *path* with a drive letter. Replace *filename* with an executable file (files that end in EXE, COM, or BAT, for example). Do not include the extension. Replace *parameter* with any parameters that must accompany the executable file. For example, if you want to start the GroupWise program from within the login script, use the following command:

```
@SYS:\APPS\GRPWISE5
```

DISPLAY

DISPLAY shows the contents of a text file when the user logs in. All characters in the file, including any printer and word processing codes, appear. To display only the text and suppress codes, use FDISPLAY. Use the following syntax:

```
DISPLAY [path] filename
```

Replace *path* with either a drive letter or a full directory path beginning with the volume name. Replace *filename* with the complete name (including the extension) of the file you want to display. You could put messages in a file called NEWS.TXT in the SYS:PUBLIC\MESSAGES directory, if you want your users to see the messages when they log in on Monday. Add the following lines to the container login script:

```
IF DAY_OF_WEEK="Monday" THEN
DISPLAY SYS:PUBLIC\MESSAGES\NEWS.TXT
END
```

EXIT

EXIT terminates execution of the login script. However, you cannot use EXIT in a login script to stop the login script and execute a program. EXIT only terminates the execution of the login script. If you want to execute a program after exiting the login script, you must use # or @ followed on the next line by EXIT.

FDISPLAY

FDISPLAY shows the text of a word processing file when the user logs in. When you use FDISPLAY to display a word processing file, the text is filtered and formatted so that only the text is displayed. Use the following syntax:

```
FDISPLAY [path] filename
```

Replace *path* with either a drive letter or a full directory path beginning with the volume name. Replace *filename* with the complete name (including the extension) of the file you want to display.

You could put messages in a file called NEWS.TXT in the SYS:PUBLIC\MESSAGES directory, if you want your users to see the messages when they log in on Monday. Add the following lines to the container login script:

```
IF DAY_OF_WEEK="Monday" THEN
FDISPLAY SYS:PUBLIC\MESSAGES\NEWS.TXT
END
```

TERM

TERM is normally used only for Application Launcher scripts, a component of ZENworks. You can use the TERM command in a login script to stop the login script and return an error code. You can also use TERM in an IF ... THEN statement, so that the login script stops, and an error code is returned only if an IF statement is true (that is, a certain condition exists). If the IF statement is false (that is, a condition doesn't exist), the login script skips the TERM command and continues executing.

Because TERM stops the login script, be sure to put this command either at the end of the login script or at a point within the script where you intend execution to stop. Do not nest the TERM command in the login script. If you add TERM to a container login script, it will prevent other profile or user login scripts from running. If you put TERM in a profile login script, it will prevent the user login script from running.

WRITE

WRITE displays messages on the workstation screen when a user logs in to the network. Text you want to display must be enclosed in quotation marks (" ").

You can display variables in the text message in several ways. The way you enter the variable in the WRITE command determines the display format, as follows:

- If you type the identifier variable as shown, with no special punctuation, only the variable is displayed on the screen.

- Enclose the identifier variable inside quotation marks, precede the variable with a percent sign (%), and type it in uppercase letters. This method is often used to combine regular text with an identifier variable, because both the text and the variable can be enclosed in the same quotation marks.

  - To join several text strings and identifier variables into a single display without enclosing the variables in quotation marks, use a semicolon between the text and the variables. If you have several WRITE commands, each one must appear on a separate line on the user's workstation. However, if you put a semicolon at the end of all but the last WRITE commands, the commands must appear as one continuous sentence or paragraph (although they might wrap onto additional lines on the workstation's screen).

Text strings can include the following special characters:

\r   Causes a carriage return

\n   Starts a new line of text

\"   Displays a quotation mark on the screen

\7   Makes a beep sound

In addition to the semicolon, you can use other operators to form compound strings (in other words, to join text and identifier variables into one command). These operators are as follows table, in order of precedence:

* / %   Multiply, divide, modulos

\+ -   Add, subtract

\>> <<   Shift left or right (1000 >> 3 becomes 1)

\7   Makes a beep sound

Use the following syntax:

```
WRITE "[text][%identifier]" [;][identifier]
```

Replace *text* with the words you want to display on the screen. Replace *identifier* with a variable you want to display, such as a user's login name. For exanple, to display the message Hello, along with the user's last name, add the following line to the login script:

```
WRITE "Hello, ";%LAST_NAME
```

To make a beep sound occur while the phrase Good morning appears on the screen, add the following line to the login script:

```
WRITE "Good %GREETING_TIME \7"
```

Other Login Script Commands

LASTLOGINTIME

LASTLOGINTIME displays the last time the user logged in.

REMARK

REMARK, REM, an asterisk (*), or a semicolon (;) enables you to include explanatory text in the login script or to keep a line from being executed during testing, when beginning a line. Any text that follows these symbols is ignored. This command and its associated text must be the only entry on a line. If a remark is several lines long, begin each line with the remark keyword (REMARK, REM, an asterisk, or a semicolon).

Identifier Variables

Identifier variables are used most often with commands such as IF . . . THEN, MAP, and WRITE. They can also be used with commands you specify a path for, such as COMSPEC. They enable you to create one login script for multiple users by replacing the variable with other text or information. You need to make sure that you type the variable exactly as shown. Identifier variables can be placed within literal text strings in a WRITE statement. Literal text must be enclosed in quotation marks, and the identifier must be preceeded by a percent sign (%). For example, using the %LAST_NAME variable substitutes the user's actual last name for the LAST_NAME variable. In a login script, WRITE "HELLO, "%LAST_NAME displays a Hello, JONES message on Mary Jones's workstation screen when she logs in. Tables A-1 to A-6 contain the identifier variables that can be used in login scripts.

Table A-1

Date variables

Identifier Variable	Function
DAY	Day number (01 through 31)
DAY_OF_WEEK	Day of week (Monday, Tuesday, etc.)
MONTH	Month number (01 through 12)
MONTH_NAME	Month name (January, February, etc.)
NDAY_OF_WEEK	Weekday number (1 through 7; 1=Sunday)
SHORT_YEAR	Last two digits of year (99, 00, 01)
YEAR	All four digits of year (1999, 2000, 2001)

Table A-2

Time variables

Identifier Variable	Function
AM_PM	Day or night (A.M. or P.M.)
GREETING_TIME	Time of day (morning, afternoon, evening)
HOUR	Hour (12-hour scale; 1 through 12)
HOUR24	Hour (24-hour scale; 00 through 23)
MINUTE	Minute (00 through 59)
SECOND	Second (00 through 59)

Table A-3

User variables

Identifier Variable	Function
%CN	User's full login name as it exists in NDS
FULL_NAME	User's unique username. It is the value of the FULL_NAME property for NDS.
LAST_NAME	User's surname in NDS
LOGIN_CONTEXT	User's context
LOGIN_NAME	User's unique login name (long names are truncated to eight characters)
MEMBER OF "group"	Group object that the user is assigned to
NOT MEMBER OF "group"	Group object that the user is not assigned to
PASSWORD_EXPIRES	Number of days before password expires
REQUESTER_CONTEXT	Context when login started
USER_ID	Number assigned to each user

Table A-4

Network variables

Identifier Variable	Function
FILE_SERVER	NetWare server name
NETWORK_ADDRESS	The internal number assigned by the network specifying where a device can be located in the network cabling system

Table A-5

Workstation
variables

Identifier Variable	Function
MACHINE	Type of computer (IBM_PC, etc.)
OS	Type of operating system on the workstation
OS_VERSION	Operating system version on the workstation
P_STATION	Workstation's node number (12-digit hexadecimal)
PLATFORM	Workstation's operating system platform
SMACHINE	Short machine name (IBM, etc.)
STATION	Workstation's connection number
WINVER	Version of the workstation's Windows operating system

Table A-6

Miscellaneous
variables

Identifier Variable	Function
ACCESS_SERVER	Shows whether the access server is functional (TRUE = functional; FALSE = nonfunctional)
ERROR_LEVEL	An error number (0 = no errors)
%n	Replaced by parameters used during login. When a user logs in, additional parameters can be entered that the login utility passes to the login script. The login utility then substitutes these parameters for any %n variables in the login script. These variables are replaced in order by the parameters the user entered when logging in.
	Users can change only four variables (%2 to %5) in the login screen. The %0 variable is replaced by the name of the NetWare server entered in the login dialog box, and %1 is replaced by the user's fully distinguished login name. The remaining variables change, depending on what the user types when executing the login utility. The %n variables must precede all command line options.
property name	You can use property values of NDS objects as variables. Use the property values just as you do any other identifier variable. If the property value includes a space, enclose the name in quotation marks.
	To use a property name with a space within a WRITE statement, you must place it at the end of the quoted string:
	`WRITE"Given name=%GIVEN_NAME" IF"MESSAGE SERVER"="MS1" THEN MAP INS S16:=MS1\SYS: EMAIL END`

APPENDIX B

WANMAN Policy Construction

The following information describes the statements and constructions that are available when creating the Declaration, Selector, and Provider sections of a WANMAN policy. These statements and constructions are generally applicable to the Selector and Provider sections of the policy. The information that is applicable to the Declarations section as well will be noted. There are six categories of statements and constructions used in WANMAN policies. They are

- Comments
- Conditionals
- Headings
- Terminators
- Mathematical Operators
- Print

Comments

Comments can be used in the Declarations section. Comments are statements used to document the policy. They are not executed. There are two ways to denote a comment

1. Comments can be set off using /* at the start of the comment and */ at the end of the comment. This notation is useful for multiline comments. For example

   ```
   /* This comment was written simply to inform you that the
   engineer creating this WANMAN policy is long-winded and enjoys
   documenting the policy structure extensively */
   ```

2. Comments can be distinguished by // at the start of the comment. Comments using this notation are terminated automatically the end of the line. For example

   ```
   IF Bob > Larry THEN  //The rest of this line is a comment.
   ```

Headings

Heading statements are used to identify the various sections of the WANMAN policy. There are two heading statements:

- *Selector* Identifies the beginning of the Selector section of the policy. A matching END statement will mark the end of the Selector section.
- *Provider* Identifies the beginning of the Provider section of the policy. A matching END statement will mark the end of the Provider section.

Terminators

Terminators are used to identify the end of a given section or statement. They are also used to pass execution back to the client that requested the WANMAN policy evaluation. There are five main terminators used in WANMAN policies:

- Semicolon (;)
- END
- RETURN
- SEND
- DONT_SEND

Semicolon (;)

A semicolon is used to terminate a single-line declaration. This includes variable definition and assignment in the Declarations section, as well as assignment and mathematical operations in the Selector and Provider sections. For example

- `X := X + 2;`
- `INT A := 5;`
- `RETURN SEND;`

END

END is used to identify the end of a multiline declaration such as an If-Then. It is also used to mark the end of the Selector and Provider sections of the WANMAN policy.

RETURN

The RETURN command is used to pass the results of the WANMAN policy calculation(s) to the WANMAN client. For example

- `RETURN 50;`
- `RETURN Y;`
- `RETURN DON'T_SEND;`

SEND

The SEND reserved word is used by the Provider section to tell the WANMAN client that it is appropriate to generate the specified NDS traffic.

DONT_SEND

The DONT_SEND reserved word is used by the Provider section to tell the WANMAN client that it cannot generate the specified NDS traffic at this time.

Conditionals

Conditional statements use the current state of the environment to determine whether or not to perform an operation. WANMAN uses a common set of conditional statements that includes

- If-Then
- Elsif-Then
- Else

If-Then

The If-Then statement is used to test a single condition and execute or bypass conditional operations accordingly. For example

```
IF X > 10 THEN
Y := (2 * X) + 3;
END
```

The Boolean expression X > 10 is evaluated for a TRUE or FALSE result. If the statement is true, the declarations that immediately follow are run. If the statement is false, all the conditional statements associated with this If-Then statement are bypassed.

Elsif-Then

The Elsif-Then statement is used to string together a series of If-Then statements. If the preceding If-Then declaration is FALSE, the Boolean Elsif declaration is evaluated for a TRUE or FALSE result. If the statement is TRUE, the declarations that immediately follow are run. If the statement is FALSE, all the conditional statements associated with the Elsif-Then statement are bypassed. For example

```
IF X > 10 THEN
        Y := (2 * X) + 3;
ELSIF Z < 30 THEN
        Y := (3 * Z);
END
```

Else

The Else statement identifies declarations that should be executed if all other If-Then or Elsif-Then statements prove to be false. For example

```
IF X > 10 THEN
        Y := (2 * X) + 3;
ELSIF Z < 30 THEN
        Y := (3 * Z);
ELSE
        Y := 1;
END
```

Mathematical Operators

Mathematical operators are used to describe the necessary calculations and assignments in a WANMAN policy. There are five categories of mathematical operators used in WANMAN policies:

- Assignment
- Arithmetic
- Relational

- Logical
- Bitwise

Assignment

The assignment operator (`:=`) assigns the value on the right side of the equation to the variable specified on the left side of the equation. The left side can specify either a standalone variable or a field of a structure. For example, assume that T1 and T2 are TIME variables, X and Y are INT variables, and B1 is a BOOLEAN variable.

```
X  := (3 * Y) / 2;
B1 := X > Y;
T1.a := T2.a;
```

Arithmetic

Arithmetic operators are the standard operations you learned in grade school. Arithmetic operators should only be used with INT variable. Do not use TIME, NETADDRESS, and BOOLEAN variable types in arithmetic expressions. The valid arithmetic operators are

- *Addition* (+) Sums two values
- *Subtraction* (−) Subtracts the second value from the first value
- *Division* (/) Divides the first value by the second value
- *Multiplication* (*) Multiplies two values
- *Modula* (MOD) Returns the remainder of a division operation rather than the quotient

Relational

Relational operators make comparisons between two different values and return a value of TRUE if the comparison is true or FALSE if the comparison is false. They are used in conditional constructions such as If-Then statements. Every relational operator can be used with variables of type TIME and INT. However, only the <> and = operators are valid with variables of type BOOLEAN and NETADDRESS. Valid relational operators include

- *Equal to* (=) Compares two values and returns TRUE if they are the equivalent

- *Not equal to (<>)*   Compares two values and returns TRUE if they are not equivalent
- *Greater than (>)*   Returns TRUE if the first value is greater than the second
- *Greater than or equal to (>=)*   Returns TRUE if the first value is equal to or greater than the second
- *Less than (<)*   Returns TRUE if the first value is less than the second.
- *Less than or equal to (<=)*   Returns TRUE if the first value is equal to or less than the second

Logical

Logical operators are used to test Boolean expressions rather than individual values and return TRUE or FALSE depending on the results of the test. The logical operators include

- *AND*   Returns TRUE if both Boolean expressions evaluate as TRUE. If one or both expressions are FALSE, the AND operation returns FALSE. For example, X < 10 AND Y > 1.
- *OR*   Returns TRUE if at least one of the Boolean expressions evaluate as TRUE. Only returns FALSE if both expressions are FALSE
- *NOT*   Returns TRUE if the Boolean expression evaluates as FALSE

Bitwise

Bitwise operators perform binary-level comparisons or manipulations on the values specified in the expression. Bitwise operators can only be performed on INT variable types. Bitwise operators return an INT value. Valid bitwise operators include

- *BITAND*   Performs a bit-level comparison of two values and returns a binary 1 if the bits are the same and a binary 0 if the bits are different. For example

Value 1:	0010 1101
Value 2:	1010 1010
BITAND Result:	0111 1000

- *BITOR*   Performs a bit-level comparison of two values and returns a binary 1 if at least one of the bits is a one. If both bits are 0, BITOR returns a 0. For example

Value 1:	0010 1101
Value 2:	1010 1010
BITOR Result:	1010 1111

- *BITNOT*   Returns the bit-level inverse of the supplied value. For example

Value:	0010 1101
BITNOT Result:	1101 0010

Order of Operations

The following precedence rules are enforced when processing complex expressions. Operators with the same level of precedence are processed left-to-right. The order is as follows:

1. Parenthesis
2. Unary (+/-)
3. BITNOT
4. BITAND
5. BITOR
6. Multiplication, Division, MOD
7. Addition, Subtraction
8. Relational (>, >=, <, <=, =)
9. NOT
10. AND
11. OR

Print

You can use the PRINT statement to send text and symbol values to the console screen of the WAN Traffic Manager server or the log file.

PRINT statements can have any number of arguments, but a comma must separate each argument. The arguments can be literal strings, symbol names or members, integer values, or Boolean values. A few notes about the PRINT statement are listed below.

- Enclose literal strings in double quotes (").
- TIME symbols are printed as follows: Month:Day:Year Hour:Minute
- NETADDRESS variables are printed as follows: 'Type' 'Length' 'Data' where
  - 'Type' is either IP or IPX.
  - 'Length' is the number of bytes in the address.
  - 'Data' is the hexadecimal address value.

APPENDIX C

Using Mailbox Manager for Microsoft Exchange

If you are migrating user accounts from Windows NT to NDS and you also use Microsoft Exchange to manage user e-mail accounts, you can reduce the time necessary for administering user information by migrating Microsoft Exchange mailbox information to NDS. Then, you can manage user information, access, and e-mail accounts by using only one NDS object (instead of two objects) in NT.

Installing Mailbox Manager for Microsoft Exchange

To install Mailbox Manager for Microsoft Exchange, complete the following steps:

1. Select Integrate Microsoft Exchange with NDS (the third option) during the initial installation of NDS on your NT server. If you need to install later, you can run the installation from I386\MM4X\SETUP.EXE and then select Integrate Microsoft Exchange with NDS.

2. Click Next to begin, and follow the on-screen instructions.

3. In the Select Components screen, make sure that you select all options, then click Next.

4. Select the tree where you want to install Mailbox, then click Next.

5. Select the NDS context where you want to install the Microsoft Exchange mailbox, then click Next.

6. Select the server where you want to install the software, then click Next.

7. Review the installation choices, then click Next.

8. Log on to the NT server as a user with administrative rights, then click Logon.

9. When the installation is complete, click Launch Import Utility Now and then click Finish. The Import utility imports Microsoft Exchange objects into NDS.

10. Click Next.

11. Select the Microsoft Exchange sites that you want to administer from NDS, then click Next.

12. Select the NDS tree from which you would like to administer Microsoft Exchange, then click Next.

13. Select the NDS Context where you want the site object to be created, then click Next.

14. Click Import.

15. Log in to NDS as a user with administrative rights. The objects are imported into NDS.

16. Review the Import Status, then click OK.

A new Mail object appears in NetWare Administrator. This object holds a Recipients Group object that contains a list of all Microsoft Exchange users (refer to Figure C-1).

To check that user mailboxes were migrated correctly, double-click the user's object. Scroll down the property pages and select the Exchange Mailbox property page (refer to Figure C-2). The user's Microsoft Exchange information should be visible.

Figure C-1

New Microsoft Exchange objects in NetWare Administrator

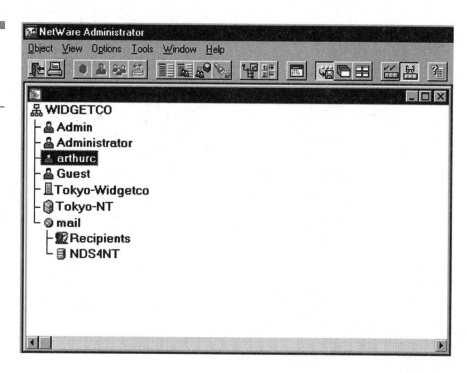

Figure C-2
Exchange property
page in NetWare
Administrator

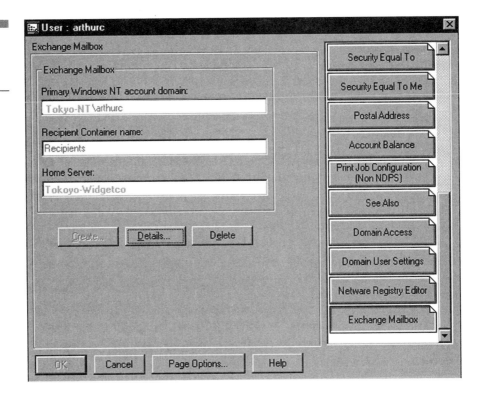

Creating a New User with a Microsoft Exchange Mailbox Account

One of the most useful features of NDS is that you can create users in NDS who are then created in the Windows NT and Microsoft Exchange databases, as well. You do not have to enter the information multiple times. To create a new user account and a Microsoft Exchange account, complete the following steps:

1. Create a new user in NetWare Administrator.
2. Double-click the user in NetWare Administrator.
3. Click the Domain Access property page, as shown in Figure C-3.
4. Click Add to associate the user with a domain.
5. Click OK.
6. Double-click the user again.
7. Click the Exchange Mailbox property page.

Figure C-3
The Domain Access
property page in
NetWare
Administrator

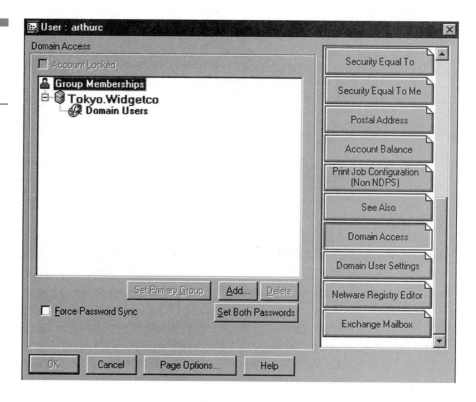

8. Click Create.

9. Browse to the corresponding Primary Windows NT account domain and select the domain.

10. Browse to the corresponding Recipient Container name and select Recipients.

11. Browse to the corresponding Home Server and select the server.

12. Click OK.

NOTE: *You might see an error stating that the main server could not be found. If you locate the main server again, the process will complete. Click Cancel to close User Information.*

To verify that the mailbox has been created, double-click the User object again and select Exchange Mailbox. Click Details to make sure that the information is correct. In Microsoft Exchange Administrator, click Recipients and make sure that the new user exists.

Creating Microsoft Exchange Accounts and Migrating them to NDS

If you must create Microsoft Exchange mailboxes once you have migrated all of the Windows NT User objects to NDS, you can still import the mailboxes and associate them with User objects. To do this task, complete the following steps:

1. In Microsoft Exchange Administrator, create a new mailbox. Click Recipients, then click File > New Mailbox.
2. Enter the mailbox information.
3. Click Primary Windows NT account.
4. Select Create NT Account, then click OK.
5. Select the primary Windows NT server, then click OK.
6. Click Apply, then click OK. The new user is created in NetWare Administrator.
7. From the Tools menu, click Import Exchange Mailboxes.
8. Click Next.
9. Select the Microsoft Exchange sites that you want to administer from NDS, then click Next.
10. Select the NDS tree from which you would like to administer Microsoft Exchange, then click Next.
11. Select the NDS Context where you want the site object to be created, then click Next.
12. Click Import.
13. Log in to NDS as a user with administrative rights. The objects are imported into NDS.
14. Review the Import Status, then click OK.

To check that user mailboxes were migrated correctly, double-click the User's object and select the Exchange Mailbox property page (refer to Figure C-4). The user's Microsoft Exchange information should be visible. You can also double-click the Mail icon in NetWare Administrator and double-click the domain object under Recipients. The name of the user you just added should exist in the Microsoft Exchange server.

Figure C-4
Recipients property
page in NetWare
Administrator

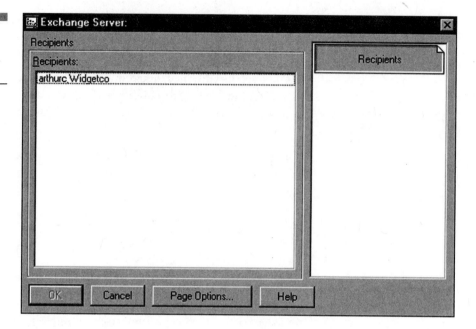

INDEX

Note: **boldface** numbers indicate illustrations

P

Index

X

Xerox support of Novell Distributed Print Services (NDPS), 317
X-refs, 416–417

Z

ABOUT THE AUTHOR

Nancy Cadjan is a technical writer for Novell and works as a freelance writer. She has worked on products such as Novell Client, Novell Internet Access Services, Novell ISP Solutions, and NDS for NT. She has edited and published other books including *Network + Certification Success Guide*. She has a Masters in technical writing.

    Jeffrey Harris is a Project Manager for Novell. He is responsible for providing technical product information to Novell's major commercial and government accounts. Previously, he spent four years in the Novell Technical Services organization supporting a variety of Novell products. Jeffrey Harris has a Bachelors degree in Computer Science and a Masters in Business Administration. He also has earned his CNE certification.